ISIS Propaganda

CAUSES AND CONSEQUENCES OF TERRORISM SERIES

Series Editors:

Gary LaFree
Gary A. Ackerman
Anthony Lemieux

Books in the Series:
From Freedom Fighters to Jihadists: Human Resources of Non State Armed Groups
Vera Mironova

Published in partnership with The National Consortium for
the Study of Terrorism and Responses to Terrorism and
the University of Maryland

ISIS Propaganda

A Full-Spectrum Extremist Message

Edited by

STEPHANE J. BAELE

KATHARINE A. BOYD

TRAVIS G. COAN

University of Exeter, UK

OXFORD

UNIVERSITY PRESS

OXFORD
UNIVERSITY PRESS

Oxford University Press is a department of the University of Oxford. It furthers
the University's objective of excellence in research, scholarship, and education
by publishing worldwide. Oxford is a registered trade mark of Oxford University
Press in the UK and certain other countries.

Published in the United States of America by Oxford University Press
198 Madison Avenue, New York, NY 10016, United States of America.

© University of Maryland National Consortium for the
Study of Terrorism and Responses to Terrorism (START) 2020

Library of Congress Control Number: 2019949818
ISBN 978–0–19–093246–6 (pbk.)
ISBN 978–0–19–093245–9 (hbk.)

1 3 5 7 9 8 6 4 2

Paperback printed by Marquis, Canada
Hardback printed by Bridgeport National Bindery, Inc., United States of America

Contents

Contributors   vii
Glossary of Frequent Arabic Terms   ix

Introduction—Full-Spectrum Propaganda: Appraising the
"IS Moment" in Propaganda History   1
Stephane J. Baele

1. The Strategic Logic of Islamic State's Full-Spectrum
   Propaganda: Coherence, Comprehensiveness, and
   Multidimensionality   20
   Haroro J. Ingram

2. Situating Islamic State's Message: A Social and Theological
   Genealogy   50
   Mehdi Laghmari

3. The Matrix of Islamic State's Propaganda: Magazines   84
   Stephane J. Baele, Katharine A. Boyd, and Travis G. Coan

4. Shock and Inspire: Islamic State's Propaganda Videos   127
   Stephane J. Baele, Katharine A. Boyd, and Travis G. Coan

5. Islamic State's Propaganda and Social Media: Dissemination,
   Support, and Resilience   155
   Laura Wakeford and Laura Smith

6. From Music to Books, from Pictures to Numbers: The Forgotten
   Yet Crucial Components of Islamic State's Propaganda   188
   Stephane J. Baele and Charlie Winter

7. Countering Islamic State's Propaganda: Challenges and
   Opportunities   219
   Tobias Borck and Jonathan Githens-Mazer

8. Terrorist Propaganda After the Islamic State: Learning,
   Emulation, and Imitation   242
   *Paul Gill, Kurt Braddock, Sanaz Zolghadriha, Bettina Rottweiler,
   and Lily D. Cushenbery*

Afterword: The Uniqueness of Islamic State   265
    Thomas Hegghammer

Appendix 1: *List of* Anashīd *Produced by the Islamic State*   271
Appendix 2: *Example of a Provincial News Report from Al-Bayan Radio*   275
Index   277

Contributors

Stephane J. Baele, PhD
Senior Lecturer in International Relations
Politics Department
University of Exeter
Exeter, UK

Tobias Borck
Associate Fellow
Royal United Services Institute for
    Defence and Security Studies (RUSI)
London, UK

Katharine A. Boyd, PhD
Senior Lecturer in Criminology
Sociology, Philosophy, and
    Anthropology Department
University of Exeter
Exeter, UK

Kurt Braddock, PhD
Assistant Teaching Professor
Department of Communication Arts
    and Sciences
Penn State University
University Park, Pennsylvania, USA

Travis G. Coan, PhD
Senior Lecturer in Quantitative Politics
Politics Department
University of Exeter
Exeter, UK

Lily D. Cushenbery, PhD
Associate Professor of Management
College of Business
Stony Brook University
Stony Brook, NY, USA

Paul Gill, PhD
Professor
Department of Security and Crime
    Science
University College London
London, UK

Jonathan Githens-Mazer, PhD
Associate Professor
Institute of Arab and Islamic Studies
University of Exeter
Exeter, UK

Thomas Hegghammer, PhD
Senior Research Fellow
Norwegian Defence Research
    Establishment (FFI)
Kjeller, Norway

Haroro J. Ingram, PhD
Senior Research Fellow
Program on Extremism
George Washington University
Washington, DC, USA

Mehdi Laghmari, PhD
Reseacher and Consultant
Institute of Arab and Islamic Studies
University of Exeter
Exeter, UK

Bettina Rottweiler
PhD Candidate in Security and Crime
    Science
Security and Crime Science Department
University College London
London, UK

Laura Smith, PhD
Senior Lecturer in Social Psychology
Department of Psychology
University of Bath
Bath, UK

Laura Wakeford, PhD
Postdoctoral Researcher
Psychology Department
University of Dundee
Dundee, Scotland, UK

Charlie Winter
War Studies
King's College London
London, UK

Sanaz Zolghadriha, PhD
Lecturer
Department of Security and Crime
  Science
University College London
London, UK

Glossary of Frequent Arabic Terms

Concepts (these terms are italicized throughout the book to facilitate identification):

Arabic word (Latin transliteration)	Arabic word (original spelling)	Translation (as used by IS)
ʿāqīda	العقيدة	Creed, religious belief system
Al-walāʾ wa al-barāʾ	الولاء والبراء	Unconditional adherence to the Islamist project and the group supporting it, and disavowal and disassociation of other causes and groups supporting them
Bāqiyya	باقية	Remaining
Bāqiyya wa tatamaddad	باقية وتتمدّد	Remaining and expanding
Bidʿa	البدعة	Religious innovation
Dār al-Islām	دار الإسلام	Abode of Islam
Dār al-Ḥarb	دار الحرب	Abode of war
Dār al-Kufr	دار الكفر	Abode of disbelief
Daʿwa	الدعوة	Proselytism
Fiqh	فقه	Analysis of the sources upon which *Sharīʿa* rulings are elaborated
Ghuluw	غلو	Exaggeration, excessiveness
Ḥākimiyya	الحاكمية	Divine sovereignty (and subsequent rejection of non-divine innovation)

Hijrah	الهجرة	Immigration from a non-Muslim land (*Dār al-Ḥarb, Dār al-Kufr*) land to a land implementing the Islamist project (*Dār al-Islām*)
Ḥudūd	الحدود	Religiously mandated punishments for acts deemed to be against the will of Allah
Ijtihād	الاجتهاد	Independent theological reasoning to find a solution to a specific legal question
Istishhad	استشهاد	Martyrdom
Jāhiliyya	الجاهلية	Ignorance
Jamāʿah	الجماعة	Congregation, community of believers
Jihād	الجهاد	Struggle ("great" jihad); war on the path of God ("little" jihad)
Kāfir (pl. *Kuffār*)	كافر	Unbeliever, disbeliever
Kufr	الكفر	Unbelief, disbelief
Khilāfah	الخلافة	Caliphate
Mahdī	المهدي	Messianic figure in Islamic thought, prophesized to arrive to rule and redeem the Islamic faith
Manhaj	المنهج	(prophetic) method
Mujāhid (pl. *Mujāhidīn*)	مجاهد	Jihadist fighter
Munāfiq (pl. *Munāfiqīn*)	منافق	Hypocrite
Murtadd (pl. *Murtaddīn*)	مرتد	Apostate
Nashīd (pl. *anashīd*)	نشيد	Islamic chanted hymn
Nifāq	النفاق	Hypocrisy
Rāfiḍa	الرافضة	Rejecters (pejorative label for the Shi'a)
Ridda	الردة	Apostasy
Salaf	السلف	Early companions of the Prophet
Sham	الشام	The Levant
Sharīʿa	الشريعة	Islamic legislation
Ṭaghūt (pl. *tawaghit*)	طاغوت	Tyrant

Takfīr	التكفير	Excommunication
Tamkīn	التمكين	Consolidation of power
Tatarrus	تترس	Barricading, shielding
Tawḥīd	التوحيد	Unity, unicity, and divine transcendence of God
Ummah	الأمة	The community of Muslims
Wilāya (pl. Wilāyāt)	ولاية	Province
Zakāt	الزكاة	Islamic tax

Names (individuals and groups):

Arabic word (Surname followed by forenames, Latin transliteration)	Arabic word (original spelling)
Ahl al-Hadith (group)	أهل الحديث
al-Adnani, Abu Mohamed	أبو محمد العدناني
al-Albani, Nasr dine	ناصر الدين الألباني
al-Anbari, Abu Ali	أبو علي الأنباري
al-Baghdadi, Abu Bakr	أبو بكر البغدادي
al-Baghdadi, Abu Omar	أبو عمر البغدادي
al-Dawlah al-Islamiyah (Islamic State) (group, earlier called Tawhid wal Jihad, then al-Dawlah al-Islamiyah fī 'l-'Iraq, then al-Dawlah al-Islamiyah fī 'l-'Iraq wa' al-Sham)	الدولة الإسلامية (توحيد والجهاد، الدولة الإسلامية في العراق، الدولة الإسلامية في العراق والشام)
al-Hazimi, Ahmad	أحمد الحازمي
al-Jamaa al-Salafiyya al-Muhtasiba (JSM) (group)	الجماعة السلفية المحتسبة
al-Masri, Abu Ayyub	أبو أيّوب يلمصر
al-Maqdisi Abu Mohamed	أبو محمد المقدسي
al-Muhajir, Abu Abdullah	أبو عبدالله المهاجر
al-Otaybi, Juhayman	جهيمان العتيبي
al-Qaeda (group)	القاعدة

al-Suri, Abu Khalid	أبو خالد السوري
al-Suri, Abu Mosab	أبو مصعب السوري
al-Wahhab, Mohamed Ibn Abd	محمد ابن عبد الوهاب
al-Zarqawi, Abu Mosab	أبو مصعب الزرقاوي
al-Zawahiri, Ayman	أيمن الظواهري
Ansar al-Islam (group)	أنصار الإسلام
Azzam, Abdullah	عبدالله عزام
Bin Laden, Osama	أسامة بن لادن
Ibn Taymiyyah, Taqī ad-Dīn Ahmad	ابن تيمية
Ikhwan (group)	جماعة الإخوان المسلمين
Jabhat al-Nusra (group, later called	جبهة النصرة (جبهة فتح
Jabhat Fatah al-Sham)	الشام، هيئة تحرير الشام)
Khawarij (group)	خوارج
Naji, Abu Bakr	أبو بكر ناجي
Qutb, Sayyid	سيد قطب

Introduction: Full-Spectrum Propaganda

Appraising the "IS Moment" in Propaganda History

Stephane J. Baele

As these lines are being written, the self-proclaimed "Islamic State" (IS) is still a significant force of nuisance in the Middle East and beyond. In 2016 alone, the organization's members launched more than 1,400 attacks, killing almost 11,700 (Miller & Kammerer 2017), a number that does not even include the many acts of violence conducted in the West and South-East Asia by individuals inspired by the "Caliphate." In spite of the gradual shrinking of its territory in Syria and Iraq since its apogee of 2014–2015,[1] IS nonetheless keeps on committing uncompromisingly violent actions and disseminating a wide range of propaganda products. Although the quality and sheer number of communication outputs produced by the group has fallen, IS's propaganda machine continues to inundate the online and offline worlds at levels never achieved by any terrorist group in the past (BBC Monitoring 2017; Winter & Ingram 2018). Since its origins in Iraq under the leadership of Abu Musab al-Zarqawi and throughout its subsequent avatars, IS has developed a sophisticated and exceptionally extensive propaganda system inherently linked to its actions; it has disseminated photographs; published magazines in several languages, as well as newspapers, books, and pamphlets; recorded music and speeches; broadcasted radio programs; produced short and long videos; designed infographics; created and alimented closed discussion spaces on the Internet; stimulated social media activity; organized permanent and temporary "information" points in controlled territory; and developed smartphone applications and even educational e-games for children. The sheer quantity of outputs is overwhelming. Zelin (2015a) observed no fewer than 123 different official media releases in a single week in April 2015; Farwell (2014: 51) reported "44,000 tweets a day" from IS members as they marched

---

[1] For a dynamic visualization of IS's territorial reach, see Le Monde (2017).

Stephane J. Baele, *Introduction—Full-Spectrum Propaganda: Appraising the "IS Moment" in Propaganda History* In: *ISIS Propaganda*. Edited by: Stephane J. Baele, Katharine A. Boyd, and Travis G. Coan, Oxford University Press (2020) © University of Maryland National Consortium for the Study of Terrorism and Responses to Terrorism (START)
DOI: 10.1093/oso/9780190932459.003.0001

to Mosul; Winter (2015) calculated an average of 38 "unique propaganda events" per day; and Milton (2016) counted "9,000 videos, picture reports, and photographs" uploaded over one and a half years (January 2015–August 2016). IS itself reported publishing more than 720 videos, 1,780 photo-based reports (almost 15,000 images), and 150 audio recitations and chants over the year running October 2014–2015.[2]

Our own counts in this volume further attest of this incredible productivity. Such a remarkable phenomenon warrants an in-depth study, which is what this volume offers: we provide the first comprehensive overview and detailed analysis of this propaganda effort, which, we argue here and throughout the book, constitutes an outstanding instance of "full-spectrum propaganda." The following chapters systematically unpack the "cocktail of emotional, theological and ideological appeals" (Winter 2017a: 1) that characterizes this propaganda in an accessible yet rigorous way, using a range of innovative methods and presenting the most relevant information through the lenses of pertinent theories from across the academic disciplines. Together, they offer the fullest possible picture of a complex propaganda system unprecedented in the history of terrorist organizations.

"Full-Spectrum Propaganda"

What exactly makes IS's propaganda truly unprecedented? Certainly not the originality of the themes it promotes—most were already there. Neither the formats it used—most, be it magazines or videos, had already been tried and tested by preceding groups. Rather, IS propaganda is unprecedented because it constitutes, we argue, the first sustained and largely successful attempt from a terror group to build a "full-spectrum propaganda."

We do not wish to enter the long-standing debate on the definition of "propaganda" and add yet one more volume to the list of classic monographs on the issue that dedicate their first chapter to the definition problem (likewise, we do not wish to indulge in the conceptual debate over the term "terrorism"). With World War II not even over, Henderson (1943) was already at pains to coin a consensual definition; more recent contributions still lament on the "confusion—even incoherence—over the meaning of the term" (Cunningham 2002: 5), seen as an "elusive notion" for which "it

[2] This report can be seen in Chapter 6.

is inevitable that there will be no collective agreement" (O'Shaughnessy 2004: 3; 13).[3] Extensive efforts have been made to systematically examine the many dimensions of this challenge (e.g., Cunningham 2002), which cannot be solved here. Instead, we take the pragmatic choice of accepting a noncategorical, minimal, and loose definition of propaganda based on both its everyday usage and the family resemblances between its most obvious instances (an approach inspired by Wittgenstein 1953/2009). Propaganda, in this view, can be understood as an organized attempt by a political group to shape a target audience's worldview and elicit action. It does not simply seek to influence opinions on particular matters but instead more deeply intends to structure the target audience's understanding of its social environment; it does not simply present more or less false information, but also more profoundly promotes a particular "engagement for information acquisition and interpretation, as well as a constant 'cultivation' of perceptions of the world" (Kallis 2005: 9). As such, as Cunningham claims (2002: 4), propaganda is an "epistemologically structured phenomenon" that "generates belief systems and tenacious convictions."

Propaganda is thus inseparable from culture (Cunningham 2002: 4), in the way that it "manages collective attitudes by the manipulation of significant symbols," to take Lasswell's seminal definition (1927: 627; 1927/1971), and seeks to integrate individuals in the audience within a certain imagined social group characterized by its shared codes, meanings, and desired objects (Kallis 2005: 9). We therefore situate propaganda at the heuristic level, that is, as a concerted effort to provide an audience with "cognitive shortcuts" to help it make sense of an otherwise complex, messy, and meaningless social reality (O'Shaughnessy 2004: 51), thus saving time and energy by providing simple answers to complex questions in a way that short-circuits critical thinking (Henderson 1943: 79).

Propaganda thus understood can be carried out in multiple ways. The propagandist might favor a particular format, target a specific audience, or pursue a certain level of objectives. Rarely in the history of propaganda have political actors designed a propaganda effort in such a way that it seeks to fulfil its entire potential, deliberately refusing to renounce using any particular format, targeting any specific audience, or pursuing a certain level of

---

[3] Between these two moments—the heydays of early propaganda studies right before, during, and after World War II and the recent revival of the field that some attribute to the Iraq war—the concept of "propaganda" almost disappeared and reached near "conceptual extinction" (O'Shaughnessy 2004: vi).

objectives. We call such an uncompromising effort "full-spectrum prop-aganda," echoing conceptualizations of other attempts to cover the full range and multiple processes involved in a given field of activity (such as Lenczowski's concept of a "full-spectrum diplomacy" (2011), Arnsperger's ideal of a "full-spectrum economics" (2009), or the US military's objective of achieving "full-spectrum dominance" (e.g., Batiste & Daniels 2005; Bevan 2005; Chiarelli & Michaelis 2005). Full-spectrum propaganda is thus *comprehensive* in the range of outputs it produces, *cohesive* in the way it articulates these formats together in a coherent whole, and *multidimensional* in the level of objectives it pursues and the audiences it targets. The present volume analyzes IS's communications through the ideal-typical prism of a full-spectrum propaganda, demonstrating its high performance on the three dimensions of comprehensiveness, cohesion, and multidimensionality; exploring the origins of this performance; and drawing its far-reaching consequences.

As for comprehensiveness, IS resolutely followed classic propaganda theorist Jacques Ellul's argument that the propagandist should use "all of the technical means at his disposal—the press, radio, TV, movies, posters, meetings, door-to-door canvassing. . . . There is no propaganda as long as one makes use, in a sporadic fashion and at random, of a newspaper article here, a poster or radio program there" (1962/1973: 9). In this regard, the multiplication of media channels brought about by the Internet[4] constituted both at once an opportunity but also a challenge for IS: expanding the "net" to an amplitude never attained even by a state is a dream that comes with a hefty price in terms of resources specifically dedicated to the effort. The book explores how the group grappled with this dilemma.

As for cohesiveness, IS once again seemed to follow Ellul's handbook by showing a desire to connect the messages conveyed in different ways through the multiple formats into an overarching, coherent whole. The propagandist, Ellul warned (1962/1973: 12), "must combine the elements of propaganda in a real orchestration. On the one hand, he must keep in mind the stimuli that can be utilized at a given moment, and must organize them. On the other hand the propagandist must use various instruments, each in relation to all the others." The various chapters of this volume provide evidence of IS's will to connect the many pieces of its propaganda puzzle together into a dense

---

[4] Early theorists of propaganda already claimed that propaganda is intrinsically liked with communication technology (e.g., Smith, Lasswell, & Casey 1946; Ellul 1962/1973).

"propaganda net" (Ellul 1962/1973: 10) that envelops its audience inside a single, consistent master narrative.

As for multidimensionality, IS produced propaganda to support various levels of objectives: tactical and strategic, short-term and long-term, local and global. In fact, the group's effort ticks almost all propaganda types traditionally listed. If we take Cunningham's typology, for example (2002: 66–71), we notice that IS conducted "agitation propaganda" (designed to arouse the public) and "integration propaganda" (designed to unify, integrate a society), "white propaganda" (using true information) and "black propaganda" (using false information), "disinformation propaganda" (intending to make the enemy believe and use your own biased information), "bureaucratic propaganda" (providing seemingly scientific information), "counterpropaganda" (designed to counter rivals' propaganda), "hate propaganda" (promoting hate toward particular social groups), and "propaganda of the deed" (actions conveying a propaganda message), leaving no propaganda type unused. For such a multidimensional effort to work, IS's message contains a complex mix of negative and positive contents bound together in a single big picture (in a very similar way that Nazi propaganda did; see Kallis 2005: 126; Thompson 2017), it plays on emotions as well as on reason, it criticizes enemies and praises friends, it talks to these enemies and friends as well as to those in between. The contributions to this book examine how these various dimensions emerged, combined, and evolved across time.

Full-spectrum propaganda is, of course, never entirely achieved. Yet it constitutes a horizon where IS propagandists—like their Nazi or Soviet counterparts for example[5]—were heading and neared, certainly at their peak in 2014–2015. And, as such, it constitutes a valid ideal-type against which we ought to analyze and evaluate their work.

The "IS Moment," Between Innovation and Continuity

Such a full-spectrum effort necessarily builds on earlier innovations, which is why it is important to understand it within the broader context of the historical evolution of terrorist communications in general and Salafi-jihadist

---

[5] The integration and coordination of Nazi propaganda into a single organizational system occurred gradually and took many years, and it actually never translated fully into a perfectly coherent and effective propaganda system (Kallis 2005).

propaganda more specifically. Analyzing IS's propaganda system in a vacuum, as an isolated occurrence, can only lead to mistaken conclusions and policy recommendations. As one of our contributors rightly warned in earlier work (Ingram 2016: 1), "there is a tendency in scholarly and strategic-policy fields to see the propaganda produced by groups like Islamic State and Al-Qaeda as historically unheralded. . . . This narrow perspective, in placing the current phenomenon into an historical and thematic vacuum, infers that history has little to offer contemporary efforts to understand and confront extremist propaganda." Taking this warning seriously, we situate IS's full-spectrum propaganda as the ultimate rearticulation of the Salafi-jihadist outreach tradition and as a significant new step continuing the immemorial history of propaganda (Taylor 2003; Ingram 2016). By doing so we provide insights on the past and present—but also future—of terrorist and extremist groups' communications writ large.

As affirmed earlier, most individual elements of IS propaganda, both in form and content, are indeed not new and attest to a more or less direct appropriation by the organization of established tropes and tactics. IS has advanced and mimicked some of the major trends in propaganda developed before them by other political organizations, articulating together previous successful experiences to produce its wide and dense "net." "Ultimately," Ingram explains (2016: 30), "Daesh are more strategic plagiarists than geniuses and their propaganda efforts reflect a deep appreciation of both their own history and that of their predecessors." In other words, IS has clearly learned from others' successes and failures, both in terms of techniques and message.

Regarding techniques, IS's multimodal comprehensiveness might be unprecedented for a terrorist organization but echoes the Nazis' use of all media available at their time (Kallis 2005) or, more recently, the US information spin effort surrounding the 2002 Iraq War (for an account of how images, speeches, music, and video footages combined in the US effort to frame the conflict, read Hiebert 2003). IS makes a great use of the Internet, yet this practice simply continued—albeit at an extraordinary level—the rise of the web as the primary support of propaganda, a role once again initiated by the United States during the 2002 Iraq War (especially when it comes to "orchestrating visual imagery"),[6] then cemented by jihadi organizations in the

---

[6] Heibert (2003: 251) offers this telling anecdote: "At Centcom, Combat Camera operated around the clock. Military personnel at computer stations processed 600–800 photos and 25–50 video clips from the front lines every day, of which about 80% were given to the news media. They became the images displayed on the big screens during briefings at the Pentagon and Centcom. They were also

decade preceding IS (read, e.g., Conway 2006; Zelin 2013), and today already widely used by very different violent groups.[7] As Farwell notes (2014: 49), "ISIS is not the first set of violent extremists to use such means to drive home its messages or carry out operations." Relatedly, IS's quest for creating "viral" documents is similar in essence to Ted Kaczynski's or Anders Breivik's efforts to disseminate their manifestos as widely as possible, while IS's magazines are heavily indebted to Al Qaeda's *Inspire* publications and continue a trend opened long ago by Weather Underground's *Osawatomie* periodicals or the American Nazi Party's *Stormtrooper* pamphlets. IS's notorious utilization of gruesome images has caught public imagination but only perpetuates the long-established technique of "grotesque propaganda" (read Halfmann & Young 2010 for an extensive report) and imitates in some ways Hollywood's "ultraviolence" (read Coulthard 2009).

In terms of message, most of the major themes and grievances expressed in IS propaganda are the direct heirs of older Salafi-jihadist movements' social diagnoses and agendas. At a more abstract level, IS propaganda seems to perfectly follow textbook guidelines of radicalizing political communication, including the repetition of a limited number of ideas,[8] group polarization through discourse and the creation of echo chambers,[9] or the systematic use of seemingly impermeable, reified group categories.[10] In this regard, it curiously resembles the all-encompassing mass propaganda set up by the Nazis in the 1930s and during World War II (read Thompson 2017 for a systematic comparison).

Yet IS propaganda still represents a crucial "moment" in the history of extremist and insurgent groups' communications: the group's commitment to and, at some point, success in expanding all these components and integrating them into a multidimensional, cohesive, and comprehensive full-spectrum system is remarkable. This effort brought the organization to

---

put online to news organizations and for the public, where they got an estimated 750,000 hits a day." This paragraph could be transposed to IS's central media offices with minimal change.

[7] Caiani and Parenti's analysis of extreme-right groups' online activities (2009) clearly showed that this activity was already increasing before the rise of IS propaganda, both in quantity and diversity (variety of different forms).

[8] The effects of this principle are known at least since Zajonc's work (e.g., 1968); Zimbardo and Leippe's book (1991) linked exposure to polarization.

[9] The literature on group polarization traces back to Myers's social-psychological work in the 1970s (e.g., Myers 1975; Myers & Lamm 1975) and spans until today's research on Internet-induced group polarization (e.g., Yardi & Boyd 2010).

[10] See, for example, Reicher & Hopkins (2001), Thompson (1990).

a level only seen before by authoritarian states, reflecting its hybrid status. Winter concurs (2017a: 1, 6), claiming that IS "venerates information warfare" so much that its propaganda has "enabled the group to popularize its war in a manner unparalleled by any other insurgent actor, past or present." This "IS moment" therefore means is that it is no longer sufficient to conceptualize terrorism simply as a "propaganda of the deed" that only seeks to provoke policy shifts through a visible display of violence (read, for example, Bueno de Mesquita & Dickson 2007), nor is it sound to consider IS's system as a historical anomaly preceded and likely followed by otherwise amateur terrorist propaganda. Rather, it should be seen as a quantum leap in the communication of violent political actors who will from now inevitably seek to emulate IS in proportion to their abilities and capabilities. A gold standard, resulting from the accumulation of past experiences, has been experienced, is now known, and will inspire tomorrow. As Ingram explains (2016: 30), "propaganda strategies of extremists are constantly evolving and, just as Da'esh learned from its predecessors before eclipsing them, Da'esh is already influencing the propaganda strategies of friends and foes alike." IS has shown unprecedented levels of "malevolent creativity" (Gill, Horgan, Hunter, & Cushenbery 2013; Chapter 8 in this volume) by learning from its predecessors, and its successors will take stock.

The various chapters of this book examine this "IS moment" of prodigious plagiarism by highlighting the situatedness and novelty of each of its dimensions and by detailing how these various elements combine to constitute a full-spectrum propaganda. By doing so, the book delivers conclusions that are not only relevant to IS or Salafi-jihadist groups, but also to any group using violence to reach political/ideological goals.

Such a contribution is warranted for two main, interconnected reasons. The "IS moment" is in need of a systematic, comprehensive, and scientific assessment that would, first, dissolve common misperceptions about it, and, second, provide a reference point connecting the vast amount of publications of different sorts that have blossomed on the topic.

Dissolving Misconceptions

When it comes to IS in general and the group's propaganda in particular, misconceptions and biases abound. On the one hand, the general public mostly knows IS propaganda simply as an erratic flow of gruesome beheading videos, which further nurtures deeply held misrepresentations about both terrorism and Islam. Representations of IS in the West depict a phenomenon that is both completely irrational and irreducibly "foreign," which does not encourage policymakers—who may themselves struggle or even, in extreme cases, refuse to fully grasp the nature and characteristics of the organization and its communication[11]—to design nuanced and sophisticated interventions to effectively address the challenge posed by IS and similar groups.

On the other hand, experts in the security and intelligence services are in demand for detailed analytical work employing the most rigorous scientific methods, as well as proof-of-concept guidelines, to assist them in their strenuous work gathering, analyzing, and countering the stream of propaganda and communication disseminated by IS at the high rhythm evoked earlier, predominantly in Arabic but also in languages such as English, French, Russian, German, or even Chinese. Even though the pace of this production has steadily declined (read already, Zelin 2015b; Winter 2017b; Winter & Ingram 2018), mirroring the territorial and material corrosion of the "caliphate" and reflecting the organization's shifting objectives, governments still struggle to understand, in real time and without being influenced by a range of sometimes deeply entrenched preconceptions, what is really going on in this propaganda, how it is crafted, who it targets, and which mechanisms of radicalization it elicits (among both potential supporters and opponents).

This book constitutes a reference point not only for researchers but also for the public, policymakers, and the intelligence services, one that aims to strengthen their understanding of IS propaganda and brush away misperceptions with a clear presentation of the overall puzzle and a detailed analysis of each of its many pieces. Because today "the terrorist act does not simply speak for itself . . . but is amplified through a vast constellations of modern media" (O'Shaughnessy & Baines 2009: 227), such a task is vital.

Uniting the Literature

The second reason why the present volume is timely is more pragmatic and relates to the need to unite the literature on the issue. Current scholarship

---

[11] One prominent example is former French Prime Minister, Manuel Valls, who vocally assimilated attempts to explain IS with attempts to forgive it (see, e.g., http://www.lemonde.fr/societe/article/2016/03/03/terrorisme-la-cinglante-reponse-des-sciences-sociales-a-manuel-valls_4875959_3224.html).

on IS propaganda suffers from being scattered across various academic fields, different kinds of research and advocacy institutions, and the several types of actors interested in the phenomenon for various, though sometimes conflicting, reasons. Since the spectacular breakthrough—and press coverage—of IS in 2013–2014, research on the organization, its tactics, and message has boomed, up to the point that reviewing it has become almost impossible. This profusion adds to the spectacular growth of research on terrorism in general and jihadist violent groups in particular that took place after 9/11.

The result is a fascinating but extremely dispersed field of inquiry, one where description is very often favored to theorization and observations made from anecdotal evidence usually preferred to studies based on well-thought representative samples.[12] Important contributions have been published by academics in scientific disciplines as diverse as media studies (e.g., Winkler, El Damanhoury, Dicker, & Lemieux 2016), psychology (e.g., Bhui & Ibrahim 2013), political science and international relations (e.g., Molin Friis 2017), cultural studies (e.g., Awan 2007), terrorism and radicalization studies (e.g., Zelin 2015; O'Halloran et al. 2016), computer science (e.g., Chatfield, Reddick, & Brajawidagda 2015), and social philosophy (e.g., Leander 2016), among others. While connections do exist between these fields, there is unfortunately no sense of a coherent dialogue. To add to the complexity of the situation, the most up-to-date work has arguably been produced outside or at the margins of academia, in semi-academic or nonacademic think-tanks, government-sponsored centers, and private institutes for research—organizations like Quilliam (e.g., Hussain & Saltman 2014; Winter 2015) or the International Centre for the Study of Radicalisation and Political Violence (e.g., Winter 2017a) in the United Kingdom, the Brookings Institution in the United States and Doha (e.g., Berger & Morgan 2015), the International Centre for Counter-Terrorism in the Netherlands (e.g., Whiteside 2016), or the Geneva Centre for Security Policy (e.g., Schori Liang 2015). The circulation of ideas, data, and results between these hubs and academic researchers is not inexistent but far from optimal, which leads to contributions being written in very different formats (policy brief, research notes, academic articles) that do not always speak to one another and very often substantially repeat one another without being fully comparable.

---

[12] This is not actually a specificity of studies on IS; rather, it reflects the methodological challenges associated with terrorism research in general (read, e.g., Sageman 2014; Silke 1998, 2001; Victoroff 2005).

Another fault line exists between security and intelligence professionals and researchers. A wealth of information and analysis is produced in-house by counterterrorism experts in government agencies such as the MI5, MI6, Home Office, or Government Communications Headquarters (GCHQ) in the United Kingdom, or the Central Intelligence Agency (CIA), the Director of National Intelligence (DNI), and the National Security Agency (NSA) in the United States, yet this work almost never travels to academics and independent researchers—and the reverse is almost as rare.

In this context, this volume aims to gather, connect, and advance the literature from across the academic spectrum and the different types of contributors, offering what we believe to be the first book-length effort to unify and advance the field. As an offshoot of a research project commissioned by the UK's Centre for Research and Evidence on Security Threats (CREST), this book contributes to bridge the gap between practitioners and researchers. CREST—the UK's "national hub for understanding, countering and mitigating security threats"[13]—has made it possible for the editors of this volume to meet and share information with UK counterterrorism experts and to maximize the impact of these various chapters in the government's intelligence community. The publication of the volume as part of the START series will undoubtedly reinforce this aspect.

The Question of IS Propaganda's Impact

Two caveats are warranted at this stage. First and foremost, we do not assess the true impact of IS propaganda. Indeed, we do not conduct direct measurements of the effects of IS propaganda on its audience(s). Such an endeavor is plagued by almost unassailable methodological and ethical problems. Some of the chapters evaluate the reach of IS's "net," identify the audiences of particular outputs, or hypothesize their effects in terms of cognition and radicalization, yet what these outputs do in reality cannot be fully known beyond more or less educated suppositions.

Second, we do not take a definitive position on the thorny question of the propagandists' and propagandees' respective agencies; in other words, their

---

[13] See https://crestresearch.ac.uk/about/ for more information on CREST and https://crest-research.ac.uk/projects/isis-online-propaganda/ for an overview of the research program that led to this volume. As such, the editors of the volume acknowledge the support of, and express their gratitude for the CREST/ESRC award ES/N009614/1.

inspiration and motivation. The reader attuned to the field will know that several confronting interpretations currently face each other, without much dialogue. The rise of the group in 2014 and the wave of violence that ensued in fact reopened an older, heated debate among scholars and experts on how to conceptualize the nature of violent Islamist groups. On the one hand, some who could be labeled "jihadologists" (such as Aaron Zelin, Thomas Hegghammer, or Romain Caillet) conceptualize jihadism as an ideology and its militants as political actors rationally pursuing their ideologically inspired interests (e.g., establishment of the caliphate, undermining of the Saudi dynasty, ousting of US forces from Muslim lands). On the other hand, detractors of this view, who could tentatively be labeled "nihilists," contest the claim that the driving force of IS's actions is Islamic ideology, criticizing this new current as "neo-essentialist"[14] and dismissing any religiosity or political project for most of IS's motivations and actions; this is epitomized by Olivier Roy's "islamization of radicalism" thesis,[15] which considers people who join the group as marginal misfits who are largely ignorant of religion and geopolitics and bereft of real historical grievances.

This view tends to present IS militants as being attracted by the radicalism and the violence of the group rather than by its political or religious agenda and as irrational actors manipulated by the very top of their hierarchy and external actors for their own personal material profits, in a way reminiscent of Collier and Hoeffler's famous "greed" thesis on civil wars (2004) and Kaldor's description of "new wars" (1999).[16] Facing this minefield, this book does not advocate a simplistic answer in line with either approach. Rather, opening as we do the black box of IS's full-spectrum propaganda makes possible the emergence of a better, more sophisticated, and nuanced account of the many different roles simultaneously played by IS's message among

---

[14] This directly echoes the older debate between "essentialist" and "contextualist" analyses of political Islam of the 1980s and 1990s (read, e.g., Kuru 2005; Brynen 2010).

[15] In reaction to the last attacks on Paris, Olivier Roy (2017) argued that the individuals joining IS now would have joined leftist terrorist groups 40 years ago, claiming that "radical Islam is more an Islamization of radicalism rather than a radicalization of Islam."

[16] A subset of this second broad approach offers a "neo-Baathist" explanation, according to which IS's jihadist label and frames mask the criminal nature of the organization, where resources are extracted in controlled territory for the benefit of the remnants of Saddam Hussein's Baathist elite now piloting IS. Another, very different subset of this second approach, defended, for example, by Meriam Benraad, considers that IS's excesses mirror the West's entertainment society, whereby the group's ideology and theology serve as an excuse for the release of violence indirectly produced by the Western civilization, paradoxically against the West itself. Connected to these interpretations is the popular view among the media and elites of the Arab World that IS does not promotes "true Islam" (a discourse called "normative Islamology" by Burgat 2015).

multiple audiences and disseminators. This is not the equivalent of taking a lukewarm middle-ground in the debate. Rather, it reflects the book's ambition to offer a broader and deeper exploration of IS's information campaign that exposes its sophistication and the many complex ways through which it operates, beyond broad stereotypes. This analysis highlights both at once manipulation and belief, greed and grievances, emotion and reason, religion and (post)modernity.

The Book

The volume contains eight chapters in addition to the present introduction and an afterword. Written by some of the most authoritative experts of the field, these contributions have been ordered and carefully edited to provide the reader with a continuous and snowballing narrative gradually revealing the "net" of IS's full-spectrum propaganda, tracing a coherent thread from IS's past to its probable future, and emphasizing its full-spectrum character. The aim has been to provide the reader with an overarching, systematic, rigorous, and theoretically informed analysis of IS propaganda. Overarching, in that it covers each of the many constitutive components of IS propaganda, explains their roles within the strategic logic of IS's information warfare, shows how they contribute to the composition of a full-spectrum system, and situates these components and logic both within their social, historical, and political context and against the backdrop of their likely consequences. Systematic, because it both at once separates these various elements for specific analyses and gradually builds a multifaceted yet coherent analysis of IS propaganda, so that reading the entire volume gives the reader a clear map of IS's full-spectrum propaganda.

Each chapter also provides the reader with multiple connections to pertinent information offered in other chapters and operates within the conceptual field laid out in this introduction and more substantially in the first chapter, deepening and expanding it in an effort to offer theoretically grounded interpretations and explanations that move beyond purely descriptive stances. This strong theoretical commitment ensures that the volume offers a rich, multidisciplinary, and plural—yet integrated—explanatory viewpoint on IS propaganda. Contributions also use rigorous methods of information gathering, data generation, and visualization borrowed from across the social and computational sciences. Among others, the chapter authors make use of quantitative and qualitative content and discourse analysis, coding-based visual analysis, and interpretive methods. Most of the data collected through these methods and not visible in the book are available upon demand by the authors.

The book is organized into three main parts. The first two chapters operate at the macro-level, stressing the general and structural characteristics of IS propaganda. The following four contributions zoom in on the individual components of the propaganda system. The last two chapters step back to offer an assessment of IS's full-spectrum propaganda in terms of counterterrorism efforts and future terrorist threats. A glossary of the Arabic concepts (and their respective meaning) used in IS propaganda and hence in the chapters helps the reader to navigate through the discussions.

Chapters 1 and 2 therefore constitute the backbone of the volume. Chapter 1, "The Strategic Logic of Islamic State's Propaganda: Coherence, Comprehensiveness, and Multidimensionality," by Haroro Ingram expands and deepens the conceptual field opened in this introduction and is concerned with the organization and structure of IS propaganda. It provides the reader with a schematic map of all its major constitutive components, explaining how they work together in a synchronized way as part of a sophisticated strategy of information operations targeting different audiences simultaneously. In other words, the chapter clarifies the defining formal lines of IS's full-spectrum propaganda, canvassing its strategic logic by examining how its key constituent parts are designed to interlock in an approach to communications that is comprehensive, multidimensional, and cohesive—the three fundamental elements merely sketched earlier. The chapter considers how these elements have evolved through the "boom-bust" evolution of IS and exposes the formal institutional and bureaucratic structures and dynamics holding the many pieces of the propaganda puzzle together in service of the group's strategic, tactical, and organizational goals. It does so by positioning IS's propaganda innovation/plagiarism within the tradition of insurgent information warfare.

Chapter 2, "Situating Islamic State's Message: A Social and Theological Genealogy," by Mehdi Laghmari shifts from structure and logic to content and meaning, offering a fine-grained presentation and analysis of the message constituting IS propaganda. The chapter does so by looking at the present through the prism of the past, tracing back the social, ideological, and theological origins of IS's message with an extremely detailed genealogy of Salafi-jihadism—from Ibn Taymiyyah to Abu Abdullah al-Muhajir—and its core concepts—from *Al-walā' wa al-barā'* to *takfīr*. Offering such a genealogy is crucial to situate IS's claims within the lineage of (non-)radical Islamist groups from across the Middle East, as well as to understand the way that each component described in the ensuing chapters is mobilized.

Building on these two macro-level chapters, the following four contributions zoom in on the constitutive components of IS's propaganda net, providing detailed information and analysis of IS's magazines (Chapter 4, by Stéphane Baele, Katharine Boyd, and Travis Coan), videos (Chapter 3, by Stéphane Baele, Katharine Boyd, and Travis Coan), social media (Chapter 5, by Laura Wakeford and Laura Smith), and the many lesser-known, seemingly disparate yet nonetheless crucial outputs such as photo reports, literature, infographics, news broadcast, and music (Chapter 6, by Stéphane Baele and Charlie Winter). Each of these chapters gives an account of what and how much exactly IS has produced, when, and by whom. It also provides in-depth analysis of how each of these particular propaganda products works (technical aspects), to whom it is disseminated and why (anticipated impact), how it participates in the constitution of a full-spectrum system, and how innovative/copycat IS has been in its use. These chapters openly acknowledge, connect, and critically review the important work already conducted, on which the authors then build novel insights using various theories and cutting-edge methods. Together, these four contributions considerably strengthen our understanding of IS propaganda, demonstrating that its efficiency is due both at once to its simplicity (ability to convey a straightforward message through mass repetition) and its sophistication (complex standardization and synchronization of the message across many outputs, ability to target different audiences simultaneously in different ways).

Reflecting on these six contributions, Chapter 7, "Countering Islamic State's Propaganda: Challenges and Opportunities," by Tobias Borck and Jonathan Githens-Mazer then offers an argument on what IS full-spectrum propaganda means in terms of counterterrorism. It takes into the equation the dominant features of IS propaganda highlighted in the book in order to assess the conditions of an efficient counterpropaganda effort, as far as such an endeavor is even possible. This reflection then paves the way for the final Chapter 8, "Terrorist Propaganda After Islamic State: Learning, Emulation, Imitation," by Paul Gill, Kurt Braddock, Lily Cushenbery, Sanaz Zolghadriha, and Bettina Rottweiler, which draws on both the literature on extremist groups' historical trajectories and research on innovation dynamics in organizations to raise the hypothesis of future extremist groups learning from IS's full-spectrum approach. The chapter goes back to the claim that IS is, to take Ingram's words evoked earlier (2016: 30), a major "plagiarist," evaluating IS's "radical" and "incremental" innovations in order to show that the most visible and plainly successful elements of IS propaganda are unfortunately likely to be mimicked in bespoke ways by already-existing and future extremist groups across the ideological spectrum. Finally, the book closes with an afterword by Thomas Hegghammer, who reflects on the main insights of the book, using them as starting points for further thinking and research on IS, extremist propaganda, terrorism, and the West.

Together, these contributions depict IS propaganda as an unprecedented effort from a terrorist or insurgent group to design and produce a full-spectrum propaganda targeting various audiences simultaneously, extensively recycling old symbolic imagery and narratives into a not-so-new political message, institutionalizing the production of this message for maximal coherence and adaptability to external and internal events, and aiming not only to promote ideas but also, more deeply, to disseminate a certain culture and transform their enemies' own worldview. To some extent, the organization has worryingly been able to bring this effort to fruition in ways detailed in the following pages, which makes the present volume not only an in-depth study of IS propaganda but also a point of departure for prospective thinking not only on the future of violent groups' communications but also on the reactions to it by democratic and authoritarian societies.

References

Arnsperger C. (2009) *Full-Spectrum Economics: Toward an Inclusive and Emancipatory Social Science*. London: Routledge.

Awan A. (2007) "Virtual Jihadist Media: Function, Legitimacy and Radicalizing Efficacy", *European Journal of Cultural Studies* 10(3): 389–408.

Batiste J., Daniels P. (2005) "The Fight for Samarra: Full-Spectrum Operations in Modern Warfare," *Military Review* 85(3): 13–21.

BBC Monitoring (2017) "Analysis: Islamic State Media Output Goes into Sharp Decline." Online document available at https://monitoring.bbc.co.uk/product/c1dnnj2k.

Berger J., Morgan J. (2015) "The ISIS Twitter Census. Defining and Describing the Population of ISIS Supporters on Twitter," *Brookings Project on US Relations with the Islamic World Analysis Paper* 20.

Bevan B. (2005) "Full Spectrum Dominance," *Arab Studies Quarterly* 27(3): 51–56.

Bhui K., Ibrahim Y. (2013) "Marketing the 'Radical': Symbolic Communication and Persuasive Technologies in Jihadist Websites," *Transcultural Psychiatry* 50(2): 216–234.

Brynen R. (2010) "Political Culture and the Puzzle of Persistent Authoritarianism in the Middle East." Online document available at http://www.mcgill.ca/icames/files/icames/IPSA.pdf.

Bueno de Mesquita E., Dickson E. (2007) "The Propaganda of the Deed: Terrorism, Counterterrorism, and Mobilization," *American Journal of Political Science* 51(2): 364–381.

Burgat F. (2015) "The Appeal of the Islamic State," *Global Dialogue* 5(4): 7–9.

Caiani M., Parenti L. (2009) "The Dark Side of the Web: Italian Right-Wing Extremist Groups and the Internet", *South European Society and Politics* 14(3): 273–294.

Chatfield A., Reddick C., Brajawidagda U. (2015) "Tweeting Propaganda, Radicalization and Recruitment: Islamic State Supporters Multi-Sided Twitter Networks," *Proceedings of the 16th Annual International Conference on Digital Government Research*: 239–249. doi:10.1145/2757401.2757408.

Chiarelli P., Michaelis P. (2005) "Winning the Peace. The Requirement for Full-Spectrum Operations," *Military Review* 85(4): 4–17.

Collier P., Hoeffler A. (2004) "Greed and Grievance in Civil War," *Oxford Economic Papers* 56(4): 563–595.

Conway M. (2006) "Terrorism and the Internet: New Media—New Threat?," *Parliamentary Affairs* 59(2): 283–298.

Coulthard L. (2009) "Torture Tunes: Tarantino, Popular Music, and New Hollywood Ultraviolence," *Music & the Moving Image* 2(2): 1–6.

Cunningham S. (2002) *The Idea of Propaganda: A Reconstruction.* Westport: Praeger.

Ellul J. (1962/1973) *Propaganda. The Formation of Men's Attitudes.* New York: Vintage Books.

Farwell J. (2014) "The Media Strategy of ISIS," *Survival* 56(6): 49–55.

Gill P., Horgan J., Hunter S., Cushenbery L. (2013) "Malevolent Creativity in Terrorist Organizations," *Journal of Creative Behavior* 47(2): 125–151.

Halfmann D., Young M. (2010) "War Pictures: The Grotesque as a Mobilizing Tactic," *Mobilization: An International Quarterly* 15(1): 1–24.

Hegghammer T., ed. (2017) *Jihadi Culture. The Art and Social Practices of Militant Islamists.* Cambridge: Cambridge University Press.

Henderson E. (1943) "Toward a Definition of Propaganda," *Journal of Social Psychology* 18(1): 71–87.

Hiebert R. (2003) "Public Relations and Propaganda in Framing the Iraq War," *Public Relations Review* 29: 243–255.

Hussain G., Saltman E. M. (2014) "Jihad Trending: A Comprehensive Analysis of Online Extremism and How to Counter It," *Quilliam Working Papers*, https://www.quilliaminternational.com/jihad-trending-a-comprehensive-analysis-of-online-extremism-and-how-to-counter-it-executive-summary/.

Ingram H. (2016) "A Brief History of Propaganda during Conflict: Lessons for Counter-Terrorism Strategic Communications," *ICCT Research Paper*. doi:10.19165/2016.1.06.

Kaldor M. (1999) *New and Old Wars: Organized Violence in a Global Era Paperback.* Cambridge: Polity Press.

Kallis A. (2005) *Nazi Propaganda and the Second World War.* Basingstoke: Palgrave Macmillan.

Kuru A. (2005) "Globalization and Diversification of Islamic Movements: Three Turkish Cases," *Political Science Quarterly* 120(2): 253–274.

Lasswell H. (1927) "The Theory of Political Propaganda," *American Political Science Review* 21(3): 627–631.

Lasswell H. (1927/1971) *Propaganda Technique in the World War*. Cambridge MA: MIT Press.

Leander A. (2016) "Digital/Commercial (in)Visibility: The Politics of DAESH Recruitment Videos," *European Journal of Social Theory* 20(3): 348–372.

Le Monde (2017) "Comment l'Etat Islamique a Perdu la Quasi-totalité de son Territoire Utile en Irak et en Syrie en Trois ans." Retrieved from http://www.lemonde.fr/les-decodeurs/visuel/2017/03/13/comment-l-etat-islamique-a-recule-en-irak-et-en-syrie-depuis-2014_5093896_4355770.html.

Lenczowski J. (2011) *Full Spectrum Diplomacy and Grand Strategy*. Plymouth: Lexington Books.

Miller E., Kammerer W. (2017) "Overview: Terrorism in 2016," *START Background Report*. Retrieved from https://www.start.umd.edu/pubs/START_GTD_OverviewTerrorism2016_August2017.pdf.

Milton D. (2016) "Communication Breakdown: Unraveling the Islamic State's Media Efforts," *Combating Terrorism Center at West Point*, https://ctc.usma.edu/communication-breakdown-unraveling-the-islamic-states-media-efforts/.

Molin Friis S. (2017) "'Behead, Burn, Crucify, Crush': Theorizing the Islamic State's Public Displays of Violence," *European Journal of International Relations* 24(2): 243–267. online first.

Myers D. (1975) "Discussion-Induced Attitude Polarization," *Human Relations* 28: 699–714.

Myers D., Lamm H. (1975) "The Polarizing Effect of Group Discussion," *American Scientist* 63(3): 297–303.

O'Halloran K., Tan S., Wignell P., Bateman J., Duc-Son P., Grossman M., Vande Moere A. (2019) "Interpreting Text and Image Relations in Violent Extremist Discourse: A Mixed Method Approach for Big Data Analysis," *Terrorism & Political Violence* 31(3): 454–474.

O'Shaughnessy N. (2004) *Politics and Propaganda: Weapons of Mass Seduction*. Manchester: Manchester University Press.

O'Shaughnessy N., Baines P. (2009) "Selling Terror: The Symbolization and Positioning of Jihad," *Marketing Theory* 9(2): 227–241.

Reicher S., Hopkins N. (2001) "Psychology and the End of History: A Critique and a Proposal for the Psychology of Social Categorization," *Political Psychology* 22(2): 383–407.

Roy O. (2017) "Who Are the New Jihadis?," *The Guardian*, April 13, 2017. Retrieved from https://www.theguardian.com/news/2017/apr/13/who-are-the-new-jihadis.

Sageman M. (2014) "The Stagnation in Terrorism Research," *Terrorism & Political Violence* 26(4): 565–580.

Schori Liang C. (2015) "Cyber Jihad: Understanding and Countering Islamic State Propaganda," *GSCP Policy Papers* 2015/1.

Silke A. (1998) "Cheshire-Cat Logic: The Recurring Theme of Terrorist Abnormality in Psychological Research," *Psychology, Crime & Law* 4: 51–69.

Silke A. (2001) "The Devil You Know: Continuing Problems with Research on Terrorism," *Terrorism & Political Violence* 13(4): 1–14.

Smith B., Lasswell H., Casey R. (1946) *Propaganda, Communication, and Public Opinion*. Princeton: Princeton University Press.

Taylor P. (2003) *Munitions of the Mind. A History of Propaganda from the Ancient World to the Present Day*. Manchester: Manchester University Press.

Thompson G. (2017) "Parallels in Propaganda? A Comparative Historical Analysis of Islamic State and the Nazi Party," *Journal of Public Relations Research* 29(1): 51–66.

Thompson J. (1990) *Ideology and Modern Culture*. Oxford: Blackwell.

Victoroff J. (2005) "The Mind of the Terrorist: A Review and Critique of Psychological Approaches," *Journal of Conflict Resolution* 49(1), 3–4.

Whiteside C. (2016) "Lighting the Path: The Evolution of the Islamic State Media Enterprise (2003–2016)," *ICCT Research Papers* Nov/2016.

Winkler C., El Damanhoury K., Dicker A., Lemieux A. (2016) "The Medium Is Terrorism: Transformation of the About to Die Trope in Dabiq," *Terrorism & Political Violence* 31(2): 224–243.

Winter C. (2015) *Documenting the Virtual "Caliphate."* London: Quilliam Foundation.

Winter C. (2017a) "Media Jihad: The Islamic State's Doctrine for Information Warfare." *ICSR Working Papers*, https://icsr.info/wp-content/uploads/2017/02/ICSR-Report-Media-Jihad-The-Islamic-State%E2%80%99s-Doctrine-for-Information-Warfare.pdf.

Winter C. (2017b) "The ISIS Propaganda Decline," *ICSR Insight*. Retrieved from http://icsr.info/2017/03/icsr-insight-isis-propaganda-decline/

Winter C., Ingram H. (2018) "Terror, Online and Off: Recent Trends in Islamic State Propaganda Operations," *War on the Rocks*, March 2, 2018. Retrieved from https://warontherocks.com/2018/03/terror-online-and-off-recent-trends-in-islamic-state-propaganda-operations/

Wittgenstein L. (1953/2009) *Philosophical Investigations*. Oxford: Wiley Blackwell.

Yardi S., Boyd D. (2010) "Dynamic Debates: An Analysis of Group Polarization over Time on Twitter," *Bulletin of Science, Technology and Society* 30(5): 316–327.

Zajonc R. (1968) "Attitude Effects of mere Exposure," *Journal of Personality and Social Psychology* 9(2): 1–27.

Zelin A. (2013) "The State of Global Jihad Online. A Qualitative, Quantitative, and Cross-Lingual Analysis," *New America Foundation Working Papers*. Retrieved from http://www.washingtoninstitute.org/uploads/Documents/opeds/Zelin20130201-NewAmericaFoundation.pdf.

Zelin A. (2015a) "Picture or It Didn't Happen: A Snapshot of the Islamic State's Official Media Output," *Perspectives on Terrorism* 9(4): 85–97.

Zelin A. (2015b) "The Decline in Islamic State Media Output," *ICSR Insight*. Retrieved from http://icsr.info/2015/12/icsr-insight-decline-islamic-state-media-output/.

Zimbardo O., Leippe M. (1991) *The Psychology of Attitude Change and Social Influence*. New York: McGraw-Hill.

1

The Strategic Logic of Islamic State's Full-Spectrum Propaganda

Coherence, Comprehensiveness, and Multidimensionality

Haroro J. Ingram

Introduction

With a history characterized by periods of extraordinary success and failure, Mosul's al-Noori Mosque became a symbol of the Islamic State's (IS) most recent period of boom and bust. From Abu Bakr al-Baghdadi's first appearance as the so-called Caliph of IS's supposed Caliphate to the destruction of the mosque's iconic leaning minaret, the al-Noori Mosque is a reminder of how narrative and imagery, disseminated and consumed in a context characterized by a complex mix of psychosocial and strategic factors, can shape how audiences perceive a conflict and its actors. Between these two iconic moments in its history, IS has demonstrated its deep appreciation for the tremendous power of timely and targeted propaganda, deploying a dizzying range of messages, media, and formats, not just for strategic but also for operational and even tactical ends. Of course, it is an appreciation forged by decades of struggle characterized by fleeting victories and crushing losses. Given the variety of components deployed by IS's propaganda machine, all of which will be explored in ensuing chapters, it is easy to miss the forest for the trees; to fixate on the components of its propaganda and miss the overarching logic that holds its campaign together.

The purpose of this chapter is therefore to expand and deepen the conceptual field of this volume that has been sketched in the Introduction. The aim is to broadly canvass the strategic logic of IS's propaganda strategy by examining how its key constituent parts interlock in a sophisticated approach to communications that is *multidimensional, comprehensive,* and *cohesive.* As

Haroro J. Ingram, *The Strategic Logic of Islamic State's Full-Spectrum Propaganda: Coherence, Comprehensiveness, and Multidimensionality* In: *ISIS Propaganda.* Edited by: Stephane J. Baele, Katharine A. Boyd, and Travis G. Coan, Oxford University Press (2020) © University of Maryland National Consortium for the Study of Terrorism and Responses to Terrorism (START)
DOI: 10.1093/oso/9780190932459.003.0002

already hinted at in the Introduction, IS appears to be acutely aware of the importance of attaining these three dimensions in order to produce a full-spectrum propaganda effort that maximizes the reach, relevance, and resonance of its message with different outputs deployed with both a singular specific purpose *and* to synchronize with other elements. It is an approach that is calibrated to create multiple, diverse, and mutually reinforcing lines of effort that compound the "effects" of IS's words and deeds while seeking to diminish the "effects" of its enemies' words and deeds. These dynamics will inevitably be more pronounced during periods of success when the group holds territory and can devote time, resources and personnel to its propaganda efforts. The challenge during times of decline is how IS can maintain these core components and competencies of its propaganda effort so it is postured to contribute to and expand during its next period of success. By broadly mapping the constituent parts of IS's propaganda strategy, explaining variations throughout the group's "boom-bust" history, and analyzing its connections with IS's military activities and territorial situation, this chapter is designed to frame the four "deep dive" chapters that explore individual aspects of IS propaganda.

To these ends, this chapter proceeds in two steps. First, it begins by exploring the role of propaganda in IS's broader campaign strategy before delving into the overarching strategic logic that drives its messaging efforts. What emerges is that while IS is broadly similar to many other violent non-state political groups in its strategic centralization of propaganda and the fundamental role it affords messaging, an analysis of "captured" IS sources and the history of its media units reveals an attitude to the power of messaging that borders on veneration. Second, the chapter details the three important traits of IS's full-spectrum propaganda campaign that are a product of and contribute to its strategic logic: multidimensionality, comprehensiveness, and coherence. The multidimensionality of IS's propaganda effort is analyzed by considering how the group uses messaging as a tactical, operational, and strategic tool. IS deploys a range of media and formats in a comprehensive approach to communication designed to maximize the reach (i.e., the ability of a message to access target audiences), relevance (i.e., the timeliness of a message and its significance within the context of immediate situational factors), and resonance (i.e., the influence of a message on audience perceptions generated by leveraging deeper identity and sociohistorical factors) of its messages across diverse and geographically disparate target audiences. The sheer array of components and messages that characterize IS's propaganda effort risks its campaign appearing ad hoc and disjointed. Yet the general coherence that tends to distinguish its messaging emerges thanks to a combination of not only IS's all-permeating strategic logic and central narrative but its branding and organizational architecture.

IS's Competitive Systems of Control and Meaning

To understand how and why IS engages in messaging and to what ends, it is necessary to first position its propaganda effort within the context of its broader politico-military campaign strategy.[1] After all, IS has engaged in a varied spectrum of politico-military activities throughout its history particularly between 2003 and 2007 and 2014 and 2017 when it controlled and then sought to hold territory across multiple theaters of operation (see Knights 2014; Whiteside 2016a). IS's spectrum of politico-military activities constitutes what Bernard Fall (1965) would describe as its "competitive system of control"—the politico-military apparatus IS uses to outcompete adversaries for territory and support. On one end of IS's politico-military spectrum, it has deployed more conventional and hybrid military operations against enemies and implemented highly bureaucratized—indeed, seemingly state-like—governance institutions in its areas of control (e.g., Raqqa, Syria and Mosul, Iraq circa 2014–2017). On the other end of the spectrum, at the fringes of its reach, IS directs its operatives or seeks to "inspire" supporters to engage in terrorism with essentially no effort to implement governance initiatives. These two extremes represent the "black" and "white" ends of a spectrum between which lies varied shades of gray, its areas of contestation where IS deploys a range of unconventional forms of violence (e.g., guerrilla warfare) and informal governance initiatives.

The different hues of IS's politico-military spectrum represent more than mere spatial cross-sections of its campaign; they are politico-military phases through which the group transitions depending on strategic and situational factors. IS actively promote its theory and practice of warfare because it rests so much of its legitimacy on the contention that it is applying the Prophetic method (*manhaj*)[2] in its pursuit of the Caliphate. The first issue of *Dabiq*

---

[1] For analyses of IS's overall propaganda strategy see Ingram 2015; Price et al. 2014; Winter 2015; Fernandez 2015; for analyses of IS' overall strategy see Berger & Stern 2015, McCants 2016, Fishman 2016; Ingram, Whiteside & Winter 2019.

[2] The reader is encouraged to refer to the Glossary of Arabic terms provided at the beginning of the volume.

magazine devoted its feature article, "From Hijrah to Khilafah" (2014), to carefully explaining the phases of its politico-military campaign strategy— *hijrah, Jamāʾah* (establishing a community of believers), destabilize the *ṭaghūt* ("idolatrous" regimes and groups), *tamkin* ("consolidation"), and *Khilāfah*— and the rationale underpinning it while *Al Naba* often promotes this strategy, if framed slightly differently, to Arabic speaking audiences. IS's adoption of a phased politico-military strategy is not unique and is broadly reflected in decades of modern insurgency thinking and practice both within the Islamist milieu (e.g., Al-Muqrin 2003/2009; Al-Suri cited in Lia 2008; see also Chapter 2) and beyond it (Irish Republican Army [c. 1950s] 1985, Tse-Tung 2000 [1937], Guevara 1998 [1961], Minh [1941] cited in O'Dowd 2013). After all, violent non-state political groups confront state adversaries who typically have significant resource, technological, personnel, and capability advantages, which compels them to engage in a phased strategy that transitions from unconventional toward more conventional politico-military activities as that asymmetry balances. IS's description of its successful Mosul operation in its newsletter *Islamic State Report* captures this strategic transition.

> This past Monday, the Islamic State of Iraq and Sham liberated the city of Mosul in its entirety . . . This followed a shift in the Islamic State's strategy, which now saw its forces leaving their desert strongholds in Iraq and making their way into the cities. Since the start of the jihad in 2003, the province of Al-Anbar has traditionally been the stronghold of the muja-hidin, with Fallujah serving as its jihadi capital. In spite of the advantage of having a strong power base, the Islamic State understood that having just a single power base in any given region would work against them by giving their enemies a point of focus for their strikes.[3]

When IS's charismatic spokesman, the late Abu Mohammad al-Adnani, flagged in his final speech in 2016 that "[i]t is the same, whether Allah blesses us with consolidation or we move into the bare, open desert, displaced and pursued" (Al-Adnani 2016), it was designed as a rallying cry to supporters and a warning to enemies that, just as IS had reemerged in 2013–2014, it would move back down its campaign phases if overwhelmed until the strategic conditions were right to escalate yet again.

---

[3] "Islamic State liberates the city of Mosul," *Islamic State Report* no. 3 (2014), pp. 1–5.

There is another crucial strategic implication that emerges from this asymmetry: modern insurgencies tend to afford propaganda a central role in their campaign strategies. Taber's seminal *War of the Flea* articulates this point perfectly.

> The guerrilla fighter is primarily a propagandist, an agitator, a disseminator of the revolutionary idea, who uses the struggle itself—the actual physical conflict—as an instrument of agitation. His primary goal is to raise the level of revolutionary anticipation, and then of popular participation, to the crisis point at which the revolution becomes general throughout the country and the people in their masses carry out the final task—the destruction of the existing order and (often but not always) of the army that defends it. (Taber 2002: 12)

IS similarly centralizes propaganda in its campaign plans. In the opening pages of IS's doctrine for propagandists, "Media Operative, You Are Also a Mujahid," it states that "The media is a jihad in the way of Allah. You, with your media work, are therefore a mujahid in the way of Allah (provided your intention is sound). The media *jihad* against the enemy is no less important than the material fight against it. Moreover, your media efforts are considered as parts of many great forms of the rite of jihad" (Al-Himma Library 2017: 6).

IS uses propaganda to provide its audiences with a "competitive system of meaning," a lens through which to perceive the conflict, its actors, and indeed the world more broadly and that must compete against the systems of meaning propagated by its enemies. As highlighted in the Introduction, its propaganda does not merely seek to shift particular opinions; it more fundamentally attempts to disseminate a certain worldview. IS learned early in its struggle just how important propaganda would be to winning local support. An analysis of "captured" IS media documents circa 2006–2008 argued that IS implemented a multiphase messaging strategy in Iraq circa 2005–2006 consisting of, "(1) emphasising the proper way to live one's life, (2) describing the cruelty being imposed on Sunnis that demanded a violent response, and (3) that al-Qaeda in Iraq/Islamic State in Iraq (AQI/ISI) is the best group to fight against this cruelty" (2016: 3). It is a battle that IS's own doctrine frames as essential to the success of their overall struggle.

The media operative brothers—may Allah the Almighty protect them—are charged with shielding the ummah from the mightiest onslaught ever known in the history of the Crusader *and* Safavid wars! They are the security valve for the *sharia* of the Merciful. They are warding off an invasion, the danger of which exceeds even the danger of the military invasion. It is an intellectual invasion that is faced by the Muslims in both their minds and their hearts, corrupting the identity of many of them, distorting their ideas, inverting their concepts, substituting their traditions, drying the headwaters of their faith and deadening their zeal. (al-Himma Library 2017: 26)[4]

At the heart of IS's system of meaning is a central narrative that is simple and decisive, more fully analyzed in the next chapter: as the world hurtles toward the Apocalypse, join us because we (IS) are the protectors and champions of the Muslims (i.e., IS-aligned Sunnis) whose crises, which are due to the words and deeds of non-Muslims (i.e., anyone who is not an IS-aligned Sunni), can only be solved with the establishment of the Caliphate based on the Prophetic method. IS thus deploys propaganda to shape the perceptions and polarize the support of target audiences—in its own words, to "light the path" and to "revive the negligent minds" (Ministry of Information of the Islamic State of Iraq, cited in Whiteside 2016b: 3)—via messages that tend to have two fundamental purposes.

The first is to deploy messages that are designed to act as a "force multiplier" for IS's system of control and a "force nullifier" against its enemy's system of control. It follows that these messages tend to make *rational-choice appeals* to target audiences by compelling them to make cost-benefit decisions contrasting IS's politico-military agenda with alternatives. The clearest examples of IS's rational-choice appeals are those that pit IS's fighting and governance efforts against those of status quo or other aspirant authorities (e.g., "On the Beat: ISR Examines How the Islamic Police Safeguards ar-Raqqah and Their Importance in State Building", 2014). This type of appeal was epitomized in the feature length movie *Flames of War* (2014) when IS's politico-military agenda was described as follows:

The Islamic State was now on show for the world to see. The courts were established; prayer was being enforced; the *hudood* were being implemented; the people were being invited to good; and the *zakat* was being collected

---

[4] For more information on the Al-Himma Library, see Chapter 6.

and distributed. Light glowed from the mujahideen, who were soft towards the believers and harsh against the *kuffar*. This harshness never wavered and was a constant trait of the brothers. So the war on the *kuffar* raged on.[5]

By interlocking messages that promote its efforts, on the one hand, and deride those of its enemies, on the other, IS's rational-choice appeals create self-reinforcing cycles. The more competent IS appear, the more incompetent its enemies appear. Such appeals are also designed to give certainty and security to audiences. As Whiteside (2016b) asserts: "In complex environments like Syria, Iraq, and Libya, the simple, consistent, and comprehensive message broadcast in tremendous volume, selling attractive products like stability and order, becomes a heuristic for humans who are craving normalcy in the midst of chaos" (Whiteside 2016b: 23). An important feature of IS's rational-choice appeals is that the group actively and proudly promotes its phased politico-military campaign strategy as tried and tested in the field. IS's *man-haj* for achieving its ultimate goal, the establishment of the Caliphate as a precursor to End Times, is central to its claims of legitimacy. Seen through this rational-choice lens, IS's brutality against enemies and harsh governance initiatives are not contradictory to those ultimate aims but intrinsic to achieving them. Put simply, IS's *manhaj* must be pursued with purity because all other options are impure and destined, ultimately, to be ineffective.

The second key purpose of IS propaganda is to win over supporters to its cause or ideology via messages that tie bipolar in-group and out-group identities to *solution* and *crisis* constructs, structuring a dichotomous worldview. It is an *identity-based messaging* dynamic crystallized by the following from Abu Bakr al-Baghdadi: "The world today has been divided into two camps and two trenches, with no third camp present: the camp of Islam and faith, and the camp of *kufr* and hypocrisy" (Al-Baghdadi 2014). Put simply, non-Muslims are evil "others" responsible for Muslim crises while IS are the champions and protectors of Sunni Muslims. To these ends, Baghdadi offers the following advice to IS fighters: "Stay awake guarding them so they can be safe and at rest. Be their support. Respond with kindness if they do you wrong. . . . Know that today you are the defenders of the religion and the guards of the land of Islam" (Al-Baghdadi 2014). Playing on these dualities—in-group identity and solution constructs with out-group identity and crisis constructs—is a potent way to leverage powerful psychosocial forces in its

---

[5] *Flames of War* is an Al-Hayat Media Center production (cf., Chapter 3; also Chapter 6).

target audiences. These identity-choice appeals seek to coax IS's audiences into perceiving the world and making decisions based on IS's in- and out-group identity constructs.

IS's dual identity-choice appeals are also designed to be interlocking and create compounding self-reinforcing cycles. After all, the more IS ties itself to solutions, the more its enemies are responsible for crises and destined to fail. Indeed IS's media doctrine encourages operatives to play upon these dualities: "the other side of the *jihadi* media work is giving glad tidings to believers, for everything that angers the unbeliever or hypocrite pleases the honest believer—it is a double-edged sword" (Al-Himma Library 2017: 19). To continue the theme of *manhaj* from the previous example, IS's methodology in the field is framed in its propaganda as not only tactically, operationally, and strategically effective given the nature of its asymmetric struggle (i.e., rational-choice appeal) but also as an identity-choice decision that all true Muslims (i.e., IS-aligned Sunnis) must follow: "For what good is there in liberating a city only to leave its inhabitants steeped in misguidance and misery, suffering from ignorance and disunity, and disconnected from the Book of Allah and the Sunnah of his Messenger."[6] This highlights a broader point central to understanding the strategic logic of IS propaganda: it is often difficult to extricate IS's rational- and identity-choice appeals.

In practice, the two broad categories of IS messaging described here—identity- and rational-choice appeals[7]—rarely operate in distinct vacuums but are woven into narratives designed to have a self-reinforcing and mutually compounding effect. After all, the more IS is seen as the champion and protector of Sunni Muslims against crisis-causing enemies (identity-choice appeals), the more IS's politico-military agenda will be seen as a preferable alternative to other options as a solution to crises (rational-choice appeals). IS synchronizes actions in the field with its messaging to help fuel perceptions of crisis and the need for solutions. In a letter to al-Qaeda leaders in 2004, al-Zarqawi expressed his intent to aggravate Sunni-Shi'a sectarian tensions as a means to fuel the conditions for winning popular Sunni support: "If we succeed in dragging them into the arena of sectarian war, it will become possible to awaken the inattentive Sunnis as they feel imminent danger and

---

[6] *Dabiq* no. 3 (2014), pp. 16–17, "Da'wah and Hisbah."
[7] For more on rational- and identity-choice decision-making see March and Heath (1994).

annihilating death at the hands of the Sabeans."[8] Milton's analysis of internal documents in the proceeding years (2006–2011) indicates that the group implemented a three-phase plan that first sought to use messaging to publish "the true faith" and explain "the jihadi system and what is needed from the people," then looked to fuel the need for the group by highlighting the value of that agenda and the dangers presented by coalition forces and Shiite militias, and, third, presented itself as the only viable solution to that crises (Milton 2016: 4–5). It has and will remain a trademark of IS's approach to war, governance, and propaganda.

The more that IS can coax supporters into adopting its system of meaning as the lens through which they perceive the world, the greater the sense of Other-induced crisis IS can generate and, in turn, increase the perceived need for solutions via its system of control. The more extreme the sense of crisis, the more extreme the solution required to address it. IS tells its propagandists that it is they who must bring these dynamics to the attention of target audiences.

[I]t is upon you—o media operative of the caliphate—to be cognisant of the need for people in general and the *mujahidin* in particular to be aware of the issues facing the Islamic *ummah*. It is upon you to guide them onto the paths of mankind's salvation from unbelief, injustice, and corruption. This is *your* responsibility! Yes, you and no one else! (Al-Himma Library 2017: 22)

What should be clear so far is that it is not possible to understand the strategic logic of IS's propaganda efforts (i.e., its competitive system of meaning) isolated from its politico-military struggle (i.e., its competitive system of control). Of course, it is important for the credibility of any political actor to narrow the difference between rhetoric and action. But this "say-do" gap issue is particularly significant for IS, whose claims to champion the Prophet Muhammad's *manhaj* (methodology) is central to its derogation of competitor Islamist groups. According to IS propaganda, establishing the Caliphate as a precondition for the Apocalypse cannot, by definition, be separated from the *manhaj* required to achieve that goal. In short, to accomplish the goal by any means other than by the Prophetic method is to not achieve the goal at

---

[8] This letter is available online on the webpage of the US Department of State: https://2001-2009.state.gov/p/nea/rls/31694.htm.

all. Unsurprisingly, when IS declared the establishment of the Islamic State of Iraq and al-Sham and then its so-called Caliphate, it inundated target audiences with propaganda across a range of formats including audio speeches by al-Adnani that were transcribed for multilingual audiences ("They Shall by No Means Harm You but with a Slight Evil" [2013], "This Is Not Our Methodology Nor Will It Ever Be" [2014], "This Is the promise of Allah" [2014], and "Sorry, Amir of al-Qaeda" [2014]), a nine-part video series titled "The Establishment of the Islamic State" (2014), and multiple articles in, for example, its English-language publications *Islamic State Report* and *Dabiq*. Moreover, a close synchronicity of actions and words has an important dual effect: actions manifest as embodiments of the message, while messages boost the real-world "effects" of actions by shaping how they are perceived. On the latter point, Winter highlights in *Media Jihād: The Islamic State's doctrine for Information Warfare* that IS believes "a well-conceived media 'missile' has the power to complement—and sometimes even substitute—military and terrorist operations" (Winter 2017: 18). As IS's doctrine declares: "verbal weapons can actually be more potent than atomic bombs" (Al-Himma Library 2017: 7). This is particularly important for IS during periods of bust when its capabilities are depleted and messaging will be crucial to it remaining relevant and maintaining the morale of supporters. For example, on 29 April 2019, in the aftermath of being routed from its last patch of territorial control in eastern Syria after years of crushing defeats, Abu Bakr al-Baghdadi appeared on video for only the second time ever to call upon the true believers to maintain an unwavering commitment to IS's strategy (The Islamic State 2019). In the months since his speech, IS's propaganda machine promoted the renewal of pledges of allegiance from established and aspirant *wilāyāt* from around the world in a video series titled "And the Best Outcome is for the Righteous".

In summary, the raison d'être of IS's propaganda campaign is to shape the perceptions and polarize the support of friends, foes, and neutrals by deploying a fusion of imagery and narrative in messages designed to appeal to rational- and identity-choice decision making in target audiences. This strategic logic drives every aspect and underpins every component of IS's propaganda campaign. It also provides the roots for the three traits that characterize its full-spectrum efforts: *multidimensionality*, *comprehensiveness*, and *cohesion*. The rest of this chapter is devoted to tracing how IS pursues these traits in its official propaganda output.

Multidimensional: Tactical, Operational, and Strategic Propaganda

There is a tendency to consider violent extremist propaganda as primarily a recruitment tool: siren calls to transform idle observers into supporters and tacit supporters into active ones. While this is, of course, an important aim of IS propaganda, it is important to develop a more holistic view of IS propaganda and understand it as a multidimensional mechanism that is deployed for tactical, operational, and strategic purposes. After all, shaping the perceptions and polarizing the support of target audiences is vital to achieving the full spectrum of IS's short-, medium-, and long-term objectives. Furthermore, like so many other aspects of IS's propaganda effort, *tactical*, *operational*, and *strategic* messaging tends to be interwoven as a means to mutually reinforce the different dimensions of its propaganda campaign. It is useful to, albeit briefly, consider how IS messaging caters to these different dimensions.

Arguably the least studied of IS propaganda, *tactical* messaging is deployed in support of operational activities. For example, prior to its capture of Mosul in June 2014, it was reported that IS operatives were sending intimidatory PSYOPS[9]-like communiques to officials and military personnel. In interviews with members of the Syrian Opposition to Assad, the author was told of similar tactical messaging being deployed against Syrian opposition groups as a means to psychologically "prepare" the battlefield. The author was told similar stories by citizens of Marawi in the Philippines whose city was briefly captured by IS militants in 2017. At a transnational level, IS's dissemination of instructional material in the "Just Terror" section of its multilingual *Rumiyah* magazine (Reed & Ingram 2017) and its efforts to incite and direct "remotely controlled attacks" (Callimachi 2017; Meleagrou-Hitchens & Hughes 2017; for a general study of the lone-actor terrorists mindset, see, e.g., Baele 2017) could similarly be considered tactical messaging given that one of its purposes is to provide its supporters with the tactical know-how to engage in terrorist operations.

Operational messaging tends to be deployed with the purpose of maximizing the desired "effects" of IS politico-military actions and diminishing the "effects" of its enemies' activities. Consequently, such messaging

---

[9] PSYOPS stands for PSYchologogical Operations.

is deployed for the full spectrum of both IS's politico-military activities and those of its enemies. In its areas of control, IS's messaging tends to focus on issues of governance and maintaining order with "media units" playing a crucial role in disseminating propaganda to local populations. As Winter explains (2016), "at once publishing houses and open-air cinemas, 'media points' are a place where literature can be downloaded and dispensed, USB sticks stocked up with images of utopia, military momentum and gore, and videos projected back-to-back before audiences of dozens. Sometimes mobile, they enable the Islamic State to extend its reach, infiltrate its message into remote regions with no online infrastructure, and sustain a constant information presence in population centers."

IS's broader propaganda efforts also deploy what could be described as operational messaging. Whenever IS propaganda promotes a particular military operation by its militants, governance efforts in a province, or a lone-wolf attack in the West, these are deployed to boost the "effects" of its actions and diminish those of its enemies (e.g., Al-Adnani A. 2015). This is a pertinent juncture at which to highlight that IS's operational messaging often seems to be deployed in the pursuit of not only first-order effects but also to set up second- and third-order messaging in response to anticipated enemy responses. It is a form of "baiting" whereby IS disseminates messages that lay "traps" designed to elicit misguided responses from its enemies. Once again highlighting that IS propagandists are more strategic plagiarists than geniuses, modern insurgencies often use actions or messages to trigger ill-conceived responses from their more powerful enemies as a means to create future opportunities for their own messaging and action in order to fuel the conditions within which supporters may radicalize toward action (a more strategic aim). For instance, IS's calls for supporters in the West to engage in lone-actor terrorism preemptively sets the conditions so that if/when a so-called inspired attack occurs, IS is ready to claim it despite having no prior knowledge of the attack or attacker. Sensationalized media reporting on such attacks, as well as on IS more broadly, can inadvertently contribute to IS's baiting strategy. As a member of the Free Syria Media told the author during an interview in 2014: "The important thing is how you react to Daesh [Islamic State] media. Daesh made a media trap and all of the Western media fell in it. They know the fears and images that the Western media is hungry for, so Daesh give it and the media spreads it." Of course, just as tactical messaging may contribute to operational messaging aims, operational messaging can have strategic ramifications that contribute to broader rational- and identity-choice appeals in IS propaganda extending beyond the immediate aftermath of an action or event.

Finally, IS deploys propaganda for *strategic* purposes, the central of which is to perpetuate the conditions within which its politico-military agenda and ideology resonate—put simply, to lure target audiences deeper into its propaganda web so that they adopt IS's competitive system of meaning as the lens through which to perceive the world. The fundamental strategic logic at the heart of IS propaganda means that almost any message—whether tactical or operational—can be used for this broader strategic purposes. Indeed, operational and even tactical messaging, particularly that produced by IS's provincial (*wilāyāt*) media units, is regularly drawn on by IS's central media units and used in its predominantly strategic media releases. The regular "Selected 10" segment that appeared in *Dabiq* and *Rumiyah*, for instance, was not only a way to promote the work of IS's provincial media units and drag viewers deeper into its propaganda web (as explained in Chapter 4), it was also a means to position operational and tactical messaging into a strategic context.

For IS, strategic propaganda is an essential mechanism for its survival during periods of bust, for glory during periods of boom, and to ensure its longevity for many decades to come. One way that IS facilitates this approach is by deploying a kind of "hedging" strategy across five pairs of key messaging themes, as shown in Table 1.1.

IS's tendency to use messaging as a simultaneous "force multiplier" for itself and "force nullifier" against enemies results in it projecting, especially via operational messaging, an image of extraordinary politico-military strength and aptitude; an image which its boom-bust history betrays. As Milton argued in late 2016, when it was clear IS were once again on the slide,

Table 1.1 Islamic State's "Hedging" Approach

Themes prioritized during periods of *bust*	↔	Themes prioritized during periods of *boom*
Struggle and sacrifice	↔	Statehood (epitomized by Caliphate)
Unconventional politico-military activities	↔	Conventional politico-military activities
Purify the ranks	↔	Build the ranks
Just terror	↔	Foreign fighters
Identity-choice appeals	↔	Rational-choice appeals

"the group also faces the prospect of increasing dissonance between what is happening on the ground and what it projects through its media campaign. The more this gap widens, the harder it may become to boost morale and attract new fighters" (Milton 2016: 1). "Hedging" acts as insurance for this dissonance potential. Depending on situational and strategic conditions at the time, IS will tend to *prioritize* a particular theme in each pairing over the other. It is an approach that ensures both a consistency of themes but also an "elasticity" in IS messaging over time.

For instance, from mid 2014 until late 2016, IS messaging tended to prioritize those themes in the right-hand column of Table 1.1 because IS was in a position of relative strength that allowed it to control swathes of territory and populations. These successes in the field were used as proof of the veracity of IS's claims of not merely statehood, evidenced by increasingly conventional politico-military activities, but the Caliphate, which required all true Muslims (i.e., IS-aligned Sunnis) to build its ranks and follow strength and momentum over weakness and decline. Many analyses of *Dabiq* highlight this messaging trend to varying degrees (e.g., Colas 2016; Ingram 2016; Winkler, el-Damanhoury, Dicker, & Lemieux 2016). As IS spokesman al-Adnani declared,

> So rush O Muslims and gather around your khilafah, so that you may return as you once were for ages, kings of the earth and knights of war. Come so that you may be honoured and esteemed, living as masters with dignity. (Al-Adnani 2014b: 4–5)

However, as losses in the field mounted, IS's propaganda themes pivoted and tended to prioritize the themes in the left-hand column of Table 1.1. Where the dominant themes disseminated by IS's propaganda machine were once for supporters to join their ranks, support their Caliphate, and be on the right side of history before the coming Apocalypse, IS's messaging circa 2016–19 increasingly emphasized the value of struggle during hardship, which now is the divinely foretold period of death and destruction when the ranks must be purified and the *ummah* tested. These were all central themes in *Rumiyah*'s contents—the first issue of which was released in September 2016—but were also captured perfectly in al-Adnani's (2016) final speech before his death.

> Were you victorious when you killed Abu Mus'ab, Abu Hamzah, Abu 'Umar, or Usamah? Would you be victorious if you were to kill ash-Shishani, Abu

Bakr, Abu Zayd, or Abu ʿAmr? No. Indeed, victory is the defeat of one's op-ponent. . . . Were we defeated when we lost the cities in Iraq and were in the desert without any city or land? . . . And victory is that we live in the might of our religion or die upon it. It is the same, whether Allah blesses us with consolidation or we move into the bare, open desert, displaced and pursued.

During its boom-bust history, IS has tended to prioritize certain themes in its messaging over others, but it is essential to recognize that those other themes rarely disappear entirely from IS's propaganda arsenal: evidence for this is clearly provided in Chapter 3, focusing on IS magazines. Consequently, when IS's fortunes change and the prioritization of themes shift, that sense of continuity demanded by the full-spectrum approach persists. For instance, when IS began to publish instructional material in the "Just Terror" section of its *Rumiyah* magazine in late 2016, this reflected its waning fortunes in the field. Indeed much was made in the media about IS focusing on "inspiring" terrorism in the West and enabling it with instructional material (Reed & Ingram 2017). Despite this shift, IS propagandists did not cease calling for foreign fighters. As the opening article in *Rumiyah* issue 4 declared: "So who-ever is unable to perform *hijrah* [migration] to Iraq and Sham [Syria], then he should perform *hijrah* to Libya, Khurasan, Yemen, Sinai, West Africa or any of the other *wilāyāt* and outposts of the *Khilafah* in the East and West."[10] Similarly, numerous videos released under IS's *Inside the Caliphate* series through 2017–2018 featured many examples of typically "boom" themes (e.g., calls to travel to IS-controlled territories), interspersed in messaging largely dominated by "bust" themes (e.g., a period of struggle and sacrifice purifying its ranks). Equally, during IS's heights through 2014–2015, its pro-pagandists still called for "lone-wolf" terrorism in the West. As IS falls deeper into another period of bust, strategic messaging will play an important role in keeping its current members and their supporters motivated until its next resurgence. Indeed, in the hands of IS's propagandists, strategic messaging is deployed to have effects over not just weeks, months, or years but intergen-erationally. As IS doctrine declares,

We consider media operatives to be from a group of knowledge seekers that the *amir* devotes to the study of *sharia* science and education. In the Words

[10] "Hijrah Does Not Cease as Long as the Kuffar Are Fought," *Rumiyah* (2017, Issue 4, pp. 2–3).

of the Almighty: "And it is not for the believers to go forth [to battle] all at once. For there should separate from every division of them a group to obtain understanding in the religion and to warn their people when they return to them so they are cautious." Therefore, it is necessary for there to be a group devoted to studying *sharia* science and educating fighters on matters of religion. If we do not provide this group, ignorance will take root among the people and it would be but a few decades before this generation of fighters in the name of Allah the Almighty would be lost and you would not be able to find anyone to continue the journey. Even if you found some left, they would not be of the level required to manage the global conflict with the evil states of unbelief. (Al-Himma Library 2017: 21–22)

Comprehensive: Multimedia and Multiformat

While it is unnecessary to analyze each of these components in great depth given that this is the purpose of other chapters in this volume, it is useful to broadly canvass the array of media and formats deployed by IS to support its messaging effort. After all, to maximize the reach, relevance, and resonance of its communiques as part of a full-spectrum approach, IS propagandists understand that it is necessary to use a mix of formats to present its messaging and deploy a range of communication media for diverse target audiences with varied access to communication technologies. While countless studies have been devoted to analyzing IS's use of online media to reach transnational target audiences, especially via social media (e.g., Berger & Morgan 2015; Burke 2016; Gill, Conway, Corner, & Thornton 2015; Klausen 2015; Chapter 5 of this volume), offline media are equally important to the group, especially in its areas of control (Price et al. 2014; Winter 2016). The greater the variety of communication media deployed in support of a communications campaign, the greater the potential reach of its messaging as the inherent limitations of any one media are compensated by other media. Utilizing a variety of formats also allows for the same key messages to be presented in different ways. Table 1.2 offers an overview of the most important formats used by IS, which, as highlighted in the Introduction, never renounced to a single one of them.

The variety of media and formats used by IS are deployed, like other components of its propaganda effort, to be interlocking and self-reinforcing. Rather than particular formats disseminating certain messages along the

Table 1.2 Multiple Formats Mobilized in Islamic State Propaganda

---

Printed word in short messages on posters, pamphlets, billboards, and online posts. Printed word has been used in longer forms such as in IS's infamous magazines (Chapter 3 presents all IS magazines and analyzes the content of some), newspapers (e.g., Arabic-language *Al-Naba*), and even books (for more, see Chapter 6). Multilingual transcriptions of speeches by IS spokesmen and leaders have also been an important format for the printed word. For example, transcriptions of Abu Bakr Al-Baghdadi's sermon in Mosul's Al-Noori mosque titled "A Message to the Mujahidin and the Muslim Ummah" (2014) and Abu Muhammad Al-Adnani's infamous "Indeed Your Lord Is Ever Watchful" (2014d) speech were quickly transcribed in a variety of languages and rapidly disseminated.

Audio releases via radio programming or the speeches of IS leaders and statements by its members. As Chapter 6 examines, emotive *anashīd* (Islamic hymns) have also been an important component of its propaganda being disseminated as audio or to accompany video imagery.

Still images have often been used to accompany IS's printed-word publications (e.g., posters, billboards, magazines, etc.). However, still images have also been used as the focal point of IS communiques, including photo reports and short online messages. Visual designs often feature in IS messaging, particularly accompanying the printed word, for example as infographics (for more, see Chapter 6).

Moving images have been used by IS in large, feature-length productions such as *The Clanging of Swords* and *Flames of War* series (Al-Furqan Media Center 2014b), which even had its own pre-release trailer. More common, however, are shorter length videos (up to 3 minutes) of which IS has a vast archive produced by its central and *wilāyāt* media units. Some that have captured the world's attention since 2014 include *A Message to America* that featured the execution of James Foley; *Although the Disbelievers Dislike It* (Al-Furqan Media Center *2014a*), which announced the death of Peter Kassig; *Healing the Believer's Chest*, showing the immolation of a captured Jordanian pilot; *The Making of Illusion*, filmed in a slaughterhouse to commemorate Eid Al-Adha, and the instructional video *You Must Fight Them O Muwahid*. IS has also produced short snapshot videos such as its *mujatweets* series that showed different perspectives of life in IS's so-called Caliphate. Chapter 4 analyzes the contents of more than 1,280 IS videos.

---

same media, IS synchronizes across its formats and media. This ensures that access to any single format will still offer a range of IS messages, while access to any single media is still likely to result in a range of echoing messages in different formats.

The period around IS's release of *Rumiyah*'s first three issues (September–November 2016) demonstrates this synchronization in practice. IS's propaganda output as a quantitative measure had been well down since its 2015 peak (Milton 2016: 21), and the emergence of *Rumiyah* in September 2016 as its flagship multilingual magazine, replacing *Dabiq* for English-speakers, *Dar al-Islam* for French-speakers, and *Constantinople* for Turkish-speakers, among others, symbolized a strategic downsizing of its propaganda campaign. For several months, it seemed that IS's streamlined efforts would be no less potent. The core of *Rumiyah*'s contents was drawn from *al-Naba* reporting, which meant that a broad linguistic range of target audiences were receiving consistent news from the Caliphate's heartlands. This content was then augmented by exclusive content addressing a particular event or issue specific to that particular audience. More broadly, early issues of *Rumiyah* synchronized with messaging in other formats. For instance, an article titled "The Kafir's Blood Is Halal So Shed It" in *Rumiyah* issue 1 was followed a week later by *The Making of Illusion*, which both coincided with Eid al-Adha—hence the blood shedding theme. For *Rumiyah*'s next issue, its inaugural "Just Terror" section featuring an instructional on knife attacks was soon augmented by the instructional video *You Must Fight Them O Muwahid*. This example of synchronicity is by no means an outlier in IS's propaganda effort, which regularly uses synchronicity across formats to reinforce key themes.[11] While *Rumiyah* has not been published since September 2017, IS has continued to publish *Al-Naba* and release videos through 2019 but in significantly diminished quantity and quality compared to years earlier.

Ultimately, IS recognize that drawing target audiences deeper and deeper into its competitive system of meaning requires more than just a variety of messages, but also an array of different formats, disseminated via a range of communication media in order to reach widely and deeply into diverse and geographically disparate target audiences. As IS's media doctrine declares: "My media operative brother, let it be known that your verbal *jihad* is not limited to speech alone, but also comprises speaking, writing, printing, audio recording and preparing scenarios for video recording and so on. All of this requires a significant amount of effort" (Al-Himma Library 2017: 13). It goes on to state,

> May Allah bless you, o media operative and bringer of glad tidings. Imagine the scale of the happiness that enters the Muslim's heart—both the mujahid one and the one who remained behind—when they watch one of the *mujahidin*'s videos regarding the victories and successes of the monotheists or the losses of the Crusaders and apostates. How much it pleases them to read

---

[11] There are, of course, many other examples such as the use of magazine articles to draw attention to the capture (e.g., "The Capture of the Crusader Pilot" 2014) and then death ("The Burning of the Murtadd Pilot." 2015) of a Jordanian fighter pilot as bookends for the release of a graphic execution video.

the pamphlets and books of the Islamic State, and o how the audio materials that are broadcast over the radio delight them, And so on and so forth. (Al Himma Library 2017: 19–20)

Coherent: Branding and Organization

Any transnational entity that is engaged in communications, whether a government promoting its foreign policy or a company selling a product, must recognize that appealing to geographically, socioculturally, and linguistically disparate audiences demands a variety of messages in both content and language, presented using a range of formats and disseminated over a multiplicity of communication media. So far, this chapter has broadly explored how IS has approached this complex set of challenges with an array of interlocking constituent elements. However, addressing this diversity problem plants the seeds for another predicament: a communication strategy that appears ad hoc and incoherent. To prevent this communication schizophrenia, IS fuses an all-permeating strategic logic and central narrative (described earlier) with powerful branding and a facilitating organizational architecture to help cohere the words and deeds that emerge from its transnational organization and network into a lucid whole, in pursuit of full-spectrum ambition.

Branding IS Symbology

The IS brand is a multifaceted construct which the group has actively and strategically fostered throughout its history. IS's brand is captured in both abstract and physical symbols, potent words, and iconic images that act as representations of its politico-military agenda (i.e., IS's system of control) and values as expressed in its propaganda (i.e., IS's system of meaning). These symbols then emerge as signposts—abstract and physical—that are placed along the fault lines of difference that distinguish IS and its supporters from its enemies. Thus, IS deploys symbols to embody the dualities which the group seeks to foment, resulting in the same symbols being interpreted in starkly different ways depending on the audience. This goes to the heart of IS's "brand reputation." Gelder argues in *Global Brand Strategy* that "brand reputation" consists of three qualities: *contextual*, which are captured in a brand's history, lineage, and creator/founder story (2010: 107); *intrinsic* qualities that a brand has come to embody over time and that inform expectations (2010: 107); and *associative*, traits "that are attributed to the brand through its association with others" (2010: 107). IS's branding, especially via its symbols, interweaves these qualities.

The most prominent of IS's abstract symbols is the group's name, which has changed several times throughout its history. IS portrays these changes as conscious signposting designed to mark its evolution and rising status as a politico-military force and ideology. Indeed, far from these changes being a source of embarrassment for the group, something to be hidden, they are celebrated in its propaganda. As al-Baghdadi proudly stated while announcing its fifth name change,

> The names of the Jihadi groups aren't names revealed from the sky or names of tribes and clans which cannot be abandoned or changed or replaced, rather they are names that were founded due to the legitimate necessity, and the supreme legitimate necessity permits to cancel and replace it with others to be at the level of growth and sublimity. The ascending needs new names that carry the fragment of Islam in its expansion and extending and spreading for the Ummah to carry the hope of returning. (Al-Baghdadi 2013: 2)

In this speech, al-Baghdadi goes on to describe the strategic rationale for each name change that took the group from its founding by al-Zarqawi as Tawhid wa al-Jihad in Afghanistan to the al-Baghdadi led Islamic State of Iraq and al-Sham (Al-Baghdadi 2013: 2–4). Al-Baghdadi carefully articulates the rationale behind the group's association with al-Qaeda during the Iraq War as well as other associations with various fighting groups and tribes throughout its history. Years later, al-Baghdadi's appearance in Mosul's al-Noori mosque to deliver his first speech as so-called Caliph of the Islamic State was shrouded in powerful symbolism that similarly boosted key aspects of IS's brand reputation. For instance, the choice of location was a homage to the group's founder al-Zarqawi. Sayf al-Adel, a senior al-Qaeda figure, wrote in his memoir *My Experiences with Abu Musab al-Zarqawi*,

> Abu Musab had an admiration for the character of the distinguished Islamic leader "Noor Al Deen Al Zinky" who led the operation of liberation and change . . . and his launch from Al Mosul in Iraq had a major role

influencing Abu Musab to move to Iraq after the fall of the [Taliban]. (Al-Adel 2015: 11)

Al-Baghdadi's two speeches are highlighted here because they capture this weaving together of the IS brand's contextual, intrinsic, and associative qualities into a cohesive whole embodied in the group's most public symbol: its name.

IS also deploys a range of physical symbols that act as rapidly recognizable embodiments of its political-military agenda and cause. From IS's flag to the uniforms of its militants, and the icons representing different politico-military and propaganda units, these physical symbols have similarly evolved with the status of the group. The use of symbolism in IS propaganda is another, perhaps more subtle, way that IS promotes its brand. Consider the videos and images of multiethnic IS members wearing the same uniforms, fighting under the same flag. The message embodied in this symbolism is clear: man-made constructs that divide, such as race, nation, and culture, do not matter here because we are all Muslims fighting, living, and dying together. The prominence and regularity with which IS propaganda featured "average" citizens and soldiers as its messengers, in contrast to senior leaders, also contributes to this idea of the IS brand as diverse yet unified, fundamentally an inclusive and accepting (of IS-aligned Sunni Muslims) entity. Indeed, one empirical study found that fewer than 1% of more than 9,000 IS messages contained "images or speeches of leadership level figures" (Milton 2016: 48). This has continued, in many respects, during its period of bust with the 2019 video series "And the Best Outcome is for the Righteous" featuring renewed pledges from geographically and ethnically diverse supporters. Of course, IS's actions are also symbolic forms of communication, "propaganda by deed," and thus physical expressions embodying its brand.

IS's symbology plays a crucial role in showcasing and communicating the IS brand to friends, foes, and neutrals. Indeed, this is a recurring theme throughout the remainder of this book, with a variety of symbols in IS's magazines (Chapter 3), videos (Chapter 4), tweets (Chapter 5), and more obscure media and formats (Chapter 6) being examined in great depth. To friends, these symbols represent IS as champion and protector, benevolent solver of crises. To enemies, those same symbols are a source of fear and anger, reminders of a seemingly omnipresent threat. This is not by chance: it is the purpose of IS's propaganda, which is designed to shape perceptions and polarize support, and its brand embodies that dichotomizing dynamic.

IS's Propaganda Architecture

The organizational architecture of IS's propaganda machine plays a functionally essential role in cohering the constituent elements of the group's messaging. This final section focuses on three specific aspects of that architecture—structure, culture, and individuals—to explore both the function of each and the compounding dynamic that results from their interaction. The tendency to think that IS's propaganda architecture is decentralized and informal with little bureaucracy and an internal institutional culture unforgiving of self-criticism is largely not supported by evidence. Analyses of captured IS documents suggest that IS's propaganda structures since 2005–2006 can be broadly characterized as multilevel (i.e., coordinated units operating at central, provincial, and intraprovincial levels) to facilitate clear delineations of responsibility and overarching central oversight. Organizationally, this structure allows IS's ground operators to collect content and make judgments about target audience requirements that then inform messages for local dissemination. With central propaganda arms providing pre-release oversight on messaging, this then allows for pertinent content to inform interprovincial and transnational efforts.

IS's synchronicity of actions and words, let alone its messaging in multiple languages and an array of formats across central and provincial media units, is a product of not only strategy but also of the structure and processes at the heart of its propaganda organization. Such a structure meant an enormous amount of editorial work for IS's central propaganda units, a trend that exponentially increased during its 2014 resurgence (Whiteside 2016b: 26). Additionally, these structures require ongoing communication, not only across IS's propaganda architecture but also in its politico-military units, too. During periods of bust when IS is operating as an insurgency on the run, greater operational risks are required to maintain the levels of communication necessary for effective coordination and oversight. As IS's fortunes have ebbed and flowed, so, too, have the structural characteristics of its propaganda architecture; but, ultimately, these principles of multilevel distribution of responsibility as enablers of both localization and centralization facilitated by controlled bureaucratic processes have been crucial to pursuing coherence across its messaging effort. As IS seeks to survive and rebuild, it will inevitably reflect on and even adopt many of the structural characteristics that facilitated its previous resurgences and successes.

Organizational culture emerges as a product of both top-down structures and guidance (e.g., doctrine) and bottom-up, often informal, processes related to personnel and their interactions. Captured internal administrative documents, the doctrine IS uses to guide its "media operatives," and the messaging it produces offer telling insights into some of the traits which its leadership hopes to imbue in the organizational culture of its propaganda units. It may surprise some to know that critical reflection on the efficacy of its propaganda efforts is important to the group. This is epitomized by the "lessons learned" document IS produced to identify what factors contributed to its demise during the Awakening circa 2006–2007 (Unnamed 2008). Fishman's (2009) analysis identified a range of recommendations stemming from across IS's politico-military spectrum, including a concern that its propaganda had generated "unrealistic expectations" for its foreign fighters that had caused negative repercussions in the field (Fishman 2009: 17). Most insightful is the document's candor in highlighting IS's poor understanding of the local population.

> Before anything we need [to] collect information about the percentage of workers, religions, sects, ethnicities, political affiliations, resources, the income per capita, available jobs, the nature of existing tribes and clans, and the security problems. It's impossible for any Jama'ah (TC: Group of brothers) to continue jihad and rule if they don't analyze the citizens' structure and know if they will be able to accept the Shari'ah for the long term, and live this life and the after-life in this manner. (cited in Fishman 2009: 17)

The primary source materials also suggests that IS is an organization that encourages a culture of "uniform innovation"; that is, creativity within the parameters of its strategy, doctrine, and brand. It is a tricky balancing act. While it is natural to focus on the slick presentations of 2014–2017, the image IS projects to the world has changed over time, mostly, it seems, by learning the lessons that emerge from experience including trial and error. As Whiteside argues (2016b: 26), "early on, IS leaned heavily on the image of the group as a militant band of brothers focused on maximizing terror in their enemies while shoring up support from its base. Later, the pressure upon IS to prove that it was a functioning state in 2007 led it to artificially mimic Western and Arab media outlets—an idea that fell flat due to its inauthenticity. By 2011 that format was gone, replaced by a newer, more exciting tempo, exemplifying combat as the true legitimacy of the jihadist."

The product of these struggles is a brand that appears to have resonance among its supporters and acts as a gravitational pull of coherence across its campaign. Yet innovation is also important for producing messages that will capture the attention of target audiences. The recurring "Selected 10" segment that appeared in several IS propaganda publications such as *Dabiq* and then *Rumiyah*, in which 10 videos from IS provincial media units are promoted, is a pertinent example of an initiative that may simultaneously encourage uniformity and innovation. Because provincial units seek to have their videos advertised in "Selected 10," this will require an adherence to the style, format, and message that is the trademark of IS content but also encourage enough creativity to stand out from the competition. A Free Syria Media operator told the author during a 2015 interview that in the early stages of the Syrian War he had shared an office building with IS media operatives. He described walking past their office and witnessing their discussions, which he described as "ISIS *Mad Men*," a reference to the American television series about an advertising firm in the 1960s, with IS's local propagandists drinking tea and debating the merits of a certain word or image. Consequently, an initiative like "Selected 10" may seem to the outside world as a simple cross-promotional initiative to coax audiences deeper into IS's propaganda web. However, internally, it may have acted as an additional means to fuel a culture of uniformity and creativity among its media operatives.

Throughout its history IS has faced two recurring challenges to its coherence which almost any state or non-state politico-military organization engaged in communications will recognize: how to synchronize its actions and words and how to attract recruits (especially the most capable) away from seemingly more glamorous fighting roles to communications ones. Indeed, the two issues are closely related. IS recognized that it was important to embed media operatives with fighting and governance units not only to capture their stories and images but also to demonstrate through action that its propagandists were on the frontlines, too. These initiatives also helped to demonstrate both the mutual benefits of forging close relationships across IS units and an appreciation for each other's roles. The title of IS's propaganda doctrine "Media Operative, You Are Also a Mujahid," is indicative of the internal challenge of attracting recruits into its propaganda wing. The media operative is promised uniquely compounding rewards for his efforts.

Inciting others to join the *jihad* is tantamount to engaging in the *jihad* oneself, as is steering others towards it and opening their eyes to it. Indeed, the one who incites is a *mujahid* in the way of Allah the Almighty and he rightfully receives a reward for every brother that embarks upon *jihad* because of his incitement. (Al-Himma Library 2017: 15)

Indeed, many of the doctrinal excerpts featured in this chapter need to be seen as rallying cries (internal propaganda) as much as indicators of the importance of messaging in IS's campaign strategy.

Finally, IS backs up the strategic centrality of propaganda in its campaign efforts and its doctrinal emphasis on messaging as crucial to survival and success by placing its most brilliant members into its media units. As Whiteside argues (2016b: 23), "IS puts its most talented commanders into the media department. It is quite remarkable how the movement has always gravitated toward educated professionals with doctorates (Muharib, Abu Bakr al-Baghdadi, al-Tai, al-Rawi), politically connected leaders from newly coopted insurgent groups (Mashadani, Muharib), and future potential emirs/caliphs (Abu Bakr, al-Adnani) to enhance the appeal of its influence campaign, a critical area of revolutionary warfare."

These brilliant individuals have been crucial to IS's survival during periods of bust and equally important during those rare periods of boom. It is no coincidence that, as IS fortunes in the field declined through 2016, rehashed speeches from the revered leaders during its last period of bust—Abu Umar al-Baghdadi and Abu Hamza al-Muhajir—have been featured in its messaging. The appearance of Abu Bakr al-Baghdadi at the bookends of IS's caliphal period—in 2014 at the announcement of its caliphate and in 2019 when its territorial demise was complete—highlights the important role of its leaders as messengers and the physical embodiment of its brand. By placing its "best and brightest" into its media units, IS demonstrates the importance of propaganda to its effort and is able to use these individuals as symbols of a coherent brand and an ongoing struggle.

Conclusion

This chapter began by positioning IS's propaganda strategy within the context of its broader politico-military strategy. What emerged is that IS seeks to synchronize the actions of its "competitive system of control" with the messages at the heart of its "competitive system of meaning." The chapter used primary sources to explore the strategic logic of IS's propaganda strategy, arguing that its central purpose was to shape the worldview and polarize the support of target audiences with a mix of rational- and identity-choice messages that are interwoven into an approach to communication that sought to be full-spectrum in character: that is, *multidimensional, comprehensive*, and *coherent*. Of course, these components operate within the broader tapestry of IS propaganda, and it is the interlocking and self-reinforcing nature of the relationship between them that is designed to compound the "effects" of IS's words and deeds (for more see Ingram, Whiteside and Winter 2019).

Indeed, this intertwining and compounding dynamic is an almost inevitable by-product of a strategic logic that is, itself, self-reinforcing in nature. This dynamic is pursued in the relationship between IS's system of control and meaning, the interweaving of rational- and identity-choice appeals in IS messaging, and the interplay of strategic and psychosocial factors *within* its rational- and identity-choice appeals. This dynamic is crucial to IS's approach to propaganda that seeks to be *multidimensional* as its propagandists interplay tactical, operational, and strategic messaging. It is present in IS's deployment of a range of media and formats to ensure its campaign is *comprehensive*. That interlocking dynamic also underpins IS's pursuit of *coherence* across its propaganda effort via an overarching strategic logic, central narrative, and brand all supported by a facilitating organizational structure. The interlocking nature of IS propaganda imbues its messaging strategy with resilience in the short to medium term and, reinforced by its tendency to "hedge" themes in its strategic messaging, in the long-term, too. This dynamic may also have a powerful psychological effect on IS supporters, whereby if an individual accepts a particular argument in IS's propaganda, they then are susceptible to the rest of its claims due to those close interrelationships.

While Chapter 7 is devoted to more holistically exploring the challenges and opportunities of countering IS propaganda, the findings of this chapter have potentially significant implications for shaping counterterrorist/countering violent extremist (CT-CVE) strategic communication efforts. The "linkage-based" approach to CT-CVE messaging (e.g., Ingram 2017) is designed to undermine the strengths and exploit the weaknesses of the strategic logic analyzed here. A key principle of that CT-CVE strategic communication approach is that while a major strength of IS propaganda is the close interconnectedness of its constituent parts creating self-reinforcing cycles of logic, these same dynamics are also a potential weakness that targeted messaging can exploit. Put simply, the potential exists for that self-reinforcing logic to work against IS, too. That is, if contradictions, doubts, or disagreements can be generated in target audiences about a particular aspect of IS propaganda, its close interconnectedness potentially renders IS's whole "system of meaning" susceptible. Of course, there is no single message presented with the perfect format that is destined for universal appeal or a particular medium that is going to reach all audiences at exactly the right moment. It follows, then, that to maximize the potential reach, relevance, and resonance of such a CT-CVE strategic communications campaign targeting inevitably diverse audiences requires a mix of rational- and identity-choice messages utilizing a variety of media and formats. Such an approach would need to reflect, if not synchronize with, actions and events pertinent to those target audiences. To a certain extent, outcompeting IS in the "information theater" will require government, private, and civil society sectors to beat them at their own game.

Acknowledgments

This chapter is based on research supported by the Australian Research Council (ARC) under the Discovery Early Career Researcher Award [DE140101123].

References

Al-Adel S. (2015) *My Experiences with Abu Musab al-Zarqawi.* Translated by L. Othman, edited by H. Ingram.

Al-Adnani A. (2013) "They Shall by No Means Harm You but with a Slight Evil," *Fursan al-Balagh Media Translation Section.*

Al-Adnani A. (2014a) "This Is Not Our Methodology Nor Will It Ever Be," *Al-Furqan Media.*

Al-Adnani A. (2014b) "This Is the Promise of Allah," *Al-Hayat Media Centre.*

Al-Adnani A. (2014c) "Sorry, Amir of al-Qaeda," *Al-Furqan Media.*

Al-Adnani A. (2014d) "Indeed Your Lord Is Ever Watchful." Retrieved from https://scholarship.tricolib.brynmawr.edu/bitstream/handle/10066/16495/ADN20140922.pdf.

Al-Adnani A. (2015) "Say 'Die in Your Rage!'," *Al-Hayat Media Centre.*

Al-Adnani A. (2016) "That They Live by Proof," *Al-Hayat Media Centre.*

Al-Baghdadi A. (2013) "'Good News to the Believers': The Declaration of the Islamic State in Iraq and Al-Sham," *Al-Furqan Media.*

Al-Baghdadi A. (2014) "A Message to the Mujahidin and the Muslim Ummah in the Month of Ramadan," *Al-Hayat Media Centre.*

Al-Furqan Media Center (2014a) *Although the Disbelievers Dislike It,* video.

Al-Furqan Media Center (2014b) *Clanging of Swords*, Part 4, video.

Al-Himma Library (2017) "Media Operative, You Are Also a Mujahid." Translated by C. Winter.

Al-Muqrin A. (2003/2009) "A Practical Course for Guerilla Warfare," in *Al-Qa'ida's Doctrine for Insurgency*, translated by N. Cigar. Washington, DC: Potomac, pp. 83–180.

Baele S. (2017) "Lone-Actor Terrorists' Emotions and Cognition: An Evaluation Beyond Stereotypes," *Political Psychology* 38(3): 449–468.

Berger J. M., Morgan J. (2015) "The ISIS Twitter Census," Brookings Project on US Relations with the Islamic World Analysis Paper 20. Retrieved from https://www.brookings.edu/wp-content/uploads/2016/06/isis_twitter_census_berger_morgan.pdf.

Berger J. M., Stern J. (2015) *ISIS: The State of Terror*. New York: Ecco.

Burke J. (2016) "The Age of Selfie Jihad: How Evolving Media Technology Is Changing Terrorism," *CTC Sentinel*, November/December issue. Retrieved from https://ctc.usma.edu/posts/the-age-of-selfie-jihad-how-evolving-media-technology-is-changing-terrorism.

"The Burning of the Murtadd Pilot." 2015. *Dabiq* (issue 7): pp. 5–8.

Callimachi R. (2017) "Not 'Lone Wolves' After All: How ISIS Guides World's Terror Plots from Afar," *The New York Times*. Retrieved from https://www.nytimes.com/2017/02/04/world/asia/isis-messaging-app-terror-plot.html.

"The Capture of the Crusader Pilot." 2014. *Dabiq* (issue 6): pp. 34–37.

Colas B. (2016) "What Does Dabiq Do? ISIS Hermeneutics and Organizational Fractures Within Dabiq Magazine," *Studies in Conflict & Terrorism* 40(3): 173–190.

Fall B. (1965) "The Theory and Practice of Insurgency and Counterinsurgency," *Naval War College Review*. Retrieved from http://www.au.af.mil/au/awc/awcgate/navy/art5-w98.htm.

Fernandez A. (2015) *Here to Stay and Growing: Combating ISIS Propaganda Networks*. Washington, DC: Brookings Institution.

Fishman B. (2009) Dysfunction and Decline: Lessons Learned from Inside Al-Qa'ida in Iraq. West Point, NY: Combating Terrorism Center. Retrieved from https://ctc.usma.edu/v2/wp-content/uploads/2010/06/Dysfunction-and-Decline.pdf.

Fishman B. (2016) *The Master Plan: ISIS, al-Qaeda, and the Jihadi Strategy for Final Victory*. New Haven: Yale University Press.

"From Hijrah to Khilafah." 2014. *Dabiq* (issue 1): pp. 34–41.

Gelder S. (2010) *Global Brand Strategy: Unlocking Branding Potential Across Countries, Cultures and Markets*. London: Kogan Page.

Guevara E. (1998) *Guerilla Warfare*. Lincoln: University of Nebraska Press.

Ingram H. (2015) "The Strategic Logic of Islamic State Information Operations," *Australian Journal of International Affairs* 69(6): 729–752.

Ingram H. (2016) "An Analysis of Islamic State's *Dabiq* Magazine," *Australian Journal of Political Science* 51(3): 458–477.

Ingram H. (2017) "The Strategic Logic of the "Linkage-Based" Approach to Combating Militant Islamist Propaganda: Conceptual and Empirical Foundations," *ICCT Research Papers*. Retrieved from https://icct.nl/wp-content/uploads/2017/04/ICCT-Ingram-The-Strategic-Logic-of-the-Linkage-Based-Approach.pdf.

Ingram, H., Whiteside, C. and Winter, C. (2019) *The ISIS Reader*, London: Hurst.

Irish Republican Army (1985) *Handbook for Volunteers of the Irish Republican Army*. Boulder, CO: Paladin Press.

"The Kafir's Blood Is Halal for You, So Shed It." 2016. *Rumiyah* (issue 1): pp. 34–36.

Klausen J. (2015) "Tweeting the Jihad: Social Media Networks of Western Foreign Fighters in Syria and Iraq," *Studies in Conflict & Terrorism* 38(1): 1–22.

Knights M. (2014) "ISIL's Political-Military Power in Iraq," *CTC Sentinel* 7(8): 1–7.

Lia B. (2008) *Architect of Global Jihad: The Life of Al-Qaeda Strategist Abu Musab Al-Suri*. New York: Columbia University.

March J., Heath C. (1994) *A Primer on Decision Making: How Decisions Happen*. New York: Free Press.

McCants W. (2016) *The ISIS Apocalypse: The History, Strategy, and Doomsday Vision of the Islamic State*. New York: Picador.

Meleagrou-Hitchens A., Hughes S. (2017) "The Threat to the United States from the Islamic State's Virtual Entrepreneurs," *CTC Sentinel* (March 2017 issue). Retrieved from https://ctc.usma.edu/posts/the-threat-to-the-united-states-from-the-islamic-states-virtual-entrepreneurs.

Milton D. (2016) *Communication Breakdown: Unraveling the Islamic State's media efforts*. West Point, NY: Combating Terrorism Center. Retrieved from https://ctc.usma.edu/v2/wp-content/uploads/2016/10/ISMedia_Online.pdf.

O'Dowd E. (2013) "Ho Chi Minh and the Origins of the Vietnamese Doctrine of Guerrilla Tactics," *Small Wars & Insurgencies* 24(3): 567–587.

"On the Beat: ISR Examines How the Islamic Police Safeguards ar-Raqqah and Their Importance in State Building." 2014. *Islamic State Report* (issue 2): pp. 5–6.

Price B., Milton D., Al-'Ubaydi M., Lahoud N. (2014) The Group that Calls Itself a State: Understanding the Evolution and Challenges of the Islamic State. West Point, NY: Combating Terrorism Center. Retrieved from https://ctc.usma.edu/posts/the-group-that-calls-itself-a-state-understanding-the-evolution-and-challenges-of-the-islamic-state

"Propagating the Correct Manhaj." 2014. *Islamic State Report* (issue 1): p. 1.

Reed A., Ingram H. (2017, May 26) "Exploring the Role of Instructional Material in AQAP's *Inspire* and ISIS' *Rumiyah*," *Europol Public Information*. Retrieved from https://icct.nl/wp-content/uploads/2017/06/reeda_ingramh_instructionalmaterial.pdf.

Taber R. (2002) *War of the Flea*. Dulles: Potomac Books.

The Islamic State (2019) "In the hospitality of amir al-mu'minin," Furqan Media Foundation.

Tse-Tung M. (2000) *On Guerrilla Warfare*. Trans. Samuel B. Griffith II. Chicago: University of Illinois Press.

Unnamed (2008) "Analysis of the State of ISI (Original Language)," West Point, NY: Combating Terrorism Center. Harmony Project. Retrieved from https://ctc.usma.edu/v2/wp-content/uploads/2013/09/Analysis-of-the-State-of-ISI-Original.pdf.

Whiteside C. (2016a.) "New Masters of Revolutionary Warfare: The Islamic State Movement (2002–2016)," *Perspectives on Terrorism* 10(4). Retrieved from http://www.terrorismanalysts.com/pt/index.php/pot/article/view/523/1036.

Whiteside C. (2016b) "Lighting the Path: The Evolution of the Islamic State Media Enterprise (2003–2016)," *ICCT Research Paper*, doi: 10.19165/2016.1.14.

Winkler C., el-Damanhoury K., Dicker A., Lemieux A. (2016) "The Medium Is Terrorism: Transformation of the About to Die Trope in *Dabiq*," *Terrorism & Political Violence* 31(2): 224–243.

Winter C. (2015) *Documenting the Virtual "Caliphate."* London: Quilliam Foundation.

Winter C. (2016) "ISIS' Offline Propaganda Strategy," *Brookings Institution*. Retrieved from https://www.brookings.edu/blog/markaz/2016/03/31/isis-offline-propaganda-strategy/.

Winter C. (2017) "Media Jihad: The Islamic State's Doctrine for Information Warfare," The International Centre for the Study of Radicalisation and Political Violence. Retrieved from http://icsr.info/wp-content/uploads/2017/02/Media-jihad_web.pdf.

2

Situating Islamic State's Message

A Social and Theological Genealogy

Mehdi Laghmari

Introduction

Four years after proclaiming its Caliphate, the so-called Islamic State (IS) is now said to be on the road to defeat in Syria and Iraq, while its affiliated groups around the word struggle to maintain their profile (Sinai, Yemen, "Khorasan," the Philippines). To be sure, military setbacks are important to constrain the group's threat; however, as this chapter seeks to show, they are far from sufficient. Indeed the group's ideological appeal, which is immaterial and can be easily disseminated, remains almost intact and is still able to inspire supporters to launch attacks across the world or attract new groups to pledge their allegiance. Furthermore, the feeling of defeat and the necessity to rationalize it and to use it to its advantage is not new to the group; in 2007–2010, when the group known then as the Islamic State in Iraq (ISI) and was cornered in Iraq and considered defeated, it showed a tremendous capacity of resilience.[1] At that time, IS articulated its resilience around its slogan "Remaining!" (*Bāqiyya*)—"The Islamic State Is Remaining!" (*Dawlat Islam Bāqiyya*), which represented the rallying cry of thousands of IS supporters and members and was used by its leaders in speeches, by its fighters after a pledge of allegiance, by its supporters in social media hashtags, and even by its prisoners who were forced to shout it as a symbol of humiliation before their execution in gruesome propaganda videos. The slogan, first voiced by Abu Omar al-Baghdadi in 2007, came to represent the group's state of mind, which has offered its survival as a sign of victory and its maximalist

---

[1] In 2010, most of the analysts considered the group on the verge of extinction—80% of its leaders were killed or jailed, thousands of its members killed, and their political goal of creating an Islamic Sunni State in Iraq was considered unachievable.

Mehdi Laghmari, *Situating the Islamic State's Message: A Social and Theological Genealogy* In: *ISIS Propaganda*. Edited by: Stephane J. Baele, Katharine A. Boyd, and Travis G. Coan, Oxford University Press (2020) © University of Maryland National Consortium for the Study of Terrorism and Responses to Terrorism (START)
DOI: 10.1093/oso/9780190932459.003.0003

objectives as sign of purity. Shouting "Remaining and Expanding" (*Bāqiyya wa Tatamaddad*) therefore represented a motivational cry and a challenge to the rest of the world, inspiring followers and sympathizers on social media (such as the "Baqiya Family")[2] and resonating in IS-made *anashīd*[3] (Islamic hymns; see Chapter 6) and videos. The group has elevated its doctrinal purity as the most important symbol of its success, more than the conquest of territories or the success of terrorist attacks around the world. It is therefore crucial that any military or intelligence operation against the group is accompanied by an in-depth understanding of its message and its origins. Such an endeavor is not only needed to prevent radicalization dynamics, but it also helps to understand the group's political and strategic decisions such as the choice of targets, the nature of its relations with rival Islamic groups, and its likely future.

While the previous chapter detailed the strategic logic and organization of IS propaganda, this chapter offers an explanation of its content, its message. The aim of the following pages is to clarify the various theological interpretations and social dynamics that constitute the foundation of this message and make it appealing for some. The key concepts structuring IS's message are highlighted, their origins and evolutions are traced, and the way these concepts have eventually come to coalesce into an autonomous message distinct from those enunciated by other Islamist groups is explained. Such a detailed effort is necessary to fully understand how this message is articulated and disseminated by the various outlets constituting IS's "full-spectrum propaganda."

This chapter is organized into three parts. First, I offer a social and theological genealogy of IS's ideology, locating its origins and evolutions within the trajectory of Salafi-jihadism and highlighting the importance of history. Second, I present the specific context in which IS's own message developed, explaining how foundational concepts evolved into a broad narrative used by the group in the battle of ideas against rival Islamist factions. Third, I briefly speculate on the future of the group's message.

---

[2] Read Miller 2015.
[3] See, for example, the *nashīd* entitled *Dawlati Baqiya* ("My State Will Remain"), which was diffused in June 2017: http://www.aymennjawad.org/2017/06/dawlati-baqiya-new-nasheed-from-the-islamic-state.

A Social and Theological Genealogy of Salafi-Jihadism

IS's ideological message is situated within the large and diverse family of Islamism. Although the term "Islamist" was first used in 1970s, the push toward returning Islam to the center of politics may be traced to the 1920s, with creation of the Muslim Brotherhood. Mandaville (2009: 57) considers that "Islamism" refers to "an ideology that has as its goal the establishment of the Islamic political order in the sense of a state whose governmental principles, institutions, and legal system derive directly from the Sharia." Islamism is considered by Feldman (2008) as a modern ideology devised in response to the secularization process of Arab and Islamic postcolonial states.

Since the 1920s, many political groups from diverse horizons have claimed to represent this ideal and political goal. Salafi-jihadism, to which IS can be attached, is the subgroup of the Islamist trend whose main sources and inspirations are, according to Zelin (2015: 160), "the socio revolutionary heritage of Sayed Qutb and doctrinal/legalistic Salafism." We can also define Salafi-jihadism by its claims, such as Hafez's identification of five core concepts (2007: 66). As noted by Maher (2016: 25), the first four—*tawhid* (simultaneously the unity and unicity of God and its divine transcendence), *Ḥākimiyya* (divine sovereignty and subsequent rejection of innovation), *takfīr* (excommunication), and *jihād* (holy struggle)—are shared by other Islamic traditions in one way or another and therefore are not unique to Salafism. The defining feature of Salafi-jihadi, when compared to other Islamist ideologies, is *al-Walā' wa al-Barā'*, the unconditional adherence to the cause and total disavowal and rejection of other ones. The objective of this first section is to situate IS's ideology in the history of groups claiming to be Islamist, simultaneously locating its sources and traditions and explaining its core concepts. We highlight the social context in which these concepts, sources, and traditions emerged, as well as how they were uniquely interpreted by IS and put at play in the group's full-spectrum propaganda.

The Struggle for the Wahhabi Legacy

At the core of IS's message is the claim that none of the states in the international system is implementing the Islamic law (*Sharī'a*) in its purest form, making them fall into "idolatrous" regimes (*tawaghit*—singular *Ṭaghūt*) that must be fought. The base of such judgment in the Islamic tradition can be traced back to the Mongol invasion of the Abbasid Empire in the 13th century, when, for the first time in Islamic history, the application of *Shari'a* was seriously disturbed and supplanted by another source of legislation. Mardin, the hometown of Ibn Taymiyah was governed Some Islamic territories were governed by the Mongols who, despite having embraced Islam, imported their tribal legal system known as the *Yasa*.[4] The basis of the modern practice of *takfir* (excommunication) aimed at a state or a group (and not simply an individual) can be traced back to Taqī ad-Dīn Ahmad Ibn Taymiyyah's (1263–1328) "Mardin Fatwa," where he declared the Mongols as heretics despite their professed allegiance to Islam because of the imposition of their legal system over *Sharī'a*.[5] His political writings[6] have been evoked—even today—as the early denunciation of secularization among Muslim rulers and as a legitimation for contemporary Salafi-jihadi theorists to declare modern Muslim states as heretic.

While the first occurrence of a proclamation of *takfir* to a state using the Sunni theological corpus in Islamic history appeared with Ibn Taymiyyah, its first practical application, which planted the seeds of Salafi-jihadism, can be traced back to what is commonly known as "Wahhabism"—that is, the predication of Mohamed Ibn Abd al-Wahhab (1703–1792) and its followers.[7] Wahhabism appeared in the central region of Najd in the Arabian Peninsula during the 19th century and subsequently played the role of ideological and religious underpinning for the establishment of the three Saudi states. Most of al-Wahhab's intellectual work was centered on the issue of creed (*'āqīda*), as he considered that the Islamic practices in the Arabian peninsula under rule of the Ottoman Empire had lost the purity characterizing the first

---

[4] *Yasa* or *Yassaq* refers to a secret written code of law created by Genghis Khan. This set of rules had the particularity to be universal and syncretic, ensuring complete religious freedom to its subjects while its laws were observed.

[5] The original transcription of this fatwa goes as follows: "*Every group that refrains from adhering to one of the clear recurring legislations of Islam from these people or others then fighting them is obligatory until they adhere to its legislations, even if they spoke the Shahadas and were adherent to some of its legislations, as Abu Bakr As-Şiddīq and the Sahabah—may Allah be pleased with them—fought those who refused to pay the Zakat. And the Scholars after them agreed after the debate of Omar with Abu Bakr may Allah be pleased with them. So the Sahabah may Allah be pleased with them agreed to fight on the rights of Islam according to the Book and Sunnah.*"

[6] In his main political text, *Siyasa al-Shariah*, Ibn Taymiyyah pointed to the negative influence the Mongols had on the Mameluke leaders. He criticized, without naming, those rulers who prioritized their own politic (*Siyasa*) over Shari'a to preserve the general interest (*maslaha*) by supplanting, replacing, or amending Shari'a. Sanctions (*ta'azir*) or policies (*Siyasat*) for cases not tackled by Shari'a, according to Ibn Taymiyyah, must defend the *maslaha* exclusively within the boundaries of Shari'a, otherwise they fall into the same category as the *Yasa* model.

[7] Al-Wahhab's most important contributions are "Book of Unicity" (*Kitab Tahwid*) and "Showing the Doubts" (*Kashf al Shubuhat*).

generation of Muslims (the *Salaf*—hence the label "Salafi"). The Wahhabi tradition is therefore first and foremost a theological doctrine built against religious innovations (*bid'a*). Al-Wahhab's followers considered that their foremost priority was to spread the call (*da'wa*) for a restoration of *Tawhid*, conceptualized by al-Wahhab as composed of three facets of equal importance: *tawhid al-Rubibibya* (proclaiming the unicity of God), *tawhid al-Asma wa Sifat* (avoiding any anthropomorphism when describing God's nature), and *tawhid al-Uluhiyaa* (worshipping God exclusively). Articulating those three components, al-Wahhab condemned many religious practices—for example, visiting tombs or calling for saints' intercession—which led to the excommunication of many Muslims (first and foremost the Shi'a and Sufi sects). For al-Wahhab, the primary enemies were deviant sects *inside* Islam, which were considered as heretics, and not the Western states or even the Arab ones.

Even though his message was first and foremost theological, he theorized two other prominent concepts that gave Wahhabism a political dimension: the disbelief in the *Taghūt* and *al-Walā' wa al-Barā'*. First, in his treaty "the Meaning of the Taghūt" (*Ma'anā at- Taghūt*), al-Wahhab established the basis for the *takfīr* of states by advancing a new polysemic nature of the concept of *Taghūt*. In Arabic, the term generally means everything that has passed and transgressed its limits. Al-Wahhab's main contribution was to extend the definition of the first pillar of Islam—the proclamation that there is no God except Allah and that Muhammad is his Messenger (*shahada*)—from not only a positive proclamation of God's unicity, but to also incorporate the simultaneous negation of all other deities as *tawaghit*. In this view, before proclaiming God's unicity, one has to first reject and express disbelief in the *Taghūt*. While most scholars at that time have interpreted it only as false gods, idols, or money, al-Wahhab introduced three new manifestations of the *Taghūt*: it can take the shape of the Devil Satan (*Shaytan*) himself, of people claiming to know the unseen (magicians), or of people being worshipped besides God. The last two manifestations hold a political dimension because they include rulers who rule by any other law than the *Sharī'a* or individuals challenging God's exclusive right to declare licit or illicit things. Al-Wahhab's definition of the *Taghūt* is used by IS in its controlled schools and centers of "repentance" where they "re-educate" fighters who deserted from the Syrian Army or other rebel factions.

Al-Walā' wa al-Barā' is the other key concept of the Salafi-jihadist literature that was first fully theorized by al-Wahhab. *Al-Walā',* or "loyalty and allegiance," refers to the commitment to the emotion and the conduct of loving and allegiance to the Muslim community (*ummah*) and more narrowly the community of "*Muwahhidin*" (the believers in the one God; the true adherents of *tawhid*). *Al-Barā'*, or "disavowal and disassociation," is rejection and animosity toward the others, whether they are disbelievers (*Kāfir*), promoters of religious innovation, or followers of the *Ṭaghūt*. To be sure, *al-Walā' wa al-Barā'* was first popularized by Ibn Taymiyyah in the Salafi creed to urge Muslims to follow the example of the Prophet Abraham. However, the term did not yet have a political connotation; it was more a call to preserve Muslims' faith by not mixing with other creeds (e.g., celebrating their holidays or wearing the same clothes). During the period of al-Wahhab's predication in Najd and throughout the 19th century, the concept started to evolve toward a marker of political identity and affiliation. A new kind of identity emerged that was based on a fraternity exclusive to the community, akin to a zero-sum game. As described by Maher (2016: 112), it became a preservationist idea which "draws the line between the group and the 'other' which corresponds to everything which is entity, action or individual." This vision of *Walā'a* and *Barā'* was repeatedly highlighted by al-Adnani (IS's former spokesman), who said in one of his speeches that "if we do not show enmity and hatred to the *Kuffār*, then *walā* and *bara* will be lost, along with the religion, and the disbelievers would be mixed with the believers."[8] The concept is also frequently repeated in IS's magazines (see Chapter 5).

The followers of al-Wahhab were divided over the posture to adopt when confronting political power. The "politicization" of *Walā'a* and *Barā* during conflicts has, as we explain later, important implications because, unlike in previous intra-Muslim conflicts, neutrality was no longer possible. During the Egyptian conquest of the Najd region against the first Saudi state in 1818, al-Wahhab's grandson labeled the Egyptian Army and the Ottoman Empire who supported them as disbelievers (Lacroix 2010: 14). Consequently, the *al-Walā' wa al-Barā'* concept was used to command authentic Muslims to break with another Muslim power and to show unconditional solidarity to the group presented as purer. A division within Wahhabism appeared that is prevailing today. The first faction, known as "exclusive" Wahhabis, called their followers to fight against the invasion and ultimately migrate by performing *hijrah* from the land conquered by the Ottomans (understood to

---

[8] See http://heavy.com/news/2016/05/new-isis-islamic-state-al-furqan-media-audio-message-that-they-live-by-proof-egyptair-flight-ms804-804-mp3-read-english-translation-text-download/.

be *Dār al-Ḥarb*, non-Muslim land where *jihād* has to be performed) to the land where pure Islam was practiced (*Dār al-Islām*). In contrast, "inclusive" Wahhabis scholars still considered the Egyptians and Ottomans to be misguided Muslims who's ruled territory was still *Dār al-Islām*.

In the beginning of the 20th century, the Saud dynasty relied on the exclusive branch of the Wahhabi tradition, inspiring Bedouin tribes in the Najd to form a militia of zealous warriors called the *Ikhwan*. Partisans of a "*jihād* without frontiers" and spearheading King Abd al-Aziz al-Saud's army, they confronted and threatened the positions of the British Empire in Transjordan. This situation, however, went out of control and ultimately pressured al-Saud to get rid of them, which was done at the Battle of Sabilla (1929). This internal struggle inside of Wahhabism led to the creation of the modern Saudi state, which has since followed an official and more pragmatic version of Wahhabism, ultimately making them a prime target for jihadi groups. Indeed, by crushing the *Ikhwan* movement in the name of pragmatism and in order to find a place in the concert of nations, the Saudi modern state planted the seeds of contestation in its model of a state led by Wahhabism—as we explain later, this decision later shaped the fate of the Salafi-jihadi ideology.

Some (e.g., Ait Yahya 2016: 205; Crooke 2015) point to the multiple resemblances between both the nature and the fate of the *Ikhwan* movement and today's IS. First, IS's *modus operandi* and the conflicting nature of its relations with all external actors reminds one of the first Saudi Emirates with the *Ikhwan*. Second, IS's interpretation and application of *Sharīa* is exclusively and systematically rooted in the "Hanbali-Wahhabi" jurisprudence and the *Ijtihād*[9] of al-Wahhab, just like the *Ikhwan* and the first generation of exclusive Wahhabis. Third, Shi'a and Sufi were considered as their prime targets,[10] and they labeled other Muslim states such as the Ottoman Empire or modern Arab states to be apostate. Finally, both the *Ikhwan* and IS were depicted by rival Muslim scholars as *Khawarij*.[11]

---

[9] In Islamic legal thought, this refers to an independent reasoning or thorough exertion of a jurist's mental faculty in finding a solution to a legal question.

[10] Kerbala was famously raided in 1852, but Ibn Bishr Najdi, the historian of the first Saudi state, wrote that al-Saud already committed a massacre in Karbala in 1801. He proudly documented that massacre, writing: "we took Karbala and slaughtered and took its people (as slaves), then praise be to Allah, Lord of the Worlds, and we do not apologize for that and say: 'And to the unbelievers: the same treatment.'"

[11] The *Khawarij* were the members of a group that appeared in the first century of Islam during the First Fitna, the crisis of leadership after the death of Muhammad. They broke into revolt against the authority of the Caliph Ali after he agreed to arbitration with his rival, Muawiyah I, to decide the

After the creation of the modern Saudi state, the conditions for strategically exporting Wahhabism from the Arabian Peninsula to other Muslim regions became more favorable. First, Wahhabi books and treatises spread to neighboring Muslim lands, and the Saudi state gained control of the Hedjaz region, place of the holiest cities of Islam (Mecca and Medina). Second, the Saudi state sought to complement this gain of legitimacy by implementing a semantic shift with the term "Salafi."

Because they follow the Hanbali theological school, Wahhabis reclaimed themselves from the *Salaf*, the pious predicessors of the Prophet's Companions. Henri Lauzière's (2016: 17) study of the preconceived notion of *Salafism* clearly demonstrates that it does not seem to have existed in the medieval period. From the 12th century, it referred exclusively to the tenants followers of the Hanbali theological school, defending a literalist lecture of God's attributes in the Quran. At the end of 19th century, the term was understood in a completely different way than the current reference to the followers of the Prophet and the first generations of Muslims. Back then, Islamic reform movement leaders, such as Mohamed Abduh and Jamal Eddine Afghani, who advocated for a new vision of Islam shaped by modern ideas such as social justice and democratic rights, were wrongfully depicted as Salafists by orientalists, such as Massignon. The utter rejection by IS of 20th-century reformists labeled as *Salafi*, such as Al Afghani and Abduh who were depicted as deviant freemasons in *Dabiq*, confirms the semantic confusion around this epithet.

Commins (2015: 155) explains that Rashid Rida—a student of Abduh and the influential editor of the leading religious periodical of the era, *al-Manar*—with other thinkers outside Arabia, published articles supporting the Saudi state by presenting the new, anti-modern credo of Wahhabism, initiating a shift in the meaning of *salafi*. According to him, true Wahhabis were the closest of all Muslims to act according to the "Prophetic tradition" (*sunnah*) and hence the *salaf*. This justification of official Wahhabism by comparing it to the *salaf*, together with the control of holy sites associated with the Prophet's tradition, legitimized the state and its doctrine. By inscribing the term "Salafi" with a new meaning confirms, as defended by Lauzière and Barkey (2016), that Salafism was a modern creation, a product of the 20th century, whose

succession to the Caliphate. Following the Battle of Siffin Ahariji, he later assassinated Ali, and, for hundreds of years, the *Khawarij* were a source of insurrection against the Caliphate and considered as apostates responsible for spilling the blood of Muslmis. Salafi Jihadist groups are often depicted as modern *Khawarij* by their detractors among Sunni scholars.

understanding has morphed. Throughout the 20th century, it lost its theological or reformist dimension and became a broad concept of purification of the dogma and the religious praxis applied to a political idea for nationalist and anticolonial purposes and, ultimately, to a totalitarian ideology.

The Influence of Sayyid Qutb

The contestation against the nature of another Arab state—Egypt—appeared during the same period. The 1920s witnessed the creation of the Muslim Brotherhood by Hassan al-Banna. The Brotherhood was the first modern organized Islamic group calling for an Islamic revival. Al-Banna's organization focused on both building up a new *Ikhwan* organizationally within the broader society and struggling against colonialism. Taking stock of the group's message and activities, one of its members, Sayyid Qutb (1906–1966), suggested shifting the rhetoric away from foreign powers' colonization to Arab states' local oppression. By declaring the Egyptian state as "apostate" and comparing the Arab society to the societies pre-dating the Prophet (which, according to tradition, lived in disorder and "ignorance," or *jāhiliyya*), he theorized the ideological basis for confrontation with the postcolonial states in the Arab world. In addition, his early experience of living in the United States as an envoy of the Egyptian Minister of Education caused him to conceptualize the "far" enemy beyond the single British Empire: British imperialism was only one aspect of a more "wide ranging sinister form of collective enmity—that of a secular, materialist, individualist and capitalist West" (Rahemna 2005: 158). He articulated the connections between this global, far enemy and the local situation in the corrupted states led by "near" enemies. This theme permeates jihadi narratives in general and IS propaganda in particular.

Qutb's return to Egypt coincided with a severe political crisis, which inspired him to fully develop his idea that pure Islam is the only cure for illnesses that plagued Egyptian (and Arab) society. First approached by the Egyptian regime to occupy prominent political positions, which he declined, Qutb was later arrested, and his book *Milestones* (*Ma'aalim fi al-Tareeq*), composed while he was in prison, constitutes a major source of inspiration for the Salafi-jihadi ideology. It articulates two key principles constituting the foundations of this thought as it has developed since then: the concepts of "divine sovereignty" (*al-Ḥākimiyya*) and "ignorance" (*al-Jāhiliyya*).

Jāhiliyya, according to Qutb, is based on an assault on God's sovereignty on earth and, particularly, against the nature of the Divine (*al-Ḥākimiyya*). In a state of *Jāhiliyya*, humans appropriate themselves "the right to set the outlook, values, legislation, laws and systems of governance as separate to, and in isolation of, the comprehensive model for living set forth by God" (Qutb 1982: 10). Based on this twofold diagnosis, Qutb pronounced the *takfīr* of his contemporary Arab modern states, as well as their societies, for living in a state of *Jāhiliyya*. Qutb was later tortured and executed by the Egyptian authorities.[12]

IS's ideological connection with Sayyid Qutb's ideology is contested. To be sure, Qutb is considered as the founding father of current Salafi-jihadism and is the only ideologue from the Muslim Brotherhood who has not been openly branded as "misguided" or "apostate" by IS publications.[13] IS's message also echoes Qutb's *takfīr* of Arab and Islamic modern states and recycles Qutb's depiction of the "West" as the prime "civilizational" enemy (which is a shift from recent Salafi-jihadist groups' focus on America, such as al-Qaeda). Yet the methodology (*manhaj*) and theological references used by Qutb and IS are different. Salafi and jihadi Salafi scholars have pointed out many incompatibilities of Qutb's theological conceptions of deity that are rejected by the Islamic Orthodoxy defended by IS (such as the three facets of *tawhid* put forth by al-Wahhab). Indeed, he is suspected to hold the idea—deemed pantheist—of believing in the "unity of being" between God and its creation. As an autodidact and a free thinker, Qutb is known to have aired critical appraisals of some of the Prophet's companions, which is completely inappropriate in most Salafi thought in general. In fact, the difference between Qutb's and IS's notions of *takfīr* is twofold. First, Qutb only judged people who are against *hākimiyya* as apostates, and he did not address those who commit innovations, such as the Shi'a and Sufi. For IS, both criteria are used to make *takfīr*. Second, Qutb considers whole Islamic societies as apostate (without distinction), while IS does not broaden its excommunication to whole societies, but rather to the security apparatus—the leaders and the supporters of the state. For these reasons, but also more tactically

---

[12] Qutb's legal and religious legitimation of *takfīr* later inspired other Jihadi theorists such as Abdu al-Salam Faraj—with his book *Jihad: The Neglected Duty* (*Al-Faridha al-Gha'iba*)—but also armed groups in the region such as the "Fighting Vanguard" (which fought against the Baath Party) and the *Jamaa Islamiyah* (responsible for killing Anwar Sadat in 1981). His excommunication of entire societies also inspired militant groups such as the Egyptian *takfīr wal Hijra*, which similarly considered the whole of Egyptian society as apostate and in a state of ignorance.

[13] See, for example, the articles in *Dabiq* 13 dedicated to the "Murtadd Brotherhood."

because Qutb was a self-made intellectual who lacked the prestige of traditional scholarship, even though many of his ideas espouse IS's paradigm, Qutb is never cited as an authoritative figure, unlike Ibn Abdu Wahhab, Ibn Taymiyah, or Abu Abdallah al-Muhajir. Nevertheless, he is neither praised nor criticized and vilified, as is Al Banna, Abu Musab Al Suri, or al-Maqdisi.

Al-Otaybi's Messianic Revolt and the Emergence of al-Maqdisi

In the 1960s, a religious movement in Saudi Arabia challenged the theological methodology of the Wahhabi-led Saudi religious establishment. Called "People of the Hadith" (*Ahl al Hadith*), its members gathered around the figure of Nasr dine al-Albani. This scholar introduced a new methodology (*manhaj*) for jurisprudence by exclusively using the hadiths,[14] reexamining their authenticity, and adopting a strict literal reading of the Quran, thereby challenging the traditional authorities. A small group of religious students inspired by al-Albani's way of challenging the religious establishment's monopoly over the interpretation of religion emerged in Medina and created another group in 1965, called *al-Jamaa al-Salafiyya al-Muhtasiba* (JSM) ("the Salafi Group that Commands Right and Forbids Wrong"). This group focused initially on moral and religious reform, not on politics. In their view, Islam had been corrupted by the introduction of reprehensible innovations (*bid'a*) in religious practice, as well as by society's deviation from religious principles (the adoption of pictures, for example). Essays were published that denounced this behavior, soon broadening the criticism of the religious and moral status of Saudi society to that of the State and the Saudi ruling family. They used the concept of *Walā'a wa Barā'* and called for its strict application. The Saud family were declared illegitimate because they were not descendants from the Prophet's tribe, the Quraysh. However, they never went as far as to declare the Saudi regime as apostate and make it *takfīr* (Hegghammer & Lacroix 2007).

On November 20, 1979, a group of approximately 300 rebels led by JSM member Juhayman al-Otaybi stormed and seized control of the great mosque in Mecca, the holiest place in Islam. They proclaimed the arrival

---

[14] *Hadiths* are the words of the Prophet Muhamad, known through compilations by his companions.

of the *Mahdī*[15] who al-Otaybi identified to be his companion, Mohamed al-Qahtani. The assault of the Saudi security forces aided by French and Pakistani security teams put an end to the siege. After storming the holy Mosque, al-Otaybi and most of his companions, including the supposed *Mahdī*, were captured and executed. Al-Otaybi's explicit use of eschatology to mobilize against the Saudi regime came from his refusal to declare the Saudi state as *Kāfir*, which meant that ending the state's corruption was only possible through a Divine intervention with the arrival of the *Mahdī* (Hegghammer & Lacroix 2007).

The security crackdown following those events pushed JSM members to flee to neighboring countries. Most of them migrated to Kuwait, where they are said to have influenced a Palestinian scholar named Abu Mohamed al-Maqdisi (Wagemakers 2009). In the early 1980s, he came into contact with the Kuwaiti branch of JSM and subsequently traveled to Afghanistan, where he published in 1984 its most important book, *Religion of Abraham* (*Millat Ibrahim*).[16] In this book, he reflected on al-Otaybi's ideas, lamenting that he never excommunicated the Saudi state (Wagemakers 2009: 282). Maqdisi became the first scholar to cross this line, presenting all the theological arguments from a Salafi and Wahhabi doctrinal reference making a *takfīr* of the Saudi state. This marks a turning point in the history of Salafi-jihadism because the *Walā* and *Bara* duality was no longer used against the Shi'a, the Sufi, or secular Arab regimes, but against the rulers of a Sunni theocracy. He claimed the Saudi state only applied *al-bara* strictly in the social sphere while failing in international relations to pose any threat to non-Muslim nations (Wagemakers 2009: 289). For the first time in the name of Wahhabism, the Saudi state and its religious establishment were to be fought ideologically and theologically. This denunciation of the Saudi regime as the epitome of the "hypocrites" is now a major theme of IS propaganda, as illustrated in Figure 2.1, taken from *Dabiq* magazine (note the caption: "The crusader Obama and his Ṭaghūt ally Salman bin Abdulaziz").

Maqdisi's second contribution to the concepts of *takfīr* and *Walā* and *Bara* was to transform the concept from a passive doctrine of not seeking the help

[15] The *Mahdī* is the just Islamic ruler who is prophesized in Islamic scriptures to appear at the end of times to lead the Islamic nation and fight the Antichrist with the support of Jesus.

[16] The full title of the book is *Millat Ibrahim: wa Da'wat al-Anbiyaa' wa al-Mursalin, wa Asaleeb al-Tughaa fi Tamyee'iha*, literally "Abraham's Creed: And the Calling of Prophets and Messengers, and the Ways in Which the Oppressors Dilute It." The book is widely available online: https://ia800309.us.archive.org/17/items/MillatIbraheem.pdf/MillatIbraheem.pdf.

Figure 2.1 Visual portrayal of Saudi "hypocrisy" (*Dabiq* no. 9).

of foreign rulers to a proactive series of obligations to confront and directly challenge political power. Following the example of Prophet Abraham who cut his relations with his father and tribe (hence the title of the book), the concept is also to be applied multidimensionally against one's family, inner circle, tribe, or country. The requirement to establish loyalty to Islam should automatically drive a person to dissociate himself from everything else. For Maqdisi, individuals also have the obligation to show enmity toward "others." This shift in interpretation may explain how "radicalization" can take place for individuals who follow this vision, leading them to cut ties with their family, friends, tribes, and country.

Maqdisi's conception of *takfir* is the same as the one advocated by IS, and it differs from the one conceptualized by Qutb. Maqdisi and IS *takfir* targets anyone who doesn't respect al-Wahhab's principles of *tawhid* and is constrained to the rulers and people who are directly engaging in abetting and helping the regime and its legislative process rather than the whole society (Wagemakers 2009: 292).

In the 1990s, Maqdisi returned from Afghanistan and was jailed in Jordan. There he met and influenced another Afghanistan veteran, Abu Mosab al-Zarqawi—the future leader of al-Qaeda in Iraq (AQI). Despite their work in tandem leading to the creation of the "Tawhid Group," the opposite personalities of Zarqawi and Maqdisi led them to follow different paths. Zarqawi was attracted to direct militant and armed struggle, while Maqdisi preferred to focus on propagating ideology, especially among his target audience, the Jordanian and Palestinian communities.

The Arrival of Azzam and His Theorization of *Jihād*

In Afghanistan, the concept of *jihād* came to be understood in a new way under the influence of a Palestinian scholar affiliated with the Muslim Brotherhood, Abdullah Azzam. A doctor from al-Azhar University often nicknamed the "father of global *jihād*," Azzam established the "Services Desk" (*Maktab al-Khadamat*) in Peshawar, coordinating the contingent of Arab fighters coming to combat the Soviets, and he was instrumental in bringing Bin Laden to Afghanistan. Religious decrees and financial incentives coming from Saudi Arabia or Egypt were also crucial to mobilize fighters from all around the Arab world to support the Afghan Mujahedeen. Azzam's energetic contribution to this effort was made by challenging the state authorities' monopoly of declaring *jihād* and the rise of the borderless concept of Solidarity *Jihād*. His charisma and writings reshaped the central notion of *jihād* by democratizing it in a way that later profoundly influenced IS's recruitment strategy.

Jihād literally means "struggle" and does not necessarily imply violence. Generally speaking, the term refers to the obligation incumbent on all Muslims to follow and realize God's will: to lead a virtuous life and to extend the Islamic community through preaching, education, behavior, writing, etc. It is well-known that there are two types of *jihād*. First, *Jihād an-Nafs*—known according to a narration of the prophet as the "the Great *Jihād*"—is a personal struggle against one's passions and desires. Second, the "Little *Jihād*" refers to the armed struggle in the path of God. Since the late 20th century, the word *jihād* has gained remarkable currency as it became widely used by resistance/liberation anticolonial movements and by terrorist organizations to legitimate their causes. Even the FLN in Algeria, a secular anticolonial movement, characterized themselves as *mujāhidīn* (people engaged in *jihād*), a term which was consistently used during the Afghanistan War (even by the Western press) to positively designate and give religious legitimacy to people involved in the *jihād* against the Red Army. Nowadays the concept of *jihād* seems to only encompass the Sunni militancy whose political goal is to build an Islamic state through violence.[17]

[17] For an extensive account of how the concept of *jihād* has been used, read Esposito 2003.

Building on Iman Ibn Nuhas's depiction of *jihād* as an obligation to defend Islam and the *ummah* community from aggression, Azzam theorized whether *jihād* could also be "offensive" in his book *The Defense of Muslim Lands (al-Dafa'a 'an Ard al-Muslimin)*.[18] This reinterpretation had a massive impact, quickly becoming the "classical jihadi " doctrine (Hegghammer 2010: 7). Three major novelties were advanced by Azzam.

First, he redefined political and theological authority in matters related to *jihād*. By producing a *fatwa* proclaiming *jihād* in Afghanistan, Azzam broke with the classical doctrinal aspect of *jihād* by challenging Muslim leaders' and scholars' exclusive right to declare it.[19]

Second, Azzam interpreted defensive *jihād* through the lens of globalization as part of his pan-Islamic vision. He theorized defensive *jihād* as an obligation for every Muslim around the world to fight any aggression against the *ummah*, contrary to the earlier doctrine that considered *jihād* as obligatory (*fard ayn*) only for the Muslim population present in an area of aggression. By both at once globalizing defensive *jihād* and making it obligatory, he created the contemporary phenomenon of Muslim foreign fighters. From all over the Arab world, hundreds of young Muslims joined Azzam to fight the Soviets, a process sometimes facilitated by US intelligence agencies. In the 1990s, worldwide calls for *jihād* resonated in Chechnya, Bosnia, Iraq (in 2003), and finally Syria, reaching unprecedented numbers with IS. IS propaganda clearly presents a unified identity of oppressed Muslims around the world, united by a common grievance that plays out differently in various parts of the world.[20]

Third, Azzam elevated defensive *jihād* as the first individual duty for Muslims, topping all five pillars of Islam.[21] He added that teenagers and members of Islamic organizations do not require their family's acceptance to perform *jihād* abroad. *Jihād* is thus democratized and placed at the center

[18] Iman Ibn Nuhas was a 14th-century scholar who wrote *Mashari al Ashwaq*.

[19] This "privatization" of *jihād* should be understood within the broader context of the "democratization" of Salafism initiated by al-Albani's movement (see earlier discussion).

[20] A good example is al-Baghdadi's "Message to the Mujahidin and the Muslim Ummah in the Month of Ramadan," released in July 2014, where he claims: "you have brothers in many parts of the world being inflicted with the worst kinds of torture. Their honor is being violated. Their blood is being spilled. Prisoners are moaning and crying for help. Orphans and widows are complaining of their plight. Women who have lost their children are weeping. *Masajid* [plural of *masjid*] are desecrated and sanctities are violated. Muslims' rights are forcibly seized in China, India, Palestine, Somalia, the Arabian Peninsula, the Caucasus, Sham (the Levant), Egypt, Iraq, Indonesia, Afghanistan, the Philippines, Ahvaz, Iran (by the rafidah [shi'a]), Pakistan, Tunisia, Libya, Algeria and Morocco, in the East and in the West."

[21] Attestation of God's Unity, prayer, fast during Ramadan, payment of the *zakat*, and pilgrimage to Mecca.

of Muslim faith. IS propaganda would go even further, warning every adult male Muslim in the world that not accomplishing *jihād* with a valid excuse and not pledging allegiance to the caliph was a major sin that brings damnation in the afterlife. To justify this claim, IS referred to a *hadith* saying that "whoever dies while not having a pledge of allegiance, dies a death of *Jāhiliyya*" (*Dabiq* no. 5). Promoting an individualist-centered interpretation of Islam, IS's underlying message is that it is not the IS that needs you, but rather you who needs to join the IS to save your soul.

The killing of Azzam in 1989, together with the arrival of al-Maqdisi in Pakistan, marked a turning point for the Salafi-jihadist movement. Bin Laden, with al-Zawahiri, would take Azzam's vision of *jihād*, but changed its *modus operandi* as well as its targets, promoting his own version of "global jihadism" from the mid-1990s. As described by Hegghammer (2010), while Azzam advocated guerrilla warfare in Muslim lands occupied by non-Muslim forces, Bin Laden called for indiscriminate mass casualty attacks on the West, particularly the United States. Bin Laden's global jihadism took priority, especially after the entrance of US troops in Saudi Arabia during the Gulf War. This contributed to the rallying of Bin Laden and other Saudi jihadists to al-Maqdisi's excommunication of the Saudi state (see earlier discussion), bringing together the various genealogical lines explored in this section. In a way, the war in Afghanistan brought together Muslim activists from different ideological backgrounds: Egyptian groups with a Qutbian heritage led by al-Zawahiri, radical Muslim Brotherhood scholars personified by Azzam, and followers of Ibn Wahab's creed such as Bin Laden and al-Maqdisi. This "ideological melting pot" contributed to and helped to create the current Salafi-jihadi movement whose flagship was al-Qaeda throughout the 1990s. However, as we will now explore, this ideology underwent yet another process of hybridization in Iraq, engendering what Fishman calls "Zarqawiism" (2016: 60), the baseline of IS's ideological message.

The Rise of the Islamic State in the Battle of Salafi-Jihadi Ideas

Iraq as an Incubator for IS Ideologues in the Making

IS built its ideology from this "melting pot" while emerging and developing in Iraq. In retrospect, one can even argue that before the arrival of al-Zarqawi to Iraq in 2003, the local Salafi scene was already presenting the characteristics of a fertile breeding ground for IS ideology. Two observations have been made. First, in the 1980s, the Iraq–Iran war and the rise in oil prices made it easy for the Saudi state to promote its brand of Salafism in Iraq, which took off with a particular anti-Shi'a tone. Second, some analysts have also highlighted the impact of Saddam Hussein's "Faith Campaign" in the 1990s, particularly among the ranks of the Iraqi military and intelligence (e.g., Orton 2015).

This second claim should, however, not be exaggerated. Former Iraqi Baath military commanders were later recruited by Zarqawi for their skills and military experience, not so much for their religious credentials, and they would not have any influence on the group's ideological doctrine. Baram (2014) explains in great detail the reasons underpinning Saddam Hussein's 180-degree shift in relation to Islam, from absolute secularism and nationalism to the promotion of Islam throughout society (construction of mosques, law, education, enforcement of Islamic punishments). The "faith campaign," conducted under the supervision of Izzat Ibrahim al-Duri (considered at that time as number two of the regime), promoted religion by following a creed much closer to Sufism than Salafism. The version of Islam that developed was apolitical and ecumenical, tightly controlled by the Baath party and thus very different from the ideological and theological views of al-Wahhab or al-Maqdisi. Most of the Iraqi leaders of the political and religious apparatus of the IS—such as the caliphs Abu Omar al-Baghdadi and Abu Bakr al-Baghdadi, or Abu Ali al-Anbari (former minister of finances)— were already part of the Iraqi Salafi underground circles in 1980s and 1990s.

Despite the involvement of IS leadership in the Iraqi Salafi movement, Whiteside (2017) argues that the Iraqi Salafi community had little to do with the official "faith campaign" but was influenced more by the rise of Wahhabism in Iraq in the 1980s. The Iraq–Iran war caused an informal alliance between Iraq and Saudi Arabia, and the latter actively promoted Salafi thought in the former, flooding Iraq with Salafi literature (Whiteside 2017). For those reasons, before 2003, the Iraqi Salafi scene was already virulently anti-Shi'a. Al-Anbari's two-part eulogy in IS media[22] shows how he was already a Salafi cleric with sharp anti-Shi'a and anti-Baath views, operating in Tel Afar prior to the US invasion. His first action with his Salafi group *Ansar al-Islam* in 2003 was to prioritize targeting Shi'a mosques (*Husayniyat*)

---

[22] See *al-Naba* no. 43.

in the Tel Afar region. Al-Zarqawi himself, a Jordanian who did not have any experience confronting the Shi'as, became vigorously anti-Shi'a after observing the Shi'a collaborate with the United States during the invasions of both Afghanistan and Iraq. Underground Salafi circles were therefore already present in Iraq in the 1990s, showing that IS's ideology does not simply result from an internal intellectual development prolonging the genealogy elaborated earlier, but also bears the mark of the impact of external influences and social context. These Salafi circles would later form the bulk of IS's key early members surrounding al-Zarqawi and form the group's religious and ideological leadership a decade later. This anti-Shi'a hatred, grounded in the rise of Salafism in Iraq during the war against Iran and later in the civil war, culminated for al-Zarqawi in June 2006 with the complete *takfir* of the Shi'a using historical and theological evidence in his audio message: "Has the Discourse of the Rafidha Reached You?" (*Hal Ataka Hadithu al-Rafidha*).[23]

From Theory to Practice: al-Zarqawi and Abu Abdullah al-Muhajir's influences

Al-Zarqawi's strategy in Iraq followed Maqdisi's idea that the consolidation of power (*tamkīn*), achieved by fighting the "near enemy" (as opposed to al-Qaeda's resolve to hit the "far enemy") should be the prime objective. As noted earlier, al-Zarqawi's former prison companion believed that contemporary rulers of the Muslim world were apostates whose unbelief should be considered worse than that of the Jews and Christians and must be fought in priority, especially Saudi Arabia (Wagemakers 2012: 289). Al-Zarqawi always defended this idea against al-Qaeda interlocutors, insisting on the strategic necessity to fight the US presence in Iraq and, more importantly, to wage an all-out war against the "Crusaders"' partners from the Shi'a majority or rival Sunni groups in Iraq.

However, despite this agreement on fighting the "near enemy," a number of differences between al-Zarqawi and Maqdisi persisted on ideological and methodological issues, which would eventually lead to a schism between the two old acquaintances. Abu Hanieh and Abu Ruhman (2015: 75) maintain

---

[23] *Rafidha* is a pejorative terms for the Shi'a. *Rawafid* is another label coming from the same root *"rafid,"* meaning to "reject," to "refuse."

that, after the first battle of Fallujah, al-Zarqawi became heavily influenced by another scholar, Sheikh Abu Abdullah al-Muhajir. Most of al-Zarqawi's methodology, which would later become trademarks of IS, were theorized and religiously justified by al-Muhajir, who pushed all the concepts evoked in the present genealogy to unprecedented levels of extremism. 0Muhajir's book *Issues in the Jurisprudence of Jihād (Masa'il fi Fiqh al-Jihād)*[24] provided the jurisprudential basis and "guidebook" for IS's message and actions. As a religious source, his frames of reference are found in the Qur'an, the Sunnah, and the jurisprudential corpus of the Hanbali School, complemented by references to the religious teachings of Ibn Taymiyyah, Ibn Qayim Al Jawziya, and al-Wahhab. The book is divided into 12 chapters, each one treating an issue related to *jihād* and bearing the marks of these thinkers, but also making the extra step toward even more radical interpretations.

In the first chapter, al-Muhajir claims that all the contemporary political systems fall into the state of "unbelief" (*kufr*) and "apostasy" (*riddah*) and must therefore be fought as they form *Dār al-Ḥarb*. He also stresses the permissibility of using all kind of weapons against this enemy, including nonconventional ones. Moreover, the blood of all the nonbelievers is considered as legal and permissible to spill unless they pay the *jizya* (the tax that would give them protection by the Muslims). When attacking nonbelievers, the presence of Muslims (whom it is unlawful to kill) among them is not sufficient to prevent those attacks. While considered *nawazil* (calamities or momentous events), suicide operations are nonetheless allowed from a religious point of view (Abu Haniyeh & Abu Ruhman 2015: 295). Another discussion justifies the beheading of infidels, which al-Zarqawi was the first to broadcast on the Internet in 2004 with the decapitation of Nicholas Berg. In comparison, al-Maqdisi was very reluctant to endorse beheadings and called to use them only in exceptional cases.

The dispute and ideological rift between al-Zarqawi and al-Maqdisi culminated in 2005 when Maqdisi published a letter to al-Zarqawi entitled "Al-Zarqawi: Advocacy and Advice, Hopes and Pains" (*Al-Zarqawi: Munasara wa Munasaha, Aamaal wa Aalaam*), in which he expresses his reservation regarding the general *takfīr* on the Shi'a, the extensive use of "martyrdom" operations, and al-Zarqawi's very permissive rules of engagement. In 2006, Maqdisi's criticisms expanded to all the doctrinal justifications for

---

[24] The book, also known as known as *The Jurisprudence of Blood (Fiqh alDimaa')*, can be accessed online: http://ia601203.us.archive.org/19/items/kotobjehad/masael.pdf.

"barricading" (*tatarrus*, using civilian populations to shield from the adversary), which was defended by al-Muhajir and used to legitimize and exonerate civilian deaths as collateral damage if they happen to be present at a legitimate target.

The Proclamation of the Islamic State of Iraq and the Final Maturation of IS's Ideology

After the proclamation of the establishment of the ISI in October 2006, the group gained autonomy from the al-Qaeda central leadership from an organizational and structural viewpoint. Since then the group began to assert its own version of the Salafi-jihadi heritage more openly and aggressively.

It is well-known today that al-Qaeda's leadership was surprised by the dissolution of its Iraqi branch into the newly created IS. Despite this surprise, Bin Laden and al-Zawahiri publicly endorsed the establishment of "this legitimate emirates" (McCants 2015: 19). Confronted with the criticism coming from other Iraqi Sunni groups regarding their activities and violent methodology, the group issued a speech in 2007 by its leader Abu Umar al-Baghdadi clearly presenting its doctrine and objectives.[25] He proclaimed adherence to the Sunni Salafi theological methodology and appealed "to all Sunnis, and to the young men of Jihadi-Salafism in particular, across the entire world." He then enumerated several points forming the basis of the group's doctrinal reference.

First, al-Baghdadi proclaimed the necessity to remove and destroy all signs of "idolatry" and innovation. He declared as apostate the Shi'as, the magicians, the tomb worshippers (the Sufi), and all the people who insult the Prophet of Islam and its companions.

At the same time, he distanced himself from the accusation of *khawarij* (see note 10) by stressing the fact that the group doesn't excommunicate Muslims who commit sins such as stealing, adultery, and consuming alcohol. From that day, the group has always tried to position its discourse between the excesses of *khawarij* extremism and the laxism of *Irja* people who separate faith from actions.

---

[25] Abū Omar Al Baghdadi's speech ("This Is Our Doctrine"—*Hadidi Aaqidatuna*) is available online in Arabic audio at https://soundcloud.com/louma3alasinna-385910377/audio-2015-09-17-21-41-55-2.

Figure 2.2 Screenshot from the Islamic State video "The End of Sykes-Picot," showing a militant contemplating a map of the Syria–Iraq border, before destroying the border control facilities.

Second, from a political point of view, the *Sharī'a* is claimed to be the only law to resolve disputes and prevail above all man-made or tribal laws. Other ideologies, such as nationalism, patriotism, communism, and ba'athism, were presented as apostasy from Islam. Other jihadi groups in Iraq were not considered as disbelievers; rather they were seen as in a state of disobedience because they did not work for the unity of Islam. Borders from the postcolonial period were considered as illegitimate (this view is later shown in the group's famous video *The End of Sykes-Picot*; see Figure 2.2). The only accepted means to change the status quo is through *jihād*,[26] understood as a military manoeuvre and a compulsory duty for all Muslims. Following Azzam's guidelines on *jihād*, Muslim lands must be defended from foreign aggressions while the territories which were once governed by *Sharī'a* reconquered. The organization also vows to fight the US occupation and the Iranian presence in Iraq. Regarding the group's legitimate targets, all countries ruled by man-made laws (and where Islam rules come second) are considered as *Dār al-Kufr* and have to be fought. Their leaders, security

[26] In Adnani's words: "We will fight, and fight, and fight until the religion is entirely for Allah. We will never beg people to accept the religion of Allah and to rule by Allah's Sharī'ah. Whoever is content, then this is the Sharī'ah of Allah. Whoever dislikes it, is discontent with it, and refuses it, then we will continue in spite of him. This is the religion of Allah. We will declare the apostates as disbelievers and disavow them all. We will take the disbelievers and polytheists as enemies and hate them."

apparatus, and functionaries are legitimate targets. Nevertheless, this does not mean that the entire population is considered as disbelievers. However, in all the Islamic countries, Christians and Jews are all considered in a state of war because they do not pay the *Jizya*. These ideological foundations presented by the leader of ISI in 2007 would not change in the year following this announcement and would remain largely the same thereafter. The declaration of the Caliphate in 2014 added a new dimension and thereby added new issues, which are discussed at the end of this section.

IS's message also took a distinctive eschatological tone, as emphasized by McCants W (2015), who claims that this constitutes a clear departure from al-Qaeda, which was reluctant to engage in this direction despite its propaganda value. For example, McCants shows that, until the war in Iraq, "apocalypticism" was unpopular among Sunni scholars and jihadi theorists, who disdainfully considered it part of Shi'a's obsession with the *Mahdī*'s return. Moreover, Otaibi's experience in proclaiming the return of the *Mahdī* in 1979 resulted in failure, which strengthened Bin Laden's conviction that it was "too risky to claim the fulfilment of prophecies and then fail" (McCants 2015: 28).

IS's ideology is therefore peculiar in that it is the first group from the Salafi-jihadi ideological matrix which relied massively on eschatology in its discourse and propaganda. Moreover, according to McCants (2015), IS's leadership sometimes acts to precipitate events depicted by the Prophet as preceding the end of times, in a kind of self-fulfilling prophecy. This was done simultaneously for strategic and tactical reasons (as explained in the next chapter), in order to appeal to an audience already influenced by apocalyptic views and conspiracy theories and because of the leaders' belief in the imminence of the end of times. The ISI minister of war after Zarqawi's death, the Egyptian Abu Hamza al-Muhajir, is said to have been deeply convinced that the days of the *Mahdī* were close, prompting him to increase attacks, which contributed to the group's errors in 2006–2007 and led to its defeat in 2010. The eschatological element became even more striking in IS propaganda after its establishment in Syria in 2013, as the use of eschatological prophecies related to *Sham* (the Levant) provided a powerful tool for recruitment and appeal in Syria for most of the religiously oriented groups already fighting in the area. Indeed, Damascus, and more precisely the Mosque of Umayyad,[27] is said to be the place of Jesus's return, while the city of Dabiq in

---

[27] It is not a coincidence that the name of the media production wing of *Jabhat al-Nusra* is called the "White Minaret" (*al-Manara Bayda*), referring to the place in Damascus where Jesus is said to return.

the region of Aleppo is where a battle between the Romans and the Muslims is supposedly due to take place before the arrival of the Anti-Christ, and the *Mahdī* is also said to have his citadel in the al-Ghouta region situated in Damascus's suburbs. At the symbolic level, the restoration of slavery; the adoption of golden and silver dinars as a currency; and the rise of an army with black banners in Khorasan (Afghanistan), Yemen, Sham, and Iraq, are all elements mentioned by prophecies and implemented by IS after the proclamation of the Caliphate.

The Battle for the Leadership of Salafi-Jihadism

This use of eschatology and symbols is one of the many tools used by IS in its bid to win the ideological battle for the theological and moral leadership of Salafi-jihadism. IS presents itself as the true inheritor of the Islamic tradition and the real successor of the Prophets' Companions, standing against deviant interpretations of Islam, chiefly the Shi'a.

IS does so in two main ways. First, its members present themselves as the authentic inheritors of al-Wahhab' tradition, in contrast to the "hypocrite" and "corrupted" Saudi state led by a supposedly Wahhabi religious establishment (framed by IS as *al-Salool*, referring to a famous hypocrite character during the time of the Prophet).[28] IS depicts a profound depletion of the Islamic faith, a crisis of unprecedented nature fueled by diverse negative foreign influences (from the "Crusaders," the "Jews," and the "corrupt" and "effeminate" "scholars" preaching for a moderate version of Islam compatible with modern life in the West).

Second, IS members assert that they continue Bin Laden's interpretation of Salafi-jihadism, as the former head of al-Qaeda is considered a *Mujaddid*[29] at the level of Ibn Taymiyyah or al-Wahhab (whereas al-Zawahiri is called *the Jew of Jihād* and said to have deviated al-Qaeda from its path).[30] Current and recent al-Qaeda ideologues[31] are therefore at the frontline of the refutation of IS's Caliphate. The conflict between IS and al-Qaeda for the leadership of

[28] The al-Saud dynasty is therefore called the "al-Salool dynasty."

[29] This refers to the Sunni tradition of the "renewer of the century" (*mujaddid al-qarn*), according to which a great scholar or leader appears at the beginning of each century to purify the religion.

[30] In reference to *Jew of Qibla*, used negatively to refer to a partisan of the *Irja*, a sect that is said to dissociate faith and action.

[31] For example Hani Sibai, Abu Qatada al-Falistini, or Tariq Abdelhaleem.

Salafi-jihadism became heated in April 2013, when al-Baghdadi announced the merger of al-Nusra and ISI, thereby forming IS. Abu Muhammad al-Jolani, the leader of al-Nusra earlier dispatched by al-Baghdadi to Syria to facilitate the future expansion of the Caliphate into the neighboring country, refused the merger and called al-Zawahiri to solve the dispute. A month later, al-Zawahiri condemned al-Baghdadi's merger and ordered each group to stay confined to its respective country. Al-Baghdadi sharply rejected al-Zawahiri's arbitration in an audio speech entitled "Remaining in Iraq and the Levant," stressing for the first time IS's doctrinal and methodological differences from al-Qaeda. As recalled by Hamming (2017: 6), the dispute evolved from an intra-movement matter "to an inter-movement contestation for power and authority." Fighting between IS and the rebellion allied to al-Nusra surged throughout 2013. The point of no return was reached in February 2014, with the killing of Abu Khalid al-Suri, a founding figure of Ahrar al-Sham sent by al-Zawahiri to Syria, and a close associate of the al-Qaeda writer Abu Mosab al-Suri. al-Qaeda officially broke ties with IS in March, and IS was given five days to return to Iraq. The conflict evolved to a full-scale confrontation in Eastern Syria, especially in the Deir-Ezzor province around Abu Mariah al-Qahtani. The religious leader of ISI in Mosul, he joined al-Nusra and was their most senior religious figure until July 2014. He represented the most anti-IS religious figure of the group, pushing for a direct confrontation against "Baghdadi's gang." Strategic considerations for the control of this wealthy region pushed both groups to release their most extreme men in the region and validate the excommunication of each other. Deir-Ezzor became the first battlefield in the zero-sum game between IS and al-Nusra, a confrontation that later expanded to elsewhere with other al-Qaeda–linked groups in Afghanistan and Libya.

This major schism in the Salafi-jihadi social movement and ideology did not topple the overall fundamental principles upon which it is founded. On the contrary, both currents still hold steadfast to these principles, which include the belief in the duty to establish the Islamic state, disavowal of the Arab regimes that do not govern by *Sharī'a*, and adherence to *al-walāʾ wa al-barāʾ*. However, they diverge so much on the methodology that an important ideological rift was created between the two. While al-Nusra and al-Qaeda are highly influenced by the operational strategy of Abu Mosab al-Suri (chiefly "The Call for a Global *Jihād*")[32] and remain committed to what Abu

---

[32] Read Brynjar 2008 for an extended analysis.

Haniyah and Abu Ruhman call the "extension of the Salafist Qutbian-Muslim Brotherhood school of thought" (2015: 141), IS's Iraqi branch was influenced by the method advocated by Abu Bakr Naji in his book *Management of Savagery: The Most Critical Stage Through Which the Islamic Nation Will Pass* (*Idarat at-Tawahhus: Akhtar marhalah satamurru biha al-ummah*).

In his "Call to Global *Jihād*," al-Suri advocates a leaderless resistance (lone-wolf attacks) and critically discusses the issue of eschatology. Reflecting on Suri's own experience of jihadi failures in Syria against Hafez al-Assad, the basis is set for a more pragmatic jihadi method. Al-Suri enumerated the following lessons that should be applied to any jihadi uprising: maintain a covert organization even in time of success, have a centralized strategy in a decentralized organization, compartmentalize the organization to avoid compromise, prefer quality over quantity of recruits, and cooperate with local groups and tribes. The cooperation with groups considered as secular, implemented by al-Nusra in Syria, pushed IS to declare al-Jolani and his group as apostates. IS further argued that whoever doesn't consider Jolani and his group a *Kāfir* is himself a *Kāfir*. In sum, if IS's methodology has drawn on al-Suri's writings (e.g., the use of lone-wolf actions, the use of eschatology to mobilize), this use has been limited compared to al-Qaeda's. Regarding *Sharīʿa*, for example, al-Qaeda stresses the importance of gaining popular support (*hadina shaabiya*) before implementing it completely, while IS considers the delay in applying *Sharīʿa* as *Ṭaghūt*. Recently, IS media clearly disavowed al-Suri's methodology of *jihād*, labeling him as a deviant.[33]

Abu Bakr Naji's work, priviliedged by IS, consists of strategic guidelines for jihadi movements to destroy governments and build a new society. Naji outlined three stages for this struggle: disruption and exhaustion, management of savagery, and empowerment. The extent to which this book was influential to explain IS's methodology is debated. IS media suggested this claim is exaggerated; however, they also claim that when al-Zarqawi read the volume he proclaimed: "it is as if the author knows what I'm planning."[34] Even though Naji's book accurately describes IS's overall strategy in Iraq, IS consider that Naji's guidelines include a few mistakes similar to those made by al-Suri, regarding the issue of cooperation with other groups who resist the full application of *Sharīʿa*.

---

[33] *Dabiq* (no. 14, p. 42): "The Murtad Brotherhood."
[34] *Dabiq* (no. 12, p. 39): "The Revival of Jihad in Bengal."

The ideological and theological roots of IS and al-Qaeda can also explain their divergence in terms of the near and far enemy strategy. IS's action is more centered on purifying Islam by attacking supposedly apostate Muslim states and scholars and by getting rid of allegedly deviant Islamic sects such as the Shi'a and Sufi. Ibn Abd Al Wahhab's and Ibn Taymiyah's foes were two non-Western powers claiming to represent Islam: the Mongols and the Ottomans. On the other hand, al-Qaeda has a more anti-Western and anticolonial paradigm inherited from its Egyptian Brotherhood and Qutbist branch. IS's political horizon goes well beyond expelling the United States from the Arabian Peninsula and destructing the state of Israel, which were the two main objectives presented by the fatwa of the "World Islamic Front for *Jihād* Against Jews and Crusaders," presenting the poltical framework of Bin Laden and Al Zawahiri's organization in 1998.

In addition to al-Qaeda, Islamist groups whose ideological matrix comes from the Muslim Brotherhood were also confronted by IS. Abu Ali al-Anbari's 40 audio lectures produced after his release from prison in 2012 represented the last update in the evolution of IS's ideological substrate in this respect. Facing a new context marked by the Arab popular uprising and the rise of Islamist parties participating in parliamentary elections with Zawahiri's approval, IS had a contrary stance. While ISI's 2007 declaration presenting its methodology and credo did not excommunicate members of the Iraqi Muslim Brotherhood (only its leadership), al-Anbari's lectures marked an evolution. IS's high cleric defended until his death (March 2016) that any Muslim joining parliaments or participating in elections was an apostate—even if he intended to Islamize the society. Al-Anbari also declared the illegitimacy of all the institutions in Muslim countries, including mosques and courts. On August 31, 2013, in a recording entitled "*Al-Silmiyya Dinu Mann?*,"[35] al-Adnani stressed that the Muslim Brotherhood's methodology and the democratic system were un-Islamic and that fighting following the Islamic methodology was the only way to change the status quo.

Later in the *Dabiq* issue dedicated to the Muslim Brotherhood, the group is said to be a "devastating cancer [that] has emerged, mutated, and spread,

---

[35] An audio recording by Abu Muhammad al-Adnani entitled "Al-Silmiyya Dinu Mann?" (literally "Whose Religion Is Peacefulness") is available (in Arabic) at the following link: http://bab-ul-islam.net/showthread.php?t=20110 and in English https://archive.org/details/PacifismIsTheReligionOfWhom

attempting to drown the entire Ummah in apostasy."[36] Hassan al-Banna is considered by IS as an apostate who founded a secularist party with an "Islamic" cloak. IS accuses these groups of having embraced democracy and nationalism (making them *tawagheet*), as well as alliances with the Shi'a (which contradicts *hakimiyah* and *al-walā' wa al-barā'a*). Consequently, IS is in open confrontation with a wide range of armed groups, such as Hamas, the Islamic Army in Iraq (which joined the Awakening Program), the *Fajr* militia in Libya, and *Ahrar al-Sham* in Syria. Even before the proclamation of the Caliphate, IS imagined itself as a state that would never have to lower its status to the level of militias.[37] Since the proclamation of the Caliphate, the group has urged in the name of *walā'* all other Islamist groups to pledge their allegiance to the Caliph. Because it elevated its status to that of a "Caliphate," IS has implicitly proclaimed itself to be the sole holder of legitimate violence in the Islamic world, and consequently no other group or militia should be tolerated. This new situation explains the inherently conflictive nature[38] of its relations with all the groups who are claiming to represent political Islam in one way or another.

The Future of IS's Message (and of Salafi-Jihadism)

Since its inception in 2004 and throughout its different manifestations as *Tawhid wal Jihād, Majliss Shura Al Mujahideen*, al-Qaeda in Mesopotamia, and eventually ISI and ISIS, IS sought to establish a specific message at the core of its full-spectrum propaganda and has been eager to elevate the question of doctrinal purity to the top of its priorities. As discussed, this message can be identified as an original fusion of multiple elements that are all deeply rooted in the history of Jihadi-Salafism. In this final section, I take stock of this picture to raise the hypothetical question of IS's future message.

[36] Cf. note 39.

[37] At the source of the conflict between IS and Syrian Rebels in 2013–2014 is IS's refusal to resolve its disputes and submit itself to a jurisdictional body composed of a Shariah Committee of other groups.

[38] As al-Adnani said: "We will divide the groups and break the ranks of the organizations. Yes, because there is no place for groups after the revival of the Jamā'ah (the Khilāfah). So away with the organizations. We will fight the movements, assemblies, and fronts. We will tear apart the battalions, the brigades, and armies, until, by Allah's permission, we bring an end to the factions, for nothing weakens the Muslims and delays victory except the factions. Yes, and we will liberate the "liberated" places, because if they are not ruled by the law of Allah, then they have not been liberated."

To do this, it is first important to observe that the ideological production of concepts such as *al-Walāwa al-barā'* is deeply *reactionary* in nature; it came from a perceived necessity to enforce a protection against foreign influence (whether Ottoman for the first Wahabbi scholars, or Western for Maqdisi and, to some extent, Qutb). *Al-Walā'wa al-barā'* was first the fruit of the division between "exclusive" and "inclusive" Wahhabism on the question of foreign intervention. Represented by scholars of the Najd, the *Ikhwan*, al-Otaybi's revolt, and the rejection of the Saudi state theorized by Maqdisi, it had a centripetal effect, attracting and bringing together a core group of Muslims, protecting them while excluding the rest. This ideological obsession with the protection of "true" Muslims from foreign corruption and "innovations" found a very fertile climate in post-2002 Iraq, a country occupied by foreign forces (the US and Iran) and deeply divided by sectarian (Sunni vs. Shi'a) and ethnic (Arabs vs. Kurds) fault lines.

It is also crucial to stress that IS's ideology is the result of successive hybridization of the Salafi-jihadi ideology, further shaped by al-Zarqawi's personal experience in the post-2003 Iraqi context. As a consequence, IS's propaganda machine is highly conscious that, to preserve its appeal, the ideological battle is most important for the leadership of Salafi-jihadism. The group has to prove that it holds the legacy of al-Wahhab, both against Saudi Arabia for the domination of Salafism and against current al-Qaeda leadership for the continuation of Bin Laden's legacy and the preponderance on jihadism. IS therefore aspires to label itself as the unique *independent* (in opposition to state-controlled scholars), *transnational* (in opposition of more local groups like the Muslim Brotherhood), and jihadi *maximalist* (in opposition to al-Qaeda and its gradualist approach to *Sharī'a*) movement in the world.

In this context, the future of IS's specific ideological stance is conditioned on the development of two elements which constituted the basis of IS's propaganda and ideological appeal at its peak in 2014 but could backlash in the future: its use of eschatology, including its claim to be a Caliphate, and its obsession with doctrinal purity.

First, IS's use of eschatological references suggesting they are chosen by God may eventually prove to be a bad choice, as envisioned by al-Suri. However, the group has proved resilient against challenges on this matter. Because eschatology is open to diverse interpretations, the group's propaganda has so far been able to adapt its narrative to fit with some prophecies. The fall of Dabiq to the Turkish-supported FSA reflects this adaptation. The city was not as important for its military strategists as it was for its media wing, so the group did not push its fighters to sacrifice for it (unlike in Kobane or Mosul), and IS's propaganda quickly revised the Dabiq prophecy, claiming that it concerned the Romans and not their servants (referring to the FSA) and changing the name of its flagship magazine to *Rumiyah* (meaning Rome), hence making another eschatological reference. IS's loss of Dabiq was an opportunity to strike a double blow on its propaganda by stressing its failed narrative and the fact that it was defeated by the very population the group says it represents. But the group has adapted its propaganda with the battle of Mosul and now prefers now to rely on the past rather than the future to frame its defeats. IS supporters and the group's media have likened the battle for Mosul to the conflict opposing the Prophet and the more numerous "Ahzab," meaning that IS will ultimately prevail just like the first Islamic state of the Prophet.

The loss of the city and the rest of its held territory, despite a fierce resistance, could nonetheless thwart IS's message of representing a Caliphate and give more weight to al-Qaeda's counternarrative. The pressure now endured in Iraq and Syria will ultimately finish its dream of territorial control and destruction of the Sykes-Picot system, on which rests its proclamation of the Caliphate and the possibility of eschatological claims. Will the group's narrative survive a dematerialized Caliphate? The answer to that question now depends on the fate of the success of its affiliated groups/provinces (*Wilāyāt*) in Afghanistan, Sinai, the Philippines, the Arabian Peninsula, Somalia, and West and North Africa. The actual trend of IS losing territory in its heartland[39] will push those groups to hasten their quest for territorial control in order to maintain the relevance of IS's discourse and utopian Caliphate— if this does not work, the eschatological dimension will be discredited for a while.

Second, IS's effort to reach doctrinal purity may prove self-destructive. A way to convince its audience that its methodology is pure has been to adopt a sharply Manichean reading of *al-Walā" wa al-Barā'*, opposing the Islamic State on the one side and a strange coalition of "enemies," such as the US-led coalition, Russia, France, Iran, the Kurds, the Turks, Israel (and more broadly the "Zionists"), Hamas, Egypt, the Taliban, the Syrian Regime, the Syrian rebels, and al-Qaeda, enmeshed in complex conspiracies (see Chapter 3). IS regularly describes itself as the "victorious group" (*taifa mansoora*) from

---

[39] Despite its loss of Mosul and imminent loss of Raqqa, the group still controls a territory as big as Belgium, with safe haven in Iraq and Syria, and the capacity to conduct large-scale guerrilla warfare from the desert of Homs/Diyala.

Islamic scriptures, standing against all other impure Islamist groups fond of innovations, concessions, pragmatism, and gradualism. The group's ideological outbidding strategy to show the purity of its doctrine led to extreme consequences, such as the widespread use of decapitation as a tool for propaganda, the enslavement of Yazidi women, or the cult of "Martyrdom operation" (Winter 2017). This has also multiplied animosity and resolve against the group.

More surprisingly, what might be a determining challenge against IS's ideology actually comes from its very own ranks, as the organization has recently witnessed the rise of a minor internal dissidence. This threat comes from a more general tendency for violent Salafi organizations to self-destroy. As suggested by Lahoud (2010), the Wahhabi doctrine's extreme focus on reaching the perfect doctrine make Salafi jihadi groups particularly vulnerable to internal fragmentation. Surprising as it may sound, members of IS have challenged the ideological unity of the group by criticizing its leadership for being "too soft" and not "pure" enough. In 2014, IS's internal security service cracked down on an "extremist" cell that wanted to make a coup and topple al-Baghdadi. Last year, the organization also replaced Abu Bakr Shekau as head of its province in Western Africa because he was making a general *takfir* on all the Muslim population which was not under his control, like the GIA in Algeria during the 1990s.[40]

In recent years, IS has also been eager to supress a radical dissidence known as the "Hazimis," a small group among IS members who follow the teachings of Ahmad al-Hazimi, a scholar based in Mecca. Although al-Hazimi is not politicized, he is very active in producing *fatwas* on Wahhabism and *tawhid*. He defends the idea that when pronouncing *takfir* on someone, ignorance cannot be an excuse; he also adds to it the fact that those who excuse the ignorant are themselves infidels and should be automatically excommunicated.[41] This extreme view led to some of al-Hazimi's followers inside the ranks of IS to declare *takfir* on Bin Laden and even al-Baghdadi.[42] IS's response was to execute the proponents of such ideology, such as Abu Umar al-Kuwaiti,[43] and to forbid its fighters from discussing the issue. IS waited three

---

[40] See the interview with al-Barnawi in *Al Naba* (issue 41).

[41] This radical stance potentially leads to absurd ad-infinitum *takfir*.

[42] Because Bin Laden never proclaimed a general *takfir* on the Shi'a, he is deemed to be *Kāfir*; because al-Baghdadi still considers Bin Laden as *mujadid* he is therefore also deemed to be *Kāfir*.

[43] "ISIS Executes One of Its Sharia Judges," *Middle East Monitor*, March 10, 2015, https://www.middleeastmonitor.com/20150310-isis-executes-one-of-its-sharia-judges/. Read also http://en.deirezzor24.net/out-of-fear-that-the-followers-of-hazimi-would-rebel-against-it-daesh-organization-arrested-and-executed-many-of-them-in-rural-deir-ezzor/.

years before finally making public its official judgment regarding this sensitive issue. In the *Rumiyah* magazine,[44] IS's religious scholars led by Turki Bin Ali[45] considered that individuals who refrain from making *takfir* on another person are not automatically *Kāfir*. One can only be declared so if one persists in refusing to make *takfir* after receiving clear evidence about the *kufr* of the person. IS's leadership knows that this disagreement could affect its legitimacy and stability. By not controlling the central matter of *takfir*, it could easily be turned against entire societies or the organization itself. After many episodes, the Hazimis–Bin Ali schism seemed to settle in favor of the defendants of Bin Ali's thesis. Days before Bin Ali's death on May 17, 2017, the Delegated Committee, which represents IS's supreme body for theological decrees, issued an important memorandum asserting *takfir* as "one of the unambiguous foundations of the religion."

Nevertheless, a few months later, on September 15, the same Delegated Committee rescinded the memorandum, stating that "'Those Who Perish Might Perish by a Clear Sign' . . . has been annulled . . . on account of its containing errors of knowledge and misleading and unreliable statements that have given rise to disagreement and division in the ranks of the mujahidin in particular, and the Muslims in general." Other audios published by the group's radio *Al Bayan* (cf. Chapter 6) eventually revoked the idea that *takfir* was a foundation of the religion rather than one of its requirements (*wajibat al-din*). What happened between the two decrees? The fate of Abu Abderaman Al-Shami can explain IS's theological shift: from being under investigation by IS's theological committee in a kind of Inquisition trial, he became appointed by al-Baghdadi as the new head of the Delegated Committee in order to correct the group's theological path. An article in *Al Nabaa* proclaiming in September 2017 the return to "the truth" seemed to indicate that the theological dispute inside the organization was settled, even though heated debates still remain in social media.

Throughout 2018, new evidence on social media has shown that the struggle between the two opposing currents was still vivid inside the organization. Bunzel (2018) highlighted the new events shaking the unity of IS's theological structure. According to Mu'assasat al-Turath al-'Ilmi, a group on social media, Abu Ya'qub al-Maqdisi—the author of the audio clips published by the group rebuking the Hazimis—was arrested. Considered an important

---

[44] *Rumiyah*, no. 2, p. 4: "Important Memorandum."
[45] Who was killed by the US coalition in May 2017. From Bahraini origins, he was a student of Maqdisi and considered the head of IS's *Sharīa* Committee.

mufti of the organization, his arrest on charges including his relationship with the abhorred cleric Abu Muhammad al-Maqdisi and his deviance from the Sunni methodology could signify the return to power of the group's more extremist wing on *Takfir* and cause the emergence of a dissidence inside the group. If al-Baghdadi ever loses control of the Delegated Committee to these extremist factions, the organization could follow the steps of the GIA in Algeria, *Takfir wal hijra* in Egypt, or Shekau's Boko Haram in Nigeria.

Despite this risk, challenging these "radical" factions, quite surprisingly from a Western perspective, serves IS's communication strategy by showing that the organization is not the most extreme one, countering the repeated accusations from al-Qaeda and mainstream Sunnis of being too extreme (*ghuluw*). Interestingly, IS's theological production feeding its ideology has tended to silence most of its famous scholars since they joined the group, such as Turki Bin Ali, the Jordanian Omar Mahdi Zayden, or Abu Abd al-Rahman al-Shami. The group has committed to communicating its theological principles exclusively through its official apparatus, its Shari'a Committee, rather than through individuals. This was a strategic decision; in order to become the theological reference for the Salafi-jihadism movement, IS has avoided promoting any individual production in order to prevent potential defections or refutations. The group is acutely aware of just how damaging "ideological revisionism" can be for groups embracing the Salafi-jihadi ideology, especially in the era of social media. Abu Ya'qub al-Maqdisi's trial and its repercussion on social media confirm this threat and stress the inherent tension facing Salafi-jihadi groups when deciding the group's ideology and methodology between the prerogative of the *Emir* as the political ruler and military leader or the authority of the mufti as a theological reference.

In conclusion, after reaching its apex in 2014–2015, IS's ideological appeal has suffered important blows, both from the outside with the demise of its "physical Caliphate" and from the inside with the rise of internal divisions. Facing those challenges, the group's ideology has nonetheless demonstrated itself to be fluid, evolutional, and hence resilient. Its propaganda production adapted to the new stakes. Its latest productions described its territorial losses as evidence of God's trial (*ibtiliaa*), promoted patience (*sabr*) as the right attitude against hardship, and explained the depletion of its ranks as God's way of purging away the deserters, traitors, and extremists in the necessary quest toward theological purity. Therefore, in spite of its difficulties, IS will probably continue to inspire hope through propaganda, mirroring its 2009–2012 regression phase in Iraq.

References

Abu Hanieh H., Abu Ruhman M. (2015) *The Islamic State Organization: The Sunni Organization and the Struggle for Global Jihadism*. Amman: Friedrich-Ebert-Stiftung Jordan & Iraq.

Ait Yahya A. (2016) *Textes et Contexte du Wahabisme*. Paris: Nawa.

Baram A. (2014) *Saddam Husain and Islam, 1968–2003: Ba'thi Iraq from Secularism to Faith*. Baltimore: Johns Hopkins University Press.

Brynjar L. (2008) *Architect of Global Jihad: The Life of Al Qaeda Strategist Abu Musab al Suri*. New York: Columbia University Press.

Bunzel C. (2015) "From Paper State to Caliphate: The Ideology of the Islamic State," *The Brookings Project on US Relations with the Islamic World, Analysis Paper* 19.

Bunzel C. (2018) The Islamic State's Mufti on Trial: The Saga of the "Silsila 'Ilmiyya," *CTC Sentinel*: 14–17.

Commins D. (2015) "From Wahhabi to Salafi," In Haykel B., Hegghammer T., Lacroix S. (eds.), *Saudi Arabia in Transition: Insights on Social, Political, Economic and Religious Change*. New York: Cambridge University Press, pp. 151–166.

Crooke A. (2015, December 29) "Middle East Time Bomb: The Real Aim of ISIS Is to Replace the Saud Family as the New Emirs of Arabia," *Huffington Post*. http://www.huffingtonpost.com/alastair-crooke/isis-aim-saudi-arabia_b_5748744.html.

Esposito J. (2003) *Unholy War Terror in the Name of Islam*. Oxford: Oxford University Press.

Feldman N. (2008) *The Fall and Rise of the Islamic State*. Princeton, NJ: Princeton University Press.

Fishman B. (2016) *The Master Plan: ISIS, Al Qaeda and the Jihadi Strategy for Final Victory*. Yale University Press.

Hafez M. (2007) *Suicide Bombers in Iraq: The Strategy and Ideology of Martyrdom*. Washington: USIP Press Books.

Hamming T. R. (2017) "The Al Qaeda–Islamic State Rivalry: Competition Yes, but No Competitive Escalation," *Terrorism & Political Violence*. Online before print.

Hegghammer T. (2010) *Jihad in Saudi Arabia: Violence and Pan-Islamism Since 1979*. Cambridge: Cambridge University Press.

Hegghammer T., Lacroix S. (2007) "Rejectionist Islamism in Saudi Arabia: The Story of Juhayman al-'Utaybi revisited," *International Journal of Middle East Studies* 39: 103–122.

Lacroix S. (2010) *Awakening Islam: The Politics of Religious Dissent in Contemporary Saudi Arabia*. Cambridge, MA: Harvard University Press.

Lahoud N. (2010) *The Jihadis' Path to Self-Destruction*. New York: Columbia University Press/Hurst.

Lauzière H., Barkey K. (2016) *The Making of Salafism: Islamic Reform in the Twentieth Century*. New York: Columbia University Press. http://www.jstor.org/stable/10.7312/lauz17550.

Maher S. (2016) *Salafi-Jihadism: The History of an Idea*. London: Hurst.

Mandaville P. (2009) *Global Political Islam*. London: Routledge.

McCants W. (2015) *The ISIS Apocalypse*. Washington: St Martin's Press.

Miller N. (2015, October 3) "Global Terror 'Family' Baqiya a Growing Concern for Security," *The Sydney Morning Herald*. Retrieved from http://www.smh.com.au/world/global-terror-family-baqiya-a-growing-concern-for-security-20151002-gk0fq5.html.

Orton K. (2015, December 23) "How Saddam Gave Us ISIS," *The New York Times*. http://mobile.nytimes.com/2015/12/23/opinion/how-saddam-hussein-gave-us-isis.html?src=twr&_r=1&referer=https://t.co/2nyZcLSEda.

Qutb S. (1982) *Ma'aalim fi al-Tareeq*. Cairo/Beirut: Dar al-Shuruq.

Rahmena A. (2005) *Pioneers of Islamic Revival*. New York: Zed Books.

Wagemakers J. (2009) "A Purist Jihadi-Salafi: The Ideology of Abu Muhammad al-Maqdisi," *British Journal of Middle Eastern Studies* 36(2): 281–297.

Wagemakers J. (2012) *A Quietist Jihadi: The Ideology and Influence of Abu Muhammad Al-Maqdisi*. Cambridge: Cambridge University Press.

Whiteside C. (2017) "A Pedigree of Terror: The Myth of the Ba'athist Influence in the Islamic State Movement," *Perspectives on Terrorism* 11(3): 2–18.

Winter C. (2017) "War by Suicide: A Statistical Analysis of the Islamic State's Martyrdom Industry," *ICCT Working Paper*. Retrieved from https://icct.nl/wp-content/uploads/2017/02/ICCT-Winter-War-by-Suicide-Feb2017.pdf.

Zelin A. (2015) "From the Archduke to the Islamic State, The Islamist Evolution that Led to the Islamic State," in Fraser T. (ed.), *The First World War and Its Aftermath: The Shaping of the Modern Middle East*. Chicago: University of Chicago Press, pp. 159–173.

3

The Matrix of Islamic State's Propaganda

Magazines

Stephane J. Baele, Katharine A. Boyd, and Travis G. Coan

Introduction: IS Magazines in Context

As explained in the preceding chapters, the Islamic State (IS) rapidly grew an ambition to develop a comprehensive and multidimensional propaganda machine, and, in this effort, magazines came to play a pivotal role at the center of the group's propaganda web. This chapter describes and analyzes this role.

IS is not the first extremist organization to publish magazines—in fact this method of appealing to sympathizers and spreading a group's message has been used by many groups in the past. In 1970, the Weather Underground issued the communiqué *New Morning, Changing Weather* that was "longer, trading slang and swagger for detail and documentation," thereby altering the format from what was used in previous public statements and setting a new trend in the type of output disseminated by radical political groups (Berger 2006: 159). The Afghan *Mujāhidīn* of the 1980s published numerous magazines, including some in Western languages, to attract fighters in their struggle against the Soviet Union. More recently, al-Qaeda issued magazines such as *Sada al-Malahim* in Arabic and *Inspire* in English to appeal to diverse populations, which was then emulated by, among others, the Taliban in Khurasan's *Azan* (2013) and the Mujahideen of Shaam in *Al Risālah* (2015), both of which are in English (see Ingram 2015, 2017). In other words, magazines have become frequent components of extremist groups' communications, including within the broad Salafi-jihadist movement.

Since the Internet has become ubiquitous and magazines can circulate online, their content and reach have dramatically changed. The advent of the web and IT more generally dramatically improved the quality of magazines (as compared to paper leaflets hastily manufactured and disseminated),

Stephane J. Baele, Katharine A. Boyd, and Travis Coan, *The Matrix of Islamic State's Propaganda: Magazines* In: *ISIS Propaganda*. Edited by: Stephane J. Baele, Katharine A. Boyd, and Travis G. Coan, Oxford University Press (2020) © University of Maryland National Consortium for the Study of Terrorism and Responses to Terrorism (START)
DOI: 10.1093/oso/9780190932459.003.0004

and, soon enough, a focus on developing and issuing attractive online propaganda became a main jihadist strategy (read for example Torres Soriano 2011). Access to technology, IT, and publishing skills to create effective communications has thus become key to group success.

In this context, while the quality and formatting style of magazines produced by IS is quite remarkable, it is not too far from its direct predecessors or contemporaries such as *Inspire*—so the group's innovation does not lie here. Rather, IS has successfully copied this genre and brought it to another level in two main ways. First, it successfully integrated this component into its full-spectrum propaganda system, making systematic efforts to integrate magazines within the broader propaganda web. As we show later (and as also mentioned in Chapter 6), these magazines occupy a pivotal position in this comprehensive propaganda system as they direct audiences to other platforms by discussing videos, linking up to new apps, or advertising books. Second, IS implemented a quantitative shift in publishing a series of different magazines to appeal to specific populations, thus expanding the "theater of terror" to a range of new spectators of this "symbolic communication" (Bhui & Ibrahim 2013: 226).[1] As discussed in Chapter 1, different IS magazines use varying proportions and types of rational- and identity-choice messaging to target specific audiences with multidimensional objectives (tactical, operational, and strategic).

This chapter discusses the main features of these magazines, focusing on the language and images used to promote the group's "master narrative," to reach specific target audiences, to establish links with other components of the group's full-spectrum propaganda, and to tap into mechanisms of radicalization. It is important, however, to qualify what information can and cannot be derived from IS magazines. We can describe trends in the data, but without more information from magazine producers, we cannot conclusively explain their decision-making processes. We occasionally speculate about the producers' motivations given information that is known about the group and battles being fought, but we must emphasize that we cannot be fully conclusive. Similarly, we pose potential causal connections between the content published in IS magazines and the effects on audiences. We cannot, however, assess the effect these magazines had on generating sympathizers, recruiting operatives, or mobilizing opposition, to name a few possibilities.

---

[1] See Weimann & Winn (1994) and Jenkins (1975) for discussions of how modern terrorism is a means of communication through violence.

We do not know how many people accessed the magazines, let alone how many read them or shared them with others. Even if we had accurate data on recruitment, it is impossible for us to isolate the effect of a single propaganda tool when each tool is integrated into a mutually reinforcing, full-spectrum propaganda apparatus. As a result, the causal inferences in this chapter and the book as a whole are only tentative, drawing on existing social science research to reinforce potential explanations.

IS Magazines: Many Publications for Many Audiences

As mentioned earlier, one of the key innovations of IS in contrast to most other terrorist groups has been to publish a range of different magazines. These magazines typically circulate online as high-quality PDFs, which are first uploaded to Internet platforms such as Archive.org and then disseminated through social media (Telegram, or, earlier, Twitter). The organization publishes both in Arabic and in a series of foreign languages, thereby expanding its propaganda net to include several different audiences, each time tailoring the content and style of the magazines.

On the one hand, publications in Arabic aim to target an audience which is either local (Syria, Iraq) or regional (e.g., Egypt, Jordan). The group's main Arabic publication is al-Naba' (meaning "The Announcement"), whose outline stands between a magazine and a newspaper (see Figure 3.1). In terms of appearance, al-Naba' is slightly more austere than IS's foreign-language magazines, focusing more on news stories. The first al-Naba' was released by IS on August 13, 2012, and the magazine was still being released at the time of writing, with Issue 193 made available in August 2019. More anecdotally, IS also started an unofficial publication of a new magazine in Arabic, al-Waqār, whose first issue was released on October 14, 2016, and the second (and, as of yet, last) issue was released just 10 days later. The magazine had a similar newsletter appearance as al-Naba'. Due to its few issues, it is yet unclear what this magazine was supposed to be in terms of its status and specific audience.

On the other hand, IS also publishes magazines in a series of foreign languages through its al-Hayat Media Center, this time targeting a series of different audiences outside the Middle East. The al-Hayat Media Center, a central media office dedicated to the production of propaganda items in non-Arabic languages (see also next chapter), created the Dabiq magazine written in English, the Dar al-Islam in French, the Istok in Russian, and the

Figure 3.1 Front cover (left) and typical page (right) of *al-Naba'* (here no. 58).

Konstantiniyye in Turkish. According to an IS defector interviewed in the *Washington Post, Dabiq*'s editorial office was located in a house in a residential area near Aleppo, where armed guards manned the entry and restricted access to few beyond the regional media emir (Miller & Mekhennet 2015). The rooms of the house had equipment for magazine production, including computers and cameras, where centralized propaganda strategy was distilled into glossy, high-quality magazines. In these magazines, IS infuses transliterated Arabic words into a major language to create a unique linguistic style conveying the group's stories (the various quotes from the magazines inserted in this chapter are typical examples), which has a polarizing effect on an audience—either one is part of the group and understands the Arabic references, or one is out of it and finds this language incomprehensible. This particular language is also a marker and producer of the broader IS "culture," in the way that the group members share a specific, recognizable way of communicating. IS magazines differ from other extremist groups' magazines, in part, by predominantly featuring unattributed articles—the authors are usually not specified. Within al-Hayat Media Center, the magazines are composed relying extensively on quotes from Islamic texts and are written in a consistent, monolithic style. The magazines are also filled with quotes from religious texts that are tedious to read, suggesting that IS does not target the impromptu reader. With the extensive use of quotes, the unattributed authorship gives the text a level of credibility and legitimacy as speaking as religious authority.

In addition to discussing the virtues of the Caliphate (*Khilāfah*) and the battles carried out by IS (some of this content being replicated in the different languages of the magazines), each of these magazines also directs extensive commentary about its specific target audience. For example, *Konstantiniyye* featured articles denouncing the Turkish president Recep Tayyip Erdogan, the PKK, and the Peoples' Democratic Party (HDP), while *Dar al-Islam* featured testimonies of Francophone IS fighters or relatives of the Paris attackers and displayed pictures of François Hollande. In that way, IS fulfilled its strategic logic to position its cohesive, central narrative within a relevant context for diverse audiences. These non-Arabic magazines show how IS propaganda sought to appeal to a wide international audience on a scale not seen by any prior terrorist group. More recently, however, in late 2016, the group replaced all these publications with the unique *Rumiyah* magazine, a tighter, more unified magazine that borrows content from other platforms and requires fewer production hours (but has nonetheless been released in various languages simultaneously).[2] This followed the last *Dabiq*, which was issued in July 2016, which was 109 days after the previous issue (the longest duration between issues, which had previously averaged 50 days between) and after the significant loss of Fallujah. Magazines in other languages stopped being issued at a similar time, with *Rumiyah* replacing these distinct magazines with a single publication issued in several languages. This served the purpose of maintaining scope and cohesion through reducing location-specific points, while reducing resource needs as the group needed to adapt to its "bust" period, IS losing territorial control since October 2015 (see Chapter 1 in this volume).[3]

---

[2] *Rumiyah* have been released in English, French, Russian, and German, as well as Indonesian and Uyghur.
[3] The size of the Khilāfah (estimated by month by Le Monde, available at: https://www.lemonde.fr/les-decodeurs/visuel/2017/03/13/comment-l-etat-islamique-a-recule-en-irak-et-en-syrie-depuis-2014_5093896_4355770.html) changed dramatically during the period in which IS was producing magazines, being 136,242 km² in June 2014 and reaching its largest size of 250,133 km² in December 2014 (when *Dabiq* no. 6 was issued); there has been a consistent decline in size since October 2015 (the month before *Dabiq* no. 12 was issued). The size of the *Khilāfah* is only one of the factors that contribute to IS's perception of "boom" and "bust," but it is one tangible measure that may reasonably help explain changes in propaganda strategies.

Table 3.1 Descriptive Information for Islamic State Magazines

Magazine	Title interpretation	Total number of issues	Duration of magazine	Average length
al-Naba' (Arabic)	The Announcement	86	Aug 2012–current	16 pages
Al-Waqār (Arabic)	Dignity, Lordliness	2	Oct 2016	22 pages
Dabiq (English)	Eschatological place in Syria[1]	15	July 2014–July 2016	61 pages
Dar Al Islam (French)	House or abode of Islam[2]	10	Dec 2014–Aug 2016	44 pages
Istok (Russian)	The Source	4	May 2015–May 2016	45 pages
Konstantiniyye (Turkish)	Transliteration of the Ottoman spelling of "Constantinople"	7	June 2015–Aug 2016	59 pages
Rumiyah (10 languages)	Rome	13	Sept 2016–September 2017	45 pages

[1] Dabiq is said to be the place of the eschatological battle that will see the final defeat of Muslims' enemies.

[2] Dār al-Islām, or literally the "house/land of Islam," is defined as "the divinely flawless abode of devout, pious Muslims" (Matusitz & Olufowote 2016: 29).

Table 3.1 provides key information on these magazines, while Figure 3.2 offers a snapshot of these publications. In addition to these magazines, the *Islamic State News* (*ISN*) and *Islamic State Report* (*ISR*) were short English-language publications with brief news stories, lots of photos, and very little text. These included 1–2 pages per province (*Wilāya*), together providing an overview of the main actions taken by IS across its territory. *ISN* and *ISR* were both test-run publications from the summer of 2014 that were quickly cast aside, with *ISN* having only three issues and *ISR* four. These were issued soon before *Dabiq* was released, after which these short publications were discontinued, suggesting that IS learned from feedback or changed strategic goals to appeal to English-speakers with more developed and content-rich magazines. Figure 3.3 shows an example of a page in *ISN*.

In spite of their roles in targeting particular audiences, IS magazines are not only important in their own right, but also importantly serve as

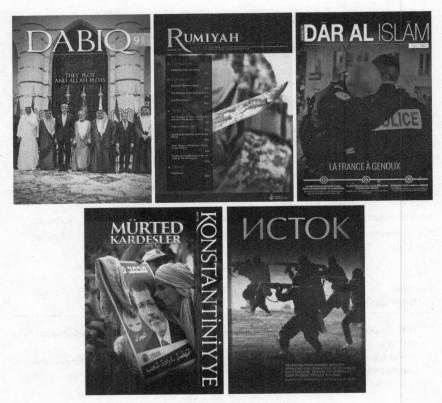

Figure 3.2 Front covers of the main foreign language magazines: *Dabiq* (no. 9), *Rumyiah* (no. 2), *Dar al-Islam* (no. 7), *Konstantiniyye* (no. 6), and *Istok* (no. 4).

central nodes in the comprehensive network of IS propaganda production. Magazines systematically advertise for other components, such as al-Himmah literary publications or new videos (see Figure 3.4). As described in Chapters 1 and 4, *Dabiq* and *Rumiyah* magazines typically contain pages dedicated to the "Selected 10" ("must see" top 10 videos) or the "Featured Videos from the *Wilāyāt* of the Islamic State—presented by *Al-Hayat*" (top 3 videos in non-Arabic languages).[4] This shows how IS magazines do not exist in a vacuum, but instead serve as a port of entry to the wider universe of

---

[4] The "Selected 10" are listed in *Dabiq* no. 9–15 and then in *Rumiyah* no. 1, and "Featured Videos" feature in *Rumiyah* no. 8–11.

Figure 3.3 Example of a page from *Islamic State News* (no. 3 p. 2).

propaganda material that is self-supporting, reiterating, repeating, and utilizes the same narratives, images, and content across platforms.

Constructing Crisis–Solution Narratives Through Language and Images

IS's magazines convey their messages through a sophisticated interaction of their textual and pictorial content, whereby images reinforce language and conversely. Over time, the organization has made a series of adjustments to its use of both images and language due to material constraints (expanding then shrinking capacities and territory) and strategic considerations (e.g., emphasis on soft "pull" images depicting the ideal *Khilāfah* versus hard gruesome images picturing dead enemies) in a way that directly

Figure 3.4 Examples of cross-medium advertisement in Islamic State magazines: Advert in *Rumyiah* for an *Al-Himmah* publication (left) and for *Al-Hayat* videos (right).

echoes Ingram's analysis of the logic of the group's information operations developed in Chapter 1. Focusing on *Dabiq* and *Rumiyah* magazines, we see that the proportion of images and words per page for each magazine differs over time. Figure 3.5 shows that the proportion of words per page generally increasing across the 15 *Dabiq* magazines, with the number of images per page following a less clear trajectory. *Dabiq* magazines, generally speaking, grew increasingly larger, with more pages and more images and words in total and per page. *Rumiyah* are different, evidencing the group's decision to downscale and simplify the message, presumably to adapt to the group's operational problems and new strategic priorities. These magazines are usually shorter than *Dabiq*, with fewer images (in count and per page, but also in terms of originality, with *Rumiyah* containing more generic pictures and images already used in the past) and fewer words.[5] This downscaling allowed

---

[5] On average, *Dabiq* has 99 images per issue (1.67 per page), while *Rumiyah* has 44 (0.98 per page). In contrast, *Rumiyah* has fewer words on average (~22,700 words per issue compared to ~25,500 for *Dabiq*, though there is greater variation across issues), though more words per page (~500 per page for *Rumiyah* and ~403 per page for *Dabiq*).

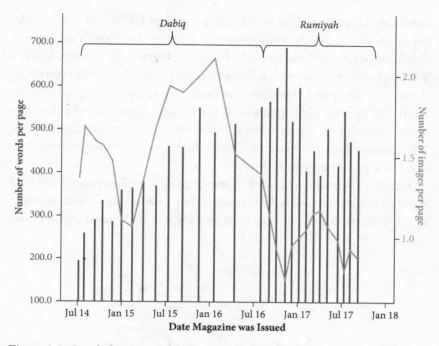

Figure 3.5 Graph depiction of when *Dabiq* and *Rumiyah* magazines were released and the number of words per page (left axis, discrete bars) and images per page (right axis, continuous line) for each issue.

the group to issue *Rumiyah* at more frequent and consistent intervals than more voluminous *Dabiq*.

Through these images and language, the magazines tell stories that together form what Halverson, Goodall, and Corman (2011) call a "master narrative," that is, "a coherent system of interrelated and sequentially organized stories that share a common rhetorical desire to resolve a conflict by establishing audience expectations according to the known trajectories of its literary and rhetorical form" (2011: 14).[6] IS magazines indeed reiterate a very limited series of storylines which, when repeated and articulated together, define the culture of the group and provide a general framework for how actions by IS and others should be interpreted. Through a systematic interaction of images and language, they tie ideological interpretation to the larger

---

[6] Halverson, Goodall, and Corman (2011) offer a thorough depiction of master narratives used by Islamist extremists.

historical and cultural dogma to provide a general framework—the master narrative—that explains who people are and how individuals and groups should behave, sometimes violently. Following Ingram (2016; also Chapter 1 in this volume), we understand this master narrative, which is therefore both at once *descriptive* and *prescriptive*, as having two sides: one emphasizing the severity of an allegedly ongoing *crisis* (which corresponds to what is sometimes referred to as the narrative's "initial situation") and one arguing that IS holds the *solution* to this crisis (which corresponds to what is sometimes referred to as the narrative's "final situation").

In terms of language, a network approach using the full corpus of *Dabiq* and *Rumiyah* magazines reveals the presence of this twofold crisis–solution master narrative. Figure 3.6 displays the most frequent words of these magazines and

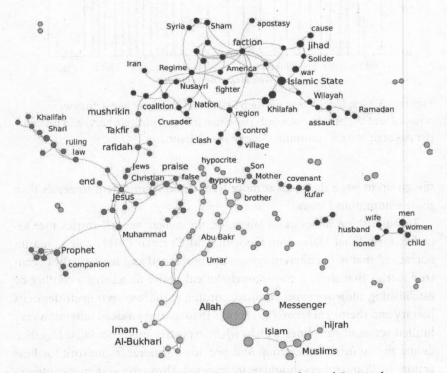

Figure 3.6 Co-occurrence network of language in *Dabiq* and *Rumiyah* magazines. The figure shows communities that were derived from the text data with the size of each circle (node) representing the number of occurrences of a word and the distance between the circles representing how closely in the text the words represented by the nodes tend to co-occur.

helps visualize the way they tend to co-occur (terms that frequently co-occur are grouped in "communities," or clusters, assuming that words that frequently co-occur either share a common meaning or are part of a relevant theme). One major cluster stands out (top of graph), formed by words relating to IS's perceived enemies ("Crusaders," "Nusayri," "Regime," etc.) and IS's war and violence against them ("jihad," "war," "fighter," etc.). Right underneath it, two large communities are formed by religious words (names of prominent *hadith* writers, names of the prophet, etc.) serving a legitimation purpose, and references to the Caliphate and its supposed positive attributes (e.g., *sharīʿa*). Using the statistics underpinning the network, we tallied the verbs associated with, on the one hand, IS or sympathizing subgroups (e.g., *mujāhidīn*) as the subject, and, on the other hand, enemies as the subject, to compare frequency of violence-related words and then to determine whether IS magazines discuss violence as a solution (against enemies) more than violence as a crisis (conducted by enemies). We found that IS-related groups are associated with more violent verbs used in greater frequency (8.8% of cases), compared to enemies who are associated with fewer violence-related verbs, which were used less (3.3% of the cases). This means the organization tends to stress the need for a violent solution more than the crisis of violent deeds by the enemy, as already highlighted by Ingram (2016). Although the United States and other out-groups are described as harming the *ummah* (e.g., "the USA decided to get involved once again in the affairs of the Muslim Ummah by conducting airstrikes against the Islamic State and its people," *Dabiq* no. 3 p. 3), IS also often describes its own violence toward its out-groups. For example, an article with John Cantlie as the byline states: "We have four dead young Americans" in an article discussing the United States and the United Kingdom's misguided resolve not to negotiate (*Dabiq* no. 14 p. 55). Another article describing military operations by IS describes "an Islamic State covert unit [that] planted and detonated an explosive device on a vehicle carrying four American soldiers" (*Rumiyah* no. 4 p. 35). Comparing words per sentence referring to the United States and the more general net of "crusaders," we found that IS featured references to the United States in greater proportion in many *Dabiq* issues, while in the *Rumiyah* there was no single issue that referred to the United States more than the "crusaders."

Figure 3.7 adds granularity to this overall picture. It displays the results of a correspondence analysis that situates the relationship between the most frequent words of these magazines and the various issues of the magazines. In other words, it reveals words' appearance patterns and in which magazines they tend to occur more frequently. This allows us to see that *Dabiq*

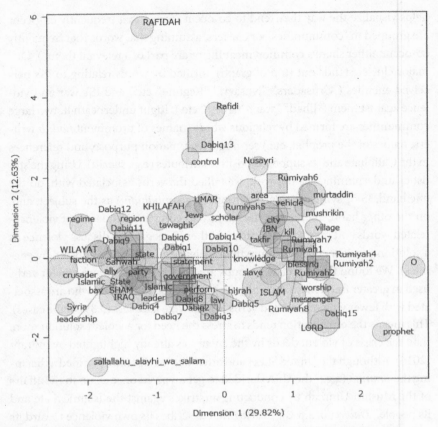

Figure 3.7 Bubble plot representing a correspondence analysis of the most frequent words in *Dabiq* (nos. 1–15) and *Rumiyah* (nos. 1–8) magazines, located on the basis of their relative saliences in each issue of the two magazines.

1–12 overall share a coherent lexical field and that there is a rupture with *Dabiq* 13, with *Dabiq* 15 to *Rumiyah* 8 sharing a different lexical field. The various dimensions of this difference are unpacked later.

In terms of images, IS magazines contain a lot of images that further accentuate the main crisis–solution master narrative conveyed by the text—in fact, some analysts even consider the text to be secondary to the pictures. As Matusitz and Olufowote, for example, argue (2016: 18), the imagery used is "the main channel for the creation and dissemination of jihadist ideas," contributing to expand the base of sympathizers and recruit new members (see also Milton 2016). As previous work on political images highlighted, pictures

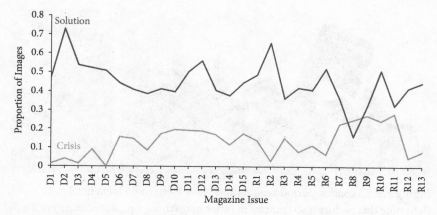

Figure 3.8 Proportion of images conveying *crisis* versus *solution* narratives across Islamic State English-speaking magazines.

"can help build or reinforce a moral position" (Campbell 2003: 72) within "an appropriate context of feeling and attitude" (Sontag 1977), and so do IS's visuals reinforce the narratives that suit the group agenda, often with captions that make the connection explicit. We conducted a coding-based visual analysis of images (with related captions) in *Dabiq* and *Rumiyah* magazines,[7] coding images as supporting either a crisis (e.g., Crusaders bomb innocent civilians, "fake" Muslim scholars corrupt Islam) or a solution (e.g., IS fighters conduct successful military operations, IS officials efficiently conduct government tasks) narrative.[8] Figure 3.8 shows that images supporting the solution dimension of the group's master narrative are systematically more numerous than those supporting a crisis diagnosis (with a single exception), again echoing Ingram's (2016) study that claimed that IS propaganda tends to focus on the solution rather than the crisis, even if this preference has tended to erode in the later magazine issues.

As highlighted in several chapters of this volume, IS's visual style is infused with symbolism, which serves to reinforce the argument that there is a crisis but more predominantly the group's claim to be the legitimate and efficient provider of the solution. The black flag, also called the "Black Banner" or

[7] A thorough description of the methodology used to code the data will be available in an upcoming paper (Baele, Boyd, & Coan 2019).

[8] Solution narratives, listed in order of frequency, include IS fighters engaging in violent jihad, utopian IS Caliphate, IS punishing enemies, and IS offering absolution unity. Crisis narratives include collusion and plotting by out-groups, the sinful enemy, Muslim victims of enemy actions, and the West occupying the holy land.

Figure 3.9 Crusades-period knights and black flag, from *Dabiq* no. 8 p. 12 (left: note this picture also features in other magazines, e.g., *Konstantiniyye* no. 3, as do many "generic" or symbolic visuals), and *Dar al-Islam* no. 10 p. 16 (right).

"Black Standard," is for instance omnipresent throughout IS magazines, with its black color symbolizing "piousness and unconditional obedience" in Islam (Matusitz & Olufowote 2016: 27), its writing at the top of the flag saying the *shahada* ("declaration of faith"), and its white circle representing the Prophet Muhammad's seal that states "Muhammad is the messenger of God" (Kovacs 2015: 55), the flag directly evokes the filiation of IS with Muhammad's own *jihād* against infidels. Several *hadith*s further state that armies would carry the black banner to change the world, which IS emphasizes to increase its "prophetic resonance" (Matusitz & Olufowote 2016: 29).[9] There are no less than 222 images that feature the black flag in the *Dabiq* and *Rumiyah* magazines, with the first *Dabiq* issue having by far the most black flag images (more than one-third of the total images in that issue) to make the prophetic filiation symbolically as obvious as possible; then, the use of the black flag in English-speaking magazines gradually decreased over time (*Rumiyah* no. 5 had for example only a single black flag image, making up ~2% of the images in that issue).

The sword is another prominent symbol that features in many IS magazine images. Gråtrud (2016) explains that "the sword has important symbolic meaning in Islamist culture," connecting contemporary "jihad to the first generation of Muslim warriors" and ultimately to Muhammad (Gråtrud

---

[9] These *hadith*s are Ahmad in al-Musnad, 14/383, Abd al-'Alim in al-Mahdi al-Muntazar, Nuaim Ibn Hammad in Kitab al-Fitan, Al-Barzanji in Isha'ah li Ashrat al-Sa'a, and Sunan Ibn Majah, 4084. For more information, see Soufan (2011), *The Black Banners*, and see 'Athamina (1989) for an exploration of the roots and mythical and messianic dimensions of this symbol.

2016: 1064). Relatedly, images of ancient warriors are frequent in IS magazines (see Figure 3.9), again to promote their current fight as part of a historic battle against blasphemy and corruption. Another symbol used in IS magazines is the orange "Guantanamo jumpsuit" (Lombardi 2015: 106). In the 28 issues of *Dabiq* and *Rumiyah*, there were 54 images that included the orange jumpsuit (which is also frequent in IS's videos; see next chapter), which serve to accentuate simultaneously IS's crisis and solution narratives. First, this symbol serves to remind the audience of the sins perpetrated by the "crusader" enemy (crisis dimension). Second, the use of this outfit, particularly for prisoners who are being executed, is a symbol that IS effectively exerts direct revenge for harms against Muslims perpetrated by the Western enemy (solution). This powerful symbolic reappropriation reinforces the branding of IS as the solution provider to the crisis allegedly facing Muslims.

The following sections look in more depth at how the magazines describe these crises (provoked by alleged presence of two radically opposed social groups, one fundamentally good [the in-group] and the other one bad [the out-group]) and solutions (on the one hand the necessity to use violence against the out-group to destroy it and end its nefarious actions, on the other hand the supposed existence of a perfect, utopian political entity—the Caliphate—where the out-group is not present).

Crisis: Fundamental Antagonism Between the In-Group and the Out-Group

Language

In its magazines, IS's main rhetorical instrument in the construction of a deep sense of crisis is its efforts to depict the world in a sharply dichotomous way, where two fundamentally incompatible groups co-exist: on the one hand, an in-group of "true" Muslims trying to live their faith without being persecuted and, on the other hand, a vast and composite out-group of all other people including the "West" (and chiefly Americans), the Shi'a, the unauthentic *taghūt* regimes, and apostate governments ruling Arab countries. Table 3.2 shows the frequencies of the main in- and out-group labels used in the *Dabiq* and *Rumiyah* magazines; notice that the in-group is overwhelmingly identified as the "Muslims," which corresponds to IS's strategy to depict itself as unambiguously Islamic, thereby labeling its members as Muslim as

Table 3.2 Labels Used to Describe In- and Out-Groups in *Dabiqs* and *Rumiyah* Magazines and Their Total Occurrences

In-group label	Number of occurrences	Out-group label	Number of occurrences
Muslim*	2,243	Crusader*	1,032
Islamic State	1,588	Murtadd*	856
Khilafah*	1,252	Rafid*	700
Mujahid*	1,091	Scholars	508
Brother*	798	Kuffar (Kafir)	382
Believer*	443	Taghut (tawaghit)	672
Ummah	312	Enem*	654
Muhajir*	216	Apostate*	450
Istishhadi*	192	Mushrik*	441
Shuhada	95	Nusayri*	311
Martyr*	77	Jew*	340
Inghimasi*	109	Christian*	305
Muwahhid*	171	American*	297
Sister*	151	United States	206
Lion*	62	Sahwah	271
		Coalition*	214
		Russia*	206
		Disbeliever*	197
		Jawlani	177
		West*	167
		Iran*	167
		Sahwat	152
		Jahili	115
		Safawi*	114
		Turkey	114
		Al Qaidah/Qaeda	156
		Pakistan	110
		Taliban	104
		Europe*	102
		Munafiq	116
		Khawarij*	70
		Kurd*	84
		Sufi*	70
		Peshmerga	66
		Jordan	63

Table 3.2 *Continued*

In-group label	Number of occurrences	Out-group label	Number of occurrences
		Shi'ah	54
		Al-Nusrah	53
		"Islamists"	50
		Murjiah	47
		Australian*	47
		Tunisia	47
		France/French	46
		FSA	43
		Qatar	36
		Puppet	36
		United Nations	35
		Egypt/Egyptian	34
		Secularists	29
		Algeria	29
		Sodomite*	25

Only labels cited more than 25 times are included.

much as possible in order to characterize the Muslims who do not endorse or join IS as de facto non-Muslims (labeling them as *murtaddīn*, *rāfiḍa*, etc.).

As mentioned, the out-group is more composite, reflecting the diversity of groups excommunicated (*takfīr*) by IS: on the one hand, the *kuffār* (disbelievers), the *ṭaghūt* regimes or organizations, and non-Sunni Muslims (*rāfiḍa*, *safawi*), and, on the other hand, the "crusaders" and Americans (as well as the "Jews"), the "West," and "disbelievers" in general. These out-groups thus perpetuate the near enemy/far enemy distinction and articulation that is central to many thinkers in Salafi-jihadism (see Chapter 2). Figure 3.10 shows the proportion of words in *Dabiq* and *Rumiyah* referring to these two families of out-groups.[10] Overall, references to the near and far enemies are roughly as frequent, although far enemies have tended to feature proportionally more often in the initial *Dabiq* issues, while near enemies have become proportionally more prominent in *Rumiyah*. This slight change in focus from the far

---

[10] The lexicon and automated content analysis used to generate this figure are available on Github at https://github.com/traviscoan.

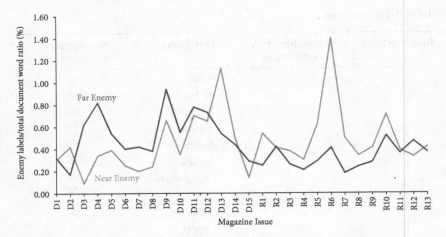

Figure 3.10 Proportion of words labeling the near and far enemy out-groups in *Dabiq* and *Rumiyah* magazines.

to the near enemy, which runs against what many intelligence officers often assume, may reflect the operational goals of IS as it has been battling to maintain territory against near enemies in more recent years (leading to more reports from the battlefield), whereas during times of boom it made more and lengthier efforts to assert a negative depiction of the far enemy being responsible for the crisis.

IS's aim, when using this sort of language in its magazines, is to convince readers that indeed the world is binarily divided between good and evil and that standing somewhere in the middle is no longer an option. IS magazines continuously reassert this state of affairs, stressing the negative characteristics and nefarious actions of the out-group and the positive traits and good deeds of the in-group. This crisis diagnosis infuses the majority of the magazines articles and is sometimes the central topic of longer interventions—for example, one *Dabiq* is entitled "The End of the Grey Zone" and features a paper stating the impossibility of being in a "grey zone" between the radical Islamist project IS promotes and its perceived enemies.

This use of impermeable binary group language is a textbook instance of the central dynamics of intergroup conflict as described by social identity scholars in psychology (from Tajfel, Billig, Bundy, & Flament 1971; see, e.g., Hewstone & Cairns 2001; Huddy 2004; Tajfel & Turner 2004). This theoretical approach suggests that individuals naturally engage in a process of categorization, of themselves and others, into social groups. The use of binary language can influence this process by reifying these group categories into sharply separated groups and attributing to them essentialist characteristics (the in-group is associated with good and virtuous traits, while the out-group is qualified by corrupt and depraved characteristics). Dualistic and polarizing language further enhances the "group homogenization effect," whereby people naturally tend to amplify perceived similarities within their in-group and within the out-groups, further distinguishing these categories. In other words, the use of sharply binary language seeks to merge the personal identity of the reader with the allegedly all-positive collective identity of an in-group while demonizing the out-group, thereby creating a simplistic worldview where the latter can be blamed for any social problem. In extreme examples such as IS magazines (but also in Nazi anti-Semitic propaganda or extremist Hutu radio shows, for example), such language ends up dehumanizing the out-group, which serves to facilitate selective moral disengagement for inhumane conduct (Bandura 2002 explains how moral disengagement comes from "cognitive restructuring"). The language used in IS magazines constantly operates the out-group versus in-group division, and distinct out-groups are characterized by unique characteristics. For example, "Jews" are uniquely associated with typical anti-Semitic adjective such as "sly" and "deceitful," while derogative nouns used for non-Sunni Muslims like *Nusayri*, *Rāfiḍa*, or *Safawi* frequently come with adjectives referring to their allegedly impure character, such as "filthy." Consider, for example, the following quote, where a stark contrast is made between the supposedly depraved West and the allegedly virtuous Caliphate:

> When you're in Dar al-Kufr [the lands of disbelief] you're exposing yourself and your children to so much filth and corruption. You make it easy for Satan to lead you astray. Here you're living a pure life, and your children are being raised with plenty of good influence around them. (*Dabiq* no. 15 p. 39)

IS qualifies the relationships between various out-groups with insolent descriptive labels and insists that these out-groups plot together against Muslims. Specifically, IS frequently calls those deemed apostate Muslims as "puppets" or "lapdogs" of the "crusaders" in the West. In the first issue of *Dabiq*, the writers argued that IS faces "the camp of kufr (disbelief) and hypocrisy . . . , the camp of the jews, the crusaders, their allies, and with them the rest of the nations and religions of kufr, all being led by America and Russia, and being mobilized by the jews" (*Dabiq* no. 1, p.11). According to IS, this exploitive manipulation is facilitated by "fake" Muslims' greed and vice-ridden desires that make them susceptible to the depraved influence of the corrupt Western leaders. As such, IS's depiction of the out-groups exceeds the sort of simple binary depictions theorized by social identity scholars: it adds a conspiratorial element that connects the out-group(s) together in complex relationships and blames them for the current state of affairs that is perceived as oppressive (e.g., American troops in Muslim lands, discriminations against Muslims in Western countries, bombings of Muslims across the world, etc.) and sinful (gradual erosion of the Muslim faith, corrupt ways of living, etc.). Many current events are depicted by IS in a convoluted manner that postulates unlikely alliances (between the West and "moderate Muslims," between *ṭaghūt* leaders and more mainstream salafi scholars, etc.) in an effort to tie loose ends together in a simplistic crisis diagnosis. The following quote is typical in this respect.

> The various apostate puppet regimes set up by the crusaders after the colonial era [fly] ... the "Arab Revolt" flag... that today represent different Arab nationalist states. .... These jahili flags essentially represent the crusaders, their apostate agents, Arab nationalism, and the puppet tawaghit loyal to the crusaders. (*Dabiq* no. 9 p. 22)[11]

Imagery

Images play a significant role in constructing this dichotomous and conspiratorial worldview. Only 10% of the images in the *Dabiq* and *Rumiyah* magazines do not depict a clearly distinguished in- or out-group. Of the rest, magazines depict the out-group members less than the in-group (37% vs. 53%), confirming the group's general preference to present itself as the provider of the solution rather than diagnosing the crisis.[12] Figure 3.11 shows

[11] The Arab nationalist states listed in this quote are Algeria, Egypt, Iraq, Jordan, Kuwait, Libya, Sudan, Syria, United Arab Emirates, Yemen, Palestine, Somalia, Morocco, Mali, and Iran, and the Ba'th party and its Naqshabandi "army."

[12] Images that do not have in- or out-group members depicted include photos of landscapes or the cosmos. Also note that some images include member of both the in- and out-group. In these photos we coded the party conducting the action being carried out (e.g., execution).

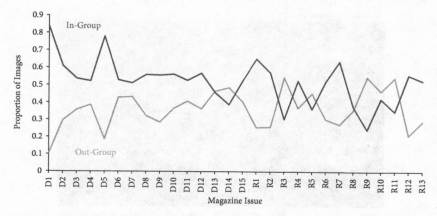

Figure 3.11 Proportion of images representing the in- and out-groups in *Dabiq* and *Rumiyah* magazines.

there are only seven magazine issues where there are more images of out-group than in-group members, yet five of these are *Rumiyah*, evidencing a shift in the group's messaging.

The magazines feature images illustrating the description of out-groups as sinful or engaging in blasphemous activity (66 such images in total [out of 2,058] in the English-language magazines). For example, *Dabiq* no. 15 features a number of images referring to gay pride and advocacy for LGBTQ rights with captions demonizing such behavior (see Figure 3.12). One image shows a child at a parade holding a poster that states: "My 2 moms are married!" with the caption: "An example of the perversion the West seeks to spread" (*Dabiq* no. 15 p. 32). In addition to disapproving Western "depraved" practices such as homosexuality, IS condemns other behaviors that do not follow their interpretation of Islam or suit their stringent lifestyle restrictions, and it disapproves of other religions and their practices of worship, especially non-IS aligned Islam. There are, for instance, numerous photos of Shi'a groups carrying out bloody mortification of their flesh by whipping or worshiping covered in mud (see Figure 3.12). Captions frame these pictures in ways that directly echo the text, further strengthening dichotomous language and frequently using dehumanizing terms (such as "swine" in our latter example). Captions closely link up what is claimed in the text and what is shown in the images, thus orienting the reader's understanding of what may otherwise be ambiguous photos in a way that confirms the worldview constructed in the text.

Figure 3.12 Pictures depicting the negative character of out-groups (top: *Dabiq* no. 15 p. 22; center: *Rumiyah* no. 9 p. 40; bottom: *Rumiyah* no. 9 p. 38).

IS also uses images to show disapproval of the use, sale, or advocacy of drugs. They include a picture of a rally in the United States with the caption, "Pagans rallying in support of marijuana" (*Dabiq* no. 15 p. 23), with the caption clearly distinguishing the actors as out-group members, which discredits their acts and creates a self-reinforcing narrative. They also discredit the Taliban for involvement in the opium trade (see Figure 3.13; the caption qualifies the Taliban as having an impure, nationalist agenda and being morally negligent for allowing forbidden behavior). These images support

Figure 3.13 Outcasting of Muslims involved in drug trafficking (*Dabiq* no. 13 p. 51).

IS's crisis narrative that out-group members engage in sinful behavior that is being imposed and proliferated through powerful political actors and institutions in *Dār al-Kufr* (the land of disbelief).

Echoing the magazines' text, images go beyond the negative representation of out-groups and display interactions between the various enemies to fuel the conspiratorial dimension of the crisis. The collusion between out-groups, specifically the West and apostate (*ṭaghūt*) regimes, is a related subnarrative that is repeatedly featured in IS magazines. Images of Western leaders, such as President Obama, with leaders of "fake" Muslim regimes are commonly featured in the magazines as proof that these distinct out-groups are working together against IS's cause (see Figure 3.14).

Figure 3.14 Pictures depicting collusion between various out-groups (left: *Dabiq* no. 9 p. 53; center: *Rumiyah* no. 5 p. 2; right: *Dar al-Islam* no. 6 p. 22).

IS repeatedly uses images of people deemed "fake Muslim scholars" whom IS claims are part of this conspiracy seeking to corrupt true Muslims and spread apostate ideas (see Figure 3.15). There are many designated out-groups that are shown together in photos with captions serving to frame the interaction in the conspiratorial narrative. IS claims the *tawaghit* regimes are plotting with the West against Muslims due to ignorance or manipulation by Western propaganda or that they are acting willingly, driven by greed. In the *Dabiq* and *Rumiyah* magazines, there are a total of 216 images (10% of the total) used to support the narrative that the out-groups are plotting against Muslims. Such images were not common in the first five *Dabiqs*, with three issues not including any images to support this narrative. In contrast, these images are more common in *Rumiyah*, where two issues have had 20% of images in that magazine depicting collusion between out-groups.

Having enunciated, through interconnected texts and images, a diagnosis of the crisis caused by the antagonistic presence of two fundamentally

Figure 3.15 Picture displaying "fake" Muslim scholars supposedly corrupting Islam under the influence of the West ("Conference of Apostates in Paris," from *Dar al-Islam* no. 4 p. 7).

opposed groups, IS magazines then articulate the solution that the organization is, in a typical narrative way, delivering with success. This solution is double: uncompromising violence to eradicate the enemies on the one hand and establishment of the prophetic Caliphate (*Khilāfah*) on the other hand, a safe and pure political entity. The following two sections examine in detail how IS's capacity to provide this double solution is constructed visually and linguistically in the magazines, and how the group has at times shifted its emphasis on one or the other aspect.

Solution 1: Punishing the Out-Group Through *Jihād* and Punishment

Language

Articles in IS magazines recurrently evoke the need to engage in violence against the many enemies faced by the organization. Countless articles depict the out-group as causing harm and conclude that IS has come to react uncompromisingly. IS indeed positions violent *jihād* as one's duty in response to the crisis created by the enemy. In his analysis of *Dabiqs* no. 1–13, Ingram (2016: 365) found that IS strategically focused less on "linking Others [the out-groups] to the crisis, preferring to focus on how IS are confronting its enemies and solving crises." In other words, when IS complains, it is generally in order to garner support for its violent actions. The following quote is an example of such utilization of a victimization claim to trigger support for an in-group solution:

> Will you leave the American, the Frenchman, or any of their allies to walk
> safely upon the earth while the armies of the crusaders strike the lands of
> the Muslims not differentiating between a civilian and fighter? They have
> killed nine Muslim women three days ago by striking a bus transporting
> them from Shām to Iraq. Will you leave the disbeliever to sleep safely at
> home while the Muslim women and children shiver with fear of the roars of
> the crusader airplanes above their heads day and night? How can you enjoy
> life and sleep while not aiding your brothers? (*Dabiq* no. 4 p. 10)

Of course IS depicts the people harmed by their acts of violence in rather different terms. IS not only justifies but also requires the infliction of brutal violence as a solution to the oppressive collusion of the various enemies. Since Muslims are victims of their enemies' evil actions, IS is obligated to engage in violent *jihād* to save the in-group. The explanation offered to justify the burning of the Jordanian pilot is a good example:

[the Islamic State had resolved to burn him [the Jordan pilot] alive as retribution for his crimes against Islam and the Muslims, including his active involvement in crusader airstrikes against Muslim lands. When the news of the video broke out, the tāghūt of Jordan who at the time was in Washington to meet with his masters at the White House—as is the habit of the crusader puppets—cut short his trip. (*Dabiq* no. 7 p. 5)

Figure 3.16, which presents the combined saliency of 10 most frequently used English-language words in *Dabiq* and *Rumiyah* magazines that unambiguously refer to violence (which are *jihād*, war, army, battle, kill, fight, attack, destroy, target, and weapon), shows that discussions of war and violence have never been absent from the pages of the two publications and does not reflect any clear decision to publish more or less "violent" issues, apart perhaps at the time of the first few *Rumiyah*.[13]

A related subtheme of violence against the enemy relates to martyrdom. The *Dabiq* magazine has a recurring column called "Among the Believers Are Men," wherein peoples' deaths are memorialized and featured as sacrifices for the cause. IS attributes its success, in part, to these actors; one can, for example, read that "the Islamic State will remain because it was built upon the corpses of martyrs . . . it will remain because of the success granted by Allah in this jihad" (*Dabiq* no. 5 p. 32).

Based on the combined frequency in *Dabiq* and *Rumiyah* of words depicting martyrdom (*martyr, inghimasi* [suicide fighter], *shahid* or *shaheed* [both meaning "witness," denoting martyr, and plural *shuhada*], and *istishhad* [heroic death, death of martyr]), Figure 3.17 clearly shows that references to martyrdom, which were infrequent during the group's "boom" period, sharply increased as it entered its period of "bust," with consistently greater salience since *Dabiq* no. 12 when IS was losing territorial control. IS's increased reference to martyrdom operations in later

---

[13] There is no statistically significant difference in violent references between *Dabiq* and *Rumiyah*, and there is no relationship between the use of violent terminology and the size of the Caliphate. Substantively, the data show that IS uses a violent lexicon with relatively consistent fluctuation in frequency over time.

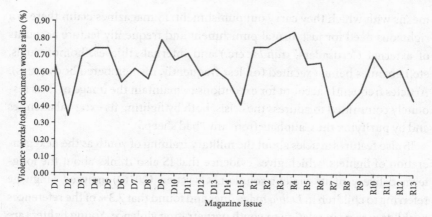

Figure 3.16 Proportion of violence-referring words across *Dabiq* and *Rumiyah* magazines.

issues could therefore be interpreted as an effort to normalize and encourage this type of extreme military tactic in an increasingly difficult environment.

Another way that IS magazines discuss the organization's commitment to violently face its enemies to solve its perceived crisis is by exposing the brutal

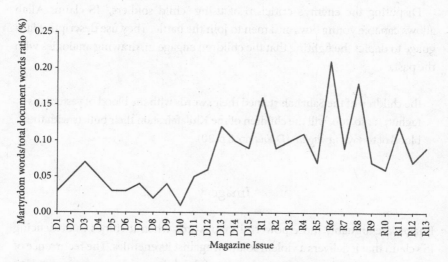

Figure 3.17 Proportion of martyrdom words across *Dabiq* and *Rumiyah* magazines.

means with which they carry out punishment. IS magazines claim there is a righteous need for just, brutal punishment and frequently feature accounts of external ("crusaders," *rāfiḍa*, etc.) and internal (thieves, homosexuals, etc.) enemies being executed (or, less frequently, dismembered body parts). Articles frequently account for executions to maintain the image of IS as resolutely committed to address the crisis, both by fighting its external enemies and by purifying the Caliphate from any "bad sheep."

IS also features articles about the military training of youth as the next generation of fighters, which gives evidence that IS also thinks about the long-term delivery of its violent solution. Christien (2016) analyzed language referring to children in *Dabiq* magazines and found that 7.3% of the references to children were in relation to youth perpetrating violence. Young fighters are often referred to as "lions" or "lion cubs" being reared for future battle. *Dabiq* 9, for example, features an article called "Cubs of the Khilafah," which says,

> There is a new generation waiting in the wings, eagerly anticipating the day that it is called upon to take up the banner of iman. These are the children of the Ummah of jihad, a generation raised in the lands of malahim [fierce battles] and nurtured under the shade of Shari'ah, just a stone's throw from the frontlines. (*Dabiq* no. 8 p. 20)

Disputing the enemy's criticism of using "child soldiers," IS claims Allah allows capable young boys and men to join the battle. They use descriptive language to depict the fighting that the children engage in, drawing analogies with the past,

> the children of the Sahabah stained their swords with the blood of yesterday's taghut; . . . so, too, will the children of the Khilafah stain their bullets with the blood of today's *tawaghit*. (*Dabiq* no. 8 p. 20)

Imagery

Images are arguably more powerful than words when it comes to evidencing IS's claim that it delivers a violent solution against its enemies. The recurrence of war scenes and violence, with a subgenre of shocking and gruesome images, is a key trait of IS magazines.

Figure 3.18 Image of armed Islamic State soldiers (*Dar al-Islam* no. 10 p. 20).

Images of *jihād* are very frequent. In the 27 issues of *Dabiq* and *Rumiyah*, there are 541 images depicting IS fighters engaging in violent *jihād*, which is more than 25% of all images in the magazines. These images feature consistently across magazine issues, though they are in slightly greater proportion in *Rumiyah* than in *Dabiq* (30% and 25%, respectively). Many of these images are of targets exploding or weapons being fired (the quality of the images differs depending on the magazine and prominence of the image in the issue), with significantly fewer images of Muslims being victimized by their enemies' violence (only 42 such images in the 27 issues of *Dabiq* and *Rumiyah*, with nine issues not including any).[14] Again, these findings match Ingram's (2016) claim that IS prefers to present itself as a solution provider than to engage in lengthy descriptions of the crisis itself.

Pictures of heavily armed soldiers, which are "an important cornerstone of the Jihadist visual representation" (Kovacs 2015: 59), also abound (see Figure 3.18 for an example). Most of the weapons displayed in such pictures

[14] The majority of these images depicting in-group victimization (50%) are also gruesome, most often featuring images of slaughtered children or noncombatants. Such shocking images trigger emotions and profound questioning that elicits strong feelings of group solidarity, and thereby reinforces polarization (see, e.g., Halfmann & Youngs 2010). Individuals who identify with the depicted victims are more likely to feel an increased cohesion to the group and distance from the perceived perpetrators of the harm.

Figure 3.19 Islamic State soldiers visually memorialized as martyrs (all pictures from *Dabiq* no. 8 pp. 46–49).

in IS magazines are firearms; however, fighters also pose with knives, swords, tanks, and even drones.[15] In addition to battlefield images, these representations promote the claim that IS is willing and able to carry out violent *jihād* against its enemies.

Images of individual IS fighters featured as suicide bombers (*istishhadi*) play a comparable role, evidencing the ultimate determination characterizing IS members in their conduct of *jihād*. The above-mentioned "Among the Believers Are Men" column in *Dabiq* often shows images of the martyrs, sometimes with photos of the attack (e.g., image of an explosion), its aftermath (e.g., first responders at the scene, physical destruction of building), and occasionally an image of the deceased martyr (see Figure 3.19 for an example).

The epitome of the visual representation of IS's violent solution is certainly executions and brutal punishment images, which are present in magazines in very graphic ways (and famously also feature regularly in videos; cf., next chapter). There are 145 images bolstering the narrative that IS issues brutal punishment. Figure 3.20 shows how punishment images have been used in varying amounts across the 27 issues of *Dabiq* and *Rumiyah*, displaying no clear strategic choice, although the proportion of such images has generally declined, with 3 of the 10 *Rumiyah* magazines not including any images of IS punishment.

Previous research on gruesome images shows that such images can trigger emotions relevant to political attitudes; however, they do not

---

[15] More than a third of the images in *Dabiq* and *Rumiyah* feature some type of weapon (respectively, 35% and almost 36% of images).

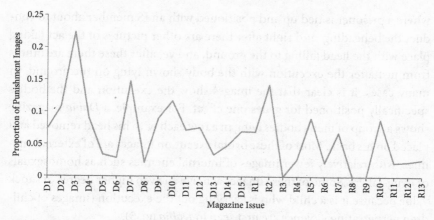

Figure 3.20 Proportion of images depicting Islamic State issuing punishment against enemies in *Dabiq* and *Rumiyah* magazines.

produce a uniform reaction across populations (Halfmann & Young 2010). These images can provoke diverse reactions, from severe upset and disgust by the out-group to feelings of reverence and fascination by the in-group. Gruesome images can both "transfix" and "anesthetize," thereby having the power to "deaden [the] conscience [as much] as arouse it" (Sontag 1977: 20). Halfmann and Young (2010) suggest that such images are used strategically by groups to target a potentially sympathetic minority who may start to question their preexisting beliefs and, simultaneously, as a psychological weapon to disturb and frighten the enemy.[16]

Gruesome execution and punishment images provide strong reinforcement of the claim that IS punishes its enemies using brutal, uncompromising, and definitive acts of justice. These images are presented through the prism of this claim to encourage selective moral disengagement that allows one to endorse these acts. Magazines contain very detailed images of some of the most infamous executions, including the above-mentioned burning of Jordanian pilot Moaz al-Kasasbeh in February 2015 or the beheading by explosives necklaces of a series of "spies" that same year. Usually, several moments of the execution are depicted, in a way reminiscent of the stereotypical sequencing found in execution videos (see next chapter): for example, there is an image

[16] Although grotesque imagery may disturb viewers, Carrabine (2011: 9) points out that such violence "is deeply embedded in human storytelling" and the "desire for disturbing imagery and horrific stories is not pathological departure from social norms."

where a prisoner is tied up and positioned with an IS member about to conduct the beheading, and right after there are other pictures of the act taking place with the head falling to the ground, and yet after these there are others from just after the execution with the body shown lying on the ground. In many cases, it is clear that the images show the execution and the bodies specifically positioned for gruesome effect. For example, a *Dabiq* magazine shows a group of men's bodies lying in a row each with his head removed and placed on his back. Most of these brutal execution images are of external enemies, with relatively fewer images of internal enemies such as homosexuals or drug-takers. Some of these images achieve an even higher degree of shock value because it is a child who is carrying out the execution (images of children perpetrating violence are first seen in *Dabiq* no. 5).

Solution 2: The Prospect of an Idyllic Islamic Caliphate

Language

In addition to claiming that IS successfully fights internal and external enemies to solve the alleged crisis, the group's magazines offer a second dimension to the solution: the real existence of a political entity where Muslims can safely live the purest form of their faith, the prophetic Caliphate (*Khilāfah*: more on the origin of this claim in Chapter 2). IS magazines contain many articles lauding the Caliphate, legitimizing the need and value of the religiously ordained institutional rules that govern it, and depicting the allegedly high quality of life in its territory. *Sharīʿa* law underpins the governing social order, so the Caliphate is not simply a nation state, but is also meant to be "more a theocratic totalitarian entity, with no borders and no separation of religious and secular life" (Wignell, Tan, & O'Halloran 2017: 7). The term *Khilāfah* is used no less than 1,009 times in the English-language magazines, indicating the importance of this word and subject to IS, and religious scriptures and terms are quoted, often out of context, in an effort to boost the group's legitimacy in establishing the Caliphate (Kendall 2016).

In addition to declaring the legitimacy and religious affirmation of the Caliphate, IS seeks to explain how life in the Caliphate is ideal and superior to life elsewhere. This is done in various ways. First, the Caliphate is described in illustrative, idyllic adjectives and attributes, such as honor, pride, prophetic, unity, blessed, or legitimate, in order to build a positive and motivating lexical field around it. Second, IS magazines make frequent reference to the Caliphate being a place free of corruption and sin, where one can go to worship freely and properly, in contrast to the sinful West where Muslims are discriminated against and incapable of practicing their faith. Third, IS magazines claim that obedience to *Sharīʿa* results in all aspects of society working effectively and properly, with great care for the poor, excellent welfare and social services, absent crime due to efficient and uncorrupt justice, thriving commerce, and happy family life. *Dabiq* no. 9, for example, features an article devoted to discussing the allegedly effective healthcare system provided in the Caliphate.

> The Islamic State provides the Muslims with extensive healthcare by running a host of medical facilities including hospitals and clinics in all major cities through which it is offering a wide range of medical services, from various types of complicated surgery to simpler services such as hijamah. This infrastructure is aided by a widespread network of pharmacies run by qualified pharmacists and managed under the supervision and control of the Health Diwan. Just as the medical staff in the hospitals and clinics are made up of qualified, trained professionals, the pharmacies are likewise only run by qualified and certified pharmacists. (*Dabiq* no. 9 p. 25)

The magazines not only attempt to present an idyllic Caliphate, they also actively encourage Muslims to come live in it, calling sympathizers to perform *hijrah*, in an analogy to the journey the Prophet and his followers made from Mecca to Medina to escape persecution. People have traveled to join IS in the Caliphate from far away, which Wignell, Tan, and O'Halloran (2017: 18) argue, "demonstrates the viability and attraction of ISIS as a 'state' and immigrants [making the journey] also serve as inspiration and role models for other potential immigrants." The use of the term *hijrah* across the *Dabiq* magazines is shown in Figure 3.21, which evidences the regularity of the topic across time, with perhaps less enthusiasm during the "bust" *Rumiyah* period when it became extremely hard to emigrate from the West to the shrinking Caliphate.

In this figure, the spike in *Dabiq* no. 3, whose front page title is "A Call to Hijrah," is mainly due to a long article titled "Hijrah from Hypocrisy to Sincerity." In this article, *hijrah* is positioned as an obligation with warnings

Figure 3.21 Proportion of *Hijrah* across the *Dabiq* and *Rumiyah* magazines.

that those who do not travel are hypocrites and disavowed. The article also explains the groundbreaking nature and the benefits of taking this journey.

> the only way for a man . . . to preserve his faith would be to leave the West. Before, such an idea might have sounded impossible for some, but now there is a Khilafah prepared to accept every Muslim and Muslimah into its lands and do all it can within its power to protect them while relying on Allah alone. (*Dabiq* no. 3 p. 27)

The article also highlights how individuals can contribute to the Caliphate by obeying the duty of *hijrah*, contributing to make the prophetic entity a reality:

> Every Muslim professional who delayed his *jihad* under the pretense of studying . . . should now make his number one priority to repent and answer the call of *hijrah*, especially after the establishment of the Khilafah. This Khilafah is more in need than ever before for experts, professionals, and specialists, who can help contribute in strengthening its structure and tending to the needs of their Muslim brothers. (*Dabiq* no. 3 p. 26)

One repeated subtheme to this solution narrative is how the Caliphate provides an ideal environment for families, especially women. IS magazines depict a strict patriarchal society, as shown, for example, in an article titled "The Flesh of Your Spouse Is Poisonous" describing the proper relationship between husband and wife (*Rumiyah* no. 7 p. 30). "To Our Sisters" is a recurring column written specifically for a female audience, featured in *Dabiq* 7–13[17] and dominated by patriarchal themes and hypermasculinity. Women are invited to live a supporting life at home, obeying their husbands' wishes, supporting them, and making sure they get pregnant. Consider the two following examples:

> My sisters, be bases of support and safety for husbands, brothers, fathers, and sons. Be advisors to them. They should find comfort and peace with you. Do not make things difficult for them. (*Dabiq* no. 7 p. 51)

> My Muslim sister, indeed you are a *mujahidah*, and if the weapon of the men is the assault rifle and the explosive belt, then know that the weapon of the women is good behavior and knowledge. (*Dabiq* no. 11 p. 44)

This is not a secondary theme—women are referenced in the 28 issues of *Dabiq* and *Rumiyah* more than 1,500 times.[18] This exceeds most other forms of IS propaganda, which is largely due to the strict rules IS enforces forbidding the depiction or portrayal of women. There are no images of women in their magazines, nor do women feature in their videos or songs. There is an image of a woman's prayer book that is meant to represent the female in one of the "To Our Sisters" articles, but this is the only visual representation. Many scholars have discussed women in relation to IS,[19] and, according to the existing literature, these articles in *Dabiq* constitute an attempt from the organization to tailor parts of its message to them, but also to potential male sympathizers who may be attracted by a very patriarchal society.

Imagery

In contrast to the images of the corrupt, sinful world promoted by out-groups in *Dār al-Kufr*, IS uses specific images of the *Khilāfah* to portray the utopian world described in the articles. To do so, IS magazines make frequent use of iconic, symbolic images to depict the idyllic *Dār al-Islām*, with a total of 155

[17] "To Our Sisters" (*Dabiq* no. 7 p. 50; *Dabiq* no. 8 p. 32), "From Our Sisters" (*Dabiq* no. 9 p. 44; *Dabiq* no. 10 p. 42), "To Our Sisters: A Jihad Without Fighting" (*Dabiq* no. 11 p. 40), "To Our Sisters: Two, Three, or Four" (*Dabiq* no. 12 p. 19), and "To Our Sisters: Advice on Ihad" (*Dabiq* no. 13 p. 24).
[18] This includes references to woman, women, sister(s), female(s), daughter(s), girl(s), mother(s), she, she's, wife, wives.
[19] See Hoyle, Bradford, & Frenett 2015; Khelghat-Doost 2017; Lahoud 2017; Peresin & Cervone 2015; and Saltman & Smith 2015.

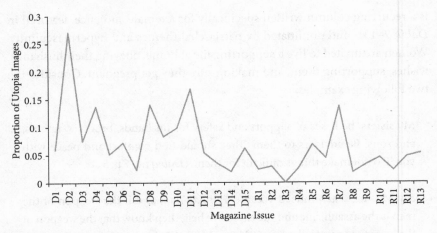

Figure 3.22 Proportion of utopian images of the *Khilāfah* across *Dabiq* and *Rumiyah* magazines.

such images across the *Dabiq* and *Rumiyah* magazines. These images are not consistently used across magazines, as shown in Figure 3.22, yet the impact of the group's "bust" clearly appears, with *Dabiq* magazines having significantly more images of the idyllic Caliphate than the *Rumiyah* ones (8.9% vs. 4.2%) as it became increasingly difficult for the group to put forward original and credible photos of a well-working place. The average proportion of utopian images in *Dabiq* magazine issues is more than twice the proportion of these images in *Rumiyah*, which corresponds to the reduced size of the *Khilāfah* in more recent months. Although the size of the *Khilāfah* may not fully represent IS's perception of "boom" and "bust," it may reasonably help explain changes in propaganda strategies and the decrease in the use of utopian images specifically.

These utopian images have several variants. First, magazines frequently include pictures of Muslims worshiping or engaging in religious activities (an individual calmly reading a holy book, a group conducting one of the daily prayers or enthusiastically reasserting allegiance to the *Khilāfah*). These images promote the narrative that IS consists of true Muslims and that the Caliphate is a place where one can truly live and worship properly and safely and experience a deep religious inner peace.

Second, IS recurrently uses images of the social services the state supposedly provides. A prime example is the visual representation of healthcare (as in Figure 3.23. These images show the latest medical technology available

Figure 3.23 Visual utopian representation of healthcare in the *Khilāfah* (all from *Dabiq* no. 9, pp. 24–26).

(such as medical imaging and advanced neonatal services) and what appear to be competent staff expertly conducting medical tasks (such as physiotherapy). IS magazines include images of other services allegedly run with great efficiency by the Caliphate (such as food distribution and support for orphans), which supports the solution claim that the Caliphate is a pure safe haven where true believers can live in harmony.

Third, IS magazines uses numerous images showing happy children partaking in various activities, portraying the Caliphate as a wonderful place to live and raise a family (see Figure 3.24). IS even advertises in the magazines' pages a series of online learning opportunities—with cartoon weapons—for children to learn the Quran and learn to read (see Figure 3.24 as well). The placement of weapons in an advertisement targeting parents shows how IS subtly draws multiple themes together in an identity-choice appeal that reifies perceptions of obligation—both to one's own children and to the group cause.

Fourth and finally, IS magazines also include many group pictures of enthusiastic IS members getting together, in order to convey the camaraderie and support allegedly binding group members. In *Dabiq* and *Rumiyah*, these images occur in 83 photos, though they are not used with the same frequency across issues. The first *Dabiq* featured the greatest proportion of such images, while *Rumiyah* 5–8 and 11–12 do not have any unity-inspired images, denoting a gradual abandonment of this type of visual representation. As exemplified in Figure 3.25, these images often portray people from different origins or ethnicities to show that IS is an inclusive community for all Muslims, regardless of where they come from, which is particularly meaningful for magazines issued in a variety of languages targeting different demographics (in several of these cases, the caption makes this explicit, for example, contrasting IS brotherhood with "American racism"). In these

Figure 3.24 Pictures presenting the Caliphate as an ideal place for children (left: *Dabiq* no. 15 p. 39; center: *Dar al-Islam* no. 6 p. 32; right: *Rumiyah* no. 13 p. 42).

photos men often stand with arms around each other or hands together in a display of power to show unity and group solidarity. These images suggest that joining IS will provide both physical and existential support.

IS Magazines and Mechanisms of Radicalization

IS magazines are one the many formats adopted by the group in view of disseminating its crisis–solution message and purpose with the presumed hope of generating more sympathizers, supporters, and recruits. In this fashion way, these magazines are one of the various means by which IS seeks to catalyze radicalization among readers: radicalization being broadly understood here as "the development of beliefs, feelings, and actions in support of any group or cause in conflict" (McCauley & Moskalenko 2011: 4). It is useful to consider that IS propaganda seeks to radicalize following the same methods used to market consumer goods; that is, "to enlist the consumer in beliefs

Figure 3.25 IS members getting together in *Dabiq* no.11 p.18 (left), *Dabiq* no.11 p.63 (center), and *Dar al-Islam* no.7 p.38 (right). Note the caption of the first picture ("Wala and Bara' versus American racism").

and actions that are complicit with the intentions of the provider of information; such that this leads to take up of messaging, interpreting the messages in the process" (Bhui & Ibrahim 2013: 224). IS magazines seek to do this by binding extremist ideological narratives with reference to the Quran and Islamic tenets and current conflicts with the historic struggles of the *Ummah* to position the concept of being a true believer with an obligation for violent *jihād* or martyrdom.

The language and images used in IS magazines facilitate a number of mechanisms of radicalization identified by scholars. For example, the binary, polarizing language used by IS facilitates hatred toward the out-group, which is conceptualized as a form of negative identification, rather than simply an emotion. Hatred is associated with dehumanization, which necessarily elevates the perceived virtue of the in-group and can help justify violent actions toward the out-group. McCauley and Moskalenko (2011) state that hatred of the out-group is enabled when it is easy to generalize and identify a clear "other"; presenting material in a binary format, as IS does in its magazines, is a "technique of persuasion" that facilitates this process (Bhui & Ibrahim 2013: 225).

Studies also show that a perceived common threat and/or goal increases group cohesion (see McCauley & Moskalenko 2011; Sherif et al. 1961). The utopian Caliphate is IS's group aim, and they have identified multiple, interconnected threats. Binary language and repetitious delivery of points keep IS on message with the ability to exploit these social tendencies so that the audience will align views with the in-group and generate cohesion. Also, IS magazines nurture group-based grievances elicited by the perceived harm and victimization of in-group Muslim members at the hands of the "crusaders" or *ṭaghūt* leaders. The generation of group-based grievance is a known mechanism of radicalization that relies on people's group identification and feelings of sympathy for those victimized with the hope of inspiring people's willingness to sacrifice for the group. The few references to Muslim victimization in IS magazines suggests that this is not the primary means by which IS has gained sympathizers and radicalized recruits. In fact, we argue that perhaps IS has learned to target propaganda in a fashion that taps into a particular mechanism of radicalization identified by McCauley and Moskalenko (2011) but rarely given much credence: "risk and status." Together with previous research, our chapter shows that IS magazines focus on *jihād* and issuing violence more than on victimization—in other words, they promote solutions above crises. Such a "solution construct" radicalizes individuals by providing a tangible solution to a crisis and therefore acts as a "pull factor" (Ingram 2016). The violent images and narratives may mobilize youth in a way not previously anticipated by evoking youths' desire to achieve status and defy risk in a way that is not offered in their home societies. More research is needed to test this claim.

Conclusion

IS has attracted tens of thousands of Muslim recruits and sympathizers from around the world (Bunzel 2015), suggesting that IS made effective use of a comprehensive, cohesive, and multidimensional propaganda strategy aimed at audiences well beyond its territorial reach or "natural" public. Not only has IS been successful at recruiting people to join them in the Caliphate, IS also has successfully mobilized people to conduct terrorist attacks abroad as well. The group's magazines played a central role in these two successes. Their relentless depiction of the two sides of IS's master narrative—the crisis and its solution—as well as their constant use of sharply dichotomous language and their systematic advertisement for other components of the organization's propaganda have been effective. What's more, the more recent issues of *Rumiyah* have also offered practical advice on how to carry out attacks: a recurring column called "Just Terror Tactics" describes how to use a specific method to most effectively incite terror (knives in no. 2 p. 12, vehicles in issue no. 3 p. 10, arson in issue no. 5 p. 8, hostage-taking and trucks in issue no. 9 p. 46–56), explaining how to select the ideal weapon (e.g., vehicle with raised chassis and bumper), how to acquire the weapon (e.g., rent, buy), and ideal targets (e.g., parades, small groups, etc.). These articles serve group tactical strategies to facilitate people in engaging in violence anywhere in the world without the direct oversight or direction of command by IS. In 2017, IS was linked to five attacks involving a vehicle and nine attacks with knives in countries targeted by these magazines.[20,21] We cannot definitively state whether these attacks are a result of people reading these articles, but it is interesting to note that the five

[20] These incidents involve known IS members, people who acted on behalf of the group, or people suspected to have sympathies for the group.
[21] Arabic-speaking countries were excluded from this list, in part because IS has controlled territory in a number of these countries, and they are not targeted with *Rumiyah*. The foreign countries included where these attacks took place are Australia (2), Austria (1), Bangladesh (3), Belgium (1), France (1), Georgia (1), India (1), Indonesia (4), Italy (1), Norway (1), Russia (7), Spain (1), Sweden (1), the United Kingdom (4), and the United States (2).

vehicle attacks, occurring in the United Kingdom, United States, Spain, and Sweden were all perpetrated after the "Just Terror Tactic" article on vehicles was issued (November 2016), whereas there were no vehicle attacks linked to IS in foreign countries in 2014–2016.

Although access to (and dissemination of) these magazines is illegal in many countries, particularly in the West, this material is still available online to inspire people around the world. More worryingly, perhaps, these magazines now constitute a new "gold standard" that extremist groups from across the ideological spectrum will inevitably want to copy.

References

'Athamina K. (1989) "The Black Banners and the Socio-Political Significance of Flags and Slogans in Medieval Islam," *Arabica* 36(3): 307–326.

Baele S, Boyd K, Coan T. (2019) "Lethal Images: Analyzing Extremist Visual Propaganda from IS and Beyond", *Journal of Global Security Studies*, in press.

Bandura, A. (2002) "Selective Moral Disengagement in the Exercise of Moral Agency," *Journal of Moral Education* 31(2): 101–119.

Berger, D. (2006) *Outlaws of America: The Weather Underground and the Politics of Solidarity.* Oakland, CA: AK Press.

Bhui K., Ibrahim Y. (2013) "Marketing the 'Radical': Symbolic Communication and Persuasive Technologies in Jihadist Websites," *Transcultural Psychiatry* 50(2): 216–234.

Bunzel C. (2015) "From Paper State to Caliphate: The Ideology of the Islamic State," *The Brookings Project on US Relations with the Islamic World.* Analysis Paper 19.

Campbell D. (2003) "Cultural Governance and Pictorial Resistance: Reflections on the Imaging of War," *Review of International Studies* 29: 57–73.

Carrabine E. (2011) "Images of Torture: Culture, Politics and Power," *Crime Media Culture* 7(1): 5–30.

Christien A. (2016) "The representation of youth in the Islamic State's propaganda magazine Dabiq," *Contemporary Voices: St Andrews Journal of International Relations* 7(3).

Gråtrud H. (2016) "Islamic State Nasheeds as Messaging Tools," *Studies in Conflict & Terrorism* 39(12): 1050–1070.

Halfmann D., Young M. (2010) "War Pictures: The Grotesque as a Mobilizing Tactic," *Mobilization: An International Quarterly* 15(1): 1–24

Halverson, J., Goodall, Jr., H. L., & Corman, S. (2011). *Master Narratives of Islamist Extremism.* New York: Palgrave Macmillan.

Hewstone M., Cairns E. (2001) "Social Psychology and Intergroup Conflict," in Daniel Chirot & Martin E. P. Seligman (eds.), *Ethnopolitical Warfare: Causes, Consequences, and Possible Solutions.* Washington DC: American Psychological Association, pp. 319–342.

Hoyle C, Bradford A, & Frenett R. (2015) "Becoming Mulan? Female Western Migrants to ISIS," *Institute for Strategic Dialogue.* https://www.isdglobal.org/isd-publications/becoming-mulan-female-western-migrants-to-isis/

Huddy L. (2004) "Contrasting Theoretical Approaches to Intergroup Relations," *Political Psychology* 25(6): 947–967.

Ingram H. (2015) "An Analysis of the Taliban in Khurasan's *Azan* (Issues 1–5)," *Studies in Conflict & Terrorism* 38(7): 560–579.

Ingram H. (2016) "An Analysis of Islamic State's Dabiq Magazine," *Australian Journal of Political Science* 51(3): 458–477.

Ingram H. (2017) "An Analysis of *Inspire* and *Dabiq*: Lessons from AQAP and Islamic State's Propaganda War," *Studies in Conflict & Terrorism* 40(5): 357–375.

Jenkins, B. (1975) *International Terrorism: A New Mode of Conflict.* Los Angeles: Crescent.

Kendall E. (2016) "Jihadist Propaganda and Its Exploitation of the Arab Poetic Tradition," in Kendall E., Khan A. (eds.), *Reclaiming Islamic Tradition. Modern Interpretations of the Classical Heritage.* Edinburgh: Edinburgh University Press, pp. 223–246.

Khelghat-Doost H. (2017) "Women of the Caliphate: The Mechanism for Women's Incorporation into the Islamic State (IS)," *Perspectives on Terrorism* 11(1): 17–25.

Kovacs A. (2015) "The 'New Jihadists' and the Visual Turn from Al-Qa'ida to ISIL/ISIS?Da'ish," *Biztpol Affairs* 2(3): 47–70.

Lahoud N. (2017) "Can Women Be Soldiers of the Islamic State?" *Survival* 59(1): 61–78.

Lombardi M. (2015) "Islamic State Communication Project" *Sicurezza, Terrorismo e Società* (1): 99–133.

Matusitz, J., Olufowote, J. (2016) "Visual Motifs in Islamist Terrorism: Applying Conceptual Metaphor Theory," *Journal of Applied Security Research* 11: 18–32.

McCauley, C., Moskalenko, S. (2011) *Friction: How Radicalization Happens to Them and Us.* New York: Oxford University Press.

Miller G., Mekhennet S. (2015, November 20). "Inside the Surreal World of the Islamic State's Propaganda Machine," *The Washington Post.* Retrieved from https://www.washingtonpost.com/world/national-security/inside-the-islamic-states-propaganda-machine/2015/11/20/051e997a-8ce6-11e5-acff-673ae92ddd2b_story.html?utm_term=.323620ee7e88.

Milton, D. (2016) "Communication Breakdown: Unraveling the Islamic State's Media Efforts." West Point, NY: Combating Terrorism Center, United States Military Academy. Retrieved from https://ctc.usma.edu/v2/wp-content/uploads/2016/10/ISMedia_Online.pdf.

Peresin A, Cervone A. (2015) "The Western Muhajirat of ISIS," *Studies in Conflict & Terrorism* 38(7): 495–509.

Saltman EM, Smith M. (2015) "'Til Martyrdom Do Us Part': Gender and the ISIS Phenomenon," *Institute for Strategic Dialogue.* https://www.isdglobal.org/isd-publications/till-martyrdom-do-us-part-gender-and-the-isis-phenomenon/.

Sherif M., Harvey O. J., White B. J., Hood W. R., & Sherif C. W. (1961) Intergroup conflict and cooperation. *The robbers cave experiment. Oklahoma.*

Sontag, S. (1977) *On Photography.* London: Penguin.

Soufan, A. (2011) *The Black Banners.* New York: W. W. Norton.

Tajfel H., Billig M., Bundy R., Flament C. (1971) "Social Categorisation and Intergroup Behaviour," *European Journal of Social Psychology* 2(1): 149–178.

Tajfel H., Turner J. (2004) "The Social Identity Theory of Intergroup Behavior," in Jost J., Sidanius J. (eds.), *Key Readings in Social Psychology. Political Psychology.* New-York: Psychology Press, pp. 276–293.

Torres Soriano M. (2011) "The Road to Media Jihad: The Propaganda Actions of Al Qaeda in the Islamic Maghreb," *Terrorism & Political Violence* 23(1): 72–88.

Weimann G., Winn C. (1994) *The Theater of Terror: Mass Media and International Terrorism.* New York: Longman.

Wignell P., Tan S., & O'Halloran K. (2017) "Violent Extremism and Iconisation: Commanding Good and Forbidding Evil?" *Critical Discourse Studies* 14(1): 1–22.

4

Shock and Inspire

Islamic State's Propaganda Videos

Stephane J. Baele, Katharine A. Boyd, and Travis G. Coan

Introduction

Videos are arguably the most widely known element of the Islamic State's (IS) highly visual propaganda. While this is likely due to IS's deliberate strategy of disseminating large quantities of videos and to regularly include gruesome footage in these clips, another important factor is the frequent reporting on the most violent newly released videos in the mainstream press across the world, which informs large audiences on supposedly new "trends" in the genre. From tabloids such as the United Kingdom's *Daily Express* that went as far as streaming execution footage on their websites,[1] to high-end newspapers like France's *Le Monde*,[2] the United States' *Washington Post*,[3] Israel's *Haaretz*,[4] or the United Kingdom's *Independent*,[5] the media has contributed to establish IS's videos as "instant icons" that shape the dominant visual representation of IS and Islamism more generally among Western populations (Molin Friis 2015: 733). As Tinnes explains (2015: 77), "the traditional mainstream media remain of high importance for terrorists, who try to exploit

---

[1] For example: *Daily Express*, "WATCH: Islamic State Drowns 'Spy' in FISH TANK in Latest Sickening Video," January 5, 2017, http://www.express.co.uk/news/world/750804/ISIS-Islamic-State-terror-Afghanistan-Iraq-Mosul-death-video-drowning

[2] *Le Monde*, "Boko Haram publie une vidéo d'exécution sur le modèle de l'Etat Islamique," March 14, 2017, http://www.lemonde.fr/afrique/article/2017/03/14/boko-haram-une-video-d-execution-sur-le-modele-de-l-etat-islamique_5094396_3212.htmlno. muKpc9y6PeY5hfdE.99.

[3] *Washington Post*, "Islamic State Video Shows Beheading of Russian Intelligence Agent," May 9, 2017, https://www.washingtonpost.com/world/islamic-state-video-shows-beheading-of-russian-intelligence-agent/2017/05/09/a880cb00-3498-11e7-b4ee-434b6d506b37_story.html?utm_term=.8a865e4d527b

[4] *Haaretz*, "ISIS Publishes First-ever Video in Hebrew: 'Not a Single Jew Will Remain in Jerusalem,'" October 23, 2015, http://www.haaretz.com/israel-news/1.682060

[5] *The Independent*, "ISIS Threatens China and Vows to 'Shed Blood Like Rivers,'" March 1, 2017, http://www.independent.co.uk/news/world/middle-east/isis-china-threaten-terror-attack-muslim-islamist-group-islamic-state-a7606211.html

Stephane J. Baele, Katharine A. Boyd, and Travis G. Coan, *Shock and Inspire: Islamic State's Propaganda Videos* In: *ISIS Propaganda*. Edited by: Stephane J. Baele, Katharine A. Boyd, and Travis G. Coan, Oxford University Press (2020) © University of Maryland National Consortium for the Study of Terrorism and Responses to Terrorism (START)
10.1093/oso/9780190932459.003.0005

them as a powerful echo-chamber for enhancing the radius of their message."
An NBC/*Wall Street Journal* (WSJ) poll from 2014, for example, revealed
that 94% of Americans had "seen, read, or heard the news coverage about
the beheadings" carried out by IS.[6] As such, IS's videos play a key role in the
group's ability to inspire terror.

This high visibility has not only played a role in potential recruits' or
isolated individuals' radicalization,[7] it has also produced "reverse" radicalization of Western audiences and politics—that is, their increasing hostility
toward the terrorist organization and decreasing willingness to address
the Iraq/Syria crisis through nonviolent means (Molin Friis 2015: 727).
Whiteside (2016: 6) adds that the mass production and wide dissemination of videos conveying IS's extremist radical *takfiri* worldview and featuring explicit violence sought to gradually sharpen initially less extreme
discourses, following the logic of the so-called "Overton window," whereby
the "ideas that lie beyond the range of acceptable beliefs can be popularized and normalized through repetitive discourse to the point of eventual
inclusion by audiences outside the fringe." The continuous flow of videos
produced by the various IS media offices described in this chapter pursued,
he argued, the aim of shifting the doctrinal lines of the global Salafi-jihadist
movement, "especially concerning the use of violence and the principle of
takfir (excommunication)" (2016: 6). In brief, IS's videos have had a wide,
diverse, and deep impact on public perceptions and attitudes across the
spectrum of their compound audience, even if other kinds of outputs constituting IS's multifaceted propaganda have been by far more numerous
(see Chapter 6).

Yet in spite of their iconic dimension, IS videos cannot be understood as
free-standing elements: they not only constitute a piece of IS's full-spectrum
propaganda, but also pertain to the much wider contemporary visual political culture (read, e.g., Baudrillard 1994; Bleiker 2015; Griffin & Lee 1995;
Hansen 2015) and therefore are by no means a radical innovation in themselves. Bolt (2012) has shown how the strategic production and dissemination of violent footage has already been used by militant groups—as well as

---

[6] See http://newscms.nbcnews.com/sites/newscms/files/14901_september_nbc-wsj_poll.pdf.
[7] The extent of this role is impossible to assess, yet evidence indicates that recent attackers had seen
videos at one point in their radicalization: see, for example, Amedy Coulibaly's wife's depiction of
him watching videos, as reported in IS's French-language magazine *Dar al-Islam* ("ses yeux brillaient
à chaque fois qu'il visionnait les vidéos de l'État Islamique et il disait: 'Il ne faut pas me montrer ça' car
cela lui donnait envie de partir immédiatement").

states—who sought to influence enemies and potential sympathizers. In this sense, IS is not the first insurgent group or jihadist organization to embrace visual imagery and to produce and disseminate videos to elicit reactions— for example, al-Qaeda's leadership famously published videos to expose their worldview. However, IS clearly stands out as the first terrorist organization to mass produce propaganda videos with a high degree of standardization; as we will see, the sheer amount of videos produced by the organization is incomparable to the production of other violent extremist groups across the political spectrum and within the violent jihadist constellation. As such, with its videos, IS simultaneously both simply *continues* the "massive 'visual turn' of certain radical Islamist movements at the beginning of the 21st century" (Kovacs 2015: 66), further developing some of its main themes and tropes, and sharply *accelerates* this trend while creating "its own visual world" (Kovacs 2015: 51), where extreme violence is one of the most noticeable— yet by no means the sole—distinctive features.[8] In sum, echoing the overall thread of the present volume and the discussion offered in Chapter 8, IS videos have to be understood as a significant innovation within a continuity of propaganda practices.

Against this backdrop, this chapter seeks to provide a systematic over- view of IS video production, highlighting its key features and its role in the group's full-spectrum propaganda effort. There have been a number of previous attempts made in the literature to analyze IS video content, and this work has led to a series of important insights (see, e.g., Winter's de- tailed analysis of one video [2014b], Lesaca's report on the use of Western pop culture in IS videos [2015], or Leander's reflection on the "commer- cial" character of IS videos [2016]). These studies tend to focus on short time periods and limited samples. Moreover, the lack of a rich quantita- tive literature on IS videos is hardly surprising: it is notoriously hard to analyze videos, let alone videos containing violence and extremist con- tent, with multiple barriers ranging from the technical (how to find the videos online, how to accurately transcribe their content, etc.) to the methodological (how to locate variables of interests, how to systematically examine moving images, etc.), not to mention the ethical (how to store illegal content, how to analyze large volumes of graphic content without

[8] The extreme visuality of jihadist videos is somewhat at odds with the Islamic tradition of refusing images, yet videos have such a potential in terms of communication that they can no longer be ignored in contemporary propaganda. This tension has led to a series of theological debates and ad- justment behaviors (read Kovacs 2015 for an account).

psychological harm to the researcher, etc.). The goal of this chapter is to thus build on and further complement previous systematic studies on IS video content (e.g., Zelin 2015; Milton 2016) and to articulate findings to the general reflection on the full-spectrum character of the group's propaganda.

To provide a general overview of the state of IS video production, we draw on a large sample of 1,280 videos spanning the period from December 2014 to January 2017. Specifically, this chapter is organized around the following questions:

1. How much video content does IS produce? How does video production vary across the organization's so-called "provinces" (*Wilāyāt*) and across time? What can these trends teach us in terms of strategy and constraints?

2. What messages are prominent in the sample? Using the concept of a "script," we examine how standardized messages fit within the context of IS's full-spectrum propaganda, specifically to its constitutive narratives highlighted in the previous chapter.

3. Which of these scripts and narratives does IS strategically prioritize in its "Selected 10" featured videos (this refers to the list of videos suggested in *Dabiq* magazines, as explained in the previous chapter)? Is the focus of these videos similar to or different from IS video content more generally?

We address these questions through a combination of quantitative, descriptive analysis of overall video production and qualitative analysis of the sequencing of moving images. We proceed in four parts. First, we depict the organizational landscape of IS video production. Second, we use quantitative tools to provide a general overview of the main trends, in terms of production volume and quality, of the corpus of 1,278 videos spanning from December 2014 to January 2017. Third, we deepen this quantitative overview by offering a qualitative discussion of the major "scripts"—that is, frequent standardized combinations of spoken and visual components constructing micro-narratives that partake of IS's broader propaganda master narrative as defined in the previous chapters of this book—found in a 50-video sample taken from this corpus. Fourth and finally, we focus on the "Selected 10" videos to compare and contrast their characteristics to those of the 50-video sample.

Decentralized Yet Standardized: The Organizational Structure of IS Video Production

As highlighted in Chapter 1 in general terms, IS propaganda is not solely produced by a single central office, but instead comes from a series of independent yet connected and hierarchically organized offices. IS videos follow the same logic: production obeys a three-tier organization defined by regional and role lines. As evidenced by Milton's work on declassified official IS/ al-Qaeda in Iraq (AQI) memos, media production is heavily bureaucratized (Milton 2016: 6), with top-down regulations and directives and compulsory down-top reporting. Each production unit has its own carefully designed logo, which usually appears in an animated form at the beginning of each video and very often remains in the top right-hand corner of the screen for the duration of the video, sometimes reappearing full-screen between sequences.

The first group of video producers is constituted of IS's central media organizations directly dependent on IS's Department of Media (*diwan al-Ilam*), the same units that are responsible for the production of other propaganda outputs such as magazines or audio messages. Three central offices share work on the basis of their respective roles. The first one, *al-Furqan Media*, is the truly pivotal media office, in charge of producing and releasing propaganda videos in Arabic, some of them coming in series, such as the 22-episode *Messages from the Land of Epic Battles*. Al-Furqan is the oldest group, having started to release material back in the early days of the proclamation of the Islamic State in Iraq (ISI) in October 2006; it remains central in drawing the lines of official propaganda (al-Furqan literally means "the reference"). *Al-I'tisam Media* (meaning "adherence") is the second central group producing videos in Arabic, most notably the series *Windows on the Land of Epic Battles*. While the office's status vis-à-vis al-Furqan Media is unclear, its more recent foundation in 2013 seems to indicate that it was created to accompany the group's expansion to Syria. *Al-Hayat Media Center* (meaning "life"), founded in 2014, is IS's media wing designed to produce propaganda in foreign languages targeting non-Arabic audiences. Well-known in the West for its production of a series of magazines (see previous chapter), it releases videos in many different languages from English to French, from German to Indonesian. Al-Hayat also records its own *anashid* (Islamic chants, see Chapter 6) in foreign languages as well, which are both released independently and used as soundtracks for

Figure 4.1 Logos of the Islamic State central media offices. From left to right: al-Furqan Media, al-I'tisam Media, and Al-Hayat Media Center.

al-Hayat videos. Figure 4.1 shows the logos of these three central media offices.

The second group of video-producing units comprises the many decentralized "media offices" attached to the "provinces" (*Wilāyāt*) of the IS, which also produce other material such as photo reports (see Chapter 6). As al-Tamimi explains, with IS primarily governed by its various departments (*diwans*) such as health or education, provinces are chiefly used to "give an impression of territorial control" (2016: 31) and therefore serve an important propaganda function. Media operatives working for a provincial media center are attached to a particular city or area within the province and work under the supervision of the head of *Wilāya* media operations. Each provincial media office has to produce videos that follow strict directives from the top, and each has to report to the top in a detailed manner. Hence, while the production of videos is indeed decentralized, as Milton rightly warns (2016: 6), it is a misconception to consider this production as a flexible structure with extensive freedom and significant powers devolved to the provincial units.

This said, it is also useful to distinguish within this group between "core" and "peripheral" provinces—that is, between provinces belonging to the territory controlled (or once controlled) by IS in Iraq and Syria and those provinces established elsewhere as local groups have emerged, pledged allegiance to IS, and started to produce their own media content within the more or less strict control of the central offices. As we will detail, the quantity and quality of video products varies between core and peripheral provinces. Also, while the vast majority of videos released by provincial offices is in Arabic,[9] peripheral media offices located in non–Arabic-speaking regions (e.g., Nigeria,

---

[9] Some core *Wilāyāt* do occasionally produce content in a foreign language (e.g., sequences seeking to appeal to foreigners).

Figure 4.2 Two examples of the logos of provincial media offices. From left to right: al-Furat Media Center and al-Khayr Media Center (both core *Wilāyāt*).

Caucasus) regularly produce content in foreign languages, sometimes subtitled in Arabic. Figure 4.2 provides two examples of provincial media offices' logos, while Tables 4.1 and 4.2, together with the map in Figure 4.3, offer a list of existing provinces and indications of their location.

In fact, as we detail later, even though provincial videos are less well-known in the West, where attention has mainly been attracted by al-Hayat or al-Furqan productions, these provincial media offices produce together the bulk of IS video propaganda and tend to include gruesome content even more regularly (see later discussion). Provincial offices are therefore by no

Table 4.1 List of Core *Wilāyāt*, with Their Location

Iraq	Iraq/Syria	Syria
• *Ninawah*	• *al-Furat*	• *Dimashq*
• *Shamal-Baghdad*		• *Hamah*
• *Baghdad*		• *Halab*
• *Kirkuk*		• *ar-Raqqah*
• *Diyala*		• *al-Khayr*
• *Salahuddin*		• *al-Barakah*
• *al-Anbar*		• *Idlib*
• *al-Jazirah*		• *Hims*
• *al-Janub*		
• *al-Fallujah*		
• *al-Dijlah*		

In the absence of accurate and clear *Wilāyāt* map, this one is the least imperfect one, retrieved from the open Reddit thread "[OC] Islamic State Wilayahs - Syria & Iraq" https://www.reddit.com/r/syriancivilwar/comments/3qmbft/oc_islamic_state_wilayahs_syria_iraq/). Imperfect efforts to localize peripheral provinces exist; see, e.g., *Washington Post* (2015) "Map: The world according to the Islamic State," May 29, 2015, available at https://www.washingtonpost.com/news/worldviews/wp/2015/05/29/map-the-world-according-to-the-islamic-state/?utm_term=.52da7045878c."

Table 4.2 List of Peripheral *Wilāyāt* (and in Two Cases Their Subcomponents Sometimes Advertised as Provinces), with their Location

Libya	Egypt	Algeria	Yemen	Af-Pak	Nigeria	Saudi Arabia	Caucasus
• al-Barqah • Fazzan • Tarabulus	• Sinai	• al-Jazâ'ir	• Yaman	• Khurâsân	• Gharb Ifrîqiyyâh	• Haramayn • Najd • al-Hijaz	• Qawqâz
			- Sanaa - Ibb wa Taiz - Lahij - Adan-Abyan - Shabwah - Hadramawt - al-Bayda - Ataq				- Kabika - Daghistan - al-Shishan - Inghushiyya

Figure 4.3 Map of core IS Wilāyāt.

In the absence of accurate and clear *Wilāyāt* map, this one is the least imperfect one, retrieved from the open Reddit thread "[OC] Islamic State Wilayahs - Syria & Iraq" https://www.reddit.com/r/syriancivilwar/comments/3qmbft/oc_islamic_state_wilayahs_syria_iraq/).

Figure 4.4 Example of the two logos used by an unofficial media office, al-Battar Media Foundation.

means secondary to the central offices when it comes to video production, even though their work is tightly directed and monitored by the central offices, leading to the recurrence of the standardized footages described later.

The final group in IS's three-tier structure of video-producing units is constituted by unofficial media organizations. As explained in several chapters of this volume, IS propaganda is not simply dependent on the work of its official agencies, but also heavily relies on individuals and groups without official status acting as disseminators and, in some cases, creators (read, e.g., Milton 2016: 13; Chapter 5 of this volume).[10] Groups such as *al-Battar Media Foundation* or *al-Ghuraba Media* have statuses that are sometimes hard to decipher,[11] yet they produce videos that mobilize the same themes, claims, and visual tropes as those of official IS footages, and display similar logos. They have regularly released short videos celebrating IS-linked terrorist attacks in the West (e.g., after the Brussels and Orlando attacks), but have also produced longer, more generalist content—for example, al-Battar released in May 2014 a 50-minute video called *Why the Islamic State?*, which makes it one of the longest videos propagandizing the group's message. Figure 4.4 shows the logos of one of these unofficial media offices.

This three-tier, decentralized yet bureaucratized structure is responsible for the production of propaganda videos at an unprecedented scale for a terror group and is a testimony to the group's commitment to combine mass production of videos with overall coherence in terms of content and to its

---

[10] This situation, due to IS's strategy of favoring open large-scale dissemination over closed and targeted communication, creates tensions related to the need to control the organization's message. Discussing these tensions is beyond the scope of this chapter.

[11] For example, al-Battar Media Foundation is thought to be linked to the group Katibat al-Battar, of Libyan origin and with some degree of autonomy within the IS structure.

efforts to disseminate messages that target different audiences while remaining recognizable.

IS video production involves strict control and coordination. According to IS defectors, media operatives went through training programs, and only they were allowed to have cameras in the Caliphate (Miller & Mekhennet 2015). IS operatives would receive instructions on where to go to shoot staged events, with multiple cameramen sometimes filming the same event from different angles, sometimes with cue cards for "actors" to read. Not only did IS determine how executions or utopian images would be captured through coordinated efforts by multiple cameramen, but the compiling and editing process for productions by the central offices also was highly controlled. In fact, a cameraman defector says that media operatives were told to transfer footage taken each day to memory sticks and leave these at "drop sites" where production teams would compile footage from multiple sources, adding titles and *anashīd*. This process shows the effort and attention that IS paid to ensuring the videos portrayed a cohesive narrative.

A Quantitative Overview of IS Video Production

With an understanding the organizational structure in hand, our next set of questions turn to variation in production across various levels of the hierarchy. Are most videos produced by the central IS media machine, or is most content provided by the provinces? How does production vary over time? In this section, we explore the who, where, when, and how much of IS video production. We complement earlier attempts to quantify this output—for example, Zelin (2015), who counted no fewer than 24 videos released in a single week of April 2015, or Winter (2017) who more recently counted more than 100 videos released over the second month of 2017 (although most of this set was made of unedited, free-standing footage with only a tiny fraction consisting of edited official videos).

Data

While these and similar counting endeavors already indicate the extent of IS's propaganda effort, they are open to numerous potential biases—for example, the chosen week or month might have been unusually active or calm—and offer neither long-term trends nor a comparative vision across types of producers/videos. Using the *Jihadology* online repository,[12] which is by far the most systematic and comprehensive source of Jihadi material, we have referenced 1,280 unique, edited videos released by official IS media offices during the 2-year period between December 2014 and January 2017, a number consistent with Milton's count of 875 videos over the 1½ years from January 2015 to July 2016 (Milton 2016). This amounts to a bit more than one official video released per day on average, suggesting that Zelin's effort took place during an unusually productive week. IS official videos have an average length of 10'17" (a bit longer than Milton's 8'37"), yet the distribution of duration is skewed (median duration is roughly 8 minutes; with the majority of videos lasting between 3 and 10 minutes, and a handful of longer productions going well above that, reaching 30–40 minutes and almost 1 hour in a few cases). In this constant flow of videos, some come in series exploring a given theme, representing specific situations, or following a particular format—for example, the notorious "Mujatweets Episodes" (short clips depicting positive scenes of daily life in the so-called Caliphate) or the already mentioned *A Window Upon the Land of Epic Battles* (50 combat-ridden episodes released by al-I'tisam in 2013–2014). However, this large number hides great variation in output across time and space, as well as in terms of quality. The remainder of this section explores this variation in greater detail.

Variation Across Space

The vast majority of videos (more than 850) are produced by core *Wilāyāt* taken together, not by the central offices or the peripheral *Wilāyāt*. Figure 4.5 shows this domination. This is a crucial observation highlighting the decentralized character of IS's video propaganda structure, where each province is responsible for producing video content that is region-specific yet follows established scripts (see the later, qualitative discussion). Moreover, production across provinces—both peripheral and core—is spread very unequally, with some provinces producing high amounts of videos (e.g., *Ninawa*, *al-Khayr*, or *ar-Raqqah*) while others release very few output (e.g., *Baghdad*, *Diyala*). Figure 4.5 also reveals that state of affairs. This diversity is easily understood when taking into account a series of material factors, chiefly the

---

[12] http://jihadology.net/. This repository is led by Aaron Zelin.

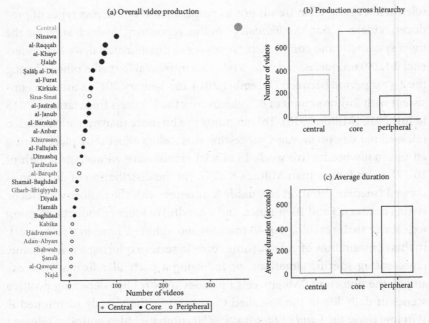

Figure 4.5 Descriptive information on Islamic State video production (December 2014–January 2017). (a) Plots the overall number of videos produced by the Central media office (grey dot on top of graph), core *Wilāyāt* (black dots), and peripheral *Wilāyāt* (hollow dots). (b) Plots the number of videos by type of producer and (c) displays the average video duration for each producer in the organizational hierarchy.

stability of IS power in the province (e.g., the provinces surrounding IS's long-standing strongholds of Raqqa and Nineveh are the two top producers). This means that peripheral provinces, which "vary widely in operational circumstances and capabilities" (Bauer 2016: xvi), have very different and generally low output levels.

Variation Across Time

Figure 4.6 demonstrates variation in video production across time by the type of producer. Turning first to the core *Wilāyāt*, these data suggest a gradual decline in video output and are thus consistent with Milton's data (2016: 21) and Winter's more recent observations (2017) and further illustrate the

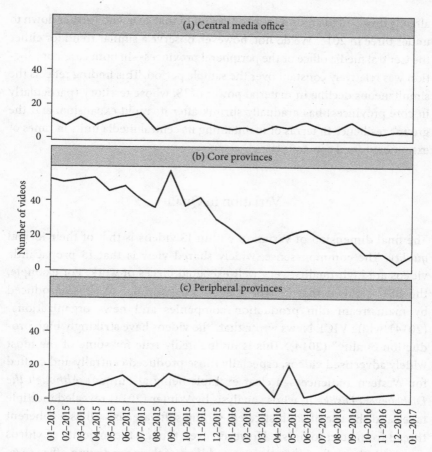

Figure 4.6 Number of video by type of producer (January 2015 to January 2017). As demonstrated in the figure, while the production of the central media office remained more or less stable over time, the production of the core provinces diminished gradually as Islamic State (IŚ) territory shrank, leading to a steady tarnishing of IS overall video production.

boom-and-bust cycle described in Chapter 1.[13] While there are declines across the board among core provinces, *Wilāyāt* such ar-Raqqah, al-Khayr, and Ninawa experienced a precipitous drop. Each of these *Wilāyāt* produced between five and ten videos per month in early 2015, but production had

---

[13] As shown by Ingram in the first chapter of this volume, media output and situation in the field are inseparable. We can thus use such increase/decrease measures simultaneously as shifts in media strategies designed to weather bust cycles and indirectly as indicators of success or failure on the field.

already dropped to around four by the end of that year, and further down to under three in 2016. We do not, however, observe a similar trend for either the Central media office or the peripheral provinces—in both cases, production was relatively constant over the sample period. This finding reflects the simultaneous decline in material power of IS, whose territory (particularly in core provinces) has gradually shrunk after its rapid expansion, and the group's resilience in terms of maintaining its central media units in times of extreme external constraints.

Variation in Quality

The final dimension of variation within IS videos is that of their formal *quality*. The common-sense, widely shared view is that IS propaganda videos are high-quality, very well-executed pieces of work. For example, the BBC claimed that IS videos are "not dissimilar to those produced by mainstream film production companies and news organizations" (2014), while VICE News wrote that "the videos have strikingly high production quality" (2014). This is undoubtedly true for some of the most widely advertised videos, especially those produced centrally and crafted for Western audiences—a clear example being al-Furqan's *Although the Disbelievers Dislike It*, whose analysis by Winter (2014) revealed multiple takes and the use of sophisticated editing software, as well as a coherent thread from start to finish. However, even though the majority of videos start with the well-executed animated logo of their producing office (e.g., al-Furqan Media or al-Khayr Media Center), many are low-quality productions realized with basic video-editing software requiring no professional skills. Scores of videos have no coherent thread, juxtaposing without transition raw battlefield footage characterized by loud noise as background to individuals' messages to their enemies or fellow *mujāhidīn*, or to executions. The omnipresence of *anashīd* chants, although inherently significant (as explained in Chapter 6), sometimes trumps the spoken message. To sum up, while a limited group of highly visible, top-profile videos display strong formal characteristics, most videos released by IS media offices result from a balance struck between, on the one hand, producing the required, recognizable standardized scripts (as described later) and, on the other hand, functioning with readily available software and tight time pressure.

A Qualitative Analysis of IS Videos: Scripts and Meta-Narrative

While the descriptive analysis in the previous section helps clarify the overall picture of how much video propaganda is being released, when, and by whom, we have yet to explore the actual content of our video data. To achieve this objective, we conducted a qualitative assessment of a sample of videos, noting the commonalities in terms of sequencing across videos. More specifically, from the total corpus, we selected a stratified, random sample of 50 videos (with strata determined by the three main groups according to their relative frequency: 22% ($n = 11$) from IS's central offices, 66% ($n = 33$) from core provinces, and 12% ($n = 6$) from peripheral provinces). The two main advantages of such a complement is first to be able to identify and closely analyze potential differences between videos and second to see how moving images are enmeshed with language to co-construct particular narratives. Together with the quantitative viewpoint, this approach helps us to understand how videos operationalize the major strategy structuring IS propaganda already highlighted in Chapter 1 of this book and echo the master narrative constructed by magazines (see previous chapter).

To do so, we identify here five recurrent *scripts*—understood as particularly standardized sequences of moving images and sound—that predominantly feature in videos, and we explain how these scripts relate to each other and contribute to the construction of IS's propaganda message. Together, these scripts make most of the footage time in our sample. A close qualitative viewing of the sample indeed immediately revealed their highly repetitive character: the videos constantly reiterate new versions of a limited number of particular and standardized sets of sequences. This can be understood as a result of IS's decentralized yet bureaucratic media system already evoked earlier: working with original AQI/IS memos, Milton indeed revealed that IS leadership has gradually refined its propaganda content by "tracking progress and identifying best practices," leading to increased standardization of authorized outputs (2016: 9). Even though IS propaganda videos do feature gruesome executions, which are perhaps, in themselves, the most standardized script, they do extent beyond this most famous aspect by covering (a very limited series of) other themes. We identify five scripts: *message, utopia, punishment, war,* and *istishhad*.

These codified sets of sequences regularly feature the same prominent jihadist symbols found in other IS propaganda outlets and jihadi culture in general, such as the *raayat as-sawdaa* black flag (read Wignell, Tan, & O'Halloran 2017a on the prominence of this symbol in IS literature; see also previous chapter) and the Kalashnikov (which has, as shown by Kovacs 2015, moved from mere weapon to jihadi symbol).[14] As explained by Bhui and Ibrahim (2013), these recurring symbols are building blocks in the formation of a group culture, thereby shaping individuals' identities as members of the group (on the "jihadi culture," read Hegghammer 2017). They do so in a way similar to the linguistic symbols highlighted by Kendall in her detailed analysis of jihadi texts (2016): they constitute the group by reinforcing its legitimacy through historical links (the black flag refers to the prophet and his companions, the Kalashnikov to the already mythicized Afghan *jihād*, etc.).

Script 1: Message

A first recurrent script is the *message*, where an individual (usually a fighter accompanied by a couple of associates) directly apostrophizes the watcher, who is assumed to be either an enemy who is therefore threatened (e.g., the United States, France,[15] Shi'a militias, apostates, etc.) or a group of potential sympathizers who are therefore incited to join or commit attacks (e.g., Muslims in Jordan or France). Another version of the message script similarly features one fighter or a small group speaking directly to the camera, but this time to pledge allegiance to the Caliphate or praise it. This is the simplest possible script, "made with only basic visual skills, a static camera and fully focused on the text, missing the full potential of visual propaganda" (Kovacs 2015: 56). Inherited from al-Qaeda's older as-Sahab productions featuring Osama Bin Laden and al-Zawahiri, the message script is the easiest form of footage to execute; it therefore comes as no surprise that in our sample, 4 of the 6 videos produced by peripheral provinces consist exclusively of one or several message scripts, reflecting their limited ability to produce anything more sophisticated.

Messages are regularly staged with symbolic elements in the background. The black flag, traditional clothes, Kalashnikovs, and the raised index finger symbolizing the belief in the oneness of God (*shahada*) are frequent and

[14] Wignell, Tan, and O'Halloran (2017b) have documented the omnipresence, in IS magazines' imagery, of the Kalashnikov as a symbolic icon.

[15] In the case of messages to foreign audiences, scripts can contain non-Arabic language even when produced by *Wilāyāt* (as for example al-Furat's video *And Verily Our Soldiers Will Be Victorious*).

Figure 4.7 Top: Screenshots of three instances of the *message* script (left: *Wilāya Dijlah*, "A Declaration of Innocence and Cutting of Family Link"; center: *Wilāya al-Khayr*, "Oh Commander of the Faithful, Leave Space Between Us and Them"; right: *Wilāya Khurasan*, "You Won't Dream of Being Secure"). Bottom: Instances of the *message* script in two al-Qaeda videos.

often combined. Figure 4.7 shows three variations of the message script in IS videos, compared to two very similar instances of the script in al-Qaeda videos.

Script 2: Utopia

A second script is constituted of images of the perfect, utopian life lived under the Caliphate: footages of bustling street life, well-stocked shops, happy playing children, state-of-the-art hospitals, impartial and functioning government services, and the like. Although this script is less codified than the message one, it is almost as straightforward, featuring simple footage of the perfect scene (say, a market) accompanied by one or several interviews of participants (e.g., a doctor, a child)[16] insisting on how perfect that particular situation is. The "Mujatweets" series already mentioned epitomize this script, which is also very present in 12 out of the 33 videos sampled from core provinces, making it a very frequent script.

In contrast to the message script, the utopia script is unique to IS, which has been the only jihadi group to achieve sufficient territorial gains to be able to produce it (and credible in doing so). IS videos' insistence on how well the

---

[16] An analysis of the recurring presence of children in IS propaganda can be found in Christien (2016). For a more general discussion on children in the IS, read Horgan, Taylor, Bloom, and Winter (2017).

Figure 4.8 Screenshots of two variations of the *utopian* script (left: *Wilāya Ar-Raqqah*, "The Atmosphere of 'Id al-Fiṭr in the City of al-Raqqah"; Right: *Wilāya Halab*, "To the Light").

Caliphate is organized and how happy its inhabitants are seeks to both establish the Caliphate as a real state (as opposed to merely an insurgent group holding territory) and to reinforce its appeal to potential immigrants[17] or inhabitants of zones close to those controlled by IS. Figure 4.8 shows two variants of the utopia script, which directly echoes one of the "solution" themes stressed in the organization's magazines, thus evidencing the group's willingness to disseminate a coherent and cross-fertilizing message across the various media of its full-spectrum propaganda.

Script 3: Punishment

In accordance to IS's sharp *takfiri* discourse insisting on the disappearance of any "grey zone" between true believers and their opponents (see Chapter 2), this utopian life can only be offered and guaranteed in a society purified of its enemies. This is why the third script, that of punishment of IS's enemies, is central and frequent: the punishment of both internal and external enemies constitutes the link between the internal-facing enforcement of law and order in order to construct a perfect life and the external-facing *jihād* warfare, both of which are crystallized in a different script (utopia and war, respectively).[18]

---

[17] Hence the recurring insistence on immigration to the Caliphate (*hijra*) in these scripts.

[18] While the frequent juxtaposition of great care for its citizens and brutal violence against its enemies can seem incomprehensible, it closely matches Michel Foucault's seminal analysis of state fascism (1997), whereby some states' growing concerns with the security and productive life of its defined in-group come to depend on the elimination of all members perceived as endangering the health and purity of this in-group. Just as in Nazi Germany's "Aryan" *lebensraum*, the good, utopian life of IS's in-group simply cannot be realized with enemies living on its mythic soil.

IS can be credited for the invention and frequent implementation of highly ritualized—and therefore heavily scripted videos of—punishments, most of them being executions but a noteworthy minority being violent yet nonlethal punishment such as foot or hand amputations. This new trend traces back to the al-Zarqawi period (and was at that time famously rebuked by al-Zawahiri in his 2004 letter).[19] One-third of the videos produced by core *Wilāyāt* in our sample include a punishment script (nonlethal in two instances) featuring either internal enemies enduring Shari'a-governed punishments (*ḥudūd*)[20] or external enemies ("spies," shi'a fighters, foreign fighters or journalists, etc.).

The archetypal structure of the script, followed rigorously in 6 of our 50 sampled videos (and only slightly more loosely followed in the other cases) goes as follows. First, one or several individual(s) (dressed in orange if "external" enemy) confess(es) his/their crime at length (e.g., spying, stealing, adultery), stressing how wrong and vain his/their action was given IS's power and righteousness. Second, the individual(s) appear(s) with the executioner, who offers a statement. Third, the individual(s) is/are executed or punished (most of the time by gun, often by beheading, and often through unusual means like drowning, stoning, throwing from the top of a building, or exploding). This makes the punishment script invariably shocking.

As Halfmann and Young's study of gruesome images in anti-abortion and anti-slavery campaigns claimed, such "grotesque" images produce "strong emotions that increase the intensity and emotional resonance of movement frames" (Halfmann & Young 2010: 4). In other words, they are not only made to elicit terror, but also to reiterate the most important narratives advocated by the group and intensify the emotional reaction that goes with them. With anti-abortion groups like the Army of God, images of dead fetuses are, for example, juxtaposed to those of corpses in Nazi concentration camps, thus reinforcing the narrative of abortion as genocide and strengthening the audience's emotional reaction. For IS, strictly codified executions reiterate the group's claim to be the only one that really punishes those who harm

---

[19] The letter is available at https://www.ctc.usma.edu/posts/zawahiris-letter-to-zarqawi-original-language-2.

[20] Scenes of *ḥudūd* might well follow the same script as executions of "external" enemies because they mostly target local audiences. As Winter indeed (2015b: 34) explains, "the principal message it is trying to convey is that the 'caliphate' is a 'caliphate of law' where civil crimes like murder, banditry, theft and drug-taking are punished, swiftly and unwaveringly. To many in the region, civil security—even if harshly imposed—is enticing. Besides this, depictions of the hudud punishments for religious 'crimes' like adultery, insulting God and homosexuality, attract and gratify ideological supporters.... Reports on Islamic State's 'justice' seek to provoke outrage among the international community, a key tenet of the group's international outreach strategy."

Figure 4.9 Screenshot of a typical *execution* script from an Islamic State propaganda video: confession (left) followed by execution (right) of prisoners wearing Guantanamo-like suits (*Wilāya al-Furat*, "Implementation of the Rule of God Upon the Corrupters in the Land").

Muslims—a clear example of this is the notorious video showing the execution of the Jordanian pilot, who is burned because he has purportedly burned Muslims with his bombs. The heavily ritualized execution sequences reinforce this emotional effect even more: indeed, for individuals who have already watched a few videos, the mere appearance of a person confessing or wearing an orange suit is sufficient to trigger the emotional reaction associated with the execution itself, in a Pavlovian way.

Symbols are extensively used by IS in these videos to reinforce the link between the punishment script and this claim that IS provides a real solution to the crisis. As Tinnes for example observes (2015: 77), IS's "execution videos are laden with colour symbolism. Often, the captive is forced to wear an orange jumpsuit—a reference to the prison uniforms at Guantanamo Bay. . . . The executioner is usually clad in black clothes—symbolically representing the concepts of jihad and the caliphate by creating a historical link to both the prophet's black battle flag and the medieval Abbasid Caliphate." Figure 4.9 shows the first and second steps of the punishment script; notice the prisoners' orange jumpsuits and executioners' black clothes.

Script 4: War

War is probably the dominant theme of IS propaganda and is omnipresent in videos. From our 50 videos sample, 19 feature battlefield scenes, which roughly confirms the approximately 2:5 ratio provided in Winter's analysis of one month of IS propaganda content (2015b: 24). As he puts it, such a

Figure 4.10 Screenshots from two instances of the *war* script (left: An example of *training*: *Wilāya Halab*, "To the Light"; right, an example of *firing*: *Wilāya Halab*, "Progress of the Battle with the Nuṣayrī Army").

prominence is not surprising as "war is Islamic State's raison d'etre, its primary agent of change and revolution." War is not only the means to establish the religious goal of the Caliphate; as with punishment, it is also presented as a retributive action to punish the harm done by the various out-groups—the title of a war-filled video released by the Tarabulus province, *From Humiliation to Dignity*, illustrates this idea.

The war script is not as heavily codified as the other ones; rather, it comprises a series of slightly different footages, each documenting one particular aspect of war. In the *training* type, images show well-geared and equipped IS *mujāhidīn* flawlessly performing in perfect synchronization hard exercises and military drills. In the *shooting* type, images show IS fighters aiming and firing their weapons (light weapons, mortar, embarked heavy machine guns, etc.) at an unseen enemy. In the *aftermath* type, a moving camera films a recently won area (e.g., a building, a village), focusing on the image on enemies' dead bodies, abandoned buildings, and newly gained weapons (which are usually shown aligned together on the floor or against a wall to emphasize the quantity of the booty).[21] Each of these types is clearly standardized and frequently appears in videos (see Figure 4.10).

Script 5: *Istishhad*

The final prominent script that we highlight is that of *istishhad*, or martyrdom. Equally as tightly codified as the punishment script, it consistently

---

[21] These three subtypes partly align with Winter's six subthemes of the war narrative in IS propaganda (2015a: 24): preparation, martyrdom panegyrics, offensive, defense, aftermath, and attrition.

Figure 4.11 Screenshot of a typical *istishhad* script from an Islamic State propaganda video: goodbye from the ecstatic truck driver (left), departure of the explosive truck (center), explosion of the truck with supporters shouting "Allahu Akbar" (right) (*Wilāya al-Furat*, "Implementation of the Rule of God Upon the Corrupters in the Land").

involves the exact same three sequences (see Figure 4.11 for an illustration of this sequence). First, a man is seen entering or sitting in an armor-plated truck; the man is invariably happy and sometimes chats with the cameraman while setting up cables and devices. Second, the truck leaves the IS lines, driving toward the enemy. Third, a static recording shows a huge explosion (allegedly that of the truck) on the skyline, always followed by loud cheers for the martyr who just exploded. This exact sequence features in 7 of the 50 sampled videos (all from provinces, none from centrally produced videos), a significant proportion which reveals both the amplitude of suicide tactics in IS warfare[22] and the importance given in its culture to the martyr figure (*istishhadi*), who is regularly glorified in propaganda magazines as well as in radio reports and "martyrologies" (see Chapter 6).

As already noted, most videos contain more than one of these scripts, as well as some unscripted material; a typical 5-minute video would, for example, have a utopian script, then move on to a lengthy war script, with eventually a message script and some unscripted images. While in some cases the transitions between the scripts make sense, most of the time they fail to build a coherent message for the full video: one sampled video, for example, offers scenes of well-run street market shops (utopia script), then without transition or explanation shows an enemy armored truck exploding on a landmine (war script). Yet in spite of these formal problems, the relentless repetition of these scenarios contributes to reiterate the overarching, simplistic crisis–solution narrative disseminated by IS

---

[22] If we hypothesize that this proportion is true for the entire video corpus, it would mean that almost 200 suicide operations have been recorded following to this script.

propaganda (read previous chapters; also Ingram 2016): (1) the *messages* diagnose the problems and identify once again the enemies and friends; (2) the *war* footage shows that IS is a powerful and successful organization in charge of addressing this problem, attracting friends, and retaliating against the enemies for the harm they have done to Muslims; (3) the display of numerous *istishhad* operations shows the unlimited determination and faith of IS fighters as well as their potential for devastation in the conduct of war; (4) the *utopia* script proves that the Caliphate is the perfect political entity caring for its members; and, finally, (5) the *punishments* demonstrate that IS is ruthless and impartial in its implementation of law and order, as well as the only efficient and uncompromising organization committed to the retaliatory project against Muslims' oppressive enemies ("Crusaders," Shi'a, "apostates," etc.).

A Closer Look at the "Selected 10" Videos

While the previous sections offer a broad description of IS video production and the specific "scripts" that reoccur throughout IS videos in general to disseminate its message, it is useful to also explore the types of videos that IS seeks to strategically prioritize. We offer an initial examination of this question by taking a closer look at the "Selected 10" videos first introduced in Chapter 1. To refresh, IS's *Dabiq* and *Rumiyah* magazines highlight 10 videos from across the *Wilāyāt* media outlets to encourage provincial video production, draw susceptible viewers deeper into their web of propaganda, and support the promotion of particular strategic, operational, and tactical messages. In this section, we take a comparative view of the "Selected 10," not only describing basic features of this subset of content, but also highlighting similarities and differences with IS video content more generally.

Data

First, we began by collecting the "Selected 10" videos for both *Dabiq* (nos. 10–15) and *Rumiyah* (nos. 1 and 9) magazines. As shown in Figure 4.12a, the distribution of provinces making it into the top 10 is highly concentrated in the core *Wilāyāt*, with Salah al-Din ($n = 10$ videos) and Ninawa

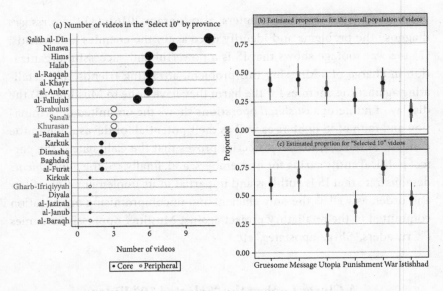

Figure 4.12 A comparison to the "Selected 10." (a) Plots the number of videos in the selected 10 across the core *Wilāyāt* (black dots) and peripheral *Wilāyāt* (hollow dots). (b) Estimates the proportion of videos with each narrative (or script) for the full sample, while (c) displays the estimated proportion for the selected 10. The thick (1 standard error) and thin (2 standard errors) tails represent uncertainty around the estimated proportions.

($n = 7$) representing a considerable proportion of the overall videos. Of the 80 videos collected as part of this analysis, 69 videos are from the core provinces (86%), and thus the representation conforms generally to the breakdown in overall production highlighted in Figure 4.1. Second, to provide a more detailed analysis of the video content, we selected and viewed a random sample of 15 videos. For each video, the authors noted general characteristics such as quality, visual style, and the use of symbols, while also coding for the presence or absence of the main scripts presented in the previous section. We use these data to (1) provide some general reflections on the "Selected 10" and (2) provide an initial comparison of the prominence of narratives and themes in the full and selected subsample.

Reflections on the "Selected 10"

Overall, the sample of videos is notable for its high-quality production. Moreover, consistent with IS videos more generally, the videos are similar in structure, appearance, and substance, further demonstrating IS's efforts to promote a cohesive and easily recognizable message. These videos also highlight a number of "innovations" used to draw in the viewer. For instance, several videos featured footage from a sniper scope with the target in the cross-hairs, eventually zooming in as the viewer watches the victim being struck. There were also scenes featuring first-person footage in which the camera was placed on the weapon, thus imitating the modern first-person video game experience. More generally, the drone target-tracking, sniper-scope, and first-person view footage has been noted by Lesaca (2015) as tapping into Western pop culture, mimicking TV shows (e.g., *Person of Interest*), films (e.g., *American Sniper*), and popular video games (e.g., Halo). This constitutes one clear example of a well-thought articulation between two of the many components of IS's full-spectrum propaganda in order to target one specific audience. Drawing on these existing cultural references, moreover, arguably assists in spreading IS's appeal to the non–Arabic-speaking viewers baited by *Dabiq* or *Rumiyah*. Despite all the videos being filmed in Arabic (often with Arabic captions), the narratives are easy to follow, even for non–Arabic-speakers.

Comparing the Messages: How Does the Selected 10 Differ from the Full Sample?

The similarity in appearance of IS videos is complemented by the cohesive message promoted across the full and "Selected 10" sample. Although each video has a central focus—often easily identified by the title of the video—most of the videos featured some combination of the "scripts" outlined in the previous section. For instance, the top-ranked video in *Dabiq* no. 15, *Racing to the Villages to Spread Guidance* predominantly features a utopian script, with many scenes showing happy children listening and learning from IS members and even features a playful handshake between an IS member and a young boy. Yet, near the end of this video, starts an *istishhad* script and a violent *war* script.

While the overarching message and scripts were consistent across the full and subsample of selected videos, the relative emphasis of videos differed in a handful of areas. As highlighted in Figure 4.12b,c, the overall pattern across scripts is similar: both samples tend to focus on "the message" and "war" narratives, while also displaying a significant portion of gruesome visual content. However, to the extent that the two samples differ, the "Select 10" is less likely to feature the *utopian* script and more likely to feature the *istishhad* one. It is also important to note that the overall percentage of gruesome content was much higher in the selective subsample—these videos were *extremely* gruesome, often displaying heinous acts of violence alongside footage of in-group victimization. This overrepresentation of gruesome footage in the videos selected to be advertised to Western audiences most probably denotes a strategic choice made by the group.

Conclusion

For the Western public, videos arguably constitute the most well-known component of IS propaganda. Images of gruesome executions are now part of the general representation of the terrorist group and perhaps Salafi-jihadism in general. Yet this chapter has shown that behind the videos produced for— or/and advertised to—this particular audience, a much bigger flow of videos is produced by an array of media offices bound together in a multilayer organization, with many interwoven objectives and target audiences.

We have also shown that even though there has been a precipitous decline in the production of core provinces (which are responsible for most of IS's videos), the Central office's resilience (and to a lesser extent the fluctuating activity of peripheral provinces) denotes the group's ability to adapt to its environment with a media organization that has a variable geometry built around a solid center. Even though the group's "bust" had a significant effect on the overall production of videos, the group's flexible model could easily be re-expanded around its center if opportunities arise.

Our multilayered methodological approach has also revealed the highly standardized content of the group's videos, which confirms Milton's organizational claims. Videos are highly consistent in terms of the scripts they follow, across all levels of the organizational hierarchy. However, while the general themes are consistent, the relative emphasis of the videos differs across groups of videos depending on their target audience and producer—for example, the "Selected 10" are clearly distinct from the full sample even though they mobilize the same scripts (they are more gruesome, they feature less the utopia script, and their editorial quality was much higher) in order to match the target audience's expectations, desires, or cultural affinities.

References

Al-Tamimi A. (2016) "Governance," in Bauer K. (ed.), "Beyond Syria and Iraq. Examining Islamic State Provinces." The Washington Institute for Near East Policy. Retrieved from https://www.washingtoninstitute.org/uploads/Documents/pubs/PolicyFocus149_Bauer.pdf, pp. 30–35.

Baudrillard J. (1994) Simulacra and Simulation. Ann Arbor: University of Michigan Press.

Bauer K., ed. (2016) "Beyond Syria and Iraq. Examining Islamic State Provinces." The Washington Institute for Near East Policy. Retrieved from https://www.washingtoninstitute.org/uploads/Documents/pubs/PolicyFocus149_Bauer.pdf.

BBC (2014, October 21) "Slick, Agile and Modern—The IS Media Machine." Retrieved from http://www.bbc.co.uk/monitoring/slick-agile-and-modern-the-is-media-machine.

Bhui K., Ibrahim Y. (2013) "Marketing the 'Radical': Symbolic Communication and Persuasive Technologies in Jihadist Websites, Transcultural Psychiatry 50(2): 216–234.

Bleiker R. (2015) "Pluralist Methods for Visual Global Politics," Millennium: Journal of International Studies 43(3): 872–890.

Bolt N. (2012) The Violent Image: Insurgent Propaganda and the New Revolutionaries. New York: Columbia University Press/Hurst.

Christien A. (2016) "The Representation of Youth in the Islamic State's Propaganda Magazine Dabiq," Journal of Terrorism Research 7(3): 1–8.

Foucault M. (1997) Il faut défendre la société: Cours au Collège de France, 1976. Paris: Gallimard-Seuil.

Griffin M., Lee J. (1995) "Picturing the Gulf War: Constructing an Image of War in Time, Newsweek, and U.S. News & World Report," Journalism & Mass Communication Quarterly 72 (4): 813–825.

Halfmann D., Young M. (2010) "War Pictures: The Grotesque as a Mobilizing Tactic," Mobilization: An International Quarterly 15(1): 1–24.

Hansen L. (2015) "How Images Make World Politics: International Icons and the Case of Abu Ghraib," Review of International Studies 41: 263–288.

Hegghammer T., ed. (2017) Jihadi Culture: The Art and Social Practices of Militant Islamists. Cambridge: Cambridge University Press.

Horgan J., Taylor M., Bloom M., Winter C. (2017) "From Cubs to Lions: A Six Stage Model of Child Socialization into the Islamic State," Studies in Conflict & Terrorism 40(7): 645–664.

Ingram H. (2016) "An Analysis of Islamic State's Dabiq magazine," Australian Journal of Political Science 51(3): 458–477.

Kendall E. (2016) "Jihadist Propaganda and its Exploitation of the Arab Poetic Tradition," in Kendall E., Khan A. (eds.), Reclaiming Islamic Tradition. Modern Interpretations of the Classical Heritage. Edinburgh: Edinburgh University Press.

Kovacs A. (2015) "The 'New Jihadists' and the Visual Turn from Al-Qa'ida to ISIL/ ISIS?Da'ish," *Biztpol Affairs* 2(3): 47–70.

Leander A. (2016) "Digital/Commercial (in)Visibility: The Politics of DAESH Recruitment Videos," *European Journal of Social Theory*. Online before print.

Lesaca J. (2015) "On Social Media, ISIS Uses Modern Cultural Images to Spread Anti-Modern Values," *Brookings Institution*. Retrieved from https://www.brookings.edu/ blog/techtank/2015/09/24/on-social-media-isis-uses-modern-cultural-images-to-spread-anti-modern-values/.

Miller G., Mekhennet S. (2015, November 20). "Inside the Surreal World of the Islamic State's Propaganda Machine," *The Washington Post*. Retrieved from https://www. washingtonpost.com/world/national-security/inside-the-islamic-states-propaganda-machine/2015/11/20/051e997a-8ce6-11e5-acff-673ae92ddd2b_story.html?utm_ term=.323620ee7e88.

Milton D. (2016) "Communication Breakdown: Unraveling the Islamic State's Media Efforts," *Combating Terrorism Center at West Point Report*. Retrieved from https://www.ctc.usma. edu/posts/communication-breakdown-unraveling-the-islamic-states-media-efforts.

Molin Friis S. (2015) "'Beyond Anything We Have Ever Seen': Beheading Videos and the Visibility of Violence in the War Against ISIS," *International Affairs* 91(4): 725–746.

Tinnes J (2015) "Although the (Dis-)Believers Dislike It: A Backgrounder on IS Hostage Videos—August—December 2014," *Perspectives on Terrorism* 9(1): 76–94.

VICE News (2014, July 12) "ISIS Has a Really Slick and Sophisticated Media Department." Retrieved from https://news.vice.com/article/isis-has-a-really slick-and-sophisticated-media-department.

Whiteside C. (2016) "Lighting the Path: The Evolution of the Islamic State Media Enterprise (2003–2016)," *ICCT Research Paper*.

Wignell P., Tan S., O'Halloran K. (2017a) "Violent Extremism and Iconisation: Commanding Good and Forbidding Evil?," *Critical Discourse Studies* 14(1): 1–22.

Wignell P., Tan S., O'Halloran K. (2017b) "Under the Shade of AK47s: A Multimodal Approach to Violent Extremist Recruitment Strategies for Foreign Fighters," *Critical Studies on Terrorism*. Online first. doi: 10.1080/17539153.2017.1319319.

Winter C. (2014) "Detailed Analysis of Islamic State Propaganda Video: Although the Disbelievers Dislike It," Quilliam/TRAC. Retrieved from http://www.quilliaminter-national.com/shop/e-publications/detailed-analysis-of-islamic-state-propaganda-video-although-the-disbelievers-dislike-it/ (paywall).

Winter C. (2015a) "The Virtual 'Caliphate': Understanding Islamic State's Propaganda Strategy."

Winter C. (2015b) "Documenting the Virtual 'Caliphate'," *Quilliam Research Paper*.

Winter C. (2017) "The ISIS Propaganda Decline," *ICSR Insight*. Retrieved from http://icsr. info/2017/03/icsr-insight-isis-propaganda-decline/

Zelin A. (2015) "Picture or It Didn't Happen: A Snapshot of the Islamic State's Official Media Output," *Perspectives on Terrorism* 9(4): 85–97.

5

Islamic State's Propaganda and Social Media

Dissemination, Support, and Resilience

Laura Wakeford and Laura Smith

> The Internet has replaced Afghanistan as the terrorist training
> ground, and this should concern us the most.
> —Ronald Noble, Secretary General of Interpol, 2000–2014,
> writing in 2011; as cited in Conway 2012

> The move to social media in the wake of the conflict in Syria and, in
> particular, the subsequent IS media operations on Twitter are one
> of the most remarkable developments of the online jihad in the past
> decade.
> —Prucha 2016

Introduction

On May 22, 2017, a suicide bomber detonated an improvised explosive device packed with nuts and bolts in the foyer of the Manchester Arena at the end of a performance by the US artist Ariana Grande. The bomb killed 22 people and injured 116. Many of the casualties were children. While there was no official claim of responsibility for the attack by any terrorist group, supporters of the Islamic State (IS) celebrated the bombing on social media. IS supporters hailed the bombing as a victory against "the crusaders." After the attack, they used the encrypted Telegram messaging service to circulate more IS films than usual that threatened Britain and other Western democracies. It was widely reported that, in one film, an English-speaking supporter of IS held up a homemade sign with the word "Manchester" and the date of

Laura Wakeford and Laura Smith, *Islamic State's Propaganda and Social Media: Dissemination, Support, and Resilience* In: *ISIS Propaganda*. Edited by: Stephane J. Baele, Katharine A. Boyd, and Travis G. Coan, Oxford University Press (2020) © University of Maryland National Consortium for the Study of Terrorism and Responses to Terrorism (START)
DOI: 10.1093/oso/9780190932459.001.0006

the attack, stating "This is only the beginning. The lions of Islamic State of Iraq and Sham are beginning to attack all the crusaders." In this way, IS used social media to harness the publicity of terror attacks committed by jihadists who were unaffiliated with IS or those who acted alone to spread their own message, to radicalize and mobilize supporters, and to instill fear in the citizens of the countries they targeted. They "outsourced" the dissemination of propaganda to their decentralized networks of online supporters who both spread the messages of IS social media operatives and created their own—the ominously named *media mujāhidīn*.

IS was not the first organization to use the Internet to socialize, radicalize, and recruit members. As noted in the Introduction and Chapter 1 of this volume, IS propaganda is best conceptualized as a series of incremental innovations rather than as a new phenomenon in itself: its use of the Internet and social media is no exception. Indeed, Hezbullah pioneered insurgent marketing as early as the 1990s. IS's most notable peer—al Qaeda (AQ)—maintained a presence on social media since its advent, a tactic both endorsed by their late leader Osama bin Ladan (see Klausen 2015) and extensively exploited by its members (e.g., Anwar al-Awlaki). In other ideological contexts, social movements have formed and reformed (at least in part) through social media interactions (McGarty, Thomas, Lala, Smith, & Bliuc 2014; Smith, Gavin, & Sharp 2015; Smith, Thomas, & McGarty 2015; Thomas et al. 2015). For example, Smith, Gavin, and Sharp (2015) demonstrated that the Occupy Wall Street movement formed through interactions on a Facebook event page that enabled people to coalesce around a shared norm for taking action to redress perceived economic and social injustices. While groups such as IS and the Occupy movement obviously differ ideologically, in this chapter we propose that they share common psychological underpinnings through their online activities. However, due to the fact that IS's supporters' communication of jihadist ideology contravened many social media platforms' codes of conduct, the group developed a unique ability to innovate and adapt online in response to interventions that aimed to curtail its social media activity. In fact, despite the inherent difficulties associated with quantifying a group's online success,[1] by 2013, IS's use of social media

---

[1] Many factors obscure the relative support for a group on social media—especially proscribed groups like IS. For example, the criterion used to define an account as "radical" is often subject to disagreement (Berger & Perez 2016; Fisher 2016b), a single user could be operating multiple accounts, it is problematic to count accounts that have been suspended and quickly been replaced multiple times, such successive (as opposed to independent) accounts are not always easy to identify as such, some

had surpassed that of its peers both in terms of presence and global reach (Prucha 2016).

In this chapter, we describe how IS used social media in innovative (but also less novel) ways to advance its full-spectrum propaganda, which—as set out in the Introduction to this volume—encapsulates a comprehensive, cohesive, and multidimensional approach to developing and propagating material. Crucially, we explain *how* and *why* their strategies are effective from a social psychological perspective. On the pages that follow, we demonstrate how IS responded to technological developments in online and social media to develop a sophisticated media strategy and how, at the same time, social media played an instrumental role in the development and evolution of IS itself. Whereas in the past other jihadist groups utilized online media primarily for the purpose of recruitment, IS's ability to weave its application into almost all aspects of their battle for the Caliphate created an entirely new form of online jihadist collective identity. Significantly, while in this chapter we examine a discrete temporal snapshot of online jihadism, in doing so we provide an opportunity to critically examine methodological challenges, future research opportunities, and the conceptual implications of studying the activities of IS online. Thus, in this chapter, we describe how IS was able to develop a coherent and cohesive shared *social identity* (Tajfel & Turner 1979) and "brand" by combining full-spectrum propaganda with social media (particularly Twitter) interactions.

Caveats: IS Propaganda and the Current Limitations of Social Media Research

At this juncture, it is important to explain the limitations and challenges of social media research methods and how they shape the statistics cited about IS's (and other groups') reach on social media. First, the majority of research on IS-affiliated accounts has been conducted in the absence of what computer scientists call *ground truth*. For this purpose, we can define ground truth as independent verification of the identity (e.g., group affiliation) of the users within a sample. For example, to investigate the nature and behavior of members of IS online, one would need to independently verify that the

accounts might be operated by outgroup intelligence operatives, and a reduction in online presence does not necessarily equate to reduced productivity (Fisher 2016a).

user accounts identified as IS-affiliated are indeed run by individuals affiliated with IS (in that they are recognized by IS and/or the media *mujāhidīn* as a group member). One way in which a researcher would go about establishing ground truth is to obtain a sample of social media user accounts that are known to originate from convicted IS foreign fighters or terrorists. Needless to say, such datasets are difficult—if not virtually impossible—to obtain and are often limited in their scope (e.g., in terms of the number of accounts in the sample). This means that researchers who publish figures on numbers of accounts associated with IS on various social media platforms must first identify the "features" (the online characteristics, behaviors, and metrics) associated with IS accounts (which will vary according to the nature of each social media platform and over time) and then find accounts that display those IS features. This means that the number of accounts identified will depend on the inclusivity and discriminatory ability of the features. A broad set of "somewhat radical" features (such as following an official IS account) will "capture" a greater number of accounts than will a narrow set of more extreme features (such as displaying an IS flag and proclaiming allegiance to IS). Figures about the reach of IS on social media sites should be understood with these caveats in mind.

A second important caveat is that, of the social media accounts identified as pro-IS, the majority are likely to be "clicktivists" rather than "activists." That is, while they are willing to show support for IS online, they are unlikely to take their support offline. "Clicktivism" (also known as "slacktivism") is the phenomenon that occurs when low-cost, low-risk actions on social media—such as liking or sharing a post—forecloses engagement in higher risk actions because clicking satisfies the motivation to act (see also Lee & Hsieh 2013). Thus, someone might be willing to retweet a link to an IS film or select a pro-IS avatar for their social media account, but this does not mean that they would be willing to build and detonate an improvised explosive device or travel to Syria to become an IS foreign fighter. While there is evidence that communicating opinions online can leave a psychological legacy (Carlisle & Patton 2013; Schumann & Klein 2015) and affect the broader online community or "milieu" (Conway 2012), online actions do not translate to offline actions: it is not a "slippery slope"; rather, the expression of online attitudes and offline actions are two very different "slopes." Having said that, the role and reach of IS on social media refutes the suggestion that IS's engagement through social media and its effect on intergroup relations was a tidal wave of reaction to external events that quickly subsided (cf., Morozov

2009). Rather, communicating opinions online resulted in substantive social and psychological changes at the community level (Harlow 2012; McGarty et al. 2014; Smith, Gavin, & Sharp 2015; Thomas et al. 2015; Wojcieszak 2009). This suggests that accounts of clicktivism are overly simplified; they do not take into account the way in which communicating opinions and ideology can color social relations and the broader social milieu and can in turn lead to sustained individual- and group-level changes.

What is missing in the general understanding of these phenomena is empirical evidence for causal connections between online social media interactions and offline terrorist behavior/radicalization (which brings us back to the problem of the absence of ground truth data). Current evidence for causal connections is either anecdotal, stemming from individual case studies that cannot be generalized, or arises from secondary sources. But where researchers are claiming that tens of thousands of user accounts on each social media platform are authored by IS supporters, we need to harness the power of that sample size to begin to understand general longitudinal causal connections between online and offline behaviors.

Given these limitations, this raises the question of how the impact of online counterterrorism interventions can be evaluated. While social media platforms have been given multiple mandates by governments to deny extremists a safe space in which to communicate (Home Affairs Committee 2017), without the methodologies that can accurately assess the reach of extremists online, and the social, psychological, and practical impact of interventions, these companies will be working on the untested assumption that their interventions decrease the threat posed by the group. Of course, it is possible that interventions could worsen as well as alleviate the threat posed by terrorist groups.

Notwithstanding the limitations of current social media research methods, there are specific conceptual, practical, and methodological lessons that we can learn from IS's online strategy and propaganda. In this chapter, while acknowledging and alluding to the cross-platform nature of IS social media activity, we have chosen to focus in greater depth on IS's activity on a single social media platform: Twitter. The reasons for this are threefold: first, we could not do justice to all of the relevant platforms within the space confines of this chapter. Second, the majority of research on IS social media activity has been conducted on Twitter, and therefore, by focusing on this platform, we can take advantage of the insights of this literature. The third reason for this focus (both within this chapter and in past literature) is that Twitter has

a relatively open application programming interface (API) that, in combination with Twitter's policy, makes a substantial volume of publicly posted
Twitter data ("tweets") available to researchers. Put simply, Twitter data are
easier to access than data on other, more private and/or encrypted social
media platforms, and therefore these data are available for study. However,
there are limitations in focusing on an analysis of IS activity solely on
Twitter, and the majority of past research has not fully acknowledged these
limitations. For example, while different people play different roles within
the media *mujāhidīn* (disseminator, creator, passive "consumer"), it is not
straightforward to identify these roles using Twitter data. Furthermore, IS
uses a very wide variety of interconnected online platforms, each of which
plays a different role in its overall online activity. These additional platforms
include well-known sites such as Facebook, WhatsApp, and Telegram, but
also lesser known locations such as diaspora, surespot, kik, Wordpress, ar-
chive.org, and justpaste.it. Only through multiplatform analyses can research
establish the full range of activities and the reach of IS online.

Keeping these caveats in mind, here we describe how the uniquely innovative nature of IS online enabled the group to build on the tried-and-tested
online strategies of other groups (see Chapter 1 for more on IS as plagiarists)
and to adapt and strengthen as both a group and "brand" as the Internet
evolved and social media were invented. As will be seen, IS's use of full-
spectrum propaganda in conjunction with social media allowed the group
to connect a diverse audience with like-minded others at a scale never seen
before, at least not for a terrorist organization. Together, this environment
provided the conditions for users to interact, share reaffirming or polarizing
information, and modify theirs and other's "understanding of their social
environment" (see Introduction) while developing a sense of group membership and collective pride and self-esteem by promoting the group to the
world. The implications of this combination on the group's evolution provide
the overarching theme of this chapter.

Online Jihadism: The Shift from Passive to Active Online Activity

IS's online media campaign was not built in a void; it rested on almost three
decades of experimentation by other Sunni jihadist groups. In 2001, the coordinated attacks on the Twin Towers propelled AQ's brand of extreme Sunni

jihadism into homes the world over, and, as Prucha (2016) notes, the Internet has played an important role in maintaining this brand of jihadism ever since. In this section, we will explain the background to jihadist propaganda and how it developed with the evolution of the Internet.

Following Zelin's (2013) framework, it is useful to consider jihadism as divided into four temporal phases. The first phase predated the use of the Internet (e.g., sermons, newsletters, magazines, videotapes, etc.); however, the subsequent three phases were differentiated based on shifts in online strategy, thus providing a useful framework from which we can begin to understand how IS's social media strategy fitted into the wider online jihadist movement from which it was born. The first phase of jihadist propaganda occurred offline. During this time, jihadist groups such as AQ used newsletters, magazines, and videotapes to disseminate propaganda to their network of supporters. The second phase of online jihadism began in the mid-1990s, after the advent of Web 1.0, when jihadist-based websites began proliferating (Zelin 2013). In Web 1.0, information on websites was mostly static, the data were only updated occasionally, and content was not interactive: only webmasters could edit content of webpages. Thus, end users of these websites could not connect or collaborate: they remained "consumers" of the content. This meant that, during the era of Web 1.0, AQ—the predominant brand of Salafi-jihadism at the time—retained a large degree of control over its online presence. It achieved this by collaborating with ideologically aligned media groups, such as the al-Shabab Media Production Company. These companies, who produced AQ's websites, were granted privileged access to exclusive interviews with the group's leaders and, among other things, disseminated sermons, published first-hand jihadi stories, and produced historical short films (Rogan & Stenerson 2007). The relatively static nature of Web 1.0 and the centrally controlled nature of these sites meant that AQ had tight control over the content published. Information transmission was thus unidirectional and top-down: from AQ to interested end users. Webmasters determined the information that was on the websites, and this information could be viewed or downloaded.

Web 2.0 came into common usage in the mid-2000s. Increasingly, users could connect, interact, and collaborate with each other and content providers; had more input into the nature and scope of Web content; and, in some cases, could exert real-time control over it. This gave Web 2.0 an inherently social nature. Through Web 2.0, chat forums gained traction among the online jihadist community, marking entry to Zelin's third phase. These forums allow globally displaced, like-minded ideologues to interact with relative anonymity. While such sites permit users a sense of autonomy in directing debate, they are administered and "steered" by site administrators who can control the brand by banning users, deleting threads, and hushing or removing ideologically incongruent dialogue (Zelin 2013). Furthermore, jihadist media groups could influence the ebb and flow of activity within these forums by releasing (branded) propaganda in synchronized and simultaneous waves, making them "force multipliers" who capitalized on events, such as terrorist attacks, in order to maintain their momentum (Rogan & Stenerson 2007).

With Web 2.0, the increasing prevalence of Software as a Service (SaaS), web apps, and cloud computing rather than locally installed programs and services enabled users to share content. Mobile computing allowed users to connect from anywhere in the world, enabled by the proliferation of smartphones, tablets, and other mobile devices in conjunction with readily accessible Wi-Fi networks. Social networking sites like Facebook, Twitter, WhatsApp, Diaspora, and Telegram meant that supporters of jihadist groups could expand their number of social contacts by making connections through friends and followers. Through platforms that enabled user-generated content (UGC) (e.g., video content on YouTube), propaganda not only became freely available online by the individuals who created it, but users could also create their own. Thus, as Web 2.0 enabled *social* media, it was far more sociable, dynamic, and interactive than Web 1.0. With Web 2.0, control over content was shifted from the webmaster to the user. With the rise of social media, the end users from Web 1.0 became *connected content creators* in Web 2.0. This was Zelin's (2013) fourth phase.

This shift in dissemination strategy from the relatively local distribution of offline propaganda (Phase 1; prior to the World Wide Web), to passive consumption by end-users (Phase 2; Web 1.0), to active participation and co-creation of propaganda (Phases 3 and 4; Web 2.0) allowed, as Rogan and Stenersen (2007) put it, online jihadists to become "self-sustainable." With a team of members and sympathizers mobilized and ready to share new and relocated sites, they could circumvent the problem of government "takedowns" by simply republishing their webpage at a different web address and letting the media *mujāhidīn* advertise their relocated sites. Thus, the introduction of forum-based communities made the task of policing the Internet exponentially more difficult.

Chat forums and social media platforms tend to provide an insular space within which ideologues could interact privately with like-minded users, reaffirming their beliefs in an echo chamber–like environment (see Krasodomski-Jones 2016). Online echo chambers are insular networks formed by friends and followers who share a worldview. This means that users operating within an echo chamber are likely to share similar content that aligns with their shared worldview; thus this content will serve to reinforce and validate their preexisting beliefs, and, at the same time they are less likely to be exposed to content that is critical of their worldview. Unlike chat forums, social media platforms such as Twitter could overcome these echo-chamber effects and expose jihadist users to countermessages and dissent to some extent[2]. Salient opposition—especially when encountered in an online environment—can have the undesired impact of polarizing groups, causing extremists to become more steadfast in their ideological convictions (see Turner 1982; Turner, Wetherell, & Hogg 1989).

Using an "open" or public platform such as Twitter creates the opportunity for radical Islamists to fulfil, with relative ease, their obligation to call others to Islam (*da'wa*), or, more precisely, their extreme version of Islam. Indeed, an official IS document, *Media Operative, You Are a Mujāhid, Too*, published in 2015, promoted the idea that the production and dissemination of IS propaganda was a legitimate form of worship and, furthermore, that it was a valid form of *jihād* (Winter 2017b). As Zelin (2013) notes, jihadists had entered a "golden age of online *da'wa*" (p. 6). This was likely an important reason why jihadist groups such as IS flourished on social media: these platforms allowed sympathizers to gain group-member status by simply promoting the group; as we return to later, such inclusivity is particularly seductive to those who feel marginalized within their own country (Reicher & Haslam 2016). Of course, the degree to which *da'wa* can truly be achieved will depend entirely on the network the user has established on social media. In fact, the network of friends and followers of an IS sympathizer on social media is likely to restrict *da'wa* since it could be argued that their "voice" rarely penetrates the echo chamber from within which they are operating.

---

[2] Although in Twitter users are likely to only see content shared by friends and followers in their echo chamber if they stay within their "news feed" and do not read other feeds.

IS and Social Media: Why the Success?

On June 29, 2014, IS claimed to have formed a Worldwide Caliphate, with Abu Bakr al-Baghdadi appointed as Caliph (leader). The powerful rhetoric of the group's spokesman, Abu Muhammad al-Adnani, together with its willingness to embrace social media as an outreach tool (most likely spear-headed by IS's then media emir Dr. Wa'el al-Rawi; Whiteside 2016), provided a unique media opportunity for IS to infiltrate and multiply in online spaces. As we explain later, through this channel, the group was able to disseminate highly tailored material that "spoke" to a diverse range of individuals. Social media meant that its propaganda "net" was unbounded and functioned to point newly connected users to a range of materials now accessible online (e.g., links to official IS magazines and videos). A history of appointing young IT-literate ideologues in senior positions (e.g., AQI/IS's first spokesman: Abu Maysara al-Iraqi) undoubtedly helped IS to mount a successful online media campaign, which, toward the end of 2014, encompassed almost 90,000 sup-porters on Twitter alone (Berger & Morgan 2015).[3] Thus, the online success of IS can be attributed, at least in part, to the shift from passive to active inter-actions already taking place online during the mid-2000s and the group's forethought to capitalize on this change in the online landscape.

The reasons for IS's success on social media were threefold. First, the group's brand was strong—its name alone provided a powerful message: they had successfully implemented an ideology that AQ had spent three decades building and promoting (see Stern & Berger 2015 for an overview of how IS evolved). As such, its audience was already established and listening, with IS militants and media companies being quick to adopt the IS name (Bodine-Baron, Helmus, Magnuson, & Winkelman 2016).

Second, and critically, the media *mujāhidīn* were ready to promote the brand to a worldwide audience (Bodo & Speckhard 2017; Prucha 2016). Indeed, the media *mujāhidīn* were instrumental in IS's success: they weath-ered relentless suspensions on Twitter by working as a group, evolving and reforming (Fisher 2015) to maintain their group-level presence. Their ability to do this meant that a constant stream of wide-ranging IS propaganda fil-tered onto Twitter, so that interested users simply followed a URL to view and/or download extreme material. At the individual level, the media

---

[3] Although it is important to keep in mind the distortions that potentially exist in such data; see note 1.

mujāhidīn's online presence was vulnerable, but, at a group-level, they proved formidable.

The third reason for IS's success on social media is that it had a team of media operatives who armed the media *mujāhidīn* with a plethora of professionally produced, highly targeted materials. This full-spectrum propaganda encompassed a range of output media, including but not restricted to magazines, posters, videos, news broadcasts, and music, all tailored for specific audiences. Together, these outputs bore all the hallmarks of a considered, comprehensive, and cohesive message and thus represented a strong brand the media *mujāhidīn* had confidence in promoting. IS used these materials as weapons (Winter 2017b), and, as such, their production was highly prized by the group. In a series of interviews with captured IS media operatives/defectors, the *Washington Post* published a rare insight into the value IS attached to their media personnel (Miller & Mekhennet 2015). Cameramen attested to receiving higher salaries than IS soldiers; were provided with nice cars, houses, and high-end equipment; and senior media personnel received "emir-like" status equivalent to their military equivalents and were involved in key military decisions. The employment positions within the media wing were vast and ranged from roles such as cameramen, lighting and sound engineers, and hackers to paper and film editors. This diversification and specialism of their media wing resulted in an equally diverse and specialized array of media outputs, ready for dissemination by the media *mujāhidīn* to the outside world.

To protect its media operations from the perils that accompany running an effective media operation in a war zone, IS had a decentralized network of media offices. During a month-long harvesting period of Twitter data, Winter (2015) documented official IS outputs from 38 different media units spanning 11 different geographical regions, with most media units based at the *Wilāyāt* (provincial) level (see also Zelin 2015). In mid-2007 alone, during IS's early days, coalition raids resulted in the destruction of eight different media offices throughout Iraq; however, the decentralized organizational structure adopted by IS ensured a continuous stream of propaganda regardless of the destruction of individual media offices (Whiteside 2016).

Now that we have described *how* IS effectively utilized social media, we should consider *why* it chose to invest such resources in its online operatives. Taylor, Holbrook, and Joinson (2017) attach importance to three distinct opportunities that the Internet affords, namely: *instrumental opportunities* (e.g., to gain information; e.g., Manchester bomber Salman Abedi allegedly learned how to build the explosive device through watching YouTube videos), *identity opportunities* (e.g., ideological; see Chapter 1), and *relational opportunities* (e.g., making connections, developing social networks and affiliations). Recent research suggests that the degree to which these opportunities are utilized online interacts with the opportunities present offline; that is, the Internet is a facilitative tool that fulfils the needs not otherwise fulfilled offline. From this perspective, Taylor and colleagues argue that online and offline activities can be thought of as "two sides of the same coin" (Gill et al. 2017; Taylor et al. 2017), although they are not psychologically equivalent (see, e.g., Postmes, Spears, Sakhel, & de Groot 2001).

Through IS's carefully constructed social media strategy, the group met potential and existing supporters' instrumental, identity, and relational needs. Regarding instrumental needs, the media *mujāhidīn* used platforms such as Twitter to share URLs to other websites that had a more stable presence: these URLs linked to document and film repositories (e.g., Archive.org) that contained information about, for example, how to use social media to maximum effect and avoid suspension or how to build an improvised explosive device. While an individual Twitter account may have been suspended for sharing a URL linked to terrorist material, the website hosting the material would not necessarily be affected. Other Twitter users retweeted the initial tweet containing the URL, and thus Twitter's attempts to suspend users became a game of "cat and mouse" that ultimately ended with the cat (Twitter) chasing an exponentially growing number of "mice" (the media *mujāhidīn*). IS supporters' identity and relational needs were met through similar mechanisms: IS supporters disseminated ideological content on Telegram (e.g., by advertising the online locations of new editions of *Dabiq* and new official IS films and statements), which the media *mujāhidīn* disseminated to the wider population on Twitter.

With respect to identity needs, the content of social media communications by IS and its supporters was designed to resonate with the lives and experiences of those who sought out those communications. Social media users take an active role in seeking out content that aligns (at least to an extent) with their own identity (their beliefs, opinions, and values; see Durodié & Chia 2008). For example, an IS sympathizer may have chosen to locate the latest tweet by a well-known IS media agency. Social psychological research tells us that people are more likely to believe and trust information that concurs with their preexisting views, thus reinforcing and validating these opinions (DiFonzo & Bordia 2007). This is psychologically significant because social validation of our opinions can function to turn subjective beliefs into those considered objective and widely shared (Festinger 1954). Social media content such as YouTube sermons then functioned as a gateway to connection: once interested parties became aware of relevant YouTube channels and watched ideological content, they used messaging platforms like WhatsApp and Telegram to engage with other sympathizers and built relationships with individuals already embedded within networks of IS supporters. If we conceptualize the role of social media in terms of need fulfillment in this way, it is unsurprising that IS was so successful online: IS's and the media *mujāhidīn*'s use of social media (both by design and fortuitously) fulfilled the instrumental, identity, and relational needs of individuals following an extremist trajectory, all of which might otherwise have acted as barriers should individuals have been confined to their offline environments.

Through having these needs fulfilled at the individual level, IS supporters were able to develop a shared sense of social identification online, thus creating a psychological entity at the group level. People who share a common social self-definition and coalesce around a group ideology or set of norms are said to share a *social identity*—that is, they are members of a common social psychological group, and their attitudes and behavior are guided by the norms and ideology of that group (Bliuc, McGarty, Reynolds, & Muntele 2007; Smith, Thomas, & McGarty 2015; Tajfel & Turner 1979; Turner, Hogg, Oakes, Reicher, & Wetherell 1987). Importantly, social identity is a dynamic construct: one social identity can become more (or less) salient at any one point in time as elements of the context and framing change. Propaganda, like that espoused by IS in the way that it frames the ingroup and outgroup identities (see Chapter 1), has the potential to increase the salience of ingroup identity, altering ingroup members' understanding of their shared social environment (see Introduction). If individuals identify with (i.e., feel emotionally and cognitively attached to) a group, they will share that group's worldview and it will become self-defining, which, as Ingram (Chapter 1) suggests, has the potential to increase their need for solutions following an "Other-induced crisis." Critically, communication (e.g., via social media) is the underlying process that enables individuals to feel connected to a group, and it aids the development of social identification (Smith, Gavin, & Sharp 2015; Smith & Postmes 2011; Smith, Thomas, & McGarty 2015). The nature of online (relative to offline) communication, shaped by IS propaganda, may have sharpened and hastened the transformation of individual users into psychological group members (i.e., caused the radicalization of individuals into the IS ingroup). Thus, whereas in Chapter 2, Ingram argues that the effect of IS propaganda on supporters was to increase their need for solutions, we argue that this is because of the propaganda's ability to work with the communicative affordances of social media to evoke and shape a shared social identity, one situated within the sociostructural (intergroup) context.

Early research on computer-mediated communication in Web 1.0 demonstrated that when online communications allow individuals to remain anonymous, they tend to be shaped more by social cues than when individuals are identifiable (Postmes et al. 2001). As offline interactions contain more identifying cues than online interactions, this means that online interactions may be more likely to be shaped by social cues than offline interactions are. To explain this phenomenon, let us imagine, for a moment, that the media *mujāhidīn* on social media represented a "crowd" of sorts. Indeed, they were a close-knit, cohesive group of individuals who shared social identification with a jihadist ideology and who also shared a coherent set of norms for online behavior. More than 20 years ago, before the advent of Web 2.0 and social media, Reicher, Spears, and Postmes (1995) proposed the *social identity model of deindividuation effects* (SIDE) to describe the cognitive and strategic factors involved in social identity definition and enactment (see especially Drury & Reicher 2000). According to SIDE, individuals within crowds act in normative and controlled ways. These norms are specific to the salient social identity of the crowd. Thus, rather than feeling "deindividuated" and experiencing the freedom associated with anonymity, the individual recategorizes him- or herself as having a common group affiliation with the crowd. Returning to the IS online "crowd," we can apply the principles of SIDE to suggest that when members of the crowd communicate via social media, they do so in terms of the social norms of IS and related subgroups. Anonymous individuals interacting online are more aware of shared group affiliations than they would be in offline interactions (in which they are more aware of their idiosyncratic personal identity due to the online environment being less "rich" in nonverbal communication cues; see media richness theory; Daft & Lengel 1984; Postmes et al. 2001), and therefore they are more likely to conform to group norms (Reicher et al. 1995). Therefore, when IS supporters interacted online, they were potentially more likely to interact in terms of salient IS norms than when they would hypothetically interact offline. This has the potential to flavor online interactions with a sharper, more polarized edge and accelerate the process of radicalization (or, in social-psychological terms, the development of social identification with a radical group).

While the online activity of the media *mujāhidīn* had psychological effects in terms of developing the group and recruiting new IS supporters, it has also been implicated in physical gains offline, such as IS's taking of Mosul in 2014. In the lead-up to and during this military campaign, IS militants' uploaded visual evidence of their advancement toward Mosul, documenting in detail the fate of their opponents. A Twitter bot set up by the group ("The Dawn of Glad Tidings," or just "Dawn") allowed sympathizers to follow the group and to tweet on their behalf. They celebrated IS's ferocity, advertising their gains and warned: "We are coming, Baghdad." In 1 day alone, Berger (2014) reports that more than 40,000 tweets originated from the bot, making a Twitter search for "Baghdad" generate an IS image. This bombardment of Twitter via the media *mujāhidīn* was implicated as a contributing factor in how IS militants were able to overpower Iraqi soldiers in Mosul despite outnumbering IS 10:1, with it being widely reported that Iraqi soldiers simply abandoned their positions in fear. It seems the media *mujāhidīn* exploited social media to accomplish the old Chinese proverb (which some have argued to be "the first pillar of terror"; Prunckun 2014): "kill one, frighten ten thousand" (Sun Tzu, cited in Prunckun 2014).

To aid the media *mujāhidīn*, IS's media wing produced a deluge of skillfully crafted pieces of media every day, spanning (but not limited to) posters, high-definition movies, interviews, and war reports. This material was targeted (see Winter 2015; Zelin 2015), carried a clear and coherent message (Fisher 2016b), and often was released to coincide with terror attacks (thus taking advantage of the "publicity" for IS's ideology that such attacks afford). The primary tool for dissemination: social media.

People living in the West were typically unaware of both the breadth and depth of propaganda that was being released by IS. This was, in part at least, orchestrated by IS, which only released a small proportion of its media in English—most of which was intended to incite terror. This targeting was strategic, and the biased reporting of Western media provided a platform from which IS's (tailored) message could propagate in the West. As Reicher and Haslam (2016) noted, IS instigated a situation in which co-radicalization could flourish: Westerners become fearful and distrusting of Muslims, and, as a result, Muslims felt marginalized. As Reicher and Haslam (2016) summarized, "terrorism is all about polarization. It is about reconfiguring intergroup relationships so that extreme leadership appears to offer the most sensible way of engaging with an extreme world" (p. 38). Indeed, online discussions about intergroup actions can shift individual users' pre-discussion opinions and attitudes to a more extreme position, in the direction in which they already tended (group polarization, see Moscovici & Zavalloni 1969; also Myers & Bishop 1970; Turner 1991). IS's carefully framed and targeted propaganda functioned to polarize sympathizers and opponents, leading to a notable increase in attacks and reprisals by sympathizers with no known official connection to the group (e.g., the 2017 Westminster attacker, Khalid Masood) and reactionary Islamophobia in the United States and Western Europe. Such co-radicalization elicited large-scale societal changes, such as President Trump's executive order to ban immigrants from Muslim countries in 2017, and subsequent "ripple effects," whereby several groups formed and polarized in multiple different directions. This demonstrated that audiences online are affected by geopolitical events. To capitalize on this phenomenon, "Islamic State's media strategists understand that it is not enough to interact with sympathizers alone and, therefore, its propaganda seeks out friend and foe in almost equal measure" (Winter 2017b: 19).

Of course, the media *mujāhidīn*, armed with a comprehensive library of propaganda, were poised and ready to offer a sense of belonging and identity to those in the West who found themselves cast into the outgroup. This interaction between the IS media wing (who created division) and the media *mujāhidīn* (who offered a shared social identity) proved a potent combination, no doubt accounting for many of the 4,500 Western foreign fighters (Bodine-Baron et al. 2016) who were inspired to join the Caliphate or to act in its name through lone-wolf attacks in the West. In a recent American presidential debate, Hilary Clinton went so far as to suggest that Donald Trump—known for his skepticism of the Muslim faith—was one of IS's "best recruiters" (Farand 2015).

As discussed in Chapter 2, the narrative adopted by IS was transient, shifting according to the group's objectives at the time. In "Documenting the Virtual 'Caliphate'", Winter (2015; see also Zelin 2015) analyzed all media output produced by IS over a 1-month period (mid-July to mid-August 2015). During this analysis period, the theme of war only accounted for 37% of IS's online media output at that time, while other common themes related to victimhood (7%) and the Caliphate as a utopian society (53%); mercy, belonging, and brutality combined accounted for less than 4% of the sample. Both Zelin and Winter credited IS with shifting its narrative according to its priorities at the time, a process Ingram refers to as "hedging" (see Chapter 1); these shifts over time likely account for some of the variation in themes between these studies. Indeed, following the loss of physical ground, Winter

(2017a) reported that, by 2017, utopian-related propaganda had dropped by 74% from 2015 compared with a 100% increase in war-related propaganda.[4]

Together, Zelin's (2015) and Winter's (2015) research demonstrated IS's unique understanding of and willingness to fulfill the online identity and ideological needs of its diverse followers. This marks an important departure from other significant jihadist groups, such as AQ, which tended to focus on the ideological aspects of their message (e.g., via historical videos, online sermons, or battle scenes). Thus, IS did not simply "luck into" the advent of social media; we must also credit the group with the forethought of considering the broad spectrum of needs of its users and investing heavily in satisfying these needs. This investment in its online following was rewarded: IS had a loyal fan base of media *mujāhidīn* who, as we will see in what follows, have been instrumental in helping the group weather online assaults on their Twitter distribution networks. Efforts by Twitter have largely failed to taper the rate with which propaganda continues to be distributed (Winter 2015).

Twitter

IS was commonly assumed to have a large presence on Twitter, and this presence had a global effect: owning a Twitter account was not a prerequisite for viewing (public) tweets, therefore IS's presence on Twitter had the potential to reach everyone who had access to the Internet, which at the time included almost half the world's population.[5] A large number of IS supporters were active on the platform at any one time. At the peak of its popularity in 2014, Berger and Morgan (2015) estimated that, between September and December of that year, as many as 46,000 Twitter accounts overtly supported IS, a figure that doubled (90,000) when the count was extended to all supporters.[6] As noted by Winter (2015), Twitter provided an efficient environment for IS: material could be disseminated at great speed and in a targeted

---

[4] Winter acknowledged that in "higher impact propaganda videos," the utopian image continued to feature heavily in 2017.

[5] A report published in 2015 predicted that, by the end of 2015, 3.2 billion of the world's 7.2 billion people would be online (the International Telecommunications Union (ITU, 2015, cited by BBC News, 2015).

[6] Note that the number of accounts active at any single point in time will be less than the figures quoted since Berger and Morgan's (2015) analysis period covered a 4-month window, within which not all accounts were active at the same time.

fashion, which, together with the use of hashtags, made Twitter the ideal platform for its outreach activities.

IS's targeted "marketing style" made the group relevant to an extremely diverse range of supporters, many of whom openly supported the group on Twitter and dedicated their time to promoting it. Furthermore, the media *mujāhidīn*, together with IS's official Twitter accounts, demonstrated an astonishing degree of speed, agility, and resilience in responding to sustained attempts to temper pro-IS activity on Twitter, such as account suspensions (Fisher 2015). This blend of marketing, loyalty, and intragroup strategizing and restrategizing resulted in a formidable, dynamic opponent that was winning the digital battle, if not the physical war (Bodo & Speckhard 2017).

Official IS Twitter Accounts

In 2012, IS (or, more precisely given this period, the Islamic State of Iraq, or ISI) created its first Twitter account: al-I'tisam (Whiteside 2016), which was responsible for the distribution of official IS material. However, graphic videos published under this account name, including the beheadings of Western journalists and aid workers, soon resulted in the account's suspension by Twitter. Al-I'tisam underwent a series of reincarnations, each being pointed to by a slightly different Twitter handle; however, this method of dissemination soon proved inefficient and only partially effective since Twitter could detect and suspend the new versions of al-I'tisam just as quickly as the media *mujāhidīn* were able to reestablish their connections with it.

In response, IS shifted its strategy. Since official IS accounts, such as al-I'tisam (and, indeed, many other similar accounts) were easy for Twitter to identify and suspend, IS began disseminating its material via hashtags, which were neither suspended nor blocked by Twitter (Winter 2015). The path of IS propaganda passed through three "tiers" on Twitter: first, the media was released to Twitter via an official IS member. Second, "several dozen activists" retweeted the material (often via a URL), retweeted one another's tweets, and constructed new tweets, all using a common hashtag. Third, these tweets were then picked up by the *ansar mujāhidīn* (general supporters), who replicated tier two's strategy, allowing the message to multiply on Twitter (Stern & Berger 2015).

Of course, IS Twitter accounts remained vulnerable to suspensions, but by delegating the act of propagation to the media *mujāhidīn*, they were harder for Twitter officials to detect and shut down. By having several IS accounts running in tandem, even if a dissemination account was located and suspended, other accounts would continue to produce the media for IS members/sympathizers to propagate. By engaging in this strategy, IS effectively removed its need for centralized advertising accounts while still maintaining and managing a productive output (Berger 2015; Winter 2015).

Prior to IS becoming established on Twitter, the platform was used by activists in Syria trying to bring humanitarian atrocities to a global audience. Such material, published by nonviolent groups, was soon adapted by jihadists to fit with their narrative and to legitimize their existence: to defend the Sunni population in Syria (Prucha & Fisher 2013). In addition to exposing Assad's regime, IS was particularly proactive in distributing images of coalition bombings in Syria, such as airstrikes in Aleppo. Images of civilian destruction, including dead, dying, maimed, or injured civilians—including children—provided powerful propaganda material for the group. While groups had used "gruesome propaganda" in the past (see Introduction), IS media operatives demonstrated a unique awareness that disseminating visceral images of individual victims and the harm that befell them at the hands of outgroups, was more relatable—and thus more effective for their propaganda purposes—than demonstrating the scale of death and destruction in Syria and the Levant. *Mortality salience*—that is, awareness of the inevitability of death—is known to have a significant impact on collective behavior. One protective response to the anxiety associated with mortality salience is immersion in a cultural worldview or loyalty to membership of a group that will endure beyond death (Burke, Martens, & Faucher 2010). For example, when citizens feel threatened, mortality salience can lead to increased support for heads of state (Landau, Solomon, Greenberg, Cohen, & Pyszczynski 2004) and aggression toward the threatening target (McGregor et al. 1998). Thus, images of the death of vulnerable individuals could function to further polarize supporters of IS against Assad and Western democracies. Furthermore, advertising civilian destruction and causalities communicates a sense of grievance that can act as a catalyst for collective action. In other words, propaganda that focuses on grievances and injustice can mobilize people to support IS and act on its behalf and in accordance with its norms and values. Such propaganda will aid recruitment and enhance consensus, politicization, and cohesion within the organization and its wider network of sympathizers (see Smith, Thomas, & McGarty 2015).

A common misconception in the West was that IS's media output focuses almost exclusively on brutality, such as released footage of executions. In fact, such media accounted for less than 2% of the content analyzed by Winter (2015; see earlier discussion) and just 1% of all releases published via IS's Twitter accounts during a 1-week period in April 2015 (Zelin 2015). The misconception that IS portrayed itself in its propaganda as a "completely irrational and irreducibly foreign group" (see Introduction) has also been shown to be false for other modes of IS propaganda, including videos (see Chapter 3) and magazines (see Chapter 4). Instead, in Winter's (2015) analysis, "utopia" was the most dominant theme.[7] This theme allowed Twitter users to consume material that portrayed IS as the only legitimate state, one that offered decisive justice and a healthcare system located within an idyllic location where life continued as normal despite it being a war zone. Such spread and depth of propaganda had the advantage of satisfying a diverse audience who were inspired to support or join IS for a myriad of reasons. This strategy attracted online users from Middle Eastern or North African countries that had been marred by years of unrest, political injustice, and war or from farther abroad, attracting foreign fighters and jihadi brides under IS's online mirage of the Caliphate.

As already touched on earlier, IS was particularly skilled at attaching relevant imagery to its messages, from graphics of a utopian society at one end of the spectrum to the use of gruesome propaganda (discussed earlier) at the other. Indeed, 88% of its overall output for a 1-week period in July included graphics, such as photographs and videos (Zelin 2015). IS's ability to weave such graphics into its range of diverse and highly tailored narratives made its message all the more potent to its equally diverse audience. To disseminate full-spectrum propaganda in this manner was unprecedented—especially by a terrorist organization—and the use of social media in particular allowed IS to cast its net, quite literally, across the globe.

Media *Mujāhidīn*

So far, we have concentrated on the official IS message circling the IS network on Twitter, but what features (collective behaviors) did the media *mujāhidīn* share at the level of the individual user? An important step toward answering

---

[7] However, such themes are transient, see earlier discussion and Winter, 2017a, 2017b.

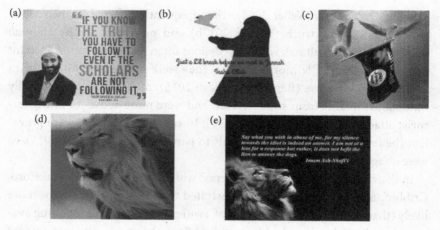

Figure 5.1 Popular Islamic State (IS) imagery on Twitter: (a) a poster shared by an IS supporter quoting the late al-Qaeda cleric Anwar al-Awlaki; (b) and (c) images featuring green birds; (d) and (e) lion imagery.

this question was taken by Berger and Morgan (2015) in their oft-cited ISIS Twitter Consensus. Briefly, of the 20,000 accounts they had identified as being pro-IS during their 3-month analysis period, 18% had selected English as their default language, while 75% had chosen Arabic. There was a strong trend that revealed that the media *mujāhidīn* openly identified with IS, often using display names that referenced the group (e.g., *Dawla*, which is "state" in Arabic, and *bāqiyya*, which is an important IS slogan—"remaining"), with account avatars depicting significant jihadis (such as AQ's Bin Laden or IS's Jihadi John or al-Baghdadi) or a variation of the IS flag (e.g., Figure 5.1c). This latter trend was, however, restricted to medium-sized accounts (those with 150–1,000 followers), with smaller accounts often opting to retain the Twitter default "egg" avatar, while larger accounts typically adopted unrelated imagery, which Berger and Morgan suggested could have reflected a suspension-avoidance strategy. More than one in three of their sample's tweets pointed to a URL, while the most popular hashtags among the group's 200 most recent tweets included variations of the group's name (ISIS).

Research found a preference, in Arabic at least, for the media *mujāhidīn* to refer to themselves as "Islamic State" rather than by abbreviations such as "Daesh" (perceived as derogatory; Bodine-Baron et al. 2016) or "ISIS" [8]

---

[8] Which both researchers report as being indicative of anti-IS support.

(Magdy, Darwish, & Weber 2015). They frequently referred to themselves as followers of the truth (Winter 2017b) and protectors of the *Ummah* (Community of Muslims), while discussions often revolved around account suspensions (Berger & Morgan 2015). They were most active following an IS propaganda release (Berger & Morgan 2015), often lifting (occasionally innocuous) images from such releases, and were more active following terrorist attacks (Bodo & Speckhard 2017). Images of green birds were prevalent (believed to carry a martyr's souls to paradise; e.g., see Edgar 2015), as were images of lions (see Figure 5.1).

In their analysis of 110 IS supporters' Twitter accounts, Smith, Wakeford, Cribbin, and Barnett (2017) demonstrated that IS supporters were more likely (than a neutral control sample of Twitter users) to use IS-defining avatars (e.g., the IS black and white standard flag), threatening images, images of weapons, symbols of *tawḥīd*, cat and lion imagery, and the default "egg" avatar (Table 5.1); they were less likely to use neutral imagery. As noted by Ingram in Chapter 2, IS' "symbology" was intended to promote the IS brand to "friends, foes and neutrals," thus creating a "media trap." The wide spread of avatar categories reported here appears to embody this notion, with some even achieving this simultaneously (e.g., weapons can be viewed as either a sign of strength or something to be feared, depending on your perspective). Indeed, Ingram suggests that presenting dichotomous messages simultaneously was a distinguishing trait of the group (see Chapter 1).

It would seem from this analysis, therefore, that many of the media *mujāhidīn* wore the pro-IS badge with pride. However, from late 2014

Table 5.1 Avatar Differences Between the Media *Mujāhidīn* and Control Sample

Avatar category	IS	Control
IS-defining	12$_a$	0$_b$
Threatening	5$_a$	1$_a$
Weapons/war	22$_a$	0$_b$
Tawḥīd	7$_a$	0$_b$
Cat/lion	15$_a$	4$_b$
Neutral	37$_a$	79$_b$
Default "egg"	11$_a$	0$_b$

Percentages on rows with different subscripts differ significantly at p < .05.

onward, the media *mujāhidīn* found themselves targeted by Twitter suspensions. Searching just a handful of key English and/or Arabic words on the platform quickly betrayed an IS sympathizer as such (Prucha 2016).

Given the ease with which jihadist accounts continue to be detected, both manually and via Twitter's own network facilitation tool (e.g., through their "who to follow" tool; Berger & Morgan 2015), it is perhaps unsurprising that, from late 2014 onward, IS media *mujāhidīn* also suffered repeated suspensions (Berger & Perez 2016). Thus, displaying pro-IS features was a risky strategy as far as vulnerability to account suspensions goes, but the group had a remarkable ability to survive multiple suspensions through "shoutouts." This feature refers to pro-IS accounts advertising the new Twitter handle of a previously suspended account. Given the insular network of these users, such a strategy allowed previously suspended users to reconnect with their network almost instantly. Indeed, boasting about their number of suspensions appeared to signify a badge of honor among the media *mujāhidīn* (Fisher 2016b). Stern and Berger (2015) compared IS's response to suspensions to the children's game "Whack-a-Mole," where new accounts simply popped up in replacement of suspended ones.

Suspensions: Enduring and Evolving

In the following section, we concentrate on the impact that account suspensions had on the reach of the media *mujāhidīn*, together with the impact they had on IS's ability to distribute official material. Twitter's suspensions campaign only really began in August 2014, when they suspended 12 official ISIS provincial news accounts (Friedman 2014). But, by August 2016, Twitter reported that, since mid-2015, it had suspended a total of 360,000 accounts due to violations of its policies on the promotion of terrorism.[9]

There is some disagreement regarding the degree to which suspensions impacted IS's online reach, partly because there is no agreement on the metrics for success or the methods for independently establishing the group affiliation of users (see earlier discussion). Berger and Perez (2016) reported that, between June and October 2015, IS's activity on Twitter was "stagnant, or in slight decline," which they attribute, for the most part at least, to suspensions.

---

[9] Note that this figure will include accounts associated with other terrorist organizations in addition to IS.

By concentrating a subset of analyses on the four most suspended accounts in their sample, they showed that both network (e.g., number of friends and followers) and activity (e.g., number of tweets) were negatively impacted by suspensions and that the effects appeared to be long-lasting, with replacement accounts rarely as productive as their associated pre-suspension accounts.

However, others, such as Fisher and colleagues from the VORTEX project in Vienna, disagree with this analysis (see Fisher 2015, 2016a, 2016b). Instead, they suggest that account suspensions merely forced the media *mujāhidīn* to (successfully) adapt their online strategy. Using network analysis, Fisher has shown that the media *mujāhidīn* operate through a "dispersed network of accounts," which he suggests undergoes constant reformations akin to how a flock of birds or bees instinctively reconfigure in midflight. Fisher thus refers to the media *mujāhidīn* as a "swarmcast," the defining features of which include speed, agility, and resilience. Using dynamic social network analysis, which included 3.4 million jihadist-related tweets, Fisher has shown that new accounts simply replace suspended ones. He further points out that Berger and Perez (2016) report that both the "size" and "reach" of the network remained flat overall, despite some larger accounts sustaining repeated suspensions. This suggests, according to Fisher, that the group evolved to allow other accounts to pick up the slack of those who had been targeted by repeated suspensions.

As Fisher (2016a) noted, IS's strategy was not to gain Twitter followers; it was to disseminate material, a task at which the media *mujāhidīn* excelled. For example, an English version of the IS video *No Respite* was downloaded or viewed approximately 400,000 times in just a few days on Archive.org. Given the obscure video titles and links typically employed by the group, Fisher (2016b) suggests that such tallies cannot be attributed to Google searches alone; rather, the swarmcast must have signposted where the video could be located. They argue that to counter online jihadists, we need "strategic approaches to disrupt the system-wide emerging structures and collective behaviors" (n.p.); suspensions will always be an inconvenience, but little more.

Fisher (2015) likens IS media operations on Twitter to "netwar." In defining netwar, Fisher quotes a recent RAND paper that suggests it is an "emerging mode of conflict in which the protagonists—ranging from terrorists and criminal organizations on the dark side, to militant social activists on the bright side—use network forms of organization, doctrine, strategy, and technology attuned to the information age" (n.p.). Furthermore, he states that netwar is distinct from state-controlled conflict since it is driven from societal (not state) forces. Such a description certainly appears to encapsulate the essence of the media *mujāhidīn*'s activity on social media, and, as we will see, such a strategy requires a novel counterapproach if we wish to stem IS's global reach on social media.

Despite the widespread use of suspensions, to date, there has been no empirical evaluation of the efficacy of this strategy in dissipating the psychological conditions for dangerous group-based behavior. Suspension could be a useful strategy if the aim is to remove or reduce extremists' "safe space" in which to recruit members and disseminate material. Suspensions could also be a useful triage process that "weeds out" peripheral supporters, only motivating those who are highly affiliated and psychologically attached to the group to set up new accounts. It may be only those latter group members who move to encrypted platforms once suspended from the mainstream platforms. Further empirical evaluation of the psychological impact of suspensions is essential because they have the potential to make online groups more dangerous: that is, through processes of polarization, the threat that suspended users pose could increase or decrease (or stay the same) after suspension. While some preliminary work has evaluated the impact of Twitter's suspension policy on the activity of jihadist groups (Berger & Perez 2016; Conway et al. 2017), these groups' online activity is rarely restricted to a single online platform. Although this work provided some evidence for how a group was affected by suspensions in terms of the number of accounts removed, it did not elucidate the longitudinal psychological impact of the suspensions on the suspended users or remaining community. To understand *why* interventions have an impact on the nature of a group and the substantive nature of that impact on the behavior of the individual members, evaluations need to assess the longitudinal *social and psychological processes* affected by disruption strategies on a group *across multiple platforms*.

Telegram

Telegram is an encrypted open source messaging platform that bears some similarity to the chat forums discussed earlier. The "group chat" environment is private, heavily encrypted, and unpoliced by platform owners. By 2016, given Twitter's suspension efforts, Telegram was the group's preferred distribution for media releases (Berger & Perez 2016). Data requests from specific governments were not honored because the storage of data was dispersed across the globe, as was the associated decryption key, which was further split and never stored in the same place as the data themselves. Due to this architecture, Telegram stated that, "we can ensure that no single government or block of like-minded countries can intrude on people's privacy and freedom of expression" (Telegram n.d.). Telegram thus provided IS with a safe space within which to interact with like-minded individuals.

Telegram allowed users to broadcast material over public channels to an unlimited audience. However, following the 2015 attacks in Paris, these channels were subjected to suspensions, with (at least) 78 IS-related channels being suspended by 2016 (Berger & Perez 2016). Nevertheless, Prucha (2016) reported that IS members and sympathizers were responsible for passing more than 30,000 messages across hundreds of dedicated channels every week. Indeed, Telegram became a hub for retrieving IS-related propaganda and coordinating its distribution on other social network platforms, thus allowing IS to organize *ghazawat* (raids) on platforms such as Facebook and Twitter. Prucha summarized that "Telegram is central to the supply of text for tweets, disseminating new hashtags, the timing of such raids [which are often event-driven, e.g., post attack], and the flooding of comments on Facebook pages and so on" (Prucha 2016: 52). By branching into Telegram, IS successfully secured another gateway through which the media *mujāhidīn* could smuggle IS-related material ready to propagate strategically to the wider masses.

We should emphasize, however, that IS's media wing cautioned against the media *mujāhidīn* confining themselves to Telegram since it restricted the operatives' commitment to *da'wa* (calling others to Islam; see earlier discussion). In an official two-page letter to the media *mujāhidīn*, al-Ghazzi implored: "do not isolate yourself on Telegram!" (al-Ghazzi, cited in Prucha 2016: 55). Thus, while Telegram was—for the reasons just described—a central tool for IS, the group was also keen for the media *mujāhidīn* to continue weathering the suspensions on Twitter. It seemed that it was acutely aware that its online global success was driven by engaging with the wider population, whether that included fellow sympathizers already following a radical trajectory or opponents, whom they used as pawns in their strategy of co-radicalization.

Moving Forward: Countering Terrorism in Online Spaces

In her foreword to Vidino and Hughes's research paper, "ISIS in America: From Retweets to Raqqa" (2015), Harman, head of the Wilson Center and chartered by Congress to bridge the worlds of scholarship and policy, writes that the Internet has "overhauled radicalization," and, consequently, our response to it must evolve to reflect this change (p. vii). Google, Facebook, Twitter, and Microsoft have recently committed to working together to build a database capable of detecting terrorist images and videos via a set of "unique digital fingerprints" (Facebook 2016); however, governments are calling for more to be done (e.g., Home Affairs Committee 2017).

So, how can we tackle radicalization on social media? Interventions (e.g., account suspensions, content withdrawal) may attempt to reduce dissemination of propaganda or proactively compete with the ideology of the group (i.e., counternarratives). However, developing robust counternarratives is not straightforward. A central theme throughout this chapter has been that IS's success online rested on the stable foundations of a strong Sunni jihadist brand. Winter (2017b) argues that it was not enough to simply delegitimize IS's claims of forming an Islamic state; government stakeholders needed to learn from IS, investigate and understand what made them so influential, and harness that in their own counterterrorism efforts. As we have seen, IS propaganda was multidimensional, therefore any countermessages should address each of these dimensions. According to Bodine-Baron et al. (2016), anti-IS propaganda needs to tackle themes as diverse as religious justification, belonging, threat against Islam, and dehumanization of enemies. Furthermore, they argued that anti-IS activists should be armed with this material, in much the same way as IS armed their media *mujāhidīn*; anti-IS Twitter accounts outnumbered pro-IS 10 to 1 (Bodine-Baron et al. 2016), but without effective material to disseminate, they could not be as influential or effective. Similarly, countering online radicalization should be tackled from multiple vantage points. To be most effective in countering IS's online influence, multiple actors must be employed across a range of channels, both online and offline (Winter 2017b).

To maximize the influence of a counternarrative, one must consider the source(s) of the message. A recent study into gambling and social media showed that responsible gambling accounts rarely reached their target audience due to a "disconnect" between pro-gambling and responsible gambling accounts (Miller, Krasodomski-Jones, & Smith 2016). This research shows that counternarratives must propagate from sources that hold some influence over a group. By using a combination of (a) community detection analyses, (b) lexical analysis, and (c) social network analysis, Bodine-Baron and colleagues (2016) identified four online "metacommunities" and described the relationship of the interactions among and between them to identify the source from which anti-IS material would be most influential: "The core of the Syrian *mujāhidīn* metacommunity serves as an important connection between the Shi'a metacommunity, some Sunni communities, and the ISIS supporter metacommunity, who are otherwise disconnected. It is therefore possible that individuals within the Syrian *mujāhidīn* community could serve as influencers of ISIS supporters and connect ISIS opponents together" (Bodine-Baron et al. 2016: xii–xiii).

Given the vastness of the Internet, any one intervention or even combination of interventions is unlikely to shut IS down completely online: there are practical limitations that mean it is not possible to deny terrorism a safe space to propagate. However, ultimately, given that terrorist groups are commonly underpinned by a cohesive shared social identity, interventionists need to understand and harness those social psychological mechanisms underlying the groups. That is, interventions need to be rooted in an understanding of the impact they have on social psychological processes to be effective. As yet, no research has attempted to systematically understand this impact, and thus this is an important direction for future research.

Conclusion

In the fourth phase of jihadism (Zelin 2013), IS's online jihadists became *connected content creators* through the functionalities and reach of social media. During this time, IS's online responsivity to external events and interventions enabled it to make innovations at the collective level, such as multiplatform resource sharing, the move to encrypted messaging and chat rooms, and the use of shoutouts in response to suspensions, meaning that IS remained flexible, potent, and agentic online. Perhaps more significantly, through a combination of the affordances of social media (through which IS could satisfy supporters' key instrumental, identity, and relational needs), the decentralized nature of the group, and the unique psychological processes that occur through online interactions, IS created a new and innovative form of online, shared *social identity*. IS developed a recognizable ingroup "brand" or identity that could only be fully understood in relation to outgroup identities (e.g., the US, Assad's regime) and the political activities of those groups. The Islamophobic actions of foreign politicians, in combination with the rise of populism, solidified and polarized the IS brand. In light of research into intergroup polarization, to counter terrorist brands like IS, Western politicians should carefully consider the strategic and symbolic political communications and gestures that can psychologically shape both the perceptions of Western countries and, in turn, terrorist groups.

IS's innovative, sophisticated, and prolific use of social media enabled it to connect with like-minded others across the globe. However, a focus on IS's official social media strategy and the work of its social media officers obfuscates the source of its online strength. The activities of IS's wide network of supporters and sympathizers—the media *mujāhidīn*—served to further decentralize and stabilize the group online and perpetuate and protect the functions of its propaganda officers. Of course, the reach of IS's officially produced social media content—in terms of its spread through social networks—affected its impact. Yet, more significantly, due to the decentralized nature of the media *mujāhidīn* and IS's multifaceted narrative, the IS online network was relatively immune to the impact of account suspensions and robust against counternarratives. Online, IS developed an innovative and illusive new form of collective identity that thwarted traditional attempts to curtail its activities and the content that gave supporters compelling reasons to choose IS (Chapter 1). To counter the future threats created by online jihadism and other forms of extremism, we must develop equally dynamic and diversionary, multifaceted, multimedia, and multiplatform interventions that harness the psychological processes that give online interactions their power.

References

BBC News. (2015) *Internet Used by 3.2 Billion People in 2015*. Retrieved from http://www.bbc.co.uk/news/technology-32884867.

Berger J. (2014) *How ISIS Game Twitter*. Retrieved from https://www.theatlantic.com/international/archive/2014/06/isis-iraq-twitter-social-media-strategy/372856/.

Berger J. (2015) "The Metronome of Apocalyptic Time: Social Media as a Carrier Wave for Millenarian Contagion," *Perspectives on Terrorism* 9(4): 61–71.

Berger J., Morgan J. (2015) "The ISIS Twitter Census: Defining and Describing the Population of ISIS Supporters on Twitter," *The Brookings Institution* 20. https://www.brookings.edu/wp-content/uploads/2016/06/isis_twitter_census_berger_morgan.pdf.

Berger J. M., Perez H. (2016) "The Islamic State's Diminishing Returns on Twitter: How Suspensions Are Limiting the Social Networks of English-Speaking ISIS Supporters," *George Washington University's Program on Extremism. Occasional Paper*: 1–20. https://extremism.gwu.edu/sites/g/files/zaxdzs2191/f/downloads/JMB%20Diminishing%20Returns.pdf.

Bliuc A., McGarty C., Reynolds K., Muntele D. (2007) "Opinion-Based Group Membership as a Predictor of Commitment to Political Action," *European Journal of Social Psychology* 37(1): 19–32.

Bodine-Baron E., Helmus T., Magnuson M., Winkelman Z. (2016) *Examining ISIS Support and Opposition Networks on Twitter.* RAND Corporation Santa Monica United States. https://www.rand.org/content/dam/rand/pubs/research_reports/RR1300/RR1328/RAND_RR1328.pdf.

Bodo L., Speckhard A. (2017) *The Daily Harvester: How ISIS Disseminates Propaganda over the Internet Despite Counter-Measures and How to Fight Back.* Retrieved from http://www.icsve.org/brief-reports/the-daily   harvester-how-isis-disseminates-propaganda-over-the-Internet-despite-counter-measures-and- how-to-fight-back/.

Burke B., Martens A., Faucher E. (2010) "Two Decades of Terror Management Theory: A Meta-Analysis of Mortality Salience Research," *Personality and Social Psychology Review* 14(2): 155–195.

Carlisle J., Patton R. (2013) "Is Social Media Changing How We Understand Political Engagement? An Analysis of Facebook and the 2008 Presidential Election," *Political Research Quarterly* 66: 883–895.

Conway M. (2012) "From al-Zarqawi to al-Awlaki: The Emergence and Development of an Online Radical Milieu," *CTX* 2(4): 12–22.

Conway M., Khawaja M., Lakhani S., Reffin J., Robertson A., Weir D. (2017) "Disrupting Daesh: Measuring Takedown on Online Terrorist Material and Its Impacts," *VOXPol* 1–45. http://www.voxpol.eu/download/vox-pol_publication/DCUJ5528-Disrupting-DAESH-1706-WEB-v2.pdf.

Daft R., Lengel R. (1984) "Information Richness: A New Approach to Managerial Behavior and Organizational Design," *Research in Organizational Behavior* 6: 191–233.

DiFonzo N., Bordia P. (2007) *Rumor Psychology: Social and Organizational Approaches.* Washington, DC: American Psychological Association.

Drury J., Reicher S. (2000) "Collective Action and Psychological Change: The Emergence of New Social Identities," *British Journal of Social Psychology* 39: 579–604.

Durodié B., Chia N. (2008) "Is Internet Radicalization Possible?" *RSIS Commentaries* 122: 1–3.

Edgar I. (2015) "The Dreams of Islamic State," *Perspectives on Terrorism* 9(4): 72–84.

Facebook (2016) *Partnering to Help Curb Spread of Online Terrorist Content.* Retrieved from https://newsroom.fb.com/news/2016/12/partnering-to-help-curb-spread-of-online-terrorist-content/.

Farand C. (2015) "Donald Trump Is ISIS' Best Recruiter, Says Hilary Clinton in Democratic TV Debate," *The Independent.* Retrieved from http://www.independent.co.uk/news/world/americas/us-elections/donald-trump-isis-best-recruiter-says-hillary-clinton-in-democratic-television-debate-a6780321.html.

Festinger L. (1954) "A Theory of Social Comparison Processes," *Human Relations* 7(2): 117–140.

Fisher A. (2015) "How Jihadist Networks Maintain a Persistent Online Presence," *Perspectives on Terrorism* 9(3): 3–20.

Fisher A. (2016a). "Interpreting Data About ISIS Online." *CPD Blog*. Retrieved from https://uscpublicdiplomacy.org/blog/interpreting-data-about-isis-online.

Fisher A. (2016b, March 16) "ISIS Strategy and the Twitter Jihadiscape." *CPD Blog*. Retrieved from https://uscpublicdiplomacy.org/blog/isis-strategy-and-twitter-jihadiscape.

Friedman D. (2014) "Twitter Stepping Up Suspensions of ISIS-Affiliated Accounts: Experts." Retrieved from http://www.nydailynews.com/news/world/twitter-stepping-suspensions-isis-affiliated-accounts-experts-article-1.1906193.

Gill P., Corner E., Conway M., Thornton A., Bloom M., Horgan J. (2017) "Terrorist Use of the Internet by the Numbers," *Criminology & Public Policy* 16(1): 99–117.

Harlow S. (2012) "Social Media and Social Movements: Facebook and an Online Guatemalan Justice Movement That Moved Offline," *New Media & Society* 14(2): 225–243.

Home Affairs Committee (2017) "Hate Crime: Abuse, Hate and Extremism Online." Retrieved from House of Commons: http://www.parliament.uk/homeaffairscom.

Klausen J. (2015) "Tweeting the Jihad: Social Media Networks of Western Foreign Fighters in Syria and Iraq," *Studies in Conflict & Terrorism* 38(1): 1–22.

Krasodomski-Jones A. (2016) "Talking to Ourselves: Political Debate Online and the Echo Chamber Effect." Retrieved from https://www.demos.co.uk/wp-content/uploads/2017/02/Echo-Chambers-final-version.pdf.

Landau M. J., Solomon S., Greenberg J., Cohen F., Pyszczynski T. (2004) "Deliver Us from Evil: The Effects of Mortality Salience and Reminders of 9/11 on Support for President George W. Bush," *Personality and Social Psychology Bulletin* 30(9): 1136–1150.

Lee Y. H., Hsieh G. (2013) "Does slacktivism hurt activism?: The effects of moral balancing and consistency in online activism," in Proceedings of CHI 2013. ACM Press, pp. 811–820.

Magdy W., Darwish K., Weber I. (2015) "#FailedRevolutions: Using Twitter to Study the Antecedents of ISIS support." arXiv preprint arXiv:1503.02401.

McGarty C., Thomas E., Lala G., Smith L., Bliuc A.-M. (2014) "New Technologies, New Identities, and the Growth of Mass Opposition in the Arab Spring," *Political Psychology* 35(6): 725–740.

McGregor H., Lieberman J., Greenberg J., Solomon S., Arndt J., Simon L., Pyszczynski T. (1998) "Terror Management and Aggression: Evidence That Mortality Salience Motivates Aggression Against Worldview-Threatening Others," *Journal of Personality and Social Psychology* 74(3): 590–605.

Miller C., Krasodomski-Jones A., Smith J. (2016) "Gambling and Social Media." Retrieved from https://www.demos.co.uk/wpcontent/uploads/2016/02/Gambling-Social-Media-Demos-and-RGT.pdf.

Miller G., Mekhennet S. (2015, November 20). "Inside the Surreal World of the Islamic State's Propaganda Machine," *The Washington Post*. Retrieved from https://www.washingtonpost.com/world/national-security/inside-the-islamic-states-propaganda-machine/2015/11/20/051e997a-8ce6-11e5-acff-673ae92ddd2b_story.html?utm_term=.323620ee7e88.

Morozov E. (2009) "Iran: Downside to the 'Twitter revolution,'" *Dissent* 56(4): 10–14.

Moscovici S., Zavalloni M. (1969) "The Group as a Polarizer of Attitudes," *Journal of Personality and Social Psychology* 12(2): 125–135.

Myers D., Bishop G. (1970) "Discussion Effects on Racial Attitudes," *Science* 169(3947): 778–779.

Postmes T., Spears R., Sakhel K., de Groot D. (2001) "Social Influence in Computer-Mediated Communication: The Effects of Anonymity on Group Behaviour," *Personality and Social Psychology Bulletin* 27: 1243–1254.

Prucha N. (2016) "IS and the Jihadist Information Highway—Projecting Influence and Religious Identity via Telegram," 10(6): 48–58.

Prucha N., Fisher A. (2013) "Tweeting for the Caliphate: Twitter as the New Frontier for Jihadist Propaganda," *CTC Sentinel* 6(6): 19–23.

Prunckun H. (2014) "The First Pillar of Terror—Kill One, Frighten Ten Thousand: A Critical Discussion of the Doctrinal Shift Associated with the 'New Terrorism.'" *The Police Journal*, 87(3): 178–185.

Reicher S., Haslam A. (2016) "Fueling Extremes: The Psychology of Group Dynamics Goes a Long Way Toward Explaining What Drives Ordinary People Toward Radicalism," *Scientific American Mind* 27: 34–39.

Reicher S., Spears R., Postmes T. (1995) "A Social Identity Model of Deindividuation Phenomena," *European Review of Social Psychology* 6: 161–198.

Rogan H., Stenerson A. (2007) *Al-Qaida's Use of the Internet*. Oslo: Norwegian Defense Research Establishment (FFI).

Schumann S., Klein O. (2015) "Substitute or Stepping Stone? Assessing the Impact of Low-Threshold Online Collective Actions on Offline Participation," *European Journal of Social Psychology* 45(3): 308–322.

Smith L, Gavin J., Sharp E. (2015) "Social Identity Formation During the Emergence of the Occupy Movement," *European Journal of Social Psychology* 45(7): 818–832.

Smith L., Postmes T. (2011) "The Power of Talk: Developing Discriminatory Group Norms Through Discussion," *British Journal of Social Psychology* 50(2): 193–215.

Smith L., Thomas E., McGarty C. (2015) "'We Must Be the Change We Want to See in the World': Integrating Norms and Identities Through Social Interaction," *Political Psychology* 36(5): 543–557.

Smith L., Wakeford L., Cribbin T., Barnett J. (2017) "Prediction of Online Radicalization Through Language and Social Interaction." Unpublished manuscript, University of Bath.

Stern J., Berger J. (2015) *ISIS: The State of Terror*. London: Harper Collins.

Tajfel H., Turner J. (1979) "An Integrative Theory of Intergroup Conflict," in Worchel S. & Austin W. G. (eds.), *The Social Psychology of Intergroup Relations*. Monterey, CA: Brooks/Cole, pp. 33–47.

Taylor P., Holbrook D., Joinson A. (2017) "Same Kind of Different: Affordances, Terrorism, and the Internet," *Criminology and Public Policy* 16(1): 127–133.

Telegram. (n.d.) "Telegram FAQ: Do You Process Data Requests?" Retrieved from https://telegram.org/faq.

Thomas E., McGarty C., Lala G., Stuart A., Hall L., Goddard A. (2015) "Whatever Happened to Kony2012? Understanding a Global Internet Phenomenon as an Emergent Social Identity," *European Journal of Social Psychology* 45: 356–367.

Turner J. (1982) "Toward a Cognitive Redefinition of the Social Group," in Tajfel H. (ed.), *Social identity and inter-group relations*. Cambridge: Cambridge University Press, pp. 15–40.

Turner J. (1991) *Social Influence*. Milton Keynes, UK: Open University Press.

Turner J., Hogg M., Oakes P., Reicher S., Wetherell M. (1987) *Rediscovering the Social Group: A Self-Categorization Theory*. Oxford: Blackwell.

Turner J., Wetherell M., Hogg M. (1989) "Referent Informational Influence and Group Polarization," *British Journal of Social Psychology* 28: 135–147.

Whiteside C. (2016) "Lighting the Path: the Evolution of the Islamic State Media Enterprise (2003–2016)," *The International Centre for Counter-Terrorism—The Hague* 1–36. https://icct.nl/wp-content/uploads/2016/11/ICCT-Whiteside-Lighting-the-Path-the-Evolution-of-the-Islamic-State-Media-Enterprise-2003-2016-Nov2016.pdf.

Winter C. (2015) *Documenting the Virtual "Caliphate."* London: Quilliam Foundation.

Winter C. (2017a) "ICSR Insight: The ISIS Propaganda Decline." Retrieved from http://icsr.info/2017/03/icsr-insight-isis-propaganda-decline/.

Winter C. (2017b) "Media Jihad: The Islamic State's Doctrine for Information Warfare." Retrieved from http://icsr.info/2017/02/icsr-report-media-jihad-islamic-states-doctrine-information-warfare/.

Wojcieszak M. (2009) "Carrying Online Participation Offline: Mobilization by Radical Online Groups and Politically Dissimilar Offline Ties," *Journal of Communication* 59: 564–586.

Zelin A. (2013) *The State of Global Jihad Online: A Qualitative, Quantitative, and Cross Lingual Analysis.* Washington: New America Foundation.

Zelin A. (2015) "Picture or It Didn't Happen: A Snapshot of the Islamic State's Official Media Output," *Perspectives on Terrorism* 9(4): 85–97.

6

From Music to Books, from Pictures to Numbers

The Forgotten Yet Crucial Components of Islamic State's Propaganda

Stephane J. Baele and Charlie Winter

Propaganda must be total. The propagandist must utilize all of the technical means at his disposal—the press, radio, TV, movies, posters, meetings, door-to-door canvassing. There is no propaganda as long as one makes use, in sporadic fashion and at random, of a newspaper article here, a poster or a radio program there, organizes a few meetings and lectures, writes a few slogans on walls; that is not propaganda.

—Jacques Ellul (1973)

Introduction

Islamic State (IS) videos, magazines, and social media networks have so far attracted the bulk of scholarly, expert, and everyday commenting on the group's communication. While this state of affairs is quite legitimate given the importance and visibility of these three components (explained in detail in the previous three chapters), they are far from alone in IS's propaganda toolkit. Indeed, in terms of prevalence, they are actually quite marginal to it. In reality, the organization has produced a myriad of other elements that are neither add-ons embedded in magazines or videos nor subordinate material disseminated through social media, but rather have an independent existence and are truly important in their own right. Although these components might be less familiar to Western audiences and consequently attract less

Stephane J. Baele and Charlie Winter, *From Music to Books, from Pictures to Numbers: The Forgotten Yet Crucial Components of Islamic State's Propaganda* In: *ISIS Propaganda*. Edited by: Stephane J. Baele, Katharine A. Boyd, and Travis G. Coan, Oxford University Press (2020) © University of Maryland National Consortium for the Study of Terrorism and Responses to Terrorism (START)
DOI: 10.1093/oso/9780190932459.003.0007

attention, they nonetheless deliver specific and singular contributions to IS's propaganda efforts, especially among non-Western publics.

In this chapter, we explore these "forgotten" yet no less crucial components of IS propaganda. We scrutinize five components in particular: religious chants (*nashīd* when singular and *anashīd* when plural),[1] photo galleries/reports, infographics, books, and news communiqués (by al-Bayan Radio and A'maq News Agency). Only by incorporating these five elements can a comprehensive picture of IS's full-spectrum approach toward propaganda emerge, one that clarifies its well-known visual and linguistic universe. Contrarily to the previous three chapters, this one does not claim exhaustive analysis of the components it deals with. Rather, it simply provides a presentation and initial discussion of these elements, highlighting their most important characteristics and roles, stressing their novel or bygone character, with a view to paving the way for more systematic and in-depth future research on each one of them.

Overall, this chapter shows that these elements play a tripartite role in the establishment of a full-spectrum propaganda. First and foremost, their ubiquity and repetitive character heavily contribute to the relentless reiteration of the master frame constructed in other IS propaganda outputs (diagnostic/prognostic, crisis/solution), using the same narratives and core binary concepts. As exemplified by Ellul's earlier quote (which is also discussed in the Introduction of this book), a full-spectrum propaganda system by definition seeks to use all possible "technical means at his disposal," with the aim of creating continuity in the diffusion of the message. To take Ellul's words again, the individual being targeted "must not be allowed a moment of meditation or reflection in which to see himself vis-à-vis the propagandist . . . the individual must not be allowed to recover, to collect himself, to remain untouched by propaganda during any relatively long period, for propaganda is not the touch of the magic wand. It is based on slow, constant impregnation . . . it must create a complete environment for the individual, one from which he never emerges" (Ellul 1973: 17–18). Propaganda, when full-spectrum, thus seeks to occupy even moments of relaxation—in this context, propaganda texts are replaced by films, music, or games. As Kallis observes in his in-depth study of Nazi propaganda, even in these moments "the audience [should] remain the recipient of cultural symbols which it then processes with reference

---

[1] Most analyses in English use *nasheed* for the singular and *nasheeds* for the plural. In line with this volume's Arabic glossary, we prefer to remain faithful to the Arabic and use *nashīd* for the singular and *anashīd* for the plural (see Glossary of Frequent Arabic Terms at the beginning of the volume).

to its overall perception of reality" (2005: 10). As such, more than simply "filling the gaps," the less noticeable components are essential in elevating IS propaganda into the higher levels of what some authors have called a "jihadi culture" (Ramsay 2013; Hegghammer 2017), a holistic worldview that comes with its norms, tastes, preconceptions, and practices.

Second, these components *accentuate the emotional impact of propaganda* by adding music and pictures, very often recycling ancient symbolic tropes. "Each usable medium," Ellul writes, "has its own particular way of penetration" (1973: 9) that must be used to ensure that the target audience is caught in a tight propaganda "net." Third, these elements *reinforce IS's legitimacy* by tapping into old Islamic traditions, like poetry or martyr biographies. While magazines and videos attempt to include hints that their source is legitimate (e.g., by quoting *hadiths*), a martyr biography or a poetry volume is, in itself, an item that conveys a certain weight in terms of legitimacy. These three reasons make clear that what truly makes IS propaganda an unprecedented full-spectrum system is its colossal use of these less publicized outputs. As highlighted in the Introduction, none of these components constitutes a revolutionary innovation by IS—rather, it is their well thought-out and coordinated inclusion into the group's propaganda system and strategy, as well as their production in extraordinary quantities, that is new.

Anashīd

The first component we examine are *anashīd*, which are a-cappella Islamic chants. Often overlooked, they are nonetheless, as Grâtrud argued in one of the rare studies specifically dedicated to the genre, "a vital part" of IS output (2016: 1050). Just as for videos or magazines, IS's use of *anashīd* is not an innovation in itself. Indeed, despite the perennial controversy over music in Islam (read, e.g., Shiloah 1995, 1997), the *nashīd* is a popular and widespread type of Islamic religious hymn that has "always existed in Islam" (Grâtrud 2016: 1051) and has already been used in one form or another by violent Islamist groups like the Taliban (Johnson & Waheed 2011; also read Pelevin & Weinreich 2012) or Hamas (Berg 2012). As we will also see, it prolongs a long tradition of jihadist poetry. However, and again just as is the case for videos and magazines, IS's use of *anashīd* is characterized by unprecedentedly high quantities as compared with other jihadist organizations. Incidentally, IS's strict stance on music means that their *anashīd* only feature male a-capella singing—and occasionally rapping—which is subjected to heavy digital editing.

The main unit for the production of official Arabic *anashīd* is the Ajnad Foundation, which was founded in 2013 (*Mu'assasat Ajnad*, see Figure 6.1). Production in foreign languages is done by the al-Hayat Media Center (and, to a lesser extent, by the Furat Foundation), just as for other types of outputs. To have a unit whose only preoccupation is the production of music and Quranic recitations is notable for a terrorist organization and shows that IS has learned from the successes and failures of Hizbullah (Khatib, Matar, & Alshaer 2014: 76) and Hamas (which also tactically "produces, performs, records, and uses" music as one of its "resistance tools," Berg 2012: 297). There is, however, no certain knowledge of how these units conduct their music production on a daily basis. As Schatz notes (2015), "no one outside of ISIS knows exactly who does the musical arrangements." While some reports—which were later corroborated by his appearance in a number of its releases—suggested that German rapper Denis Cuspert played a prominent role in al-Hayat Media Center's musical operations, the proceedings of the Ajnad Foundation remain largely unknown.

Anashīd appear in IS propaganda in two contexts. First and most visibly, they are omnipresent in IS's provincial and central media office videos, most of which have their soundtrack saturated by background *anashīd*. In this instance, the lyrics and rhythms of the carefully chosen *anashīd* are used to reinforce the message delivered on the screen, as shown by Winkler and colleagues' multimodal approach (2017): slower and more religious *anashīd* tend to complement calmer meditative sequences of videos (such as declarations and prayers of future martyrs), while *anashīd* with more aggressive lyrics and faster rhythms tend to accompany more violent fighting sequences. Second, *anashīd* are circulated online and on radio as stand-alone

Figure 6.1 The two alternative logos of the Ajnad Foundation.

Figure 6.2 Example of cover picture advertising and accompanying an IS *nashīd*, whose main theme is martyrdom ("My Right Hand Is on the Button," August 2013).

products, to be later integrated into videos. Such stand-alone *anashīd* are released regularly (sometimes together with English translations) and advertised, sometimes with a cover picture that relates to their main theme (as in Figure 6.2). They then circulate widely on the web through platforms like Reddit and Archive.org, but also on much more openly accessible platforms like YouTube.

Counting from various Reddit threads on IS's *anashīd*,[2] and cross-checking from various IS sympathizer websites known for disseminating the organization's music,[3] we counted 104 original official *anashīd* released as stand-alone items between February 2013 and March 2017. Appendix 1, at the end of the book, provides their titles (in English), their release dates,[4] and the language used (e.g., Arabic, German). Figure 6.3 shows the chronological distributions of these 104 *anashīd*.

Two key observations can be drawn from this figure and Appendix 1. First, while *anashīd* were first exclusively produced in Arabic, there has been a shift toward much more diversity in terms of language. *Anashīd* have appeared in foreign languages like German, French, or Turkish, and there have even been noteworthy uses of Uyghur and Mandarin (in an explicit bid to speak to the Muslim minority in Western China's Xinjiang region), Bengali, and Urdu. This turn not only represents a will to talk more directly to potential

---

[2] For example, https://www.reddit.com/r/DankestNasheeds/comments/42s7xi/islamic_state_nasheed_master_thread/, or https://www.reddit.com/r/DankestNasheeds/comments/4ohds4/the_islamic_state_nasheed_archive/.

[3] For example, https://khilafatimes.wordpress.com/nasheeds/.

[4] We cannot claim to have perfect accuracy on this data, so this information is subject to caution. However, deviations are likely to be minimal.

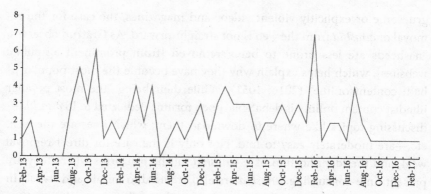

Figure 6.3 Chronological evolution of Islamic State *anashīd* production (number of new *anashīd* released per month, February 2013–March 2017).

sympathizers, but also represents IS's willingness to perform, in practice, its postnational project; in other words, to project its utopian image of the diverse (composed of individuals from all backgrounds, origins, races and ethnicities) yet strongly unified and eschatological conception of the Muslim *ummah*. It is worth noting that this trend of linguistic diversification has been apparent across IS propaganda operations between 2014 and 2017, and has been facilitated by the abilities it accrued from foreign fighter inflows. The second observation is that *anashīd* have been produced at an irregular rhythm, with a vague drop to around one or two releases per month after the February 2016 spike (July 2016 seems like an outlier), down from between two and four *anashīd* released per month in the period from the end of 2013 to the very beginning of 2016. This decline echoes, although in a markedly less clear way, the decline in video productions and magazine content (as measured in number of pages and number of different publications) highlighted in the previous chapters.

Building on the literature studying the roles played by music in conflict in general (e.g., Johnson & Cloonan 2008) and on the uses of Islamic hymns by Islamist groups of the recent past in particular (Said 2012; Berg 2012; Massad 2005; Johnson & Waheed 2011), we suggest that IS produces in-house *anashīd* for four main reasons, each contributing to the group's ambition to produce a comprehensive, multidimensional, and cohesive full-spectrum propaganda.

First, producing *anashīd* is a way to publish a form of propaganda that is hard to counter. *Anashīd* indeed have a significant tactical advantage: unlike gruesome or explicitly violent videos and magazines, the case for the removal of *anashīd* from the web is not straightforward. As Gråtrud observes, "nasheeds are less prone to being removed [from prominent all-public websites], which helps explain why they have become the most popular jihadi content online" (2016: 1051). While their being "the most popular jihadist content online" is debatable, open forums dedicated to IS *anashīd*— discussing topics like where to download them, which ones are the best, etc.—are moderately easy to find. Not only is the case for direct removal weak and the identification of IS *anashīd* on the platforms where they are present time-consuming, *anashīd* are also are hard to mimic and "twist" in counternarrative efforts, which can more easily produce appealing texts or even images providing a convincing counterdiscourse. Johnson and Waheed (2011) already noticed this advantage in their study of the traditional hymns used by the Taliban, which were particularly hard to counter because of their very specific genre, language, and mobilization of local traditions. Berg concurs, noting that in Palestine, militant music "creates a political space that the Israelis cannot control" (2012: 297).

A second reason to produce *anashīd* can be found in IS's understanding that, as Ingram explains in Chapter 1 of this volume, "a comprehensive messaging strategy uses a range of messengers, media, and formats to maximize the reach, relevance, and resonance of a campaign across diverse target audiences." *Anashīd* are simply another type of content to add to the already huge flow of propaganda material released by the organization to promote its worldview. As Gråtrud has shown (2016), IS's hymns indeed repeat its most important messages as much as possible, reiterating once again its master narratives and major themes by using a restrictive list of key identity-marking concepts, symbols, and binary oppositions (e.g., *ṭawaghīt*, crusaders, brothers). In their study of chants as a "little understood Afghan Taliban propaganda tool" (2011: 3), Johnson and Waheed already observed that the many repetitions of simple mottos by the singers ensure that the main messages "stay in people's consciousness" (2011: 5). Through the reverberation of major themes, reinforced by *anashīd*'s very repetitive structure, IS's *anashīd* production pursues the same three aims identified by Berg (2012) in Hamas music: spreading the organization's message, exhorting resistance, and strengthening social cohesion.

Even though the issues dealt with in the course of a given IS *nashīd* can vary according to situational exigencies faced by the group at the time of composition, there is undeniably a significant predominance of war-related themes in

IS *anashīd*.[5] Gråtrud's analysis (2016) reveals four major themes: "Jihad is the solution," "Fighters are role models," "War and brutality," and "IS is the leader and protector of Islam"—other themes are present but are less prominent. Just like the other propaganda outputs it reinforces, *anashīd* thereby provide a "narrative" with "clear diagnostic, prognostic, and motivational elements" (Gråtrud 2016: 1063). The two following excerpts illustrate this.

> So arise, O brother, get up on the path of salvation, So we may march together, resist the aggressors / Raise our glory, and raise the foreheads, That have refused to bow before any besides the Lord / Clanging of the swords is the Nasheed of the reluctant, The path of fighting is the path of life / So amidst an assault, tyranny is destroyed. ("Clanging of the Swords, Nashīd of the Defiant")

> Regiments of my State, arise, revive our glory / And restore the crown of our Ummah on its head, arise / Regiments of my State, arise, revive our glory / And restore the crown of our Ummah on its head, arise.
> Destroy every Taghut, light your roasting fire / Gain dominance over soldiers by any means, draw breath by any means / Destroy every Taghut, light your roasting fire / Gain dominance over soldiers by any means, draw breath by any means.
> Regiments of my State, arise, revive our glory / And restore the crown of our Ummah on its head, arise / Regiments of my State, arise, revive our glory / And restore the crown of our Ummah on its head, arise.
> And no, have no mercy on the filthy one, his tongue practises distortion / He gets drunk by night, and fills his day with transgression / And no, have no mercy on the filthy one, his tongue practises distortion / He gets drunk by night, and fills his day with transgression.
> Regiments of my State, arise, revive our glory / And restore the crown of our Ummah on its head, arise / Regiments of my State, arise, revive our glory / And restore the crown of our Ummah on its head, arise.
> The men of the State have been and continue to be loyal to us / May Allah preserve them alive as knights in Baghdad first / The men of the State have been and continue to be loyal to us / May Allah preserve them alive as knights in Baghdad first. ("Regiments of My State")

[5] Gråtrud clearly notes that "IS nasheeds are more important in preparing for war than for depicting the softer sides of life in the IS" (2016: 1050).

Note that there is a clear continuation of the major themes of Taliban hymns as highlighted by Johnson and Waheed (2011): invasion and oppression of foreigners and apostates, armed *jihād* against them, and nefarious impact of non-Islamic activities. These themes are, in general, close to those present in the communication of other Islamist groups. Compare the preceding IS *anashīd* with, for example, the two following *anashīd* from Hamas and the Taliban, respectively, each of which encourages listeners to stop bowing down and start resisting violently against the near and far enemies.

Oh Afghan, the foreigners are present in your country, your past enemies are present in your country / They are the your past enemies whom your ancestors defeated, and then they ran away / Today they are the rulers who dominate your soil / They hit you by huge bombs, cruise missiles and napalm bombs. (Taliban hymn, cited by Johnson & Waheed 2011)

Hit the qassam rocket, shoot in the liver of the oppressive, hit your terror as a pending reaction, storming roaring bombs / Hit, the glory is calling us, Trembles the nests of our enemies. (Hamas hymn, cited by Berg 2012).

The third motive appears to be to elicit or reinforce the emotional reactions experienced by the audience of the propaganda, both when the *nashīd* stands alone and when it supports a particular video footage, as explained earlier. Although the exact mechanisms by which it works are not well understood, music is well-known to trigger emotions (e.g., Juslin & Sloboda 2001; Koelsch 2005; Juslin & Vastfjall 2008). In the case of *anashīd*, this effect is reinforced by the very repetitive character of *anashīd* and by their use of symbols— indeed, just as in Islamist poetry, prominent Islamic symbols abound in IS *anashīd*: "guns and bombs feature as swords; cars and motorbikes as steeds; firefights as epic battles; jihadists as knights or lions" (Kendall 2016: 237). In the preceding example, the "knights" in Baghdad evoke early Muslim fighters.

Fourth and finally, *anashīd* are a powerful way to reinforce the legitimacy of the group, which is one of IS's central concerns. This is because *anashīd* directly appeal to the venerable tradition of poetry in Islamic thought in general and the jihadist tradition in particular, explained in more detail later. In this sense, *anashīd* are directly linked to the phenomena identified by Kendall that poetry is significant "in winning hearts and minds for the militant jihadi cause" (Kendall 2016: 223); they help IS to situate its project as the direct heritage of the millennial project of holy *jihād*.

Photo Galleries and Reports

While the visual dimension of IS propaganda has already been discussed in previous chapters, one prominent component of IS's "own visual world" (Kovacs 2015: 51) has not yet been addressed: photo reports, understood as small sets of pictures organized around a common theme, with a title and very limited accompanying text, and which circulate online.

This is not a minor phenomenon; in fact, most experts on IS communication agree that, aside from news bulletins, photo reports have consistently constituted, in terms of the raw number of propaganda items or "events" released by IS, the biggest part of the group's propaganda effort. In the Hijri year 1436, which roughly equated to October 2014 to October 2015, IS boasted of having released no fewer than 14,523 photographs and a further 1,787 formally arranged photographic reports, a figure that is consistent with data collected by Winter (2015). According to Zelin's count of IS propaganda items during 1 week in April 2015, no less than 63% of IS's releases are photo reports (77 releases, as compared to 24 videos or 6 radio reports). Winter's count of 30 days of propaganda in July and August 2015 goes even further, showing that 78% of IS propaganda circulating online consists of these short photo galleries (2015). In a later study (2018), Winter found that 61% of IS's output comprised photo reports, a figure that roughly correlates with Milton's data (2016). In that sense, IS photo reports bear strategic value that constantly accumulates as a result of their repetition. It is worth noting that almost all of these photo reports come from the provincial media offices, with the aim of providing snapshots of daily life and prominent events across the territory controlled by IS. These reports' quantity has thus plummeted, corresponding with the shrinking size of the "Caliphate" through 2017. Figure 6.4 provides an example of a photo report.

As stressed elsewhere in this book, it is well known that photos can have a significant impact on the successful dissemination of political ideas, taking an "increasingly important role . . . in global politics" (Bleiker 2015: 872). Rather than having an intrinsic power, images accentuate both particular political messages and core elements of broad meaning systems, reinforcing particular political perceptions and opinions. The power of images in political communication is therefore not as much one of self-sufficient direct persuasion as one of frame accentuation: visuals activate preexisting frames of interpretation of political events in a more effective way than language (Brothers 1996; Hansen 2011, 2015). For example, IS's images of its prisoners

Figure 6.4 Example of a photography report: "The Markets' Activity Shortly Before al-Id in al-Mayadin," produced by the al-Khayr provincial media center (images have been slightly reorganized to use less space).

dressed in orange Guantanamo suits does not convey meaning *in abstracto*, but rather immediately evokes both the torture of mainly Muslim prisoners by the United States and the existence of an opportunity for revenge in IS.

Building on Galtung's seminal opposition between "peace journalism" and "war journalism" (1986), many analyses of photo reporting on controversial political issues and conflicts have shown that groups tend to use very narrow visual landscapes; that is, they have a propensity to visually represent the conflict with a limited series of images. The frequent repetition of particular types of images constructs biased perceptions of events and, when done strategically, contributes to establish a specific framing of the overall situation (e.g., Rohlinger & Klein 2012 on the abortion debate; Fahmy & Neumann 2012 on the 2008–2009 Gaza war; Griffin & Lee 1995 on the US news coverage of the first Gulf War; Bleiker et al. 2013 on the visual depiction of refugees). Limited visual landscapes can be used to reflect, crystallize, and further disseminate already existing meaning in a condensed way.

Hansen's recent work on pictorial "icons" (2015) highlights the effects symbolic images can have when they are strategically articulated to support political messages or systems of meaning. As Domke, Perlmutter, and Spratt (2002: 148) have explained, this accentuation and condensation of frames is operated as images reinforce the association between cognition and evaluations, on the one hand, and emotions, on the other hand. In other words, well-chosen images are better than text at eliciting the emotions usually felt by a particular public when facing a particular issue; they have a unique potential to dramatize social groups' appraisal of a particular social problem. To use Bleiker and colleagues' words, "dominant imagery emotionally frames" discussions on political issues (2013: 399; also Hansen 2011: 55; O'Neill et al. 2013: 414). It follows that specific types of images trigger specific emotions, some of which (anger, sadness, joy, hatred, or fear) are known to play an important role in political attitudes (e.g., Halperin 2015).

IS's use of photos—many of which are taken by adolescent or preadolescent media operatives in Iraq and Syria—displays both a limited visual landscape and a strategic choice of images picked up for the emotions they are expected to trigger: pictures of dead children after a "crusader" bombing are chosen to trigger anger (and therefore an urge to retaliate); pictures of happy people doing their shopping in well-stocked markets (as in Figure 6.4) will trigger serenity or happiness (and therefore stimulate a desire to join that place, if not yet there); pictures of a "crusader" president shaking hands with a *ṭaghūt* leader are circulated to provoke hatred (and therefore a desire to both move away from the enemy and to punish him).[6]

Just like *anashīd*, images reinforce the frames and narratives put forward by IS by eliciting emotions. They are consistent, carefully selected, and, within their respective themes, monolithic. Taken together, those that are overtly civilian in nature fill in the gaps in IS's construction of reality, offering

---

[6] On the action tendencies of hatred, read Halperin 2008.

"evidence" of the "fact" that it administers a functioning proto-state encompassing all walks of life. Conversely, the photographs that focus on its military pursuits offer the group—and its supporters—something else: they are a way to mark territory and declare supremacy. As a consequence of this, IS has historically used images more tactically than it has videos and publications. IS offered images as a way to directly respond to enemy information operations and counterpropaganda; a reliable tool that could selectively cut through the anti-IS "lies" peddled in the mainstream media.

Infographics

The third component reviewed here are *infographics*. An infographic can be defined as "an illustration (as in a book or magazine, or on a website) that uses graphic elements to present information in a visually striking way,"[7] or as "a visual representation of information or data."[8] The *Oxford Dictionary* offers the maxim that "a good infographic is worth a thousand words."[9] They are a specific genre that stands at the intersection of visual images, language, and quantitative data. Each of these aspects, as well as how they interact, is important when assessing infographics' impact on their audiences. Aside from Winkler's brief 2016 analysis and Adelman's 2018 article, there is currently no scholarly work on the use of quantified language (numbers, graphs, statistics, etc.), let alone infographics, by extremist groups in general and IS in particular.

Similar to *anashīd*, IS infographics are both important in their own right and as add-ons to other outlets. They first appeared as stand-alone news events developed by the A'maq News Agency to present suicide operation statistics in the fall of 2015. By the end of that year, they had also begun to appear as add-ons embedded in the Arabic-language newspaper *al-Naba*,[10] and they were produced by the unit in charge of it. Infographics were integrated to *al-Naba* from its inception, with the first infographic appearing in the first issue (see Figure 6.5). Since then, the quality and sophistication of infographic design has been self-evident (see the four examples in Figure 6.6),

---

7 https://www.merriam-webster.com/dictionary/infographic.

8 https://en.oxforddictionaries.com/definition/infographic.

9 https://en.oxforddictionaries.com/definition/infographic.

10 *Al-Naba* means "the announcement," which is the title of the 78th *sura* of the Quran. While it exists in newspaper form now, prior to IS's declaration of the Caliphate, it was more akin to an annual operational report.

Figure 6.5 First appearance of an infographic embedded in an Islamic State magazine (*al-Naba* no. 2).

and, somewhat surprisingly, the genre was only recently integrated into outlets targeting Western audiences. In the context of the al-Hayat–produced magazines, they never appeared in *Dabiq* (with one exception related to healthcare in issue 9), but became a regular feature of subsequent productions such as *Rumiyah* magazine, as Figure 6.7 shows. This clear distinction between *Dabiq*, *al-Naba*, and *Rumiyah* suggests a conscious tactical choice.

In its West-facing magazines, infographics are always accompanied by the *al-Naba* Arabic logo, sometimes accompanied by the words "al-Naba

Figure 6.6 Four examples of Islamic State infographics.

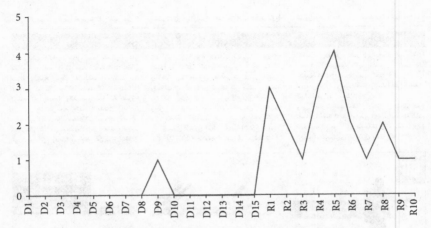

Figure 6.7 Chronological distribution of embedded infographics in Islamic State English-speaking magazines (from *Dabiq* no. 1 to *Rumiyah* no. 10).

Infographics," which suggests that a small unit within the *al-Naba* staff is in charge of producing these visuals. Given the presence of repeating motifs and styles, it is probable that the *al-Naba* team overlaps in its operations with the A'maq News Agency. It should be noted that the *al-Naba* team also produces well-crafted, one-page thematic computer visuals akin to infographics but without numbers (as in Figure 6.8, which similarly mostly circulate embedded in magazines. Yet infographics also circulate alone and are important in their own right; in this case, they are also produced by A'maq News Agency (more on this "news agency" later). There is a remarkable difference between these non-numeric visuals and infographics containing data: while the former deal with a whole range of issues (religious practice, life in the

Figure 6.8 Four examples of non-numerical *al-Naba* computer graphic work.

Caliphate, etc.), the latter almost exclusively convey information about warfare (with the rare exceptions summarizing aspects of life in the Caliphate), creating through repetition a perception of IS's *jihād* as an extremely efficient, diverse, and lethal enterprise. Where infographics stand out with regards to images is in their regular use of computer-generated images instead of pictures, which arguably makes them the best-crafted genre across IS propaganda.

As noted earlier, infographics constitute a specific genre that combines textual, visual, and numerical elements. Regarding the textual dimension, infographics reinforce the main themes elaborated elsewhere in IS propaganda but with a clear preference for war/*jihād*, using the most prominent, recognizable keywords structuring the group's narratives—martyr, Islamic State, *ṭaghūt*, crusaders, *murtaddīn*, and the like. As such, they are yet another way to repeat the same message. The same applies to the visual dimension. Infographics use the same types of images that feature prominently in magazines, including the same recurring powerful and symbolic images (e.g., the black flag and the ancient knight in Figure 6.6) that appear in other IS publications. Figure 6.9 shows which symbols pertaining to IS's visual world appear in the 23 infographics embedded in *Rumiyah* magazines and how many times.

The best way to understand the importance of these infographics in the full context of IS propaganda is to move beyond their repetition of its main

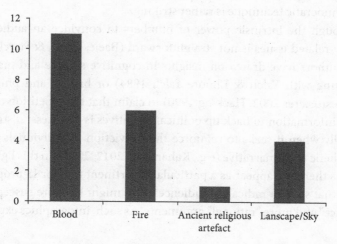

Figure 6.9 Frequency of visual symbols in infographics embedded in *Rumiyah* magazines (nos. 1–10).

linguistic and visual markers and recognize the particularity of their central component: numbers. By circulating numerical information, IS directly taps into the prominence of numbers in contemporary political communication more generally. Indeed, IS's frequent use of infographics is only the latest (and perhaps most counterintuitive) iteration of the vast, ongoing tendency to "quantify politics," the underlying assumption of which is less that numbers reflect the truth than that audiences *perceive* numbers to reflect the truth. In this sense, in spite of its hatred of the liberal world, IS mimics one of its most ubiquitous and intrinsic practices: that of political quantification. By doing so, IS follows other political organizations which understand numbers to be the most important "rhetorical weapons" of our times (Bréant 2012: 156)[11] because of the "gloss of scientificity" they apply to otherwise unverifiable or controversial information (Molle & Mollinga 2003: 537). In other words, numbers convert "what might otherwise be highly contentious normative agendas . . . into formats that gain credibility through rhetorical claims to neutral and technocratic assessment" (Broome & Quirk 2015: 813). In this sense, IS produces what Cunningham (2002, see Introduction) called "bureaucratic propaganda." In the context of the Mosul battle, IS accelerated its adoption of statistics-based denialism, producing weekly and monthly infographics that attempted to reframe its inexorable loss in the city as a strategic victory. In each graphic, it tallied suicide operations, enemy losses, vehicles destroyed and captured, and, on occasion, the number of new recruits to have signed up. To see a radically anti-modern violent group like IS using this technocratic technique is rather striking.

Although the intrinsic power of numbers to convince an audience on security-related issues is not straightforward (Baele, Coan, & Sterck 2017), many authors have drawn on insights in cognitive science and marketing (beginning with Yalch & Elmore-Yalch 1984) or history and philosophy (e.g., Desrosieres 2002; Hacking 1990) to claim that the repetition of quantitative information to back up political narratives is a successful strategy,[12] especially when it seeks to reinforce the conviction of individuals initially sympathetic to the narrative (e.g., Kahan et al. 2012; 2013). In this light, infographics therefore appear as a particularly pertinent tool for IS propaganda outlets that seek to radicalize audiences who might be more susceptible to "evidence" and more "rational" arguments. As such, infographics expand IS's

---

[11] Boswell concurs, claiming that numbers are now "important rhetorical device" (2009: 89).
[12] For cases, see, e.g., Conley 2004 or Baele, Balzacq, & Bourbeau 2017.

propaganda "net" by tapping into a different mode of persuasion than religious claims or emotional narratives.

Literature

IS also publishes a myriad of short and long self-standing books that circulate online, as well as offline in Iraq and Syria. There are two main scenarios of publication. Under the first one, books are produced and published by official IS media organizations—chiefly a unit called al-Himma Library (maktabat al-Himma) and, formerly at least, al-Furqan (on occasion, the al-Hayat Media Center disseminates translations in Roman languages, while the Furat Foundation has been known to publish translations in anything from Russian and Bosnian to Bangla and Bahasa Indonesian). Under the second scenario, new or preexisting material is edited and published as PDFs for online diffusion by unofficial support groups operating on the web. For example, Ansar al-Khilafah Media, which publishes and translates Arabic material written by figures involved in justifying IS but very often not officially part of it, like Hussain bin Mahmood (whose short books *Study on al-Khawarij, The Islamic State Is a Necessity of the Era,* or *The Issue of Beheading* clearly justify IS's existence and practices) or lower profile individuals like Abu Abdur' Rahman Raed al-Libi (*Beautiful Pearls in the Fiqh of the Islamic Khilafah*).

The scale of IS's publishing activities is impressive. According to the group, in the Hijri year 1436, for example, it prepared no fewer than 40 theological flyers, of which it printed and distributed 20,000,000 copies, along with a further 18 books, of which 255,000 editions were distributed (see Figure 6.10).

In terms of content, we identify three kinds of literature: texts related to the practice of Islam in (or advocated by) IS, poetry, and martyr biographies. In regard to the first, books related to the practice of Islam in the Caliphate offer presentations of *fiqh* (analysis of the sources upon which *shari'a* rulings are elaborated) in IS, *da'wa* prose (praises to Allah, calls to embrace Islam), or reflections on the religious beliefs and practices of prominent jihadist figures (in which case they can additionally present strategic guidance on the conduct of *jihād*). A good example of the latter sort is the series *From the Hidden History, al-Zarqawi As I Knew Him,* written by Abu Maysara al-Gharib (three very short books discussing the teachings of al-Zarqawi).

Figure 6.10 "Al-Himma Library Publications," *al-Naba* issue 4 (November 7, 2015).

We display in the next two figures examples of the cover pages of religion-oriented books (Figure 6.11: IS-produced books; Figure 6.12: unofficial IS-supporting books). It is not uncommon that religious treatises such as *fiqh* or *da'wa* texts are mobilized for political purposes. The genre has recurrently been used by previous violent Islamist groups engaged in efforts to legitimize their own projects and is routinely produced in a series of Muslim countries in efforts aiming at disseminating the official vision of Islam as well as social constructions of "others" such as Christians or Jews (Doumato 2003). Again, the IS shows here its ability to learn from other organizations' practices (the example in Figure 6.12 shows its ability to mimic even the cover designs of some of their most-despised organizations).

The second category of literature is poetry. Poetry books are rarer but should not be neglected because as they sometimes feature high-ranking figures as alleged authors. A clear example of this is *Cares and Pains*, a compilation of poetry allegedly written by none other than former al-Qaeda in Iraq (AQI) leader and later IS second-in-command Abu Ayyub al-Masri (also known as Abu Hamza al-Muhajir, killed in 2010). The cover page of this book is displayed in Figure 6.13. Using poetry to convey political ideas may

Figure 6.11 Three examples of short religion-related books published by official Islamic State media wings: al-Himma library for the two on the left (*Affairs* [on] *the Fiqh of al-Jihad: Twenty of the Most Important Affairs for the Mujahid* and *Stretch Forth Your Hands to Give the Bay'ah to Al-Baghdaadi*), and al-Furqan on the right (*From the Hidden History, al-Zarqawi As I Knew Him*). The logo of al-Himma library (read in Arabic Maktabat al-Himma) appears on top of the covers of the two books on the left.

Figure 6.12 Two examples of religion-related publications by the unofficial support website Ansar al-Khilafah Media—*Beautiful Pearls in the Fiqh of the Islamic Khilafah* and *Study on al-Khawarij*—and a Brookings Institution working paper dedicated to the Islamic State, on the right for comparison.

Figure 6.13 Cover page of *Cares and Pains* (*Humuum wa'laam*).

seem alien to Western culture (and indeed it does not seek to appeal to that audience); however, IS's practice is unsurprising. Poetry is a recurring genre in the communication of leading Islamic and jihadi thinkers and leaders— figures like al-Qaradawi, Bin Laden, al-Zawahiri, or al-Zarqawi have all produced poetry, which was also regularly featured in al-Qaeda propaganda magazines.[13]

As Kendall's seminal work on jihadi poetry stresses (2016: 225), al-Qaeda and IS simply continue a long-standing practice of using poetry in Islamist outreach tracing back to Muhammad himself, one that rests on an "extensive historical precedent for the use of poetry to connect with, sustain, encourage and document the exploits of Muslim soldiers in holy war" (Kendall 2016: 225). In this sense, IS's production of poetry and recycling of old verses chiefly seeks to reinforce its legitimacy, to situate its action and theology in the direct, centennial lineage of historical Muslim figures, including Muhammad himself. More precisely, as Kendall further explains (2016: 227), the "selective redeployment of the classic poetic heritage creates two important impressions among its primary Arab audience": first, it gives the impression "that modern interpretations of militant jihad were always part of the cultural fabric of Arab society," and second, it "re-casts Arab shared cultural history and collective memory such that it appears to have always been

[13] Even in the West, poetry has long accompanied political propaganda from the state or its opponents and is a recurring feature in history, from the Romans (e.g., Powell 1992) to English Stuart times and the Georgian period (e.g., Gerrard 1994; Norbrook 1999) or, more recently, African American civil rights movements in the 20th century (e.g., Johnson & Johnson 1991).

pointing toward a future that is today finally being realized." The mere use of classical Arabic poetry thus constitutes a formal way to reinforce the legitimacy of the message, even if this use is very often incoherent or paradoxical (distorted citations, quotes from pre-Islamic "ignorant" poets or authors who criticized bellicose Islam, etc.). In sum, "looking and sounding authentic is extremely important" in "the imperative of winning cultural credibility" (Kendall 2016: 228, 238), especially when IS tries to establish itself as the only true Islamist organization in spite of its lack of established religious credentials and its rejection of the vast majority of Muslim clerics.

The third type of literature published by IS to support its propaganda is short biographies of "martyrs" (or longer compilations of several of these biographies). IS's own series of martyr eulogies began early, when the organization was still operating under the AQI label. Since then, the collection has experienced a series of design changes that reflect the gradual establishment of IS's "brand" identity (see Chapter 1) as well as the organizational setting up of its media offices (see Chapter 1 as well; e.g., at one point [2007], the texts were officially published by al-Furqan Media). As far as we can trust the information provided with these documents (as opposed to their content), the biographies seem to have been at first single-authored by an individual called Abu Ismail al-Muhajir, and then a small group of authors joined the effort (Abu Abdulmalik and Abdula'la al-Mudari are recurring names). Once again, and as shown in Figure 6.14, martyr biographies are used by IS media offices as a support for the dissemination of its usual symbolic imagery: most cover pages display symbolic pictures, chiefly natural elements (water, fire) or dramatic cosmological landscapes (planets, dramatic skies with stars, etc.).

As with poetry, as surprising as this practice may appear to a Western audience, the genre is far from new. Indeed IS only continues a well-established trend among violent jihadi groups, employing what Halverson (2007: 542) calls the "communicative force of Muslim martyrdom narratives . . . as a literary genre." IS directly recycles the major codes of the genre without much innovation, reinforcing in print/PDF a major trope of their videos (see the "istishhad script" described in Chapter 3), magazines, or infographics. Cook (2007) studied the 120 al-Qaeda "martyr biographies" (short biographical stories of killed militants) compiled as a single volume entitled *Martyrs in a Time of Alienation* (*Shuhada' fi zaman al-ghurba*) and distributed to militant Islamist websites by the al-Fajr Media Center in 2008. His study of the genre has shown how such "martyrology" has always, in the modern period of violent jihadi Islamism, served political purposes. Stenersen concurs, stressing

Figure 6.14 Three examples of cover pages for martyr biographies. From left to right: *Abu al-Hur al-Ansari* and *Abu Turab al-Najdi* (2006), *Abu Basir al-Tunisi* (2010; note the al-Furqan logo and Islamic State flag), and *Abu Talha al-Hafrawi* (2012).

the fact that "martyr biographies are, in essence, issued for propaganda and recruitment purposes and may therefore not represent an accurate account of historical events" (2011: 173).

The content of these publications is indeed heavily marked by the recollection of the paranormal events (such as miracles) that supposedly happened during the life and death of the martyr (de la Paz 2017), echoing the content of the many reports of *mujāhidīn*'s dreams that circulate online (Edgar & de Looijer 2017). As Cook (2008: 33) summarizes, "typical of the mythical mind, jihadists utilize martyrology and miracle stories that support and strengthen their commitment to the cause of global jihad. Certain recurrent themes, such as supernatural aid for the mujahid in battle, the miraculous purification of the body of a fallen warrior, and sudden visions of paradise, characterize these tales."

The main goal is therefore not to offer an objective obituary but rather to create heroes that recruits would seek to emulate, to reinforce the audience's faith in IS's religious authenticity, and to repeat the propaganda's main themes. Indeed, for Hafez (2007: 95), martyr biographies published by violent Islamist groups in Iraq "strategically deploy emotional narratives to construct the myth of heroic martyrdom, demonize their intended targets, and appeal to potential recruits from around the Muslim world." He further observes that martyr biographies usually reassert some of the most important themes in Islamist propaganda: "humiliation of Muslims at the hands of foreigners, impotence of official Muslim governments in the face of hegemonic powers, and redemption through faithful sacrifice" (2007: 95).

More precisely, Islamist martyr biographies tend to follow the same standardized narrative structure, which is played to elicit emotional reactions. Hafez sums up this structure:

act one depicts the unmerciful humiliation and suffering inflicted on Muslims in Iraq and throughout the world, suggesting that there is a conspiracy by the Western "crusaders" to target Muslims and single them out for punishment. The second act shows the impotence of existing Muslim regimes and their collusion with the West, suggesting that they are not the true leaders of the Muslim world, but servants of their Western "masters." The final act insists on the inevitability of Muslim victory because pious and heroic cadres have stepped forward to redeem the suffering and humiliation of their fellow Muslims through faith in God, sacrifice on the battlefield, and righteousness in their cause. These three narratives are sometimes presented separately, but often they are woven together to suggest a problem, a cause of the problem, and a solution to the problem. (Hafez 2007: 96)

The three acts, which are very often present in IS martyr biographies, directly echo the diagnostic/prognostic/motivational elements found by Gråtrud in IS's anashīd (2016; see earlier discussion), as well as the crisis–solution meta-narrative of IS propaganda more generally (see Introduction and Chapters 1 and 2).

There is another, more mundane reason for which IS produces martyrologies. Especially in the post-2014 context, its streamlined eulogy notices served not just as a means of commemorating fallen fighters, reinforcing its religious aura, or reiterating key narratives, but also as a way to convey operational information regarding suicide attacks to onlookers. As chronicled by Winter (2017), by 2016, up to 10 such notices were being released each day, with each one identifying not just the suicide operative, but their target, method, and impact, too. In this sense, martyrology morphed over the course of IS's first few years as Caliphate into something that transcended the group's cultic obsession with self-sacrifice.

Al-Bayan Radio and A'maq News Agency

When one thinks of past full-spectrum propaganda, one intuitively thinks of biased broadcasted news such as that disseminated during World War II by all fighting powers, with the cases of the Soviet Union and Nazi Germany being the most studied (e.g., Horten 2002). Yanagizawa-Drott's analysis of the role played by radio in the more recent Rwandan genocide (2014) proves that radio can still contribute to triggering extreme violence. In this context, there have been surprisingly few analyses of how IS provides news to its citizens and followers. To one extent, videos participate to this endeavor (through scenes depicting daily life or significant events in the various provinces and through the announcement of victorious military/martyr operations), but they also do both much more and much less, and therefore their status as "news" providers is not evident. In fact, IS provides news through very normal means. In IS-controlled territories, there is a sustained distribution of diverse material (DVD, books, printed leaflets) in towns at local media points (*nuqat i'lamiyya*), where big screens are routinely set up in squares to broadcast videos from across the Caliphate and sound systems are plugged in to broadcast *anashīd* (Zelin 2015: 86). Yet the classical status of news provider is more evidently occupied by two media branches of IS, al-Bayan Radio and A'maq News agency.

First aired in 2014, al-Bayan Radio (literally "the dispatch"; logo in Figure 6.15, together with an advertisement for the station in *al-Naba* magazine) broadcasts a variety of programs, and IS-produced *anashīd*.[14] Crucially, it also airs daily news reports and provincial reports, in foreign languages like English, Russian, and French. Over time, the radio gradually came to function like any modern one, with reporters sent across the territory to broadcast live from different locations (NBC 2016) and with the—on-and-off—possibility to listen to the station online from February 2016, including at one point through an Android app (Site Intelligence Group 2016).

Al-Bayan Radio strived to give the impression that the Caliphate was successfully expanding through military successes, that its provinces were extremely active in establishing the millenarian project, and that the attacks from affiliated groups or individuals across the globe proved the group's

---

[14] It is worth noting that IS's station is not the only one called al-Bayan—there are several homonymic stations across the world, one of them in Australia.

Figure 6.15 Logo of al-Bayan Radio (left) and advertisement for al-Bayan Radio programs and band frequencies in *al-Naba* magazine (no. 11 p. 16) (right).

increasing influence (Washington Post 2015). In sum, and in a very similar way to Nazi radio during World War II, al-Bayan produces biased perceptions of IS's achievements and acts as yet another media repeating the group's core concepts and narratives (Appendix 2 offers an example of a daily news broadcast). The bombing of the radio's headquarters and main emitting station in Mosul in October 2016 (for an account, see NBC 2016) put an end to broadcasting.

The other news provider, A'maq, works like, or rather mimics, modern news agencies like AP or Reuters, producing short press releases. Figure 6.16 is a typical A'maq brief, sent soon after the Westminster bridge attack of

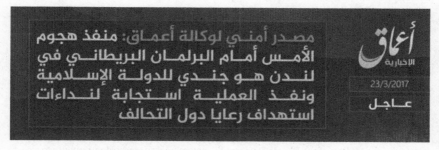

Figure 6.16 Example of an A'maq press release.

March 2017.[15] A'maq first emerged in the context of IS's assault on the town of Kobane in northern Syria. It provided its encroaching forces with media operatives whose roles roughly equated to embedded reporters: they took photographs, reported back to IS central, and produced short video clips that demonstrated IS's advances.

With time, A'maq's operations expanded, such that, by 2016, it had gained regular access to the organization's secret military information, was in charge of announcing the deaths of senior IS leaders, and regularly published operation claims from places as far afield as North America and South East Asia. On one occasion, it even disseminated video footage from inside an ongoing terrorist operation in the Iranian Parliament building in Tehran. By 2017, A'maq was perhaps the most important propaganda wing of IS—most notably, its ambiguous relationship with the central organization meant that it was regarded by some as a more trustworthy source than other IS propaganda, a characteristic that afforded its reports a regular place in the mainstream Western media.

Conclusion

It appears from the review conducted in the course of this chapter that the most well-known and visible propaganda components are far from the only important pieces in IS's propaganda strategy. The "forgotten" components explored here play a crucial role that can metaphorically be presented as the fillers or glue that bind together the more visible elements or as the finer threads ensuring the constriction of the group's propaganda "net," transforming sporadic propaganda outputs into a deeper experience that further propagates and entrenches in everyday life what scholars like Ramsay (2013) and Hegghammer (2017) call the "jihadi culture." The mass production and relentless dissemination of photo reports; the frequent release of *anashīd* and their systematic inclusion in videos and broadcasting on the radio; the daily news reports found online and on air; the embedded or stand-alone infographics; the many books, short and long, that circulate—together these outputs constituted a flood of material that constantly repeats the concepts and ideas that underpin the narratives offered by IS in its more notorious outlets.

---

[15] The brief reads: "The executor of yesterday's assault in front of the British Parliament in London was one of the soldiers of the Islamic State and the operation was executed in response to calls to target citizens of the countries of the Alliance."

Moreover, each of these components individually plays an additional, specific role in the group's sophisticated global communication strategy, the sum total of which truly makes it a full-spectrum propaganda.

References

Adelman R. (2018) "One apostate run over, hundreds repented: excess, unthinkability, and infographics from the war with I.S.I.S.", *Critical Studies in Media Communication* 35(1): 57–73.

Baele S., Balzacq T., Bourbeau P. (2017) "Numbers in Global Security Governance," *European Journal of International Security* 3(1): 22–44.

Baele S., Coan T., Sterck O. (2017) "Security Through Numbers?," *British Journal of Politics & International Relations* 20(2): 459–476.

Berg C. (2012) "Tunes of Religious Resistance? Understanding Hamas Music in a Conflict Context," *Contemporary Islam* 6: 297–314.

Bleiker R. (2015) "Pluralist Methods for Visual Global Politics," *Millennium: Journal of International Studies* 43(3): 872–890.

Bleiker R., Campbell D., Hutchison E., Nicholson X. (2013) "The Visual Dehumanisation of Refugees," *Australian Journal of Political Science* 48(4): 398–416.

Boswell C. (2009) *The Political Uses of Expert Knowledge. Immigration Policy and Social Research*. Cambridge: Cambridge University Press.

Bréant H. (2012) "Démontrer le Rôle Positif des Migrations Internationales par les Chiffres. Une Analyse de la Rhétorique Institutionnelle du Système des Nations Unies [Demonstrating the Positive Impact of International Migrations through Numbers. An Analysis of the UN System's Rhetoric]," *Mots* 100: 153–171.

Broome A., Quirk J. (2015) "The Politics of Numbers: The Normative Agendas of Global Benchmarking," *Review of International Studies* 41(5): 813–818.

Brothers C. (1996) *War and Photography: A Cultural History*. Abingdon: Routledge.

Conley T. (2004) "Globalisation and the Politics of Persuasion and Coercion," *Australian Journal of Social Issues* 39(2): 183–200.

Cook D. (2007) *Martyrdom in Islam*. Cambridge: Cambridge University Press.

Cook D. (2008) "Myth in The Service of Jihad," in Perry M., Negrin H. (eds.), *The Theory and Practice of Islamic Terrorism. An Anthology*. New York: Palgrave, pp. 33–35.

Cunningham S. (2002) *The Idea of Propaganda: A Reconstruction*. Westport: Praeger.

De la Paz A. (2017) "Jihad, Miracles, Propaganda," Paper presented at *ISA Annual Convention*, Baltimore, February 2017.

Desrosieres A. (2002) *The Politics of Large Numbers. A History of Statistical Reasoning*. Harvard: Harvard University Press.

Domke D., Perlmutter D., Spratt M. (2002) "The Primes of our Times? An Examination of the 'Power' of Visual Images," *Journalism* 3(2): 131–159.

Doumato E. A. (2003) "Manning the Barricades: Islam According to Saudi Arabia's School Texts," *Middle East Journal* 57(2): 230–247.

Edgar I., de Looijer G (2017) "The Islamic Dream Tradition and Jihad Militancy," in Hegghammer T. (ed.), *Jihadi Culture: The Art and Social Practices of Militant Islamists*. Cambridge: Cambridge University Press, pp. 128–150.

Ellul J. (1973) *Propaganda. The Formation of Men's Attitudes*. New York: Random House.

Fahmy S., Neumann R. (2012) "Shooting War Or Peace Photographs? An Examination of Newswires' Coverage of the Conflict in Gaza (2008–2009)," *American Behavioral Scientist* 56(2): NP1–NP26.

Galtung J. (1986) "On the Role of the Media in Worldwide Security and Peace," in Varis T. (ed.), *Peace and Communication*. San Jose: ULP Press, pp. 249–266.

Gerrard C. (1994) *The Patriot Opposition to Walpole: Politics, Poetry, and National Myth, 1725–1742*. Oxford: Oxford University Press.

Gråtrud H. (2016) "Islamic State Nasheeds As Messaging Tools," *Studies in Conflict & Terrorism* 39(12): 1050–1070.

Griffin M., Lee J. (1995) "Picturing the Gulf War: Constructing an Image of War in Time, Newsweek, and U.S. News & World Report," *Journalism & Mass Communication Quarterly* 72 (4): 813–825.

Hacking I. (1990) *The Taming of Chance*. Cambridge: Cambridge University Press.

Hafez M. (2007) "Martyrdom Mythology in Iraq: How Jihadists Frame Suicide Terrorism in Videos and Biographies," *Terrorism & Political Violence* 19(1): 95–115.

Halperin E. (2008) "Group-Based Hatred in Intractable Conflict in Israel," *Journal of Conflict Resolution* 52(5): 713–736.

Halperin E. (2015) *Emotions in Conflict*. London: Routledge.

Halverson J. (2007) "Martyrdom in Islam—By David Cook," *Reviews in Religion & Theology* 14(4): 542–545.

Hansen L. (2011) "Theorizing the Image for Security Studies: Visual Securitization and the Muhammad Cartoon Crisis," *European Journal of International Relations* 17(1): 51–74.

Hansen L. (2015) "How Images Make World Politics: International Icons and the Case of Abu Ghraib," *Review of International Studies* 41: 263–288.

Hegghammer T. (2017) *Jihadi Culture: The Art and Social Practices of Militant Islamists*. Cambridge: Cambridge University Press.

Horten G. (2002) *Radio Goes to War: The Cultural Politics of Propaganda During World War II*. Los Angeles: University of California Press.

Johnson A., Johnson R. (1991) *Propaganda and Aesthetics: The Literary Politics of African-American Magazines in the Twentieth Century*. Amherst: University of Massachusetts Press.

Johnson B., Cloonan M. (2008) *Dark Side of the Tune: Popular Music and Violence*. London: Routledge.

Johnson T., Waheed A. (2011) "Analyzing Taliban *Taranas* (Chants): An Effective Afghan Propaganda Artifact," *Small Wars & Insurgencies* 22(1): 3–31.

Juslin P. & Sloboda J., eds. (2001) *Music and Emotion: Theory and Research*. Oxford: Oxford University Press.

Juslin P., Vastfjall D. (2008) "Emotional Responses to Music: The Need to Consider Underlying Mechanisms," *Behavioral & Brain Sciences* 31(5): 559–621.

Kahan D., et al. (2012) "The Polarizing Impact of Science Literacy and Numeracy on Perceived Climate Change Risks," *Nature Climate Change* 2: 732–735.

Kahan D., et al. (2013) "Motivated Numeracy and Enlightened Self-Government," *Yale Public Law Working Paper* 307.

Kallis, A. (2005) *Nazi Propaganda and the Second World War*. London: Palgrave MacMillan.

Kendall E. (2016) "Jihadist Propaganda and its Exploitation of the Arab Poetic Tradition," in Kendall E., Khan A. (eds.), *Reclaiming Islamic Tradition. Modern Interpretations of the Classical Heritage*. Edinburgh: Edinburgh University Press, pp. 223–246.

Khatib L., Matar D., Alshaer A. (2014) *The Hizbullah Phenomenon: Politics and Communication*. London: Hurst.

Koelsch S. (2005) "Investigating Emotion with Music. Neuroscientific Approaches," *Annals of the New York Academy of Sciences* 1060: 412–418.

Kovacs A. (2015) "The 'New Jihadists' and the Visual Turn from Al-Qa'ida to ISIL/ISIS?Da'ish," *Biztpol Affairs* 2(3): 47–70.

Massad J. (2005) "Liberating Songs: Palestine Put to Music," in Swedenburg T., Stein R. (eds.), *Palestine, Israel, and the Politics of Popular Culture*. Durham NC: Duke University Press.

Milton D. (2016) "Communication Breakdown: Unraveling the Islamic State's Media Efforts," *Combating Terrorism Center at West Point*, October 2016. https://ctc.usma.edu/communication-breakdown-unraveling-the-islamic-states-media-efforts/.

Molle F., Mollinga P. (2003) "Water Poverty Indicators: Conceptual Problems and Policy Issues." *Water Policy* 5: 529–544.

NBC (2016, October 3) "ISIS' Al-Bayan Radio Station in Mosul Is Bombed Into Silence by IraqiJets." Retrieved from http://www.nbcnews.com/storyline/isis-terror/isis-al-bayan-radio-station-mosul-bombed-silence-iraqi-jets-n658521.

Norbrook D. (1999) *Writing the English Republic: Poetry, Rhetoric and Politics, 1627-1660*. Cambridge: Cambridge University Press.

O'Neill S., Boykoff M., Niemeyer S., Day S. (2013) "On the Use of Imagery for Climate Change Engagement," *Global Environmental Change* 23: 413–421.

Pelevin M., Weinreich M. (2012) "The Songs of the Taliban: Continuity of Form and Thought in an Ever-Changing Environment," *Iran and the Caucasus* 16: 45–70.

Powell A., ed. (1992) *Roman Poetry and Propaganda in the Age of Augustus*. Bristol: Bristol Classical Press.

Ramsay G. (2013) *Jihadi Culture on the World Wide Web*. New York: Bloomsbury Publishing.

Said B. (2012) "Hymns (Nasheeds): A Contribution to the Study of the Jihadist Culture," *Studies in Conflict & Terrorism* 35(12): 863–879.

Schatz B. (2015, February 9) "Inside the World of ISIS Propaganda Music," *Mother Jones*. Retrieved from http://www.motherjones.com/politics/2015/02/isis-islamic-state-baghdadi-music-jihad-nasheeds.

Shiloah A. (1995) *Music in the World of Islam: A Socio-Cultural Study*. Detroit, MI: Wayne State University.

Shiloah A. (1997) "Music and Religion in Islam," *Acta Musicologica* 69(2): 143–155.

Site Intelligence Group (2016) "IS Launches Website to Stream al-Bayan Radio Broadcasts." Retrieved from https://news.siteintelgroup.com/Jihadist-News/is-launches-website-to-stream-al-bayan-radio-broadcasts.html (paid access required).

Stenersen A. (2011) "Al Qaeda's Foot Soldiers: A Study of the Biographies of Foreign Fighters Killed in Afghanistan and Pakistan Between 2002 and 2006," *Studies in Conflict & Terrorism* 34(3): 171–198.

Washington Post (2015, June 4) "Islamic State has an English-Language Radio Broadcast that Sounds Eerily like NPR." Retrieved from https://www.washingtonpost.com/news/worldviews/wp/2015/06/04/islamic-state-has-a-dailyenglish-language-radio-broadcast-that-sounds-eerilylike-it-could-be-on-npr/?utm_term=.a9d8c336a5ab.

Winkler C. (2016) "Visual Images: Distinguishing Daesh's Internal and External Communication Strategies," in *Countering Daesh Propaganda: Action-Oriented Research for Practical Policy Outcomes*. Atlanta: Carter Center, pp.15–19. https://

www.cartercenter.org/resources/pdfs/peace/conflict_resolution/countering-isis/counteringdaeshpropaganda-feb2016.pdf.

Winkler C., et al. (2017) "A Multimodal Approach to Analyzing Online Messaging of Extremist Groups," Paper presented at *ISA Annual Convention*, Baltimore, February 2017.

Winter C. (2015) "Documenting the 'Virtual Caliphate'," *Quilliam Reports*, http://www.quilliaminternational.com/wp-content/uploads/2015/10/FINAL-documenting-the-virtual-caliphate.pdf.

Winter C. (2017) *War by Suicide: A Statistical Analysis of the Islamic State's Martyrdom Industry*. The Hague: International Centre for Counter Terrorism.

Yalch R., Elmore-Yalch R. 1984. "The Effect of Numbers on the Route to Persuasion." *Journal of Consumer Research* 11(1): 522–527

Yanagizawa-Drott D. (2014) "Propaganda and Conflict: Evidence from the Rwandan Genocide," *Quarterly Journal of Economics* 129(4): 1947–1994.

Zelin A. (2015) "Picture or It Didn't Happen: A Snapshot of the Islamic State's Official Media Output," *Perspectives on Terrorism* 9(4): 85–97.

7

Countering Islamic State's Propaganda

Challenges and Opportunities

Tobias Borck and Jonathan Githens-Mazer

Introduction

The Islamic State (IS) represents the latest iteration of evolving international terrorism. Since taking over and holding large swaths of territory in Iraq and Syria in from 2014 to 2017, it straddled the line between being a terrorist organization with global reach and seeking to create a proto-state-like entity that offers local governance by attracting sympathetic immigrants from all over the world. In the areas of information operation and propaganda activities, IS has also broken new paths. Terrorist organizations always seek media exposure by using propaganda to further their aims—in line with the old adage of terrorism as "propaganda of the deed." However, as the other chapters in this volume demonstrate, IS has reached new levels, including in the sheer volume, sophistication, and variety of its propaganda activities. IS has benefited from the ready availability of easy-to-use digital tools combined with the tech savviness of many of its members, but it is also clear that IS has put more emphasis on propaganda and information operations than many jihadist and non-jihadist terrorist groups in the past. This is underscored in some of the IS materials that hail the media/online *jihād* as equal to the armed struggle on the battlefield (read, e.g., Winter 2017).

As Stephane Baele outlines and Haroro Ingram details in, respectively, the Introduction and Chapter 1 of this volume, IS propaganda can be described as a "full-spectrum" approach to activity in the information environment. At its peak, when IS controlled significant territory, the group's propaganda operations were remarkably comprehensive, cohesive, and multidimensional. Propaganda material was disseminated in as many formats (audio, video, photo, text, etc.) and via as many different channels (in public, online, and in print) as possible; it was well-coordinated and tied into IS's overarching

Tobias Borck and Jonathan Githens-Mazer, *Countering Islamic State's Propaganda: Challenges and Opportunities* In: *ISIS Propaganda*. Edited by: Stephane J. Baele, Katharine A. Boyd, and Travis G. Coan, Oxford University Press (2020) © University of Maryland National Consortium for the Study of Terrorism and Responses to Terrorism (START)
DOI: 10.1093/oso/9780190932459.003.0008

branding and narrative; and it was tailored to different audiences (from local to global) and deployed in support of both short-term tactical and long-term strategic objectives. As IS has lost most of its territory, and therefore also much of the manpower, physical space, and equipment for its propaganda production, it also had to concede reductions to its propaganda capabilities. However, the ambition to retain an active posture in the information environment and act in as comprehensive, cohesive, and multidimensional manner as possible is still clearly visible.

Since information operations and propaganda activities play such an important part in IS's strategy, the international effort to counter the group has had to—and must continue to—go beyond military operations and political initiatives and include countering IS in the information environment. This chapter engages with this challenge. It combines a scholarly approach with the view of practitioners, drawing on the professional experience of the authors in this area and bringing together insights from the wider field of strategic communications and information operations. The chapter is divided into two main parts: the first discusses the challenges and opportunities associated with efforts to deny IS access to the information environment, especially online, by shutting down accounts and deleting content. The second section of the chapter addresses the possibilities and pitfalls of various approaches to directly engage and compete with IS propaganda in the information environment, including through the propagation of counter- and alternative narratives. The chapter closes with a look ahead and outlines some of the opportunities and challenges in countering IS propaganda that are beginning to emerge as the group has lost its territorial control.

Much of the discussion in this chapter may be relevant for engaging with jihadi propaganda activities in general. However, it is important to note that, in line with the other chapters in this volume, the analysis here is explicitly focused on IS and its specific full-spectrum approach to operations in the information environment.

Denying the Safe Space: Shutting IS Down Online

It has become a familiar ritual: after an IS-linked terror attack in Europe or the United States, law enforcement officials, journalists, and security analysts turn to the Internet to search for the IS statement claiming credit for the attack, a digital trail linking the culprits to IS members or sympathizers around the world, or any sign of how they may have been interacting with IS propaganda materials. Statements by politicians calling for more measures to restrict and counter IS activity online have become equally common. On the morning after three men killed eight people on London Bridge and in London's Borough Market, British Prime Minister Theresa May (2017) declared: "We cannot allow this ideology the safe space it needs to breed. Yet that is precisely what the Internet—and the big companies that provide Internet-based services—provide." She vowed to work with other governments to find ways to better regulate cyberspace to curb extremism and disrupt the planning of attacks. Statements such as this provide further impetus to the evolving debate of what governments—in coordination with Internet companies or through the introduction of legally binding regulations—can and should try to deny terrorist organizations such as IS the chance to exploit the Internet to their benefit. The United Kingdom has taken various steps in that direction; earlier this year for instance, the Home Office acknowledged its reception, from the artificial intelligence (AI) company ASI DataScience, of a tool to detect jihadist content online and block it, and its intention to encourage Internet companies to use it.[1]

There can be little doubt that technology and the Internet have played an important role in IS's rise and the group's capability to present itself as a globally relevant and powerful entity. Many, if not all, of the elements of IS propaganda discussed in this volume are in some way or another enabled by and disseminated through Internet-based technologies and services. This media exposure provides the life blood for IS. Affecting people not directly caught up in an attack by literally terrorizing them with the news or threat of violence, or demonstrating their viability and capability to potential recruits, wider supporters, and those with whom their message may resonate, can only work through the transmission of information. This transmission can take many forms, be it by word of mouth, a poster, a newspaper, a television news segment, or a Tweet. The technological changes brought about in the Information Age have made this easier. A smartphone with Internet connection allows terrorists to communicate directly with millions of people, instantaneously and in real time (Burke 2016). While IS is not the first terrorist group making use of the Internet, its online activities have broken new ground in terms of quality and quantity. It has embraced the openness of the Internet to develop its comprehensive, cohesive, and multidimensional,

---

[1] See http://www.bbc.co.uk/news/technology-43037899.

full-spectrum approach to propaganda. Furthermore, whereas its jihadi predecessors mainly used password-protected forums, IS has also actively exploited the most public platforms, sacrificing secrecy for maximum publicity. A 2015 Brookings study (Berger & Morgan 2015) into IS's use of Twitter identified at least 46,000 accounts linked to the group and dedicated to spreading its propaganda. In May 2017, Europol reported that, during a recent 48-hour crackdown on IS and al-Qaeda online activity, its investigators had identified more than 2,000 items of extremist material spread over 52 different social media platforms (Holden 2017).

The Problems with Shutting Down the Safe Space

Confronted with this issue, one of the most common demands raised by politicians and the mainstream media alike is that IS members and sympathizers should simply be denied the ability or right to use social media or even the entire Internet for their pernicious activities. However, this is simply impractical given the open and innovation-driven nature of the Internet and the wider demand among the global population for free, fair, and unfettered access to Internet. It is in light of this last aspect that such demands come up against the old debate of to what degree (at least democratic) governments should infringe upon their citizens' rights to privacy and freedom of expression in the quest of keeping them safe, a debate that echoes much of the wider debates over the cost of freedoms in light of the pursuit of security.

In practical terms, efforts aimed at denying IS the ability to use social media platforms to spread its propaganda are likely destined to follow the "Whack-a-Mole" principle: security services and Internet companies—be it voluntarily or under pressure from government legislation—would have to constantly monitor an increasing number of platforms to detect and delete accounts and content, only for the same material to immediately appear elsewhere. The cited Europol operation even found evidence that IS members have built their very own social media platforms and mobile phone applications (Holden 2017). This does not mean that this work is ineffective. On the contrary: the world's most popular Internet companies, led by Google (which owns YouTube), Facebook, and Twitter, have been keen to present themselves as taking proactive measures to stop IS members and sympathizers from exploiting their services. Google, or rather its parent company Alphabet, has created the subsidiary Jigsaw, which is dedicated to use technology to counter extremism online (Jigsaw 2017). Facebook has made very public announcements about how it is developing and using AI capabilities to detect and delete extremist content and is hiring an increasing number of specialists to counter extremism on its site where computer programs are not yet sophisticated enough (Bickert & Fishman 2017). Twitter (2016), according to its own Transparency Report, has shut down 636,248 accounts for promoting terrorism between August 1, 2015 and December 31, 2016.

J. M. Berger (2017), one of the authors of the cited study into IS Twitter usage, argues that, at least when it comes to the micro-blogging site, "there is not much more that can be done." He has found that as of March 2017, the average IS-supporting Twitter account only survives for about 24 hours before being shut down and has just 14 followers—a far cry to his 2015 findings, when accounts had an average of 1,000 followers. He therefore argues that IS activity on Twitter and Facebook have hit a point of diminishing returns for the organization. While it is possible for these companies to do even more, the majority of IS online activity has been forced to move to other, less popular, and less open social media services. This should be seen as a significant success. After all, denying IS the ability to use Twitter and Facebook to spread its propaganda means to deprive the group of the easiest method to reach the largest possible audience. Other services simply do not have the same number of users, nor do they offer the same convenient mass broadcast mechanisms. However, they may also be less willing to cooperate with governments to take action against extremists.

The Freedom of Speech Dilemma

As IS has hit a point of diminishing returns in terms of the use of platforms like Facebook and Twitter, it has turned increasingly to Telegram, which it now uses to inform its followers and spread its propaganda. Telegram offers open channels suitable for quickly disseminating material to a large number of subscribers, but these channels are also increasingly being shut down by the provider. Most IS activity on Telegram is therefore likely taking place in closed groups or peer-to-peer chats secured by end-to-end encryption. While it can therefore be argued that IS is gradually forced back into the niche forums used by its jihadi predecessors, this does pose a very different challenge to governments than simply encouraging, or legislating for, social media companies to remove openly available content or close down obvious extremism-supporting accounts. Even in the latter case, dedicated freedom of speech advocates could make a credible case that, apart perhaps from the most clear-cut cases (e.g., the spread of execution videos and speeches by known IS leaders), rights of Internet users may be at risk—to paraphrase an old cliché, one man's hate speech could very well be seen as another man's free speech.

Across Europe, governments are grappling with the question of where to draw the line between free and hate speech, while the large Internet companies are busy developing their own AI-driven detect-and-delete mechanisms to police their platforms. In Germany, for example, the government pushed through a new hate speech law in July 2017, despite much public criticism, that forces Internet companies to respond faster to user complaints about hateful content and publish regular progress reports; at the time of writing, Facebook and other affected companies continue to challenge the law in German and European courts (Tagesschau 2017). Meanwhile, Facebook is struggling to refine its hate speech–detecting algorithms to pick up on the nuances of language and has to deal with embarrassing setbacks, such as revelations that its mechanisms were triggered by phrases like "white men," but not "black children" (Vlasits 2017). To further complicate matters, as IS propaganda production and dissemination is becoming less centralized, less obviously branded with the group's insignia, and much more localized to country-specific issues—a process that appears to be ongoing in parallel with the territorial losses IS has and is suffering in Syria, Iraq, and Libya—the designation of material may well become much more difficult. This may mean that IS propaganda is losing some of its characteristic comprehensiveness, cohesiveness, and multidimensionality, but the challenge remains. In any case, however, when it comes to closed group or peer-to-peer conversations, the issue of privacy and free speech becomes even more problematic.

Telegram, WhatsApp, Facebook (through its rapidly growing messenger application), and Apple understandably insist that their users' rights to privacy have to be protected and that neither they nor the government should have the right to have access to wholesale information about their users or to the content of their conversations. Governments have become increasingly bullish on this issue, especially in the immediate aftermath of terrorist attacks. After the 2015 IS attacks in Paris and Brussels, for example, a senior Belgian official proclaimed to *The New York Times* (Peltier & Schreuer 2015) that "when we're talking about terrorists, then privacy doesn't exist." However, for the moment, governments (at least democratic ones) appear not yet ready to fully test the resolve of these Internet companies—or those of their populations, for that matter. After all, many people use Telegram and WhatsApp precisely because of the data security they offer, even if they are not at all interested in spreading extremist propaganda.

Ultimately, a full discussion of the challenge that privacy and freedom of speech issues pose to the effort to counter IS propaganda activities would far exceed the scope of this chapter—and the expertise of its authors. It is likely to occupy democratic societies' concerns for years, if not decades to come. The same is likely true for the technological challenge of completely denying extremists the ability to use the Internet or at least to detect and remove their content as quickly as possible. However, before moving on to the opportunities and challenges governments are facing when they seek to actively counter and compete with IS propaganda in the information environment, it is worth briefly highlighting three other considerations that emerge from the impulse to want to entirely deny IS the ability to use the Internet—or any other medium—to spread its message.

The Media as Accidental Amplifier

There is a strong argument that IS's message is not just disseminated by the group's members and sympathizers, but is also at least echoed by the mainstream media's coverage of IS terror, especially in Western cities (Ingram 2016b). In a way, media outlets are therefore significantly contributing to IS's ability to reach the full spectrum of the information environment. Berger (2017) highlights that this can be seen as beginning at a very tactical level: "Would-be killers do not need to follow IS on Twitter in order to learn how to drive a car into a crowd of pedestrians. They can get that from the mainstream news, which faithfully amplifies both the propaganda and attacks of IS." The media's role is arguably even more obvious when it comes to magnifying the part of IS's message that is intended to spread terror and sow divisions in the societies the group targets. The coverage of IS-linked terror attacks tends to be extremely graphic and sensationalized and is accompanied by generalizing right-wing commentary about the threats posed by immigrant and especially Muslim communities. The end result is that IS is portrayed as an almost omnipresent and existential threat and that the social cohesion of targeted societies is further undermined. For IS propagandists, this is not just a welcome side effect of how the group operates, but a core part of their communication strategy. An official IS document about media operations, entitled *Media Operative*, explains that one of the goals of IS propaganda is to "infuriate the unbelievers" and provoke knee-jerk reactions (see Winter 2017).

The challenge of preventing IS's narratives and messages from being broadcast at all has to include a focus on how the group's activities are covered in the media and the wider public discourse. To a degree, this can be done through norms and self-regulation. For example, newspapers and television stations generally no longer print or broadcast stills from IS propaganda videos showing condemned hostages in orange jumpsuits just before their executions. However, beyond such voluntary measures, it is difficult to see how governments could do much more without again wading into the above-discussed controversial issue of freedom of expression. In a way, any encroachments on the freedom of the press would run the danger of mirroring the way in which IS itself is trying to regulate what kind of information the people living in the territory under its control are exposed to. In Syria and Iraq, and for some time in Libya, the group has expended huge efforts to restrict Internet access and ensure that the would-be citizens of its "Caliphate" are only exposed to the group's very own truth (Winter 2016).

Exploiting IS Propaganda for Intelligence and Evidence

The second consideration is that IS's very publicity-seeking and relatively open, even brazen, approach to its information and propaganda operations means that the group's members and sympathizers are leaving behind a very large digital footprint that can be studied and exploited by security services. To a certain degree, this includes the possibility of gaining immediately actionable, tactical intelligence—i.e., information that could be used to identify a specific person and their location and enable police or military operations against them. The availability of tools such as virtual private networks, encrypted servers, and anonymous browsing software, however, has made it easier for IS members and sympathizers to cover their tracks online (Alkhouri & Kassirer 2016). From a more strategic-level perspective, on the other hand, IS propaganda—its content, production quality, and the way it is disseminated—remain invaluable sources of information about the group's current position, its operational focus, and self-image, let alone how it is seeking to appeal for support among what it considers to be its target audiences. The version of itself that IS presents in its own propaganda cannot be taken at face value as an accurate picture of reality, nor can declarations about what the group intends to do next or how it stands toward other extremist groups be taken as set in stone. Instead, the self-image it projects has to be understood as part of its brand-building efforts—to not only claim its persistence and capability, but also to sell its call to action to participate in high-risk activities to those who are weighing up its benefits as a brand. All of this nevertheless provides valuable insights that can at the very least serve as parts of the puzzle that security services have to piece together to get an idea of IS's strength and future path.

IS propaganda efforts are supposed to attract new recruits and terrorize its enemies, but it also allows the latter to keep a finger on the group's pulse. For the past few years, for example, it has generally been easier for watchers of the Syrian conflict to monitor what IS was doing and to identify clues about what it might be doing next than it was to do the same with al-Qaeda's affiliate in the region, Jabhat al-Nusra (now known as Hay'at Tahrir Al-Sham). Similarly, it was possible to analyze IS propaganda outputs for insights about how the group is trying to appeal to its various target audiences—be they in Iraq and Syria, Libya, Yemen, Egypt, or in Europe—by highlighting different themes. Research by the authors indicates that substantial parts of the propaganda material that came out of IS's now lost stronghold in Libya's Sirte, for example, was clearly tailored for an audience across the border in Tunisia, where the group had much more success in recruiting new members than in Libya itself. Similarly, monitoring Libya-focused IS Telegram channels in the summer of 2017 suggests that the group has adopted a much more local focus with far fewer direct links to IS *wilāyāt* in the Levant, constantly highlighting the injustices and instability of Libya's ongoing political, economic, and security crisis. While such findings cannot by themselves drive an effective strategy against IS in Libya or elsewhere, they can at least provide valuable direction.

Narrowly focusing efforts to counter IS propaganda on trying to push IS off the Internet, or at least back into the secrecy of private forums protected by passwords and—more significantly—difficult to break encryption technology, may therefore ultimately be counterproductive. In his 2015 study, while clear advocating for more concerted efforts to reduce IS room for maneuver on Twitter, Berger (2015) also warned that "if every single ISIS supporter disappeared from Twitter tomorrow, it would represent a staggering loss of intelligence." By pushing IS communications further and further to the margins of the online and social media landscape—which is, as discussed earlier, unlikely to ever actually succeed in entirely pushing IS offline—the group's members and sympathizers are essentially forced into increasingly more concentrated and closed echo chambers in which their ideas no longer even have to compete with other worldviews and opinions. It may make it harder for IS to reach its intended audience, and it may make it more difficult for someone curious about the group to find and gain access to its propaganda material. But once people are in these echo chambers, it can also be much more difficult to escape.

A final consideration—and it is related to the previous paragraphs—is that IS propaganda and its members' and sympathizers' online activity can be seen as one source of evidence should any of them ever be brought to justice in front of a court of law. While this may, of course, be a long shot, it is nevertheless something that a number of nongovernmental organizations—often with governments' support—have started to do (Bowcott 2017).

Engagement and Competition: Taking on IS in the Information Environment

Countering IS propaganda by focusing primarily on trying to address its very presence in the information space, be it through technological means (i.e., automated detecting and removing content) and/or regulations and censorship of cyberspace, is both understandable in its motive but also likely to be impossible. This means that the ideas, messages, and narratives contained within IS propaganda cannot be countered by imposing some form of an information blackout on the group. Instead, part of the strategy to defeat IS—including its information operations—has to be to engage and compete with IS in the information space.

This is a challenge that is likely to far outlive the presence of IS as a physical, territory-holding entity. Just as IS is unlikely to disappear as a threat to the national security of countries around the world once the group has lost its territory in the Levant and elsewhere, IS's propaganda, and the ideas and narratives it seeks to promote, are unlikely to lose their resonance with an—albeit small—segment of societies in the Middle East, Europe, and beyond (for a detailed explanation, read Mehdi Laghmari's Chapter 2 in this volume). It is, of course, true that one of the distinguishing features of IS propaganda has been the group's ability to not just talk of a "Caliphate" but to actually describe and depict it in its magazines and videos. However, the jihadi narrative of an Islamic state that has to be established by all means necessary, even against the seemingly overwhelming might of the supposed enemies of Islam, has existed before Abu Bakr Al-Baghdadi declared his Caliphate, and it will almost certainly continue to exist once the "Caliphate" has fallen and the caliph is dead. In fact, the notion that an Islamic state has now existed for a few years, rather than remaining a mirage painted in the words of radical scholars, has the potential to give the jihadi narrative a new lease on life: the goal is real, but it was taken away by the enemy. In short, taking on IS in the information environment requires a long-term effort; it is, and will be, a difficult and complex task for years and decades to come.

The Need for Realistic Objectives

Much has been written about how Western—and more widely nonextremist—governments and societies are "losing the battle of ideas" against IS and other extremist groups (e.g., Cottee 2015). This is not the case. Despite IS's military and recruitment success on the battlefield and in the information space, the group and its full-spectrum propaganda have only ever been able to mobilize extremely small segments of societies around the world. This does not, of course, mean that IS is not a threat or that its propaganda is not something that needs to be countered, but it is important to retain a degree of perspective on the challenge at hand. At the same time, it is also clear that many of the efforts to directly engage with and counter IS propaganda—usually led by governments—have not appeared to be particularly successful. The following discussion addresses some of the challenges that have arguably led to these apparent failures and the impression that the battle of ideas is indeed being lost. More importantly, however, it offers a number of principles and elements that can lay the foundations for a much more successful strategic communications campaign against IS.

Any effort to counter IS propaganda through some form of organized activity in the information space has to begin with a realistic discussion of what objectives can be achieved. A common assertion used by politicians is that the goal has to be "defeating this [IS'] ideology" (May 2017). However, these ambitions are as unattainable as "defeating terrorism"—at the very least, success would be extremely difficult to define. In fact, ideologies are rarely—if ever—completely defeated. For example, the ideology of Nazism, which once threatened countries around the world and was promoted through a highly sophisticated propaganda machine, was arguably never defeated. Its greatest champion and political manifestation, the Third Reich, was of course destroyed in 1945, but the ideology survives to this day. It lives on in the extreme right-wing fringes of societies, both in Germany and in countries around the world, it is glorified in various kinds of propaganda material, and occasionally it even provides the motivation for violence. This does not mean that Nazism no longer poses a threat, but that it has been marginalized to the degree that this threat can generally be kept in check by the security services. At first sight, such as scenario may seem not enough when it comes to IS ideology, the propaganda that promotes it, and the extreme violence it fuels, but it may be the only one that is actually achievable.

Selecting and Understanding the Audience

In concrete terms, this means that a more realistic objective for countering IS propaganda in the information space is not to defeat the ideology, but rather to reduce its appeal among its target audiences. In practical terms, this means helping to increase the resilience of target audiences against the narratives and messages of IS. This includes both audiences that IS sees as potential recruits and is therefore trying to attract and audiences IS considers as its enemies and consequently wants to terrorize into overreactions or submission. This chapter focuses primarily on the former, but Western governments also have to think about what they can do in the information space to reduce the effect IS has on the parts of their societies that are not at risk of being radicalized to join or sympathize with the group. This should range from steps to prevent terrorist attacks from deepening divisions between Muslim and non-Muslim communities, to engaging in public debates about how media coverage of IS and other extremist groups can be more responsible (as discussed earlier, this should not include regulations impinging on freedom of speech, but rather be focused on the fostering of societal norms), to taking active measures to prevent anti-immigrant and Islamophobic radicalization and extremism on the political right.

With regards to the element of IS propaganda that seeks to impress, attract, and ultimately help recruit new members and sympathizers, efforts to counter IS in the information space in the first instance require a detailed, honest, and continuously updated understanding of IS propaganda, its contents and principles, how it is being disseminated and consumed, and the context in which it appeals to people from various different backgrounds. Much valuable work in this direction has been done already (e.g., El-Badawy et al. 2015), and the present volume offers a capital contribution to this effort. But as Haroro Ingram explains well in Chapter 1, IS propaganda is dynamic and evolves and changes as the group's fortunes rise and fall and as its operational focus shifts. For example, the themes and points of emphasis dominating IS propaganda in a year or two, once the group has lost the bulk of its territory in the Middle East, are likely to differ significantly from what they were before or after the declaration of the "Caliphate." Perhaps most importantly, IS propaganda has always been flexible and varied enough to talk to multiple different audiences—sometimes all at once and sometimes separately—with specifically tailored campaigns. If the goal is to reduce IS's appeal among its target audiences, it is therefore imperative to determine which of these audiences a communications campaign seeks to address and then develop an understanding of both how IS is trying to appeal to this specific audience and the context in which some members of these audiences may be vulnerable and open to IS message.

All other elements of a counter-IS strategic communications campaign have to flow from this understanding of the target audience. Campaigns focused on countering IS propaganda will vary by region, state, and locale; a campaign in the Levant will be different from one in Europe (and, naturally, a campaign in France would have to be different from a campaign in the United Kingdom or Germany). The importance of properly understanding and engaging with the ultimate target audiences inevitably shines through in the following sections, which address issues surrounding the "what" (the content), the "how" (the delivery mechanisms), and "who" (the messengers) of an effective communications campaign countering IS propaganda.

Finding the Right Content

One of the most common pitfalls in designing campaign(s) to counter IS in the information space is to get too caught up in trying to refute and disprove the theological arguments of the IS narrative. It is of course true that the vast majority of Muslims do not agree with IS's interpretation of Islam and hold very different views of what *jihād* is, what an Islamic state should look like, and what Islamic scriptures say about dealing with people of different religions. However, any such arguments run the danger of leading to no more than "we say–they say" scenarios in which views become more entrenched and divisions are hardened. One of the most basic tenets of radicalization is a belief in a "revealed" truth that inspires the individual to believe that this truth, once revealed, is a link between themselves and a fundamental revelation (Githens-Mazer 2012). Arguments that counter this revelation are likely only to be viewed through this prism of revelation—and therefore efforts that counter this revelation are automatically false: the purveyor of this counter-argument is wrong because they have either not been privy to this revelation or, even worse, have rejected it.

Furthermore, a theological approach risks being immediately undermined when it can be linked to a government, which IS can simply denounce as illegitimate and un-Islamic (this includes governments of non-Muslim countries and those in the Middle East that IS generally refers to as *taghūt*). Equally ineffective are campaigns that completely ignore IS and focus entirely on promoting the virtues of an alternative system—usually the existing status—for example, by extolling liberal democratic values. Such campaigns risk simply not reaching the target audience, or worse, appearing hypocritical, self-indulgent, and ignorant of reality. Several authors in the field have therefore argued that campaigns to counter IS should not focus on theological and identity issues, but rather at engaging with and dismantling the system of meaning IS creates in its own narratives (Berger 2017; Ingram 2016a).

Ingram (2016a) explains what this system looks like: IS portrays itself and its supporters as the in-group of righteous Muslims that stands in direct conflict with the out-group—that is, the rest of the world (generally described by IS as an alliance of unbelievers including Shi'a Muslims, the crusading West, the Zionists, and, ultimately, all Muslims who do not repent and join the in-group). IS further describes the global Muslim community as suffering from a deep crisis (an argument that is fed by the socioeconomic malaise of countries in the Middle East and every case of perceived or real religious discrimination in countries around the world), which is directly caused and exacerbated by the out-group. Finally, the in-group is presented as the only force that can end the crisis and provide the solution—a better future—by fighting and ultimately defeating the out-group; all of which is then couched in religious and prophetical language (see discussion in Chapter 3).

In this context, a communications campaign that focuses entirely on the identity of the in-group—by attacking its theology, or, for example, trying to ridicule IS through the use of satire or other means—is likely only to succeed in deepening the divide between the in- and out-group. Meanwhile, it entirely ignores the "real-world" context in which IS (as the in-group) is able to interpret and instrumentalize any form of crisis or injustice perceived and/ or experienced by Muslims around the world as the responsibility of the out-group, including those that are criticizing or making fun of IS.

IS communications work because they resonate with their target audience. If the objective is to either decrease this resonance or counter its effect, the first step must to be to engage with what is resonant in its message in terms of its system of meaning. This means that the idea that IS, as the in-group, offers a viable solution for worldly problems must be challenged by illustrating the basic fact that it is ultimately IS that is responsible for a scale of almost unimaginable human suffering and that legitimate (and representative) governments and societies are in fact the most capable of providing meaningful, resonant, effective, and inclusive solutions to real-world problems. Ingram (2016a) calls this a "linkage based approach" as it ultimately attacks the linkages within IS's system of meaning. This is a challenging task and further underscores the importance of understanding the target audience. The campaign has to build on an acceptance that some form of crisis is at least real enough to be perceived as such by a segment of society. This is a difficult concept, especially in authoritarian systems in which governments often struggle to acknowledge, much less tolerate, any form of popular dissent. It becomes even more difficult when it is unclear how the crisis can be solved— be it as a result of systemic factors, a chronic lack of economic opportunities, or an intractable conflict. While it may therefore be conceivable to think of messages and narratives that demonstrate how IS does not offer a viable alternative and only contributes to and deepens the crises experienced by the target audience, generating credible content that offers real solutions to these crises is much more difficult.

This difficulty hints at a crucial reality that has to be considered with any strategic communications campaign to counter IS propaganda (or to achieve any other objective, for that matter): it cannot stand alone, but instead it has to be integrated with all other efforts to defeat the group (see, e.g., Paul 2011). This includes military and law enforcement action against IS members but, importantly, also has to stretch to political reforms, settlement of conflicts, and measures to improve the economic and social conditions of the target audience. In this context, the role of the communications campaign is to explain and creatively bring to life how every single initiative contributes to alleviating the crisis and building a better future. Only if the communications campaign works in lockstep with concrete and tangible measures can it be credible and provide a coherent, overarching narrative that builds an alternative system of meaning. It is a fundamental part of developing an approach that can be similarly—and ideally more—as full-spectrum (comprehensive, cohesive, and multidimensional) as IS's own activities in the information environment.

This principle, in turn, can also contribute to decisions about how closely the content of a communications campaign has to be linked to the truth. Much has been written about how Russia, for example, excels in using lies and half-truths—the famous *dezinformatsiya*—to erode the trust of Western societies in their governments and political systems (e.g., Giles 2016). Using such methods inevitably involves ethical considerations, and accountable democratic governments face legal and ethical hurdles to sanction deception. However, even divorced from a discussion about ethics—after all, IS propaganda does not comply with any recognized ethical codes—the operational value of disinformation in efforts to counter jihadi propaganda is limited. It may work to discredit and undermine IS in the eyes of its target audience, perhaps sowing some doubt about the group's self-portrayals. But when it comes to promoting narratives of concrete alternatives and tangible improvements to the target audience's living conditions, lies will ultimately be exposed (when nothing materializes) and therefore risk to undermine the credibility of the entire campaign.

Media Types, Formats, and Credible Voices

Just as the content of a counter-IS campaign has to be tailored to the target audience, so, too, does the way in which it is delivered. This may appear obvious but is nevertheless worth highlighting because it is easy to default to employing formats and media outlets that the architects of a communications campaign are familiar with, rather than those used by the people IS is trying to appeal to. There is no use in trying to reach potential IS supporters and sympathizers on platforms that they do not use. It may seem like a big success to place a product with an internationally known TV station, for example, but unless the station is watched by the target audience it will not be effective. An important clue, in this context, has to be taken from how IS propaganda reaches a specific target audience. An effective countercampaign does not have to strictly mirror IS communications, but in many ways IS has provided those seeking to counter it with the "area of operation," and efforts to counter its messages should ensure that they are reaching the same audiences.

More complex is the question of who is best placed to function as the messengers. As alluded to earlier, governments or individuals and entities closely associated with them are often the least credible voices and can often not just render a message ineffective, but even discredit it entirely. This is particularly the case for foreign governments. For example, the now-defunct US Department of Defense (DoD)-branded Twitter accounts that disseminated often graphic imagery in an attempt to warn people of IS's brutality and highlight the group's hypocrisy are generally considered by practitioners, analysts, and journalists to have been at best ineffective and at worst counterproductive (Miller & Higham 2015). However, it is important to note that this assessment is not based on thorough empirical research as the measurement of effect methodologies for strategic communications of this kind are still very much evolving (see next section). The DoD Twitter attempt does not mean that governments have no role to play in a counter-IS strategic communications campaign. On the contrary: when it comes to tangible measures to resolve some of the grievances of the target audience, to close the say–do gap, government action and statements are essential in confirming that a specific reform or initiative is actually going to be implemented.

In general, however, counter-IS campaigns are best delivered by voices from their potential audience who have made their own choice not to follow IS. This is not about coordination of messaging—not simply sloganeering—but ultimately about community-level action and coordination to encourage resilience to and resistance against an IS narrative. Such voices can form a diverse network of individuals and entities whose messages reinforce each other and ultimately contribute to the overarching narrative that engages with, dismantles, and reconstitutes the previously described system of meaning that IS propaganda seeks to perpetuate. This local, culturally credible, and resonant category of voices can then create and disseminate messages and narratives that shape a resonant and responsive public debate for an audience who perceives themselves to be confronted with a choice between IS and its alternatives. Such networks represent communities seeking to counter the IS message on their own terms, in ways that are resonant for their own peers and in their own contexts.

While local networks are extremely valuable, it its also important to note that, in many contexts, depending on the security situation in the specific country, this approach inevitably brings with it a security risk for all those involved, especially those who most directly speak out against IS and its practices. It therefore poses a challenge for governments and nongovernmental efforts that are supporting these kinds of local voices to devise methods and protocols to keep these (often extremely brave) individuals and entities safe without undermining their independence and therefore their credibility. Their collusion with foreign powers is indeed a prominent theme of IS propaganda, which is keen to discredit non-aligned Muslims as more or less complicit agents of the West.

Measuring Effect

Aside from the many challenges laid out in the preceding sections, arguably the most difficult issue facing any strategic communications campaign to counter IS propaganda, especially one financed by governments beholden to accountability toward taxpayers, is to provide evidence that it has effect. Measuring the effect of communications campaign is traditionally difficult, particularly when the objective does not become manifest in some kind of tangible output like the number of purchases of a specific product. There is a growing literature on this issue, but thus far no general consensus, much less a silver bullet, has emerged. The key challenge for a counter-IS communications campaign is that it is impossible to make a side-by-side comparison between a case in which the campaign is implemented and one in which it is not. There is no control group against which that effect could be measured, even if one were to focus all communications efforts only on specific countries because the context of the target audience is substantially different from case to case.

The effect of a communications campaign therefore has to be assessed over the duration of its implementation, with the implicit understanding that it takes place in a complex strategic environment in which it is often impossible to establish direct, linear causality between the systems' internal and external variables. This means that it is ultimately unknowable exactly if and how a campaign interacts with the multitude of dependent and independent other factors that ultimately affect the attitudes and behaviors of the target audience.

To surmount this complexity to a degree where at least a general assessment of the campaign's effectiveness is possible, measurement of effect methodologies therefore have to be multidimensional and combine elements such as systematic and periodic assessments of the strategic environment against a previously established baseline and a set of hypothesis of what change could look like and include qualitative and quantitative measurements of how the campaign's content is received by the target audience (through the collection of online data, for example, or the organization of focus groups). Especially when it comes to the latter, the involvement of a truly local network of activists who are themselves part and parcel of the target audience is an invaluable asset as it can provide a first set of feedback of whether the campaign has a chance to resonate or whether it misses the point.

Conclusion

Propaganda is an integral part of IS's strategy, putting the group firmly in line with the Zeitgeist of the 21st century, in which the information environment is becoming an increasingly more important and complex part of politics and conflict around the world. The dynamics of this environment and how it can be influenced, manipulated, and instrumentalized are central to many other major issues of the day, from Russia's efforts to destabilize political systems and societies in Europe and North America, to election campaigns that led to Brexit and the election of US President Donald Trump. Achieving a strategic advantage in the information environment can be just as impactful as those in more traditional political, economic, or military spheres.

The ongoing international effort to defeat IS—and comparable groups both within and beyond Salafi-jihadism—therefore has to include a strategy to counter it not just militarily (kinetic) and politically (discourse, statements, and proclamations), but also seek to work in the information space in which the group seeks to spread its terror and appeal to new members and sympathizers. Governments around the world have at least partially acknowledged this necessity, but while there are many opportunities to take effective action against IS propaganda, there are also many challenges. There is a temptation to see IS propaganda as something that can simply be censored and pushed into obscurity through technology and regulations. However, in an information environment that is increasingly dominated by the Internet, which is by

nature borderless and both driven by and constantly driving forward innovation, the notion that it is possible to deny IS all room for maneuver online
is fanciful. Moreover, the levels of regulation and censorship that would be
necessary to even come close to shutting down all IS online activity come up
against important questions around citizens' rights to privacy and freedom of
speech—both integral parts of what needs to be defended against IS and other
extremists. Limiting IS's ability to spread its propaganda and reach its target
audiences is undoubtedly important, but single-minded efforts to simply detect and delete IS propaganda also potentially remove an important source of
intelligence and evidence that can provide valuable insights about the group's
evolving situation, attitudes, operation focus, and methods.

Countering IS propaganda by engaging and competing with the group
in the information space is therefore just as important as continued efforts
to limit the group's ability to reach a mass audience. IS's own full-spectrum
approach to its propaganda activities—one that seeks to reach high levels of comprehensiveness, cohesiveness, and multidimensionality—sets
the bar for such efforts. But the design and delivery of effective counter-IS
strategic communications campaigns come with another set of challenges.
This begins with the goals such campaigns are supposed to achieve. The notion that it is IS's ideology that has to be defeated, including by attacking the
group's identity and theological legitimacy, is misguided. Ideologies can be
marginalized but are rarely completely defeated. Furthermore, efforts to attack IS's identity are likely to only lead to the further hardening of already entrenched views and the deepening of the very divisions IS needs to construct
its system of meaning in which it is defending the crisis-befallen community
of Islam from an evil enemy. The objective of a counter-IS campaign therefore has to be to reduce the appeal of IS's narrative by dismantling this system
of meaning in the eyes of the same audiences that IS is trying to appeal to and
by presenting compelling and credible alternative non-IS pathways for target
audiences to express discontent and disaffection. This, in turn, can only work
if these audiences are identified, understood, and taken seriously, and if the
communication campaigns are part of tangible measures to address their
concerns. While governments have to play their role in this, most of the work
to convince the audience that IS does not hold the answers and that change
can be achieved by different means than jihadist violence is best carried out
by a network of independent, credible, local voices. Finally, strategic communications campaigns to counter IS propaganda require a certain leap of

faith because methodologies to measure their actual effectiveness remain very much a work in progress.

Ultimately, however, the most important principle of countering IS propaganda—whether it is in efforts to deny the group space to operate online or in strategic communications campaigns engaging with and competing with IS in the information environment—is the need for continuous flexibility and adaptability. IS propaganda and information operations are not static, but dynamic and permanently changing. The understanding of IS propaganda therefore has to evolve, too, and with it the means to counter it. As the group loses its territory and its "Caliphate" disappears as a physical entity, IS is already beginning to reframe elements of its narrative. At the heart of this is the shift from portraying itself as a revolutionary state-building project toward glorifying the Islamic state that once was and that was wrongfully taken away by the enemies of Islam, supported by the ignorant masses who have forgotten what it means to be true Muslims. At the same time, IS propaganda appears to be becoming less centralized and localized. For those seeking to counter IS and its propaganda, this inevitably brings new opportunities and challenges: a decentralized and localized propaganda network may be less able to put forward a coherent and consistent narrative, but it is also more difficult to trace and potentially more capable of attaching itself to local causes. And while a narrative that focuses on glorifying the past can be less tangible, it also does not have to explain away the less appealing parts of its "Caliphate."

References

Alkhouri L., Kassirer A. (2016, July 16) "Tech for Jihad: Dissecting Jihadists' Digital Toolbox." *Flashpoint.* Retrieved from https://www.flashpoint-intel.com/wp-content/uploads/2016/08/TechForJihad.pdf.

Berger J. (2017, June 6) "'Defeating IS Ideology' Sounds Good, But What Does It Really Mean?" *ICCT Publications.* Retrieved from https://icct.nl/publication/defeating-is-ideology-sounds-good-but-what-does-it-really-mean/.

Berger J., Morgan J. (2015) *The ISIS Twitter Census: Defining and Describing the Population of ISIS Supporters on Twitter.* Washington, DC: The Brookings Institution. Retrieved from https://www.brookings.edu/wp-content/uploads/2016/06/isis_twitter_census_berger_morgan.pdf.

Bickert M., Fishman B. (2017, June 15) "Hard Questions: How We Counter Terrorism." *Facebook Newsroom.* Retrieved from https://newsroom.fb.com/news/2017/06/how-we-counter-terrorism/.

Bowcott O. (2017, March 30) "Amal Clooney Calls for Collection of Evidence of ISIS Atrocities." *The Guardian*. Retrieved from https://www.theguardian.com/world/2017/mar/29/amal-clooney-calls-for-collection-of-evidence-of-isis-atrocities.

Burke J. (2016) "The Age of Selfie Jihad: How Evolving Media Technology is Changing Terrorism." *CTC Sentinel* 9(11). Retrieved from http://www.css.ethz.ch/en/services/digital-library/articles/article.html/a7b2a4ee-4217-4cf7-8617-8600d8740487/pdf.

Cottee S. (2015, November 18) "Yes, ISIS Is Winning the 'War of Ideas.'" *The Atlantic*. Retrieved from https://www.theatlantic.com/international/archive/2015/11/isis-war-of-ideas/416553/.

El-Badawy E., Comerford M., Welby P. (2015) Inside the Jihadi Mind. London: Centre for Religion and Geopolitics. Retrieved from http://tonyblairfaithfoundation.org/sites/default/files/Inside%20the%20Jihadi%20Mind.pdf.

Giles K. (2016) *Russia's 'New' Tools for Confronting the West: Continuity and Innovation in Moscow's Exercise of Power*. Research Paper. London: Chatham House.

Holden M. (2017, May 3) "Islamic State Militants Developing Own Social Media Platform: Europol." *Reuters*. Retrieved from http://www.reuters.com/article/us-security-islamic-state-socialmedia-idUSKBN17Z1KS.

Ingram H. (2016a) "A 'Linkage-Based' Approach to Combating Militant Islamist Propaganda: A Two-Tiered Framework for Practitioners." ICCT Policy Brief, November. Retrieved from https://icct.nl/wp-content/uploads/2016/11/ICCT-Ingram-A-Linkage-Based-Approach-Nov2016.pdf.

Ingram H. (2016b) "Media as Amplifier or Disrupter of Violent Extremist Propaganda." Presentation at L'École Nationale de la Magistrature, Paris, 16 June. Retrieved from https://icct.nl/update/media-as-amplifier-or-disrupter-of-violent-extremist-propaganda-a-presentation-by-dr-haroro-ingram/.

Jigsaw (2017) "Vision: How Can Technology Make People in the World Safer?" Retrieved from https://jigsaw.google.com/vision/.

May T. (2017) "PM Statement Following London Terror Attack: 4 June 2017." Retrieved from https://www.gov.uk/government/speeches/pm-statement-following-london-terror-attack-4-june-2017.

Miller G., Higham S. (2015, May 8) "In a Propaganda War Against ISIS, the US Tried to Play by the Enemy's Rules." *The Washington Post*. Retrieved from https://www.washingtonpost.com/world/national-security/in-a-propaganda-war-us-tried-to-play-by-the-enemys-rules/2015/05/08/6eb6b732-e52f-11e4-81ea-0649268f729e_story.html?utm_term=.6eea14ca197b.

Paul C. (2011) *Strategic Communication: Origins, Concepts, and Current Debates*. Santa Barbara, CA: Praeger.

Peltier E., Schreuer M. (2015, November 19) "Leaders of France and Belgium Seek Tougher Security Measures." *The New York Times*. Retrieved from https://www.nytimes.com/2015/11/20/world/europe/france-belgium-national-security.html.

Tagesschau (2017, June 30) "Bundestag beschließt 'Facebook-Gesetz.'" Retrieved from https://www.tagesschau.de/inland/gesetz-gegen-hasskommentare-beschlossen-101.html.

Twitter (2016) "Government TOS Reports, July to December 2016." Retrieved from https://transparency.twitter.com/en/gov-tos-reports.html.

Vlasits A. (2017, July 1) "By Facebook's Logic, Who Is Protected from Hate Speech." *Wired*. Retrieved from https://www.wired.com/story/facebook-hate-speech-moderation/.

Winter C. (2016, March 27) "Totalitarianism 101: The Islamic State's Offline Propaganda Strategy." *Lawfare*. Retrieved from https://www.lawfareblog.com/totalitarianism-101-islamic-states-offline-propaganda-strategy.

Winter C. (2017) *Media Jihad: The Islamic State's Doctrine for Information Warfare*. London: International Centre for the Study of Radicalisation and Political Violence, Kings College London. Retrieved from http://icsr.info/wp-content/uploads/2017/02/Media-jihad_web.pdf.

8

Terrorist Propaganda After
the Islamic State

Learning, Emulation, and Imitation

Paul Gill, Kurt Braddock, Sanaz Zolghadriha, Bettina Rottweiler,
and Lily D. Cushenbery

Introduction

In the past, communication by terrorist groups to outsiders was largely limited to static propaganda produced by the groups and passively consumed by targeted audiences. However, the onset and global diffusion of Internet technology since the late 1990s and early 2000s has fundamentally changed how terrorist groups engage with audiences of all types. When the Internet first became widely available to the public as a communications tool, terrorist groups primarily used it to reach new audiences to which they previously lacked access. In these early days, much of what terrorist groups electronically distributed was simply a computer-mediated form of their previous propaganda—only to a larger, more geographically diverse audience. Some communicative affordances of the Internet, however, allowed terrorist groups to connect audiences in ways that had previously been impossible. For instance, often called "the first hate site on the Internet," Stormfront consisted of a series of discussion forums on which members of the site could discuss issues related to white nationalism, organize in-person meetings, share stories, and engage in a host of other activities. In a sense, Stormfront represented the first online social network specifically designed to allow those associated with an extremist ideology to connect and communicate.

Since Stormfront's genesis in 1996, Internet technology has matured and expanded. As a result, the communicative capabilities provided by the Internet have also grown more advanced. Indeed, the various chapters in

Paul Gill, Kurt Braddock, Sanaz Zolghadriha, Bettina Rottweiler, and Lily D. Cushenbery, *Terrorist Propaganda After the Islamic State: Learning, Emulation, and Imitation* In: *ISIS Propaganda*. Edited by: Stephane J. Baele, Katharine A. Boyd, and Travis G. Coan, Oxford University Press (2020) © University of Maryland National Consortium for the Study of Terrorism and Responses to Terrorism (START) DOI: 10.1093/oso/9780190932459.001.0001 this book make repeated assertions regarding the creativity and innovation embedded within Islamic State (IS) communications.

The emergence of IS as perhaps the world's most technologically adept terrorist organization (in terms of the propaganda it distributes) requires a consideration of how the new communicative techniques the group has employed may be replicated by future terrorist organizations. Moreover, the apparent effectiveness of IS propaganda suggests that the adoption of IS communicative innovations may increase the likelihood of other groups successfully filling their ranks. To understand the contagion of terrorist groups' communicative innovations, it is first necessary to consider how communicative techniques and styles diffuse more generally.

Imitation and innovation commonly occur within a terrorist organization's modus operandi. Tactical and technological innovations of one terrorist group often cross-pollinate into other groups with wildly different ideologies and from geographically diverse combat theaters. Such processes have been modeled extensively (both quantitatively and qualitatively) within the terrorism studies literature. Some refer to it as *contagion* (Moghadam 2008; Bloom 2005; Dugan, LaFree, & Piquero 2005; Midlarsky, Crenshaw, & Yoshida 1980), others as *diffusion* (Horowitz 2010; Braithwaite & Li 2007; Bonneuil & Auriat 2000), and still others (malevolent) *creativity* and *innovation* (Jackson et al. 2005; Dolnik 2007; Rasmussen & Hafez 2010; Gill et al. 2013. A similar strategy is often employed by flat-hierarchy organizations, where power distance is low, ideas are valued regardless of employee status, and sharing is encouraged (Jung, Wu, & Chow 2008). The aim of this chapter is to examine the potential imitation/emulation dynamics that extremist groups (both jihadist and other) might enter following the "success" of the propaganda produced by the IS.

There are several questions that guide the analyses that form the basis for this chapter. What factors spark imitation, creativity, and innovation within and across terrorist organizations? Are there particular traits that increase a terrorist organization's propensity for creativity and/or innovation? We make use of insight from communications, business management, and a range of psychology (social, cognitive, industrial/organizational, educational) literatures and apply this to understand (a) the degree to which IS propaganda itself is the result of imitation or innovation and (b) the potential emulation dynamics of other groups moving forward. Though it remains impossible to predict the onset of innovations within terrorist organizations, it is possible to analyze a group's capacity for creativity at a given moment in its life course.

Therefore, our focus centers on the process, behaviors, and organizational capabilities that precede the adoption of another terrorist group's innovation. This focus can offer greater insight for counterterrorism strategy focused on disrupting the abilities of terrorist organizations to communicate in a manner similar to IS. This chapter largely focuses on tactical innovation and imitation as opposed to strategic or organizational innovation more broadly. Tactical innovation and imitation encompass a terrorist organization's adoption of an entirely new method or mode of communication as well as a terrorist organization's capacity to copy and the forms of learning it engages in. Just as terrorist groups can innovate in terms of their violent operations, so, too, can they innovate in terms of their communicative activities (and, in turn, be copied by other actors). This chapter first explores what organizational psychology, business management, communications science, and terrorism studies have to say regarding creativity and innovation. We then reiterate the examples of IS emulation, creativity, and innovation depicted in the various contributions to this book before exploring their drivers and considering the likelihood of their being replicated elsewhere.

Insights into Creativity and Innovation

Insights from Communications Science

Albert Bandura's (1986, 2001) social cognitive theory (SCT) dictates that people learn behavior as a function of their involvement in social systems. Although SCT has primarily been used to describe learned behavior on the part of individuals, it also describes the process by which organizations come to adopt certain behaviors. Bandura (2001) argued that social practices are most effectively introduced to others through notable examples that illustrate the utility of those social practices for achieving organizational objectives. Organizations formalize this process through group socialization and on-boarding procedures (Bauer, Bodner, Erdogan, Truxillo, & Tucker 2007).

It follows that, as a fundamental social practice, communication behaviors are learned by organizations in the same manner as other kinds of behavior—by observing the environmental and organizational characteristics that led to their use by others. There exists some evidence to suggest that this learning process explains how individuals and organizations come to adopt different communication styles and techniques.

For instance, research on information technology has shown that users' adoption of specific communication technologies to convey information is dependent on their perceptions of the technology's ease of use and perceived usefulness (Davis, Bagozzi, & Warshaw 1992 Ilie, Van Slyke, Green, & Lou 2005), as well as on their perceptions of the technology's characteristics (Van Slyke, Lou, & Day 2002). Researchers have also shown that the intrinsic affordances of communication technologies diffuse much like the technologies themselves. For example, Chang (2010) showed that, on Twitter, hashtag adoption behavior spreads much like any other communication innovation.

In addition to communication technologies and their inherent features, there is some work that suggests that communication style also spreads in a manner consistent with theories that describe the diffusion of more tangible innovations. For example, with reference to the 2016 US Presidential election and growing discontent in the United Kingdom, Block and Negrine (2017) argued that numerous politicians (including US President Trump and UK Independence Party representative Nigel Farage) adopted populist communication styles to appeal to dissatisfied voters in both countries. In parallel, with the rise of Donald Trump to the US presidency, more politicians have adopted populist communicative styles, characterized by anti-establishment ideologies (Mudde & Rovira-Kaltwasser 2012), belligerent "plain talk" between politicians and their disenchanted constituents, and a contentious relationship with the media.

Much of the recent work on the diffusion of communication styles is found in analyses of extreme populist candidates, how they spread their ideologies, and how populism has become a learned communicative style (see Bracciale & Martella 2017; Krämer 2017; Waisbord & Amado 2017). This is appropriate for this chapter, given our focus on how the communication of another kind of extreme group, IS, may be learned and adopted by similar organizations.

Past analyses of the diffusion of communication technologies, tactics, and styles would suggest that IS's propaganda successes would lead other terrorist groups to adopt practices they had seen IS perform. SCT contends that IS's adept use of social media to disseminate its propaganda represents an exemplar of communicative behavior that can help show other groups how best to radicalize, recruit, and mobilize potential followers. Although there has been only limited work on the diffusion of communicative *style*, the successes enjoyed by IS in terms of the communicative *technologies* and *techniques* it employed gives every reason to believe that subsequent groups may at least attempt to adopt similar practices. However, the insights from organizational psychology suggest this adoption will be mediated by the degree to which their incremental innovations remain novel, relevant, elegant, and generalizable. As outlined earlier, there is a direct relationship between an innovation's novelty and its effectiveness. Therefore, as the novelty of IS communication strategies diminishes, social learning and emulation in relation to those strategies is likely to wane in parallel.

Insights from Terrorism Studies

To date, the focus of these studies has been the attacks themselves, not the communicative strategies that seek to justify, promote, and extol these attacks. That said, recent studies have emphasized a change in focus toward terrorist innovation. Previous analyses highlighted a lack of creativity and innovation within terrorist organizations. For example, Merari (1999) compared terrorism to conventional war and argued that terrorism "has not changed much in the course of a century, and virtually not at all during the last 25 years" (p. 54). Dolnik (2007) concurred with these assertions, claiming, "What we have witnessed is that this scope [of terrorist attacks] is relatively limited and remarkably unchanging. In fact when one surveys the last 50 years of terrorist operations case by case, very few incidents strike the observer as creative *in any way*" (p. 56).

Increasingly, however, there has been a growing acknowledgment that innovation regularly occurs and can be categorized in a number of ways. Crenshaw (2010) offered a typology of terrorist innovation, delineating three kinds. First, adopting new technologies to achieve unchanged objectives constitutes *tactical innovation*. Tactical innovation is not limited to attack types, but can also be extended to communicative approaches, delivery systems, the adoption of new technologies, initiation types, improvised explosive device (IED) types, and changing the profile of operatives. Second, adopting new objectives comprises *strategic innovation*. Third, changes at the organizational level in terms of structure or recruiting processes represent *organizational process innovation*.

A 2010 conference at the US Naval Postgraduate School brought together a number of terrorism experts to present on various case studies of terrorist innovation across a wide spectrum of actors and conflicts. Collectively, the analysts agreed on a number of issues. First, more resources (financial and human) can potentially lead to more prolific innovation. Second, leadership plays a central role in innovation, but conference participants failed to agree on which type of leadership facilitates innovation most. Third, innovation itself is often incremental and driven by the need to overcome security constraints.

A growing number of studies on the organizational dimension of terrorism have also begun to focus on the types of terrorist activity that are likely to be replicated and the organizational traits that make replication of another organization's tactics more likely. The majority of these studies follow in the manner of Midlarsky, Crenshaw, and Yoshida (1980) who quantitatively illustrate the contagion effect that occurred transnationally during the rise of terrorist violence between 1968 and 1974. They also examined the types of violence most likely to be replicated elsewhere. According to their analysis, bombings, kidnappings, and hijackings diffused much more readily across borders than did assassinations and raids.

More recently, suicide bombing experts such as Pape (2005), Bloom (2005), and Moghaddam (2008) utilized process-tracing techniques to emphasize the key role that success plays in a tactic's diffusion or contagion. Dugan, LaFree, and Piquero (2005) presented a time-series analysis of 1,101 attempted aerial hijackings to illustrate that hijacking rates significantly increase due to copy-cat processes (p. 340). In a highly sophisticated account, Horowitz (2010) demonstrated that external linkages and organizational capabilities facilitate a terrorist organization's ability to copy the innovation of others. For Horowitz, a terrorist organization willing to engage in suicide bombings yet missing the organizational capability or the necessary ties to others is unlikely to be able to sustain a campaign of suicide bombings.

While many studies on terrorism acknowledge that successful terrorist organizations must learn, very few show how learning occurs. According to Kenney (2007), it is unfortunate that "many government officials, policy analysts, and even researchers gloss over how . . . terrorists . . . actually *learn*, in the sense of acquiring, analyzing, and applying knowledge and experience. . . . It is not enough simply to claim, as many do, that . . . terrorists learn" (p. 13). Kenney focused on training practices and outlines the various means by which al-Qaeda has spread knowledge through its network. Examples include state sponsorship, training camps, knowledge-based artifacts such as training manuals, and "informal apprenticeships, on-the-job training, communities of practice, and combat" (Kenney 2007: 145). These learning dynamics are likely to be similar within communication styles. The terrorism studies literature therefore suggests that while emulation is likely, it is *most* likely within groups that contain members who directly learned communication strategies within IS as opposed to those who watched and studied it from afar.

Insights from Organizational Psychology and Business Management

There are a number of fundamental principles within the organizational psychology and business management literature related to creativity and innovation. First, although linked, creativity and innovation represent two distinct entities that form a collective process in the development of a product. While "creativity" refers to the generation of ideas and novel concepts, "innovation" involves implementing these ideas (Amabile 1996). Though often used interchangeably, creativity typically refers to early-stage activities such as problem solving or idea generation while innovation refers to later-stage activities such as evaluation, planning, and monitoring (Anderson, Potocnik, & Zhou 2014).

Second, for an innovation to occur, it must first go through a creative process from idea generation to full implementation. Characterizing creativity and innovation as a process requires us to understand the dynamic interactions (and the properties that govern those interactions) undertaken by multiple actors. A successful creative process requires the ability to generate ideas for a new tactic (including communications strategies) or adapt certain technologies and then use them for a new purpose. It also entails understanding how organizational structures and management systems facilitate this process. In turn, this involves understanding the drivers of creativity from both bottom-up (creativity in individuals and small groups) and top-down (leadership and intraorganizational structural effects) perspectives while also accounting for the competitive environment in which terrorist organizations operate against a much stronger foe. The creative process is multidimensional, multicausal, and dynamic (Gill et al. 2013).

Third, the result of this process ends in a novel product or process. Whether this product or process is depicted as an innovation depends on its originality, relevance, elegance, and generalizability. Creative products are novel and generate effective surprise in their beholder while remaining relevant and useful (Cropley, Kaufman, & Cropley 2008). Essentially, the product must meet both consumer and target population needs. A creative product lacking relevance and effectiveness is merely aesthetic. For terrorist communication, consumers typically include the community that the terrorist organization claims to represent, as well as the target of the violence. Spontaneous novel acts of violence generate effective surprise within the target audience. The violence and its subsequent media coverage generate an image of the terrorist organization as strong, cohesive, and relevant. Another element of creativity is the elegance of the solution. "Elegance" refers to whether the product is logical, sensible, and well-crafted. In other words, "good solutions look like good solutions" (Cropley et al. 2008: 108). Broadly speaking, organizational behavior researchers assert that creative solutions must also be generalizable. This refers to the applicability of the product, not only in terms of satisfying target population needs, but also in terms of the extent to which it sparks new ideas and inventions, challenges the status quo, and generates new ways to resolve current problems (Cropley et al. 2008).

Fourth, regardless of the innovation associated with a particular product (in this case, a communication strategy), its novelty will decay over time. Once a set of skills is perfected, terrorists may rely on the expertise associated with this set of skills to guide their future communications. However, the problem with creative, but repeated, communicative acts is the element of diminishing returns. Truly creative acts often contain novelty value. Over time, however, the novelty diminishes. Lakomy (2017: 47–48) makes this point devastatingly clear regarding IS's propaganda campaign:

Islamic State's releases are gradually losing their uniqueness, which was so striking in 2014 and 2015. . . . When the first major IS productions started to emerge online in 2014, they were fresh and unique in comparison to the earlier releases of other Islamist terrorist organizations. After two years, most potential audiences got somewhat weary with the similar issues addressed by the IS's cells over and over again. . . . It basically means that there is far less chance that these productions will draw enough attention to spark a proper viral effect.

To sidestep diminishing novelty, terrorist organizations regularly shift tactics in terms of who is targeted, attack methods, weapon components, or delivery methods. Terrorist organizations' communication strategies are likely to change in a similar fashion. This involves a return to the creative process depicted earlier. However, their innovation depends on having the right operating environmental and organizational capability (a discussion we return to later).

Fifth, as a product's novelty decays, so, too, does its effectiveness (provided countermeasures are put in place or activated) and its likelihood of being emulated by other groups. This decay in novelty will likely be accelerated by the emergence of competing products.

Finally, there are two forms of product and process innovation—incremental and radical. These variants differ in the degree to which they are revolutionary and novel. *Radical innovation* consists of fundamental changes that strike a clear departure from existing processes and products. *Incremental innovation* describes small adjustments to the current technology or product (Dewar & Dutton 1986). Radical innovation drives the creation of effective surprise and shock in consumers. Radically creative products possess the surprise factor of being rarely anticipated and thus provide a competitive advantage to the designers by making it extremely difficult for competitors to emulate the product's unique qualities. In the case of terrorist organizations' activities, innovative outcomes can include successful subway gas attacks, effective IEDs, strategic recruitment of new extremists, and responsive counterattacks against military officials. Of course, this advantage lasts only until an organization's competitors generate a more technologically advanced and desirable product. In the same way as businesses compete with one another for first-mover advantages, the war on terror is seen as a dynamic struggle between law enforcement officials and terrorists to outperform one another by employing increasingly creative means to effectively strike at their targets and evade detection (Cropley et al., 2008: 107).

IS's Imitation and Innovation

Of course, IS's communication strategy did not develop in a vacuum. As the previous chapters in this book demonstrate, IS has obviously learned a great deal from other jihadi groups from the decade prior. This should not be surprising given the insights regarding social learning outlined earlier. Less obviously, they may have also learned about effective communication strategies from the US Army, ethno-nationalist movements, left-wing revolutionaries, and Hollywood and Nazi mass propaganda (see Chapters 1 and 3). This social learning covers a range of behaviors, including:

- Using the Internet as the primary vehicle for propaganda
- Using visual imagery and "grotesque propaganda"

- Seeking "viral" documents
- Having dedicated media teams
- Using videos, magazines, and *anashīd*
- Using "martyr biographies"

IS communication strategies also imitate content, including

- Developing social diagnoses and agendas
- Reifying group categories
- Recycling old symbolic imagery and narratives
- Using eschatology

If one were to cherry-pick these examples from this book, it would be appropriate to ponder whether anything related to IS's communication strategy is actually creative or innovative. However, several claims are made in this book and elsewhere that IS's communication strategies are indeed innovative. These innovations include

- The "sophisticated" use and understanding of social media
- The quantity of propaganda outputs
- The diversity of propaganda outputs
- The lingual diversity in outputs
- Its ideological appeal being "anchored" in "exceptionalism"

The organizational psychology literature would largely depict these innovations as incremental as opposed to radical. Purely radical innovations are difficult to find. Those listed here are essentially small creative adjustments to previous efforts. Combined, they have certainly had a radical *impact*, but the innovations themselves are incremental. As the Introduction and Ingram's Chapter 1 make clear, it is IS's propaganda as a system of "full-spectrum propaganda" which is arguably unprecedented. It has built on previous innovations, but made it large scale. Kovacs (2015: 66) showed that IS incrementally improves "the massive 'visual turn' embraced by some radical Islamist movements at the beginning of the 21st Century" (2015: 66). In this book, Chapters 3 and 4 depict IS magazines as "not too far from the preceding *Inspire*" and IS videos within a "continuity of propaganda practices," respectively. What appears to distinguish IS communication strategies are their high levels of elegance and relevance, aided by the volume and diversity of outputs.

This leaves the question of whether the IS communicative strategy will likely be emulated by others? The terrorism studies and communication science literatures would both suggest that this would be a natural occurrence because the strategy has demonstrably proved to be effective. Terrorists are rational actors and conduct deliberate cost-benefit analyses, after all. However, the organizational psychology and business management literatures consistently highlight a number of caveats. The answer is more likely group-specific, and all depends on capability. As previously stated, typically multiple levels of interacting actors combine to initiate the creative process. The interplay of individuals, teams, leaders, organizations, and environments contribute to this process of creativity and innovation. Innovation therefore is typically multiply determined. We need to think about the attributes of a group that make creativity and innovation (and potentially emulation) more likely. So while groups may learn from IS communications strategies, the literature just reviewed suggests that if they do not have similar organizational characteristics, emulation may be less likely. IS communicative innovations appear primarily driven by organizational-level and environmental-level factors. Given the more nuanced accounts available from the organizational and business management literatures, we now consider some of these variables and elaborate on some of the key findings from the various literatures briefly reviewed.

IS Communicative Innovations and Organizational-Level Variables

The business management literature suggests there are several organizational-level variables of creativity that leaders can control. These include organizational structure, organizational size, offering extrinsic/intrinsic rewards, ensuring a collaborative environment, building interteam trust, engaging in participatory decision making, encouraging a unified commitment to the project, appointing principled leadership, financial resources, obtaining external support and recognition, adopting a flexible approach to roles and behaviors that accommodate emergent ideas, provision of feedback, and encouragement to "be creative" (Abetti 2000; James, Clark, & Cropanzano 1999; Carson & Carson 1993; Grant & Berry 2011). Looking at IS specifically, Miller and Mekhennet (2015) reported first-hand accounts from IS defectors who described the central role of and importance bestowed on the media team. Senior media members "are treated as 'emirs' of equal rank to their military counterparts. They are directly involved in decisions on strategy and territory. They preside over hundreds of videographers, producers and editors who form a privileged, professional class with status, salaries and living arrangements that are the envy of ordinary fighters."

The creativity literature illustrates that a flexible, organic structure, as opposed to a bureaucratic structure, is more conducive to innovation in organizations (Drazin & Schoonhoven 1996; Hunter, Bedell, & Mumford 2007). For example, in Hellstrom and Hellstrom's (2002) qualitative study, most respondents perceive organizational rules as hindering creativity. While workers depend on quick feedback because "ideas are perishable goods," informal networks possess the danger of ideas being stolen for the benefits of others. Thus, while too much structure suffocates creativity, too little structure deters idea generation, subsequent evaluation, and the processes needed for full implementation. Although a strictly hierarchical organization, IS's media department is stratified across a number of physical and virtual domains with some central coordination. This may have had the (potentially unintended) impact of creating multiple competing teams where the innovations of one quickly diffused across the organization. This same intraorganizational competition was noted as a key factor in the Provisional IRA's systematic innovations in the area of bomb development (Gill 2017).

Furthermore, Tushman and O'Reilly (1996) illustrated that larger organizations possessing complicated interlinked structures may be dependent on a network of external ties and suppliers that provide raw materials for their products and thus may hesitate to innovate in order to leave the ties undisturbed. The cost and difficulty of implementing change incentivizes some organizations to remain rooted in their structures, systems, procedures, and processes. Although a large organization's resources can be conducive to innovation, it may also lead to losing focus, which in turn leads to poor planning (Halbesleben, Novicevic, Harvey, & Buckley 2003). Leadership is also important for the creative focus. We must first distinguish what role leaders play in the creative process before distinguishing specific leadership behaviors that engender greater creativity and innovation. According to the literature, leaders provide structure and vision, facilitate idea progression, champion and promote ideas to others, provide resources and feedback, model appropriate behaviors, motivate subordinates, model open-minded thinking, extend discussions to encourage more idea generation, define problems in new ways, and grant autonomy to subordinates (Damanpour 1991; Halbesleben et al. 2003; Mumford 2000; Mumford, Hunter, Eubanks, Bedell, & Murphy 2007).

One of the clearest findings in creative leadership research is that technical expertise is critical for leader performance (Mumford et al. 2007). Expertise helps leaders appraise follower capabilities, creates awareness of professional expectations, and provides a basis for effective exercise of power (Gumusluoglu & Ilsev 2009). It is commonly perceived that newcomers to a domain may be more creative than experts because they are unhindered by locked modes of thinking. Although this may be true in some cases, research shows that, in order to conceptualize creative solutions to problems, an individual needs expertise in the problem domain (Walczyk & Griffith-Ross 2008). Experience and expertise provide individuals a framework for interpreting, gathering, and acting on information (Mumford et al. 2007; Taylor & Greve 2006). Having a broader and richer frame of reference allows individuals a larger reservoir to draw from when solving problems. Specifically, expertise promotes (a) a more rapid acquisition of knowledge, (b) use of systematic solutions rather than trial and error, and (c) applications of the principles, relationships, and prototypic cases to novel problems (Mumford 2000). The value of expertise is so great that some researchers argue most individuals take 10 years to make an important contribution in their domain (Kaufman 2009).

The preceding chapters make it clear that a key reason for IS's social media success was the organization's capacity for creating and distributing a large number of slickly produced and specifically targeted materials. Expertise and experience appear crucial to the incremental innovations embedded in this social media success. Miller and Mekhennet (2015) reported on firsthand accounts of IS defectors who described the central role of and importance bestowed on the media team. This team is stocked with individuals "whose production skills often stem from previous jobs they held at news channels or technology companies." Interviewees further claimed that "the media wing has relied on veterans of al-Qaeda media teams, young recruits fluent in social media platforms. . . . Some of them were hackers; some were engineers." The fact remains, however, that IS is beginning to lose some of these key personnel (Lakomy 2017).

While individual traits are conducive to creative work, they may also hinder collaborative efforts which themselves are often necessary to solve complex problems and require multiple areas of expertise. Indeed, the traits that allow innovative employees to break from social norms also leave them susceptible to interpersonal conflicts with co-workers (Anderson & Geistner 2007). As suggested by Feist's (1998) meta-analysis of creative personality, innovative people tend to remove themselves from social interactions more readily. Despite a creative individual's need for autonomy, workgroup support strongly predicts innovation (Baer & Frese 2003). Several reasons explain why teamwork benefits creative efforts. First, diverse expertise contributes to the pool of information available for idea generation. It also provides a greater need to articulate the problem at hand (West 2002). Work groups provide ties and networks that promote innovation (Hellstrom & Hellstrom 2002). In turn, these ties provide support in uncertain times and help lower stress. Team members serve as collaborators and provide feedback in an environment of trust (Paulus, Dzindolet, & Kohn in press; Mueller & Kamdar 2011; Pirola-Merlo & Mann 2004). Given the volume of foreign fighters within the ranks, IS's personnel is clearly a diverse pool. Chapter 6 makes a clear link between this diversity and some incremental innovations—namely, the production of *anashīd* and other propaganda outputs in a range of languages: "It is worth noting that this trend of linguistic diversification has been apparent across IS's propaganda operations between 2014 and 2017, and has been facilitated by the abilities it accrued from foreign fighter inflows."

Cohesiveness has positive effects on innovation because it increases group process effectiveness, promotes awareness of team members' skills and team mental models, aids in more efficient decision making, and builds trust and liking among group members (Ayres, Dahlstrom, & Skinner 1997; Mumford & Hunter 2005). The early years of IS and the geographical sanctity it possessed potentially allowed for this cohesiveness to develop and innovations to occur. Now that IS is under greater military pressure on the battlefield and increased pressure on the virtual space, it will be interesting to see the impact on innovation. Already this pressure appears to be impacting production quality, which many inextricably tie to IS's innovation. For example, Lakomy (2017) notes that, during 2016, some "high-profile videos contain evident editing, montage and post-production mistakes, which were previously very rare." Lakomy (2017) depicts this as "a serious creativity crisis." This fall in quality is not linked to an increase in output. Milton (2016) notes the severe reduction in content being produced through 2016.

IS Communicative Innovations and
Environmental-Level Variables

Of course, organizational-level attributes are only one side of the coin. There is an interaction effect between organizations and the environment in which they operate. Undoubtedly, IS communication strategies benefitted from their particular environmental context. So much so that some might question the degree to which we can actually credit IS with these innovations. For example, the drivers of innovation for behaviors like the use of social media and the dissemination of the quantity and diversity of propaganda appear attributable to environmental drivers outside the control of IS. Other environmental drivers can be more proximal. One such proximal environmental driver is that of external agencies *imposing* the need for innovation on a terrorist organization. As Crenshaw (2010) notes, the social movement literature embodied by Tarrow (1994: 43) suggests something similar in "that government actions as well as new opportunities and constituencies stimulate innovation in social movements and their strategies of protest."

For terrorist organizations, two types of external agencies exist in the communicative context. First, effective counterterrorism policies may force terrorist organizations to experiment with other creative acts of violence or communicative strategies. At the same time, new counterterrorism policies, while increasing the pressure to innovate, may also curtail a terrorist organization's capacity for creativity and innovation. This evokes the argument in Chapter 2 of this book that IS's reproduction of concepts such as *Al-walā' wa al-barā'* "is deeply reactionary in nature, in the sense that it comes from a perceived necessity to enforce a protection against foreign influence." Counterterrorism is no longer the sole remit of security and intelligence agencies. The pressure applied by social media organizations led to emulations of others in the use of hashtags in disseminating IS material and ultimately the switch to Telegram, which "has become a hub for retrieving IS related propaganda and coordinating its distribution on other social network platforms, allowing them to organize ghazawat (raids) on platforms such as Facebook and Twitter" (see Chapter 5).

Terrorist organizations espousing similar goals may attempt to outbid one another for community support; this represents a second form of external agency that may drive creativity and innovation for a terrorist organization. Community support for particular types of violence may also encourage terrorist organizations to innovate and fulfil these needs; this encapsulates the third form of external agency. Again, returning to Chapter 2, the central appeal of IS's communication efforts is that the group is depicted as exceptional compared to other Islamist groups and that the group is "highly conscious that its most important battle is the ideological one for the leadership of Salafi-jihadism."

Furthermore, innovation is a process of change, which is an inherently temporal phenomenon (Lubart 2001). Thus, planning is crucial for successfully releasing new products. Planning requires understanding market trends and development opportunities. However, without appropriate testing and evaluation, the product can fail. Thus, external pressure may place a greater emphasis on idea evaluation with innovative products (Mueller, Melwani, & Goncalo 2012. These findings from the organizational psychology literature resemble much theorizing from the field of social movement studies. Grievances in and of themselves fail to account for the emergence of violent contentious actions. Instead, organizational elites utilize political opportunity structures to maximize their chances of mobilizing previously passive but potential recruits and supporters. The same is true for particular manifestations of violence once mobilization has begun (see Sarma 2007). Indeed, both Zelin (2015) and Winter (2015) demonstrate IS's disposition to satisfy the broad needs of its diverse supporter pool. "This marks an important departure from other significant jihadist groups such as AQ, who tended to focus on the ideological aspects of their message (e.g., via historical videos, online sermons, or battle scenes). Thus, IS did not simply 'luck into' the advent of social media; we must also credit the group with the forethought of considering the broad spectrum of needs of its users and investing heavily in satisfying these; hence the need to turn to an organizational understanding of drivers" (see Chapter 2).

Imitation and Innovation After IS

So what does this all mean for imitation and innovation after IS? A naïve answer would suggest that because the "full-spectrum" innovation worked for IS, it is bound to be copied and incrementally improved elsewhere. However, if that were the case, we should have already seen it by now. Copying is common in industry, with only an estimated 6- to 18-month time period in which competitors have access to product development information (Levin, Klevorick, Nelson, & Winter 1987). This is especially so when the product is less complex or easier to understand and imitate, making reverse engineering easier (Pil & Cohen 2006). Additionally (and ironically), the success of a terrorist organization's innovative communication can also be its downfall, as other organizations copy the style or content and in turn make the original organization seem too mainstream. If the purpose of propaganda is to terrorize, too much exposure to it dampens the intended effect as people become habituated.

Looking at "what works" is insufficient. What the preceding section demonstrates is that we need to think about "what works, for whom and in what circumstances." All the will in the world to emulate IS communication strategies will be redundant if the individual-, environmental-, and group-level capabilities are lacking.

Where these IS innovations are most likely to be imitated will heavily depend on where IS adherents end up in other conflict zones upon the group's demise in Syria. The study of business imitation demonstrates that competitors gain knowledge through peer conversations, suppliers, customers, and employee turnover (Appleyard 1996). They will take with them the tactics, techniques, and procedures learned in Syria and adapt them to the idiosyncrasies of the local conflict and the affordances offered to them there.

What these ex-IS members bring to their new conflict will not necessarily be a reduction in the quality of communication strategy. Some research suggests an advantage to being a second mover or imitator. Chinese and Korean tech companies had initially followed this strategy with great success, allowing rapid growth and development of their own high-tech skills through acquiring information about other successful companies' methods. The second-mover advantage allows organizations to make more incremental improvements to a radical innovation, create products at a lower cost, or take advantage of a well-known and "proven" product or process once the market has already been tested for it. In a study by Golder and Tellis (1993), first movers remain market share leaders in only 4 out of 50 companies, with only a 10% market share but a 47% failure rate. In contrast, second movers had larger average market shares of 28% and lower failure rates of 8%. Thus, imitators can have a significant competitive advantage by learning from the mistakes of first movers. We might therefore expect to see less of the "full-spectrum" approach, and instead see a more fine-tuned and streamlined suite of communication products emerge.

Where innovations go next will largely be a small-scale mimicking of systematic innovations which will impact all of us benevolently. Who could have foreseen 15 years ago the ubiquity of social media in our lives and how malevolent actors could have shaped these forces for their own end? Technological changes will lead inevitably to new forms of communication strategies for both benevolent and malevolent groups.

Conclusion

The emergence of IS as perhaps the world's most preeminent terrorist organization (in terms of its communication strategy) makes it likely that others will try to replicate it. We know from the history of terrorism that this emulation is most likely going to occur within groups of a similar ideological outlook, grievance structure, and geographical proximity.

Future innovation in terrorist communications will likely depend on the affordances offered by new online innovations. It is therefore impossible to predict the timing and scale of these innovations. However, organizational psychology tells us that the right organizational and environmental variables must overlap in space and time for a group to fully make use of these innovations. Few groups will have the scale, foresight, finances, and diversified personnel that IS had. Moreover, few groups will have the relatively secure on- and offline operating space that IS benefitted from. The likelihood that a group will benefit from both at the same time is relatively unlikely. Although the Internet affordances crucial to IS's growth can be copied by other groups, these other groups are unlikely to be sufficiently capable of manipulating these affordances.

A focus on processes, behaviors, and organizational capabilities allows us to answer the "how" questions, and here there is a sparsity in the research field. Instead, analyses tend to focus on the "what" (e.g., the content of the communications) and the "why" (e.g., the instrumental reasoning behind the communication). In time, the "how" questions may become easier to answer as first-hand documents and accounts of the IS communication process become available. This book has consistently highlighted a number of innovative *products* related to IS communications. What we know too little of is the creative *process* this organization went through to make these products a reality. In particular, we know very little about issues (e.g., idea generation) that preceded the production of the innovative product. Further research is needed on the inner workings of the organization to specifically pinpoint what individual, team, leader, organizational, and environmental factors afforded its capability to relentlessly go through creative processes. This, of course, is a much more challenging research task. It will always be easier to study the *products* that IS wanted disseminated than the *processes* it tried to keep hidden from the eyes of counterterrorism. For now, we are reliant on reassurances from organizational psychology that posit that (a) communicative innovations are difficult to emulate, and (b) the sheer scope of the communicative innovations' presence diminishes their innovative effects over time. This forces terrorist groups into new communication strategies which may prove counterproductive and increase the effort required of the terrorist group to effectively communicate with targeted audiences.

Acknowledgments

This project has received funding from the European Research Council (ERC) under the European Union's Horizon 2020 research and innovation program (grant agreement No. 758834).

References

Abetti P. A. (2000) "Critical Success Factors for Radical Technological Innovation," *Creativity & Innovation Management* 9(4): 208–221.

Amabile T. M. (1996) *Creativity in Context: Update to "The Social Psychology of Creativity."* Boulder CO: Westview Press.

Anderson N., Gasteiger R. M. (2007) "Helping Creativity and Innovation Thrive in Organizations: Functional and Dysfunctional Perspectives," in Langan-Fox J., Cooper C., Klimoski R. (eds.), *Research Companion to the Dysfunctional Workplace: Management Challenges and Symptoms.* Cheltenham: Edward Elgar, pp. 422–440.

Anderson N., Potocnik K., Zhou J. (2014) "Innovation and Creativity in Organizations: A State-of-the-Science Review, Prospective Commentary, and Guiding Framework," *Journal of Management* 40(5): 1297–1333.

Appleyard M. (1996) "How Does Knowledge Flow? Interfirm Patterns in the Semiconductor Industry," *Strategic Management Journal* 17: 137–154.

Ayres D., Dahlstrom R., Skinner S. (1997) "An Exploratory Inverstigation of Organizational Antecedents to New Product Success," *Journal of Marketing Research* 34(1): 107–116.

Baer M., Frese M. (2003) "Innovation Is Not Enough: Climates for Initiative and Psychological Safety, Process Innovations, and Firm Performance," *Journal of Organizational Behavior* 24: 45–68.

Bandura A. (1986) "The Explanatory and Predictive Scope of Self-Efficacy Theory," *Journal of Social and Clinical Psychology* 4(3): 359–373.

Bandura A. (2001) "Social Cognitive Theory: An Agentic Perspective," *Annual Review of Psychology* 52: 1–26.

Bauer T., Bodner T., Erdogan B., Truxillo D., Tucker J. (2007) "Newcomer Adjustment during Organizational Socialization: A Meta-analytic Review of Antecedents, Outcomes, and Methods," *Journal of Applied Psychology* 92(3): 707–721.

Block E., Negrine R. (2017) "The Populist Communication Style: Toward a Critical Framework," *International Journal of Communication* 11: 20.

Bloom M. (2005) *Dying to Kill: The Allure of Suicide Terror.* New York: Columbia University Press.

Bonneuil N., Auriat N. (2000) "Fifty Years of Ethnic Conflict and Cohesion: 1945–1994," *Journal of Peace Research* 37(5): 563–581.

Bracciale R., Martella A. (2017) "Defining the Populist Political Communication Style: The Case of Italian Political Leaders on Twitter," *Information, Communication & Society* 20(9): 1310–1329.

Braithwaite A., Li Q. (2007) "Transnational Terrorism Hot Spots: Identification and Impact Evaluation," *Conflict Management & Peace Science* 24(4): 281–296.

Carson P., Carson E. (1993) "Managing Creativity Enhancement Through Goal-Setting and Feedback," *Journal of Applied Psychology* 27: 36–45.

Chang H. (2010) "A New Perspective on Twitter Hashtag Use: Diffusion of Innovation Theory," *Proceedings of the Association for Information Science and Technology* 47(1): 1–4.

Crenshaw M. (2010) "Innovation: Decision Points in the Trajectory of Terrorism," in Rasmussen M., Hafez M. (eds.), *Terrorist Innovations in Weapons of Mass Effect: Preconditions, Causes and Predictive Indicators.* Washington: The Defense Threat Reduction Agency (Report ASCO-2010-019), pp. 35–50. Retrieved from http://www.dtic.mil/cgi-bin/GetTRDoc?AD=ADA556986.

Cropley D., Kaufman J., Cropley A. (2008) "Malevolent Creativity: A Functional Model of Creativity in Terrorism and Crime," *Creativity Research Journal* 20(2): 105–115.

Damanpour F. (1991) "Organizational Innovation: A Meta-analysis of Effects of Determinants and Moderators," *Academy of Management Journal* 34: 555–590.

Davis F., Bagozzi R., Warshaw P. (1992) "Extrinsic and Intrinsic Motivation to Use Computers in the Workplace," *Journal of Applied Social Psychology* 22(14): 1111–1132.

Dewar R., Dutton J. (1986) "The Adoption of Radical and Incremental Innovations: An Empirical Analysis," *Management Science* 32(11): 1422–1433.

Dolnik A. (2007) *Understanding Terrorist Innovation: Technology, Tactics and Global Trends.* London: Routledge.

Drazin R., Schoonhoven C. (1996) "Community, Population, and Organization Effects on Innovation: A Multilevel Perspective," *Academy of Management Journal* 39(5): 1065–1083.

Dugan L., LaFree G., Piquero A. (2005) "Testing a Rational Choice Model of Airline Hijackings," *Criminology* 43(4): 1031–1065.

Feist G. (1998) "A Meta-analysis of Personality in Scientific and Artistic Creativity," *Personality & Social Psychology Review* 2: 290–309.

Gill, P. (2017) "Tactical Innovation and the Provisional Irish Republican Army," *Studies in Conflict & Terrorism* 40(7): 573–585.

Gill P., Horgan J., Hunter S., D Cushenbery L. (2013) "Malevolent Creativity in Terrorist Organizations," *Journal of Creative Behavior* 47(2): 125–151.

Golder P., Tellis G. (1993) "Pioneering Advantage: Marketing Logic or Marketing Legend?," *Journal of Marketing Research* 30: 158–170.

Grant A., Berry J. (2011) "The Necessity of Others Is the Mother of Invention: Intrinsic and Prosocial Motivations, Perspective-Taking, and Creativity," *Academy of Management Journal* 54(3): 73–96.

Gumusluoglu L., Ilsev A. (2009) "Transformational Leadership, Creativity, and Organizational Innovation," *Journal of Business Research* 62: 461–473.

Halbesleben J., Novicevic M., Harvey M., Buckley R. (2003) "Awareness of Temporal Complexity in Leadership of Creativity and Innovation: A Competency-Based Model," *Leadership Quarterly* 14: 433–454.

Hellstrom C., Hellstrom T. (2002) "Highways, Alleys and By-Lanes: Charting the Pathways for Ideas and Innovation in Organizations," *Creativity & Innovation Management* 11: 107–114.

Horowitz M. (2010) "Nonstate Actors and the Diffusion of Innovations: The Case of Suicide Terrorism," *International Organization* 64(1): 33–64.

Hunter S., Bedell K., Mumford M. (2007) "Climate for Creativity: A Quantitative Review," *Creativity Research Journal* 19(1): 69–90.

Ilie V., Van Slyke C., Green G., Hao L. (2005) "Gender Differences in Perceptions and Use of Communication Technologies: A Diffusion of Innovation Approach," *Information Resources Management Journal* 18(3): 13.

Jackson B., Baker J., Chalk P., Cragin K., Parachini J., Trujillo H. (2005) *Appetite for Destruction: Organizational Learning in Terrorist Groups and its Implications for Combating Terrorism*. Santa Monica, California: Rand Corporation.

James K., Clark K., Cropanzano R. (1999) "Positive and Negative Creativity in Groups, Institutions, and Organizations: A Model and Theoretical Extension," *Creativity Research Journal* 12: 211–226.

Jung D., Wu A., Chow C. (2008) "Toward Understanding the Direct and Indirect Effects of CEOs' Transformational Leadership on Firm Innovation," *Leadership Quarterly* 19: 582–594.

Kaufman J. (2009) *Creativity 101*. New York: Springer.

Kenney M. (2007) *From Pablo to Osama: Trafficking and Terrorist Networks, Government Bureaucracies, and Competitive Adaptation*. State College: Pennsylvania State University Press.

Kovacs A. (2015) "The 'New Jihadists' and the Visual Turn from al Qa'ida to ISIL / ISIS / Da'ish," *Biztpol Affairs* 2(3): 47–70.

Krämer B. (2017) "Populist Online Practices: The Function of the Internet in Right-Wing Populism," *Information, Communication & Society* 20(9): 1293–1309.

Lakomy M. (2017) "Cracks in the Online 'Caliphate': How the Islamic State Is Losing Ground in the Battle for Cyberspace," *Perspectives on Terrorism* 11(3): 40–53.

Levin R., Klevorick A., Nelson R., Winter S. (1987) "Appropriating the Returns from Industrial Research and Development," *Brookings Papers on Economic Activity* 3: 783–831.

Lubart T. (2001) "Models of the Creative Process: Past, Present and Future," *Creativity Research Journal* 13(3-4): 295–308.

Merari A. (1999) "Terrorism as a Strategy of Struggle: Past and Future," *Terrorism & Political Violence* 11(4): 52–65.

Midlarsky M., Crenshaw M., Yoshida F. (1980) "Why Violence Spreads: The Contagion of International Terrorism," *International Studies Quarterly* 24(2): 262–298.

Miller G., Mekhennet S. (2015, November 20) "Inside the Surreal World of the Islamic State's Propaganda Machine," *Washington Post*. Retrieved from https://www.washingtonpost.com/world/national-security/inside-the-islamic-states-propaganda-machine/2015/11/20/051e997a-8ce6-11e5-acff-673ae92ddd2b_story.html?noredirect=on&utm_term=.c1c809e6f60d.

Milton, D. (2016) *Communication breakdown: Unraveling the Islamic States media efforts.* US Military Academy-Combating Terrorism Center West Point United States.

Moghadam A. (2008) *The Globalization of Martyrdom*. Baltimore, MD: Johns Hopkins University Press.

Mudde C., Kaltwasser C., eds. (2012) *Populism in Europe and the Americas: Threat or Corrective for Democracy?* Cambridge: Cambridge University Press.

Mueller J., Kamdar D. (2011) "Why Seeking Help from Teammates Is a Blessing and a Curse: A Theory of Help Seeking and Individual Creativity in Team Contexts," *Journal of Applied Psychology* 96: 263–276.

Mueller J., Melwani S., Goncalo J. (2012) "The Bias Against Creativity: Why People Desire but Reject Creative Ideas," *Psychological Science* 23(1): 13–17.

Mumford M. (2000) "Managing Creativity," *Human Resource Management Review* 10: 313–351.

Mumford M., & Hunter S. T. (2005) "Innovation in Organizations: A Multi-level Perspective on Creativity," in Yammarino F., Dansereau F. (eds.), *Research in Multi-Level Issues: Volume IV*. Oxford: Elsevier, pp. 11–74.

Mumford M., Hunter S., Eubanks D., Bedell K., Murphy S. (2007) "Developing Leaders for Creative Efforts: A Domain-based Approach to Leadership Development," *Human Resource Management Review* 17(4): 402–417.

Pape R. (2005) *Dying to Win: The Strategic Logic of Suicide Terrorism*. New York: Random House.

Paulus P., Dzindolet M., Kohn N. (2012) "Collaborative Creativity—Group Creativity and Team Innovation," in Mumford M. (ed.), *Handbook of Organizational Creativity*. London: Elsevier, pp. 327–357.

Pil F., Cohen S. (2006) "Modularity: Implications for Imitation, Innovation, and Sustained Advantage," *Academy of Management Review* 31(4): 995–1011.

Pirola-Merlo A., Mann L. (2004) "The Relationship Between Individual Creativity and Team Creativity," *Journal of Organizational Behavior* 25: 235–257.

Rasmussen M., Hafez M. (2010) *Terrorist Innovations in Weapons of Mass Effect: Preconditions, Causes and Predictive Indicators*. Washington, DC: The Defense Threat Reduction Agency (Report ASCO-2010-019). Retrieved from http://www.dtic.mil/cgi-bin/GetTRDoc?AD=ADA556986.

Sarma K. (2007) "Defensive Propaganda and IRA Political Control in Republican Communities," *Studies in Conflict and Terrorism* 30(12): 1073–1094.

Tarrow S. (1994) *Power in Movement: Social Movement, Collective Action and Politics*. Cambridge: Harvard University Press.

Taylor A., Greve H. (2006) "Superman or the Fantastic Four? Knowledge Combination and Experience in Innovative Teams," *Academy of Management Journal* 49(4): 723–740.

Tushman M., O'Reilly C. (1996) "Ambidextrous Organizations: Managing Evolutionary and Revolutionary Change," *California Management Review* 38: 8–30.

Van Slyke C., Hao L., Day J. (2002) "The Impact of Perceived Innovation Characteristics on Intention to Use Groupware," *Information Resources Management Journal* 15(1): 5.

Waisbord S., Amado A. (2017) "Populist Communication by Digital Means: Presidential Twitter in Latin America," *Information, Communication & Society* 20(9): 1330–1346.

Walczyk J., Griffith-Ross D. (2008) "Commentary on the Functional Creativity Model: Its Application to Understanding Innovative Deception," *Creativity Research Journal* 20: 130–133.

West M. (2002) "Sparkling Fountains or Stagnant Ponds: An Integrative Model of Creativity and Innovation Implementation in Work Groups," *Applied Psychology: An International Review* 51: 355–387.

Winter C. (2015) "The Virtual 'Caliphate': Understanding Islamic State's Propaganda Strategy," London, UK: Quilliam Foundation.

Zelin A. (2015) "Picture or It Didn't Happen: A Snapshot of the Islamic State's Official Media Output," *Perspectives on Terrorism* 9(4): 85–97.

Afterword

The Uniqueness of Islamic State

Thomas Hegghammer

Do we really need another book on the Islamic State (IS)? In some sense no, because the market is flooded (woe to the author hoping to write a bestseller with "ISIS" in the title). In another sense, we need it more than ever because it is only now, after the dust has settled, that we can hope to truly understand what hit us a few years ago. The value of stock-taking is eminently illustrated by this volume on IS propaganda, where the contributors benefit from hindsight and a full information picture to shed new light on the IS phenomenon.

At its peak in the mid-2010s, IS's propaganda output was so large that even professional observers were losing track. Gathering propaganda products in real time was a full-time endeavor, and even then you would probably not be able to capture all materials across the full spectrum of distribution platforms. And this was just for collection; as for processing and analysis, it was beyond most individuals' capacity to view, read, or listen to all IS propaganda output in its entirety the same week it was published. Bear in mind that this happened at a time when other jihadi groups were also producing substantial amounts of material, making the overall jihadi information picture no less than overwhelming to individual researchers. In this period, it was probably only organizations and large teams of researchers that could hope to gather and process anything close to the full information picture.

Then there were all the secondary sources. The mid-2010s saw the publication of a vast number of specialized, in-depth studies on various aspects of IS's Internet activities. As highlighted in the Introduction of this volume, a rapidly expanding community of researchers produced substantial numbers of reports, articles, blog posts, and other writings in an effort to process at least some of the material being pumped into the online domain by jihadi groups. Most of these studies dealt, necessarily, with small slices of the information picture: a particular type of propaganda product, a particular

Thomas Hegghammer, *Afterword: The Uniqueness of Islamic State In: ISIS Propaganda*. Edited by: Stephane J. Baele, Katharine A. Boyd, and Travis G. Coan, Oxford University Press (2020) © University of Maryland National Consortium for the Study of Terrorism and Responses to Terrorism (START) DOI: 10.1093/oso/9780190932459.001.0009 platform, or narrower topics still, such as particular ideologists or specific films. As a result, merely keeping track of the *secondary literature* on IS propaganda was a significant undertaking. On the whole, the IS propaganda explosion happened so fast that it was difficult to see the forest for the trees. We all knew the phenomenon was large, but not precisely how large or exactly how it was strung together.

That was until this book. Thanks to the efforts of Stephane Baele, Katharine Boyd, Travis Coan, and their co-contributors, we now have a much better understanding of the scale and nature of the IS full-spectrum propaganda machine. Written by a combination of propaganda specialists and "in-the-weeds" jihadism observers, the book offers a holistic view of the phenomenon that has overwhelmed researchers and analysts for the better part of 5 years. The chapters in this book not only confirm that the IS propaganda apparatus was indeed very large; it also maps out the full range of its activities while at the same time describing in meticulous detail the depth and sophistication of its various components. The picture that emerges is that of a propaganda machinery more comprehensive, cohesive, and insidious than many analysts imagined. It establishes beyond any doubt that IS at its peak had one of the largest and most complex propaganda efforts ever seen in a rebel group.

Stock-taking, systematic efforts like this also have the benefit of producing an information baseline from which to explore comparative questions or higher order analytical issues, such as: Why exactly did the IS propaganda machine grow so large? Was the scale of the propaganda machinery a cause or a consequence of IS's on-the-ground expansion? Did IS propagandists possess unique creative or strategic talent, or did they merely fill the media space available to them with well-known techniques and formats? These are but some of the issues that scholars will need to examine in the years to come, and their job has been made easier by this edited volume.

As a long-time observer of jihadi media, I could not help reflect on IS's place in jihadi propaganda history. To what extent was the IS moment truly exceptional? What were its main contributions and innovations as compared with previous groups? These questions arise because, as demonstrated in this book, IS represents just the latest chapter in a very long history of militant Islamist propaganda, one that stretches back at least a century. For example, in 1912, when Izz al-Din al-Qassam recruited foreign fighters in Syria to wage *jihād* against the Italians in Libya, he relied on sermons, leaflets, and other methods of the day to mobilize fighters. Likewise, in 1948, when the Egyptian Muslim Brotherhood recruited volunteers to the war for Palestine they made use of the magazines and other available technologies. Throughout the 1950s and '60s, militant Islamist groups in Egypt and the Levant produced newsletters, poems, and *anashīd* in support of the cause. The 1970s saw the emergence of cassette-recorded sermons by hardline clerics, and in the early 1980s came the first jihadi videos. The war in Afghanistan saw a large increase in militant Islamist propaganda production, above all by the Afghan *Mujāhidīn*, but also by the Arab volunteers in Peshawar, the immediate forefathers of the contemporary jihadi movement. In the mid-1990s, jihadi propagandists began exploiting the Internet, and the 2000s saw them make very extensive use of the online domain. Against this historical backdrop, and with the various contributions of the present volume in mind, we can make a few observations about IS's propaganda efforts.

Regarding scale, it seems fair to assert that IS at its peak had the largest propaganda production—both in terms of product range and production rate—that we have ever seen from a single jihadi group or alliance of groups. This being said, the runners-up are not quite as far behind as one might assume. The closest competitor is probably the Afghan *Mujāhidīn* of the 1980s, who also produced a remarkable amount of propaganda, including over a hundred magazine titles, numerous videos, and other products which they distributed through information offices in many different countries around the world. *Mujāhidīn* propaganda has received much less attention by scholars, in part because the material was analogue and because the Afghan *Mujāhidīn* were not considered a security threat to anyone other than the Soviet troops in Afghanistan. Similarly, the Afghan Taliban has also run a very large propaganda operation since the early 2000s, one whose scale may not have been fully appreciated outside expert observer circles. Still, the scale of the IS propaganda output is little short of remarkable, as this volume demonstrates.

In terms of *formats*, IS's main distinctive feature appears not to have been innovation as such but rather its "full-spectrum" approach; that is, its use of a particularly broad range of different media types. Strictly speaking, IS appears not to have invented many new propaganda formats or platforms, if any at all. As Chapters 3 to 6 of this volume detail, most individual elements of IS's propaganda strategy were tried and tested methods used by previous jihadi groups. Islamist groups have published magazines since the early 1900s, and in the 1980s Afghan *Mujāhidīn* published over a hundred different magazine titles in multiple languages, including English, German,

French, Turkish, and Danish. Most of the other formats, such as films, books, statements, poems, and *anashīd* have been staples of jihadi propaganda since at least the 1980s. Similarly, jihadi groups had been at the forefront of rebel exploitation of the digital domain long before the heyday of IS. For all their backward-looking theology, jihadis were never luddites; they have always been highly pragmatic and opportunistic in their exploitation of technology and new media.

This is not to say that IS propagandists were pure imitators. For example, they were probably the first transnational jihadi group to make extensive use of radio. They also made more use of memes and infographs than their predecessors. Perhaps more significantly, they developed and improved—not to say perfected—several existing propaganda formats. For example, IS took video production to a whole new level of production quality as compared with its predecessors. Similarly, they perfected the genre of the "glossy jihadi magazine," first introduced with al-Qaeda's *Inspire* magazine around 2010. Last, but not least, IS displayed considerable creativity and innovation in the domain of distribution technologies, where its programmers developed Twitter bots, mobile apps, and other tools that allowed for the projection of propaganda products to large audiences. On the whole, however, it seems fair to say that IS was more of an incremental improver (see Chapter 8) than a radical innovator in the propaganda domain.

The same is arguably true of the *content* of IS propaganda. In terms of messaging and visual themes, there are clear lines of continuity between the propaganda of IS and that of previous groups, especially al-Qaeda and its affiliates. This is not surprising given that they share the same basic ideology and used to be part of the same organizational franchise. Still, IS did develop a certain number of new narratives and visual themes that set it apart from the jihadi propaganda of the 2000s. The most significant was probably what we might call "the showcasing of the perfect state," that is, the various films (cf., the "utopian script" described in Chapter 4), pictures (cf., magazines' visual depiction of the Caliphate analyzed in Chapter 3), and other items that showed aspects of life and governance in the Caliphate. This visual theme was part of a broader message of strength and self-confidence that was relatively new in the history of jihadi propaganda. While most jihadi groups in the 1990s and 2000s conveyed a message of Muslim weakness and victimhood by relentlessly highlighting the suffering of Muslims around the world, IS portrayed Muslims in a position of strength and superiority. A second distinctive feature was that of the "grisly execution," represented by the many films and pictures showing prisoners being put to death in particularly creative and sadistic ways. Previous jihadi groups had also committed atrocities and occasionally showcased them on video, but IS took goriness to a whole new level, shocking an entire world in the process (again consider the analysis carried out in Chapters 3 and 4). A third feature of IS messaging was the extensive borrowing of visual themes from Western popular culture. While the iconographic influence of Hollywood and the gaming industry were starting to show in al-Qaeda propaganda in the 2000s, IS took the emulation of Western pop culture several steps further. Pop culture visual themes appear to have been used primarily in propaganda products destined for Western consumption, as part of IS's sophisticated strategy of tailoring its propaganda products to different regions and audiences.

Overall, this back-of-the-envelope assessment would seem to attenuate ever so slightly the view of IS as an exceptional propaganda producer. In a longer historical perspective, the group appears as more of an incremental than a radical innovator in the propaganda domain. Both in terms of formats and themes, IS represented an extension of a long tradition of Islamist and jihadi propaganda. The group's primary distinctive feature seems to have been the sheer scale of its operation and the technical sophistication to which it took existing propaganda elements. This is not to suggest that the significance of the IS moment has been overrated, for it is by no means a given that creativity is better than scale; as the famous saying goes, "quantity has a quality all its own."

One question remains: Why was IS able to build such a large propaganda system? Two key reasons stand out. One is that IS simply was an unusually large and resourceful organization. After its capture of much of Western Iraq and establishment of a Caliphate in mid-2014, IS ran a veritable proto-state with vast resources to invest in propaganda production. To be sure, IS had a significant propaganda operation prior to the 2014 advance, but it was only afterward that it grew to the behemoth portrayed in this book. Indeed, it is a very real question for debate whether IS propaganda was a consequence or a cause of the key battlefield advances of 2014. A plausible argument can be made that the proto-state made the propaganda giant more than the other way around. In any case, at its high point in 2015, the IS propaganda system enjoyed a very high level of resources.

A second key factor behind the scale of the IS propaganda system was probably what I have called the "jihadist digital empowerment revolution." In the early 2010s, a series of technological and political developments combined to provide jihadi groups with access to much more powerful distribution and communication tools than they had previously enjoyed. In the late 2000s, jihadi groups had been constrained in their online propaganda activities by weak distribution platforms and a high risk of detection. This changed drastically in the early 2010s with the advent of social media, which not only offered much more powerful distribution but also a much lower risk of detection and arrest by authorities. Jihadi groups readily seized these new opportunities to expand their online propaganda activities. IS leveraged these opportunities more than other groups, in part because it had a long history of online propaganda production and because it enjoyed battlefield advances that offered material resources and political momentum.

Territory and technology thus seem to have been key to the scale of the IS propaganda system. If accurate, this insight has both a positive and a negative implication. On the one hand, it suggests that the IS propaganda operation grew big not due to some "evil genius" factor but for exogenous material reasons. It follows that if those material prerequisites are weakened or removed, then IS's propaganda operation is likely to suffer. That is indeed what appears to have happened since 2016: IS has been pushed back militarily in Iraq and Syria, and its ability to distribute propaganda has been curtailed by aggressive policing of jihadi Internet content. The result has so far been a significant reduction in the scale of IS propaganda, although it is still significant by the standards of the late 2000s or early 2010s.

On the other hand, if IS was not uniquely creative, then a similar phenomenon can reemerge under the right circumstances. The history of jihadism suggests that groups will exploit to the fullest extent whatever operating space and technological opportunities are provided to them. The "IS moment" is an example of what may happen when a radical group gets the space and the tools to produce propaganda almost undisturbed. A repeat of this phenomenon may seem unlikely right now, but both technology and conflict are notoriously hard to predict. Thanks to this book, we are now significantly better prepared for the next major moment in jihadi—or more generally extremist—propaganda history.

APPENDIX 1

List of *Anashīd* Produced by the Islamic State (February 2013–March 2017)

Title (in English)	Language	Release date
The Sword of Death	Arabic	Mar. 3, 2017
I Don't Care	Arabic	Feb. 6, 2017
We Came with Knives	Arabic	Jan. 21, 2017
Show the Flame	Arabic	Jan. 13, 2017
It Has Begun	Arabic	Dec. 15, 2016
The Eternal Ones	French	Nov. 16, 2016
Caravan of the Light	Arabic	Oct. 24, 2016
The Light of Shari'a	Bengali	Sept. 26, 2016
Millat Ibrahim	Uyghur	Aug. 22, 2016
Rejoice, Oh Muslims!	Turkish	Aug. 10, 2016
When War Erupts, We March to It	Arabic	Jul. 17, 2016
al-Hamdulillah	Arabic	Jul. 6, 2016
My Revenge	French	Jul. 5, 2016
Rise up, Oh Mujahid	Bengali	Jul. 3, 2016
Banner of the Eagle	Turkish	Jun. 8, 2016
Come Up!	Turkish	May 23, 2016
In the Way of God	Arabic	May 8, 2016
Blood for Blood	French	Apr. 29, 2016
Make Takbir, Oh Monotheist	Uyghur	Apr. 1, 2016
Establishment of the Caliphate	Urdu	Mar. 14, 2016
Mushtera	Arabic	Feb. 26, 2016
Ateyna Afakaroba	Arabic	Feb. 22, 2016
A Mujahid's Story	Bengali	Feb. 20, 2016
Remaining, Remaining	Afghan	Feb. 10, 2016
Thankfully, the Islamic State Is Established	Afghan	Feb. 10, 2016
Brotherhood of the Caliphate	Afghan	Feb. 10, 2016
For Allah	French	Feb. 28, 2016
Ateyna	Arabic	Jan. 25, 2016
Rise of the State [The State Has Risen]	Arabic	Jan. 16, 2016
Lions of God [Allah]	Turkish	Dec. 20, 2015
Heyya Shahid	Arabic	Dec. 10, 2015
Mujahid	Chinese	Dec. 6, 2015

ISIS Propaganda. Stephane J. Baele, Katharine A. Boyd, and Travis G. Coan, Oxford University Press (2020). © University of Maryland National Consortium for the Study of Terrorism and Responses to Terrorism (START).
DOI: 10.1093/oso/9780190932459.001.0001

Title (in English)	Language	Release date
Soon, Very Soon	Russian	Nov. 12, 2015
Sing Praises, Oh Javelins	Arabic	Nov. 10, 2015
Progress, Progress	French	Oct. 31, 2015
Return of the Caliphate	Bengali	Oct. 27, 2015
Be with God	Arabic	Oct. 17, 2015
Return of the Caliphate	Indonesian, Bengali	Sept. 12, 2015
For the Sake of God [Allah]	English	Sept. 6, 2015
We Will Move Forth to Excellence	Arabic	Aug. 30, 2015
We Have Risen Up	Arabic	Aug. 5, 2015
Come, My Friend	Uyghur	Jul. 7, 2015
Our Shariah	Arabic	Jun. 29, 2015
The Path of Jihad	Turkish	Jun. 24, 2015
Come [forward], Come [forward]	Arabic	Jun. 14, 2015
We Reject to Bow Down	Arabic	May 23, 2015
God, House the Blessed Soldier	Arabic	May 22, 2015
Extend Your Hand to Pledge Allegiance	French	May 18, 2015
Oh Brother, March Forward to the Criminal	Arabic	Apr. 27, 2015
For the Sake of God	German	Apr. 14, 2015
Oh the Soul of My Soul [Fly Away]	Arabic	Apr. 8, 2015
Oh Sons of Yemen	Arabic	Mar. 24, 2015
Descendants of the Caliphate	Kurdish	Mar. 23, 2015
Fortified Place and Patience [Be Garrisoned and Patient]	Arabic	Mar. 14, 2015
We Will Not be Beaten Down	French	Mar. 14, 2015
We Came as Soldiers for Allah [of God]	Arabic	Feb. 22, 2015
Hold Out Your Hand	French	Feb. 17, 2015
Soon, Soon	Arabic	Feb. 4, 2015
The Land of Sinai	Arabic	Jan. 16, 2015
Oh My Lord I Ask You	Arabic	Dec. 13, 2014
Our State Is Victorious	German	Dec. 9, 2014
The Path Is No Longer Restricted	Arabic	Dec.?, 2014
Shari'a of Our Lord Is Light	Arabic	Nov. 22, 2014
Our Resolve	Arabic	Nov.?, 2014
Oh Brother, Inform the Companions	Arabic	Oct. 1, 2014
We have the Sharp Swords	Arabic	Sept. 24, 2014
Say Allahu Akhbar	Arabic	Sept.?, 2014
Al-Maliki Is Vanquished	Arabic	Aug. 16, 2014
Hands Stretched in Your Bay'ah [Pledging Allegiance] to the Imam	Arabic	Jun. 29, 2014
Let's Go for al-Jihad	German	Jun. 15, 2014

Title (in English)	Language	Release date
Clanging of the Swords, Nasheed of the Defiant	Arabic	Jun.?, 2014
Soldiers of the Just Cause [Truth], Let's Go!	Arabic	Jun. 2, 2014
The Regiment of My Islamic State	Arabic	May 29, 2014
My Brother Talked About the Sahabah	Arabic	May 21, 2014
Oh Victory in Obtaining Martyrdom	Arabic	Apr. 30, 2014
The Life of Humiliation Is Not Acceptable	Arabic	Apr. 23, 2014
Lions of the Battle	Arabic	Apr. 15, 2014
Dogs of the Emergency	Arabic	Apr. 11, 2014
Oh Qadi [Judge] of the Tyrant	Arabic	Mar. 27, 2014
Martyrdom Is My Demand All the Time	Arabic	Mar. 13, 2014
Why Bowing	Arabic	Feb. 19, 2014
Sharp in My Struggle	Arabic	Jan. 31, 2014
Emir Al Baghdadi	Arabic	Jan. 15, 2014
My Ummah, Dawn Has Appeared	Arabic	Dec. 4, 2013
My Dear Mother	Arabic	Nov. 24, 2013
Ya Dawlatel	Arabic	Nov. 20, 2013
Oh Islamic State, You Are the Light of the Religion	Arabic	Nov.?, 2013
Oh Islamic State, My Love, My People	Arabic	Nov. 13, 2013
To the Front, Advance	Arabic	Nov. 8, 2013
Victory Does Not Come with Tweets	Arabic	Nov. 4, 2013
How Bad the Mention [News] of My Return to Saudi Arabia	Arabic	Oct. 25, 2013
Oh Our State, Move Forward	Arabic	Oct. 12, 2013
My Ummah Was Not Satisfied with Weakness	Arabic	Oct. 10, 2013
Peace to the Lions of the Islamic State	Arabic	Sept. 31, 2013
Overshadowed by Cowards	Arabic	Sept. 16, 2013
Be Like What They Were	Arabic	Sept. 8, 2013
They Have Closed Ranks and Pledged Bay'ah to Baghdadi	Arabic	Sept. 3, 2013
Oh My Wounded	Arabic	Sept.?, 2013
Eulogy for the Martyrs of Mannagh	Arabic	Aug. 29, 2013
Voice of the Prisoners	Arabic	Aug. 20, 2013
My Right Hand Is On the Button	Arabic	Aug.?, 2013
Qam Alilislam	Arabic	Mar. 25, 2013
The Good Spring	Arabic	Feb. 19, 2013

APPENDIX 2

Example of a Provincial News Report from Al-Bayan Radio [Excerpts]

1/6/2015 (Monday 14th of Sha'bān 1436ّ.)
Jun 2 1/6/2015 (Monday 14th of Sha'bān 1436ّ.)
Assalāmu 'Alaykum Wa Rahmatullāhi Wa Barakātuh. We thank our listeners for tuning in and present the following Islamic State news bulletin for Monday, the 14th of Sha'bān in the year 1436 of the prophetic hijrah.
The following is a glimpse at our main headlines:

- The soldiers of the Khilāfah take complete control of the strategic city of Sawrān near I'zāz, and dozens of Sahwah fighters are killed in Wilāyat Halab.
- An istishhādī attack on a Nusayrī checkpoint west of the city of al-Barakah in Wilāyat al-Barakah.
- An istishhādī attack targets Fajr Libya fighters at the Dafniyyah gate located between Misrātah and Zulaytin in Wilāyat Tarābulus.

Wilāyat Halab:

- The soldiers of the Khilāfah took complete control of the strategic city of Sawrān near I'zāz, killed dozens of Sahwah fighters, and captured various weapons and ammo as ghanīmah, walhamdulillāh.
- The mujāhidīn likewise repelled an attempted advance by PKK murtaddīn back by crusader coalition warplanes from the direction south of 'Ayn al-Islam.

Wilāyat al-Barakah:

- Our brother Abū 'Alī al-Urdunī carried out an istishhādī operation targeting the Mujayyīr checkpoint near the 122nd Regiment northwest of the city. He detonated his explosive vehicle at the checkpoint, killing and wounding dozens of murtaddīn. May Allah accept him amongst the shuhadā'.
- The soldiers of the Khilāfah likewise targeted PKK murtaddīn in the villages of al-Huwaysh and an-Nawfaliyyah in the southern countryside of Tal Hamīs with heavy machine guns and mortar rounds.

[...]

Wilāyat Salāhuddīn:

- The soldiers of the Khilāfah detonated two homes near the area of al-Mazra'ah south of the city of Bījī, targeting a gathering of Safawī soldiers and a group of Rāfidī Mobilization fighters after they entered inside. The explosions led to several of them being killed, and the mujāhidīn also captured two murtaddīn as prisoners. This was during the course of their attempted advance towards.

ISIS Propaganda. Stephane J. Baele, Katharine A. Boyd, and Travis G. Coan, Oxford University Press (2020). © University of Maryland National Consortium for the Study of Terrorism and Responses to Terrorism (START).
DOI: 10.1093/oso/9780190932459.001.0001

- The mujāhidīn likewise detonated an IED, damaging an emergency vehicle carrying dead Safawiyyīn on the highway near the region of al-Huwaysh north of the city of Sāmurrā'.
- Near the same region, Islamic State snipers shot two Rāfidī Mobilization fighters.
- Also near the region of al-Huwaysh, an IED was detonated on the highway between Sāmurrā' and Tikrīt, damaging two Rāfidī Mobilization vehicles, and killing and wounding those inside.
- West of the city of Tikrīt, a Safawī-crusader coalition drone was shot down by Islamic State antiaircraft guns.
- The mujāhidīn also burned a tank west of the city of Bījī after targeting it with a Kornet missile.

[...]

Wilāyat al-Fallūjah:

- Safawī-crusader coalition warplanes bombed Masjid Shākir ad-Dāhī, and commercial buildings in the Fallūjah market, which resulted in several Muslims, including children, being killed and injured, and led to extensive damage to Muslim property.

In closing, we cap off with a review of our main headlines once again:

- The soldiers of the Khilāfah take complete control of the strategic city of Sawrān near I'zāz, and dozens of Sahwah fighters are killed in Wilāyat Halab.
- An istishhādī attack on a Nusayrī checkpoint west of the city of al-Barakah in Wilāyat al-Barakah.
- An istishhādī attack targets Fajr Libya fighters at the Dafniyyah gate located between Misrātah and Zulaytin in Wilāyat Tarābulus.

We thank our listeners for tuning in. *Wassalāmu 'alaykum wa rahmatullāhi wa barakātuh.*

Index

Page numbers followed by *t* or *f* refer to tables and figures on respective pages.

Afghanistan War, 65, 267
aftermath type of war video
    script, 147
agitation propaganda, 5
Ahl al Hadith movement, 60
Ajnad Foundation, 191, 191*f*
al-Adel, Sayf, 39–40
al-Adnani, Abu Mohammad, 23, 29, 33,
    33–34, 55
al-Albani, Nasr dine, 60
al-Anbari, Abu Ali, 66, 75
al-Baghdadi, Abu Bakr, 26, 29, 39, 73
al-Baghdadi, Abu Umar, 69–71
al-Banna, Hassan, 58, 76
al-Battar Media Foundation, 135, 135*f*
al-Bayan Radio, 212–213, 213*f*, 275–276
al-Duri, Izzat Ibrahim, 66
al-Furat Media Center, 133*f*
al-Furqan Media, 135, 132*f*
al-Ghuraba Media, 135
al-Ḥākimiyya (divine sovereignty), 58–59
Al-Hayat Media Center, 86–88, 131, 132*f*
al-Hazimi, Ahmad, 79
Al-Himma Library
    books produced by, 205–211, 206*f*
    media doctrine, 37–38
    "Media Operative, You Are Also a
        Mujahid", 24–25, 27, 28, 29, 43–44
    strategic messaging, 34–35
Ali, Turki Bin, 80
Al-I'tisam Media, 131, 132*f*
al-I'tisam Twitter account, 173
al-Jāhiliyya (ignorance), 58–59
al-Jamaa al-Salafiyya al-Muhtasiba (JSM),
    60–61
al-Jolani, Abu Muhammad, 73
al-Khayr Media Center, 133*f*
al-Maqdisi, Abu Mohamed
    and al-Zarqawi, dispute between, 67–69
    emergence of, 61–63

al-Maqdisi, Abu Ya'qub, 80–81
al-Masri, Abu Ayyub, 206
al-Muhajir, Abu Abdullah, 67–69
al-Muhajir, Abu Hamza, 71, 206
al-Naba' magazine
    al-Bayan Radio program
        advertisements, 213*f*
    general discussion, 86, 87*f*, 89*t*
    infographics in, 200–202, 201*f*, 202*f*
al-Noori Mosque, 20
al-Nusra, 73–74
Al-Otaybi, Juhayman, 60–63
Alphabet, counter extremism initiatives
    by, 222–223
al-Qaeda
    break with IS, 69, 72–75
    enemies of, 74
    magazines produced by, 84
    martyr biographies, 209
    message video script used by, 143*f*
    poetry, production of, 206, 208
    social media presence of, 156
    use of Internet, 161
al-Qahtani, Mohamed, 61
al-Qassam, Izz al-Din, 266
al-Salool, 72
al-Saud, Abd al-Aziz, 56
al-Suri, Abu Khalid, 73
al-Suri, Abu Mosab, 73–74
Although the Disbelievers Dislike It (video),
    140
al-Wahhab, Mohamed Ibn
    Abd, 53–54, 72
al-Walā' wa al-Barā'
    Abu Mohamed al-Maqdisi and, 61
    as defining feature of Salafi-jihadi, 52
    IS interpretation of, 78, 256
    JSM and, 60
    in Wahhabism, 54–55, 77
al-Waqār magazine, 86, 89*t*

al-Zarqawi, Abu Mosab
    aggravation of sectarian tensions, 27–28
    and al-Maqdisi, dispute between, 67–69
    al-Muhajir, influence on, 67–68
    anti-Shi'a hatred, 67
    influence of, 67–69
    move to Iraq, 39–40, 65–66
    Tawhid Group, 62
"Al-Zarqawi: Advocacy and Advice, Hopes
        and Pains" (*Al-Zarqawi: Munasara
        wa Munasaha, Aamaal wa Aalaam*)
        (al-Maqdisi), 68
al-Zawahiri, Ayman, 65, 72, 73
A'maq News Agency, 202, 213–214, 213*f*
anashīd (religious chants), 190–196
    Ajnad Foundation, 192, 192*f*
    chronological distributions of, 193, 194*f*
    languages used in, 192–193
    list of, 271–273
    overview, 189
    reasons behind production of, 193–194
    stand-alone, 191–192, 192*f*
    themes in, 191–196
    in videos, 191
"And the Best Outcome is for the
        Righteous" video series, 40
Ansar al-Khilafah Media, 205, 207*f*
apocalypticism, 71–72
'aqida (creed), 53
Arabic magazines. *See* magazines
armed soldiers, magazine images of,
        113–114
audiences, decreasing effect of propaganda
        on, 230–231
audio releases, 36*t*
avatars of media *mujahidin*, 176, 176*t*
Azzam, Abdullah, 53–65

baiting strategy, 31
Baqiyya ("Remaining!") slogan, 50–51
bara, 54–55, 61–62
barricading, 69
BBC, 140
beheadings, 68, 128, 172
Berger, J. M., 177–178
Bhui, K., 123
binary group language, in magazines,
        99–104, 123
Bin Ladin, Osama, 65, 72
biographies of martyrs, 209–211, 210*f*
black flag

    in infographics, 203
    in magazines, 97–98, 98*f*
    in videos, 142
black propaganda, 5
books, 205–211
    martyr biographies, 209–211, 210*f*
    overview, 189
    poetry, 206–209
    religious, 205–206, 207*f*
boom periods, strategic messaging during,
        32–35, 32*t*, 44
branding, 38–40, 164–165
brand reputation, 38–39
brutal punishment
    magazine images of, 114–116
    video script, 144–146
bureaucratic propaganda, 5
business management, insights on
        innovation from, 248–250
bust periods, strategic messaging during,
        32–35, 32*t*, 44

Caliphate
    establishment of, 76, 78
    magazine images of, 120–122
    magazine language describing, 116–120
    in social media, 174
    utopian video script, 143–144, 144*f*,
        151–152
campaign strategy, 22–29
    central role of propaganda in, 23–24
    competitive system of control, 22
    competitive system of meaning, 24–28
    identity-choice appeals, 26–27
    phases of, 22–23
    rational-choice appeals, 25–26, 27
Cares and Pains (al-Masri), 206, 208*f*
central media offices, 131–132, 132*f*
    amount of videos produced by, 137–
        138, 138*f*
    variation of production across time,
        138–140, 140*f*
central narrative of propaganda, 25, 38
chat forums, 161–162, 163
children, care of under Caliphate, 120,
        121*f*
child soldiers, 113
civilian populations, using as shield, 69
clicktivism, 158–159
cognitive shortcuts, 3
cohesiveness of propaganda, 4, 21, 38–44

branding, 38–40
organizational architecture, 41–44
collusion between out-groups, magazine
    images of, 107–108, 108f
communications campaign, countering
    propaganda with, 228–229
    content of, 231–234
    measuring effect of, 236–237
    media types and formats for, 234–236
    realistic objectives, need for, 229–230
    target audiences, increasing resilience
        of, 230–31
communications science, insights on
    innovation from, 244–246
communication styles, diffusion of, 245
communication technologies, innovation
    in, 245
community support, innovation and, 257
competitive system of control, 22, 28
competitive system of meaning, 24–28,
    32, 37
comprehensiveness of propaganda, 4, 21,
    35–38
connected content creators, 162, 182
contagion effect, 247
content of communications campaign,
    231–234
continuity in propaganda, 5–8
control, competitive system of, 22, 28
co-occurrence network of language in
    magazines, 94–95, 94f
core Wilāyāt media offices
    amount of videos produced by, 137–
        138, 138f
    locations of, 133t, 134f
    "Selected 10" video productions, 149–
        152, 150f
    variation of production across time,
        138–140, 139f
    video production in, 132–133
correspondence analysis of magazines,
    95–96, 96f
countering propaganda
    content of communications campaign,
        231–234
    engaging and competing with IS,
        228–229
    exploiting propaganda for intelligence
        and evidence, 226–228
    freedom of speech dilemma, 223–225
    measuring effect of campaign, 236–237

media as accidental amplifier, 225–226
    media types and formats for, 234–236
    overview, 219–220
    realistic objectives, need for, 229–230
    safe space, denying, 220–222
    safe space, problems with shutting
        down, 222–223
    target audiences, increasing resilience
        of, 230–231
counterpropaganda, 5
counterterrorism measures
    effect on innovation, 257
    on social media, 159, 181–182
counterterrorist/countering violent
    extremist (CT-CVE) strategic
    communication efforts, 45–46
creativity
    business management, insights from,
        248–250
    communications science, insights from,
        244–246
    environmental-level variables, 256–257
    organizational-level variables, 253–257
    organizational psychology, insights
        from, 248–250
    overview, 243–245
    terrorism studies, insights from,
        242–249
creed ('aqida), 53
crisis–solution narratives
    general discussion, 26–28
    in magazine imagery, 96–99
    in magazine language, 91–96
crusaders, 95, 101, 104, 123
CT-CVE (counterterrorist/countering
    violent extremist) strategic
    communication efforts, 45–46

Dabiq, Syria, 77–78
Dabiq magazine
    crisis–solution master narrative in,
        94–99
    descriptive information for, 89t
    "From Hijrah to Khilafah", 22–23
    front cover of, 90f
    hedging approach, themes used in, 33
    idyllic Caliphate, images showing,
        120–122, 121f
    idyllic Caliphate, language describing,
        117–120
    images of black flag in, 98

Dabiq magazine (*Cond.*)
  in-group/out-group constructs, images
    of, 102*f*, 105–109
  in-group/out-group constructs,
    language describing, 99–104
  ISN compared to, 89
  last issue of, 88
  Muslim Brotherhood in, 75–76
  production of, 87
  punishment of out-group, images of,
    113–116
  punishment of out-group, language
    describing, 109–113
  Saudi hypocrisy portrayed in, 61, 62*f*
  "Selected 10" videos, 43, 90, 149–152
  symbolic imagery in, 98, 99
  words and images per page, 92–93, 93*f*
Dār al-Ḥarb, 56, 68
Dar al-Islam, 56, 119–120
Dar al-Islam magazine, 88, 89*t*, 90*f*, 98
da'wa, 163, 180, 205–206
*Defense of Muslim Lands (al-Dafa'a 'an Ard
  al-Muslimin), The* (Azzam), 64
dehumanization of out-group, 123
deity, theological conceptions of, 59
Department of Defense (DoD)-branded
    Twitter accounts, 235
dezinformatsiya, in Russia, 234
dichotomous worldview, 26–28
disinformation propaganda, 5
DoD (Department of Defense)-branded
    Twitter accounts, 235
Dolnik, A., 246
drug trafficking, magazine images of,
    105–106, 107*f*

echo chambers, online, 163
efficacy of propaganda, group reflection
    on, 42
Egypt, emergence of Muslim Brotherhood
    in, 58
emotional impact of propaganda, 190, 196,
    198–199
End of Sykes-Picot, The (video), 70, 70f
enemies
  global, emergence of concept of, 58
  of IS versus al-Qaeda, 74
  near, focus on, 67

environmental-level variables of creativity,
    256–257
eschatology, 71–72, 74, 77–78
evidence, exploiting propaganda for, 226–228
excommunication. *See takfir*
executions
  in magazines, images of, 114–116
  in magazines, language describing,
    111–112
  in social media output, 173–174
  in video scripts, 144–146, 146*f*
expertise, importance in leader
    performance, 254
exploiting propaganda for intelligence and
    evidence, 226–228
external agencies, innovation due to, 256

Facebook, 224
"Faith Campaign" in Iraq, 66
fake Muslim scholars, 107–108, 109*f*
films. *See* videos
fiqh texts, 205–206
flags, 40, 97–98, 98*f*, 142, 203
Flames of War (film), 25–26
focoism, 27
foreign fighters, recruitment of, 34
freedom of speech dilemma, 223–225
Free Syria Media, 31
"From Hijrah to Khilafah" (*Dabiq*
    magazine), 22–23
full-spectrum propaganda, 189,
    219–220
  cohesiveness of, 38–44
  comprehensiveness of, 35–38
  efficacy of, reflection on, 42
  general discussion, 2–5
  impact of, 11–13
  IS moment, 5–8
  misconceptions, dissolving, 8–9
  multidimensionality of, 30–35
  uniting literature on, 9–10

global enemy, emergence of concept of, 58
global jihadism, 65
Goodall, H. L., Jr., 93
Google, counter extremism initiatives by,
    222–223
grotesque propaganda, 7

ground truth, 157–158
group cohesion, effect of perceived threats on, 123
gruesome images
    in magazines, 7, 114–116
    punishment video script, 143–146, 146*f*
    on social media, 173–174
Guantanamo jumpsuit, 99, 147
guerrilla warfare, 27

Ḥākimiyya, 58–59
Hamas hymns, 195, 197
Hanbali theological school, 57
hashtags, use of, 172
hate propaganda, 5
hate speech, countering online, 224
hatred of out-groups, magazine propaganda facilitating, 123
Hazimis, 79
healthcare system, under Caliphate, 117, 121*f*
hedging strategy, 32–35, 32*t*, 170–171
hijrah, mentions in magazines of, 118–119, 118*f*
Hussein, Saddam, 66
hypocrisy of Saudi state, 61–63, 62*f*

Ibn Taymiyyah, Taqi ad-Din Ahmad, 53, 55
Ibrahim, Y., 123
ideology, 50–81
    al-Muhajir, influence of, 67–69
    al-Zarqawi, influence of, 67–69
    countering, realistic objectives in, 229–230
    establishment of ISI, 69–72
    future of, 76–81
    genealogy of Salafi-jihadism, 52–65
    Iraq as incubator for, 65–67
    leadership of Salafi-jihadism, battle for, 72–76
    maturation of, 69–72
    resilience, 50–51
    rise of IS, 52–65
identity-choice appeals, 26–27
identity opportunities, 167–168
idyllic Islamic Caliphate
    magazine images promoting, 120–122
    magazine language promoting, 116–120

in social media, 174
    video script, 143–144, 144*f*, 151–152
Ikhwan, 56, 58
imagery in magazines
    crisis–solution master narrative, 95–99, 97*f*
    of idyllic Islamic Caliphate, 120–122, 121*f*, 122*f*
    in-group/out-group constructs, 105–109
    punishment of out-groups, 113–116
imitation
    after IS, 257–259
    in IS, 250–252
    overview, 243–244
incremental innovation, 250, 251
infographics, 200–205, 201*f*
    defined, 200
    in IS magazines, 200–201, 201*f*, 202*f*
    numerical information in, 204
    overview, 189
    symbolic imagery in, 203, 204*f*
in-group identity constructs, 26–28
    countering propaganda, 231–233
    in magazine imagery, 105–109
    in magazine language, 99–104
innovation
    business management, insights from, 248–250
    communications science, insights from, 244–246
    culture of, 42–43
    environmental-level variables of creativity, 256–257
    incremental, 250, 251
    after IS, 257–259
    in IS, 5–8, 250–252
    organizational-level variables of creativity, 252–256
    organizational process, 246
    organizational psychology, insights from, 249–251
    overview, 243–245, 244–245
    radical, 251, 252
    strategic, 247
    tactical, 247
    terrorism studies, insights from, 247–249

Inside the Caliphate series, 34
instrumental opportunities, 165–166
integration propaganda, 5
intelligence, exploiting propaganda for, 226–228
intergroup conflict, 103
internal dissidence, 79–81
Internet. *See also* social media
　anashīd on, 194
　exploiting propaganda for intelligence and evidence, 226–228
　freedom of speech dilemma, 223–225
　jihadist digital empowerment revolution, 270–271
　magazine production, effect on, 84–85
　media as accidental amplifier, 225–226
　online jihadism, background of, 161
　resources needed for sharing propaganda over, 4
　safe space, denying, 220–223
Iraq, as incubator for ideology, 65–67
Iraq–Iran war, 66
Iraq War (2002), 6
ISI (Islamic State of Iraq), 69–72
Islam, books related to practice of, 205–206, 207*f*
Islamic State (IS)
　al-Qaeda, break with, 72–75
　branding, 38–40
　establishment of ISI, 69–72
　formation of, 73
　hedging strategy, 32–35, 32*t*
　internal dissidence, 79–81
　jihād as central to, 64–65
　maturation of ideology, 69–72
　name changes, 39–40
　quantity of propaganda outputs, 1–2
　rise of ideology, 65–67
　takfīr concept, 62
　as true inheritor of Islamic tradition, 72
Islamic State News (*ISN*), 89, 91*f*
Islamic State of Iraq (ISI), 69–72
Islamic State Report (*ISR*), 23, 89
Islamism, 52
islamization of radicalism, 12
Issues in the Jurisprudence of Jihad (Masa'il fi Fiqh al-Jihad) (al-Muhajir), 67

istishhad video script, 147–149, 148*f*, 151–152
Istok magazine, 89*t*, 90*f*

Jāhiliyya (ignorance), 58–59, 65
Jigsaw, counter extremism initiatives by, 222–223
jihād
　al-Suri methodology, 74
　Azzam, theorization of, 63
　basic meaning of, 63
　as compulsory duty, 65, 70
　global jihadism, 65
　magazine images of, 113–114
　media as, 24
　online jihadism, background of, 160–164
jihadi culture, 214
jihadist digital empowerment revolution, 269–270
jihadologists, 12
jizya, 68
JSM (*al-Jamaa al-Salafiyya al-Muhtasiba*), 60–61
"Just Terror Tactic" articles, *Rumiyah* magazine, 123–124

khawarij, 56, 69
Konstantiniyye magazine, 88, 89*t*, 90*f*
kuffar, 25–26

LaFree, G., 247
Lahoud, N., 79
Lakomy, M., 249, 254, 255
language in magazines
　crisis–solution master narrative, 94–95, 94*f*
　idyllic Islamic Caliphate, descriptions of, 116–120
　in-group/out-group constructs, 99–104
　punishment of out-groups, 109–113
leadership, role in innovation, 253–254
learning dynamics, 247
legitimacy, reinforcement of, 190, 196
linkage based approach, 232
literature, 205–211
　martyr biographies, 209–211, 210*f*
　poetry, 206–209

related to practice of Islam, 205–206, 207f
lone-actor terrorism, 31, 34, 74

magazines, 7, 36t. *See also specific magazines*
in context, 84–86
crisis–solution narratives in, images of, 96–99
crisis–solution narratives in, language describing, 91–96
idyllic Islamic Caliphate in, imagery promoting, 120–122
idyllic Islamic Caliphate in, language promoting, 116–120
in-group/out-group constructs in, images of, 105–109
in-group/out-group constructs in, language describing, 99–104
mechanisms of radicalization in, 121–123
punishment of out-group, images of, 113–116
punishment of out-group, language describing, 109–113
range of audiences reached by, 86–91
Mahdī, 61, 71–72
Manchester Arena terrorist attack, 155–156
manhaj
Ahl al Hadith movement, 60
in politico-military campaign strategy, 22–23, 26, 27, 28
Qutb versus IS, 59
"Mardin Fatwa", 53
martyrdom
istishhad video script, 147–149, 148f, 151–152
in magazines, 111, 112f, 114, 115f
martyr biographies, 209–211, 210f
master narrative, 94–99
meaning, competitive system of, 24–28, 32, 37
media as accidental amplifier, 225–226
media *mujāhidīn*
exploitation of social media, 169
identity needs, 166–167
instrumental needs, 166
outsourcing to, 156

recruiting messages, 170
role of, 164–165
roles within, 159
self-sustainability of, 162
social identity, 167–168
Telegram, use of, 179–180
on Twitter, collective behaviors of, 173–177, 175f
on Twitter, propagation of media through, 172–173
on Twitter, suspensions from, 177, 178
"Media Operative, You Are Also a Mujahid", 24–25, 28, 43–44, 163
media personnel, treatment of, 165, 253
media points, 31, 32, 212
media trap, 31
media types and formats for countering propaganda, 234–236
message. *See* ideology
message script in videos, 142–143, 143f, 151–152
messianic revolt, 60–61
metacommunities, online, 182
Milestones (Maʾaalim fi al-Tareeq) (Qutb), 58–59
military training of youth, promotion of, 112–113
miracles, in martyr biographies, 210
misconceptions about IS propaganda, 8–9
Mongols, 53
mortality salience, 173
Mosul, Iraq, 23, 30, 78, 171
movies. *See* videos
Mujaddid, 72
Mujāhidīn, Afghan, 84, 268
Mujāhidīn, media. *See* media *mujāhidīn*
multidimensionality of propaganda, 5, 21, 30–35
multiphase messaging strategy, 24
music. *See anashīd* (religious chants)
Muslim Brotherhood, 58, 75–76, 268

Naji, Abu Bakr, 74
name changes of IS, 39–40
nashīd. See anashīd
nawazil, 68
Nazi propaganda, 6, 7, 229–230

near enemies, 67
netwar, 178–179
news programs, 189, 212–214
nihilists, 12
novelty value of creative acts, 249
numerical information, in infographics, 204

Occupy Wall Street movement, 156
online echo chambers, 163
online jihadism, background of, 160–163
operational messaging, 30–32
orange jumpsuit, 99, 146
organizational architecture of propaganda, 41–44
organizational-level variables of creativity, 252–256
organizational process innovation, 246
organizational psychology, insights on innovation from, 248–250
out-group identity constructs, 26–28
    countering propaganda, 231–233
    hatred, role of magazine propaganda in, 123
    in magazines, images of, 105–109
    in magazines, language describing, 99–104
    punishment of, magazine images of, 113–116
    punishment of, magazine language describing, 109–113
Overton window, 128

patriarchal themes, in magazines, 119–120
"People of the Hadith" (*Ahl al Hadith*), 60
peripheral *Wilāyāt* media offices
    amount of videos produced by, 138*f*
    locations of, 134*t*
    "Selected 10" video productions, 149–152, 150*f*
    variation of production across time, 138–140, 139*f*
    video production in, 132–133
photo reports, 189, 199–200, 198*f*
physical symbols, 40
plagarism in propaganda, 5–8
pledge of allegiance, 65
poetry, 206–209

politico-military campaign strategy, 22–29
    central role of propaganda in, 23–24
    competitive system of control, 22
    competitive system of meaning, 24–28
    identity-choice appeals, 26–27
    phases of, 22–23
    rational-choice appeals, 25–26, 27
populist communication style, 245
posters, 36*t*
power of images, 197–198
printed word, 36*t*
propaganda of the deed, 5
provincial media centers, 132–133, 133*f*, 134*t*, 165
punishment of out-groups
    in magazines, images of, 113–116
    in magazines, language describing, 109–113
    video script, 144–146, 146*f*, 151–152

quality of videos, 140, 255
quantative information, backing up political narratives with, 205
Qutb, Sayyid, 58–60

radical innovation, 250, 251
radicalization
    islamization of radicalism, 12
    recruiting messages, 34, 123, 230–231
    "reverse", 128
    risk and status mechanism of, 123
    target audiences, decreasing effect of propaganda on, 230–231
    through magazines, 122–124
radio programming, 36*t*, 212–214, 276–277
rational-choice appeals, 25–26, 27
realistic objectives in countering propaganda, need for, 229–230
recruiting messages, 34, 123, 230–231
relational opportunities, 168
Religion of Abraham (Millat Ibrahim) (al-Maqdisi), 61–62
religious books, 205–206, 27*f*
religious chants (*anashīd*), 190–196
    Ajnad Foundation, 190, 191*f*
    chronological distributions of, 192, 193*f*
    languages used in, 192–193

list of, 272–277
overview, 189
reasons behind production of, 193–194
stand-alone, 191–192 192*f*
themes in, 195–196
in videos, 191
"Remaining!" (*Baqiyya*) slogan, 50–51
resilience, 50–51
"reverse" radicalization, 128
Rida, Rashid, 57–58
risk and status mechanism of
radicalization, 123
Rumiyah magazine, 30
advertisements in, 92*f*
columns with terrorist attack
instructions, 123–124
creation of, 88
crisis–solution master narrative in,
94–99
descriptive information for, 89*t*
front cover of, 90*f*
idyllic Caliphate, images showing,
120–122, 120*f*
idyllic Caliphate, language describing,
117–120
infographics in, 201
in-group/out-group constructs, images
of, 102*f*, 105–109
in-group/out-group constructs,
language describing, 99–104
instructional material in, 34
name change, 78
punishment of out-group, images of,
113–116
punishment of out-group, language
describing, 109–113
recruiting messages, 34
"Selected 10" videos, 43, 90, 149–152
strategic messaging in, 32, 33
symbolic imagery in, 98, 99
synchronization with other media
formats, 36–37
words and images per page, 92–93, 93*f*

safe space, denying
exploiting propaganda for intelligence
and evidence, 226–228
freedom of speech dilemma, 223–225
media as accidental amplifier, 225–226
overview, 220–223
problems with, 221–223
Salafi-jihadism, 7
Abdullah Azzam, arrival of, 53–65
al-Maqdisi, emergence of, 60–63
Al-Otaybi, messianic revolt of, 60–63
battle for leadership of, 72–76
core concepts of, 52
future of, 76–81
Sayyid Qutb, influence of, 58–60
Wahhabi legacy, struggle for, 52–58
Salafism, 57
salvation, *jihād* related to, 64–65
Saudi Arabia
Ahl al Hadith movement, 60
al-Jamaa al-Salafiyya al-Muhtasiba
(JSM), 60–61
creation of modern state, 56
excommunication of Saudi state, 61–63,
62*f*
promotion of Salafi thought
in Iraq, 66
scripts in videos
istishhad, 148–149, 148*f*
message, 142–143, 143*f*
overview, 141–142
punishment, 144–146, 146*f*
in "Selected 10" videos, 151–152
utopia, 143–144, 144*f*
war, 146–147, 147*f*
SCT (social cognitive theory), 244–245
sectarian tensions, 27–28
security, appeals based on, 26
"Selected 10" videos, 43, 90, 149–152
self-reinforcing cycles, 26, 27, 45–46
Sham, eschatological prophecies related
to, 71–72
Sharī'a, 70, 117
Shekau, Abu Bakr, 79
Shi'a, hatred of, 66–67
shooting type of war video script, 147
SIDE (social identity model of
deindividuation effects), 168
sinful activity, magazine images of, 105–
106, 107*f*
slacktivism, 158–159
social cognitive theory (SCT), 243–245

social identity, 157, 167–168, 182–183
social identity model of deindividuation
    effects (SIDE), 168
social media. *See also* media *mujāhidīn*;
    Twitter
  clicktivism, 158–159
  countering terrorism on, 181–182
  exploiting propaganda for intelligence
    and evidence, 226–228
  freedom of speech dilemma, 223–225
  limitations on research, 157–160
  online jihadism, background of,
    160–163
  overview, 155–157
  safe space, problems with shutting
    down, 222–223
  social identity, 157, 167–168, 182–183
  success of IS on, 164–171, 254
  Telegram, 180–181, 223–224, 256
  use by IS, reasons behind, 165–171
solution construct, 26–28
  in magazine imagery, 96–99
  in magazine language, 91–96
  punishment of out-group, in magazine
    images, 113–116
  punishment of out-group, in magazine
    language, 109–113
speeches, 36t
still images, 36t, 189, 197–200, 198f
Stormfront, 242
strategic innovation, 246
strategic logic of propaganda, 20
  cohesiveness, 38–44
  competitive system of control, 22
  competitive system of meaning,
    24–28
  comprehensiveness, 35–38
  identity-choice appeals, 26–27
  multidimensionality, 30–35
  multiphase messaging strategy, 24
  rational-choice appeals, 25–26, 27
strategic messaging, 32–35
suicide bombers, 68
  istishhad video script, 147–149, 148f
  magazine images of, 114
  Manchester Arena terrorist attack,
    155–156
  martyr biographies, 209–211
  suspensions from Twitter, 177–179
sword, magazine images of, 98–99

symbolic imagery, 38–40
  in *anashīd*, 196
  in infographics, 203, 203f
  in magazines, 97–99
  in message video script, 142–143
  in punishment video script, 146
  on Twitter, 175f, 176
Syria, social media use of images from, 173

tactical innovation, 246
tactical messaging, 30
Ṭaghūt, 54, 123
takfīr (excommunication)
  al-Hazimi, concept promoted by,
    79–80
  background of, 53–54
  change in IS concept of, 80
  Maqdisi's conception of, 61–62
  Qutb versus IS, 59
  of Saudi state, 61–63
  of Shi'a, 67
Taliban hymns, 195, 197
tamkin, 67
Tan, S., 117, 118
target audiences, increasing resilience of,
    230–231
tatarrus, 69
tawaghit, 108
tawhid, 54, 59
Tawhid Group, 62
teamwork, role in creativity, 255
Telegram, 179–180, 223–224, 256
terrorism studies, insights on innovation
    from, 246–248
terrorist attacks, magazine columns
    describing methods for, 124–125
theological arguments, countering IS with,
    231–233
Tinnes, J., 127–128, 146
training type of war video script, 147
Twitter, 169
  DoD accounts on, 235
  exploiting propaganda for intelligence
    and evidence, 227
  media *mujāhidīn* on, 174–177, 175f
  official IS accounts on, 173–174
  overview, 171–172
  safe space, problems with shutting
    down, 223
  suspensions from, 177–179

uniform innovation, culture of, 42–43
uniforms, 40
unofficial media organizations, 135 135*f*
US government propaganda, 6
utopia
   in magazines, 120–122, 120*f*, 121*f*
   in social media, 174
   video script, 143–144, 144*f*, 151–152

verbal weapons, 29
victimization, 110, 123
videos
   central media offices, 131–132, 132*f*
   istishhad script in, 147–149, 148*f*
   message script in, 142–143, 143*f*
   organizational structure of production,
      131–136
   overview, 36*t*, 127–130
   provincial media centers, 132–133,
      133*f*, 134*t*
   punishment script in, 144–146, 146*f*
   quality of, 255
   quantative overview of production,
      136–140
   scripts in, 141–142
   "Selected 10", 43, 90, 149–152
   unofficial media organizations, 135,
      135*f*
   utopia script in, 143–144, 144*f*
   variation across space, 137–138
   variation across time, 138–140
   variation in quality, 140
   war script in, 146–147, 147*f*
violent terminology, in magazines, 109–
   113, 111*f*

voices for counter-IS campaigns, 235–236
Wahhabism
   background of, 52–58
   Hazimis and, 79
   in Iraq, 66
walā, 54–55, 61–62
war video script, 146–147, 147*f*,
   151–152
Washington Post, 165
weapons, magazine images of, 113–114
Weather Underground, 84
Web 1.0, 161
Web 2.0, 161–162
West
   as enemy, 58, 59, 65
   reaction to gruesome
      videos, 127–128
white propaganda, 5
Wilāyāt media offices
   amount of videos produced by, 137–
      138, 138*f*
   media offices in, 132–133, 133*f*, 133*t*,
      134*f*, 134*t*
   "Selected 10" video productions, 149–
      152, 152*f*
   social media output from, 165
   variation of production across time,
      138–149, 139*f*
women, magazine language describing
   role of, 118–119
workgroups, role in creativity, 255

Yasa, 53
youth, military training
   of, 112–113